Monteverdi's Voices

Monteverdi's Voices

A Poetics of the Madrigal

TIM CARTER

OXFORD
UNIVERSITY PRESS

Oxford University Press is a department of the University of Oxford. It furthers the University's objective of excellence in research, scholarship, and education by publishing worldwide. Oxford is a registered trade mark of Oxford University Press in the UK and certain other countries.

Published in the United States of America by Oxford University Press
198 Madison Avenue, New York, NY 10016, United States of America.

© Oxford University Press 2024

All rights reserved. No part of this publication may be reproduced, stored in a retrieval system, or transmitted, in any form or by any means, without the prior permission in writing of Oxford University Press, or as expressly permitted by law, by license, or under terms agreed with the appropriate reproduction rights organization. Inquiries concerning reproduction outside the scope of the above should be sent to the Rights Department, Oxford University Press, at the address above.

You must not circulate this work in any other form
and you must impose this same condition on any acquirer.

Library of Congress Cataloging-in-Publication Data
Names: Carter, Tim, 1954– author.
Title: Monteverdi's voices : a poetics of the madrigal / Tim Carter.
Description: [1.] | New York, NY : Oxford University Press, 2024. |
Includes bibliographical references and index. |
Identifiers: LCCN 2024001012 (print) | LCCN 2024001013 (ebook) |
ISBN 9780197759196 (hardback) | ISBN 9780197759219 (epub) |
ISBN 9780197759226
Subjects: LCSH: Monteverdi, Claudio, 1567–1643. Madrigals. |
Madrigals, Italian—History and criticism.
Classification: LCC ML410.M77 C3706 2024 (print) | LCC ML410.M77 (ebook) |
DDC 782.5/43—dc23/eng/20240117
LC record available at https://lccn.loc.gov/2024001012
LC ebook record available at https://lccn.loc.gov/2024001013

DOI: 10.1093/oso/9780197759196.001.0001

Printed by Integrated Books International, United States of America

Contents

List of Music Examples, Figures, and Tables   vii
Acknowledgments   ix
Editorial (etc.) Principles   xi

1. Introduction   1
   - Cremona, Mantua, Venice   1
   - The *seconda pratica*   5
   - Poets, poetry, and poetics   9

2. The Apprentice Composer   13

3. The Madrigal "Book"   26
   - Printing and publishing   29
   - Formats   32
   - Production issues   38
   - The Seventh Book   42
   - Work and "work"   48

4. Monteverdi's Performers   50
   - Cleffing and ranges and modes   51
   - Musicians in Mantua   55
   - Venice   67

5. Poetic Voices   80
   - Gendered voices   83
   - He said/she said   91
   - He/she said   100
   - A pastoral conundrum   112
   - Monteverdi says . . .   117

6. Songbirds   122
   - Nightingales   124
   - Music about music   130
   - Singing and "singing"   136

7. Monteverdi's "Mistakes"   143

8. Musical (Im)pertinence   159
   - An impertinent beginning   160
   - "Ahi lasso"   170
   - Temperamental moments   174

9	The "Representative" Style	187
	The "stile recitativo"	189
	"Musica rappresentativa"	194
	The bass "I"	200
	"I"/"we"	204
	"A delightful musical aria, and beautiful"	209
10	Playing with Time	217

Bibliography 227
Index of Monteverdi's Works 233
General Index 241

List of Music Examples, Figures, and Tables

Music Examples

2.1. (a) "Chi vuol veder un bosco folto e spesso" (*Canzonette*, 1584); (b) "Se nel partir da voi, vita mia, sento" (First Book, 1587).   15

2.2. "Amor, per tua mercé, vattene a quella" (First Book, 1587).   17

2.3. (a) Marc'Antonio Ingegneri, "Mentre io mirava fiso" (Fifth Book *a*5, 1587); (b) Monteverdi, "Mentr'io mirava fiso" (Second Book, 1590).   19

2.4. (a) Luca Marenzio, "Crudel, perché mi fuggi" (Fourth Book *a*6, 1587); (b) Monteverdi, "Crudel, perché mi fuggi" (Second Book, 1590).   20

2.5. (a) Cipriano de Rore, "Cantai mentre ch'i arsi del mio foco" (First Book *a*5, 1542); (b) Monteverdi, "Cantai un tempo, e se fu dolce il canto" (Second Book, 1590).   23

4.1. (a) Luca Marenzio, "Belle ne fe' natura" (*Intermedio II*, 1589); (b) Monteverdi, "Ch'io non t'ami, cor mio?" (Third Book, 1592).   58

4.2. Francesco Dognazzi, "Ite caldi sospir'al freddo core" (*Il primo libro de varii concenti*, 1614).   66

4.3. (a) Monteverdi, "Mentre vaga Angioletta" (Eighth Book, 1638); (b) *Combattimento di Tancredi e Clorinda* (1624/Eighth Book, 1638); (c) Giovanni Felice Sances, "Venite ad me omnes" (*Motetti a voce sola*, 1638).   79

5.1. "Filli cara et amata" (First Book, 1587).   83

5.2. "Io mi son giovinetta" (Fourth Book, 1603).   94

5.3. "O Teseo, o Teseo mio" (Sixth Book, 1614).   103

5.4. (a) Giaches de Wert, "Forsennata gridava: «O tu che porti" (Eighth Book *a*5, 1586); (b) Monteverdi, "Vattene pur, crudel, con quella pace" (Third Book, 1592).   109

5.5. "Poi ch'ella in sé tornò, deserto e muto" (Third Book, 1592).   110

6.1. "Non sono in queste rive" (Second Book, 1590).   131

6.2. "Ecco mormorar l'onde" (Second Book, 1592).   134

6.3. "Mentre vaga Angioletta" (Eighth Book, 1638).   136

6.4. (a) Carlo Milanuzzi, "Sì dolce è 'l tormento" (*Primo scherzo delle ariose vaghezze*, 1622); (b) Monteverdi, "Sì dolce e 'l tormento" (in Milanuzzi, *Quarto scherzo delle ariose vaghezze*, repr. 1624).   141

7.1. "Zefiro torna e di soavi accenti" (*Scherzi musicali*, 1632).   147

7.2. "Volgea l'anima mia soavemente" (Fourth Book, 1603).   150

7.3. "O come sei gentile" (Seventh Book, 1619).   157

8.1. "O Mirtillo, Mirtill'anima mia" (Fifth Book, 1605).   161

viii LIST OF MUSIC EXAMPLES, FIGURES, AND TABLES

8.2.	"Cor mio, mentre vi miro" (Fourth Book, 1603).	162
8.3.	"Cor mio, mentre vi miro" (Fourth Book, 1603).	166
8.4.	"Anima del cor mio" (Fourth Book, 1603).	168
8.5.	"Oimè il bel viso, oimè 'l soave sguardo" (Sixth Book, 1614).	169
8.6.	"Cruda Amarilli, che col nome ancora" (Fifth Book, 1605).	170
8.7.	"Oimè, se tanto amate" (Fourth Book, 1603).	171
8.8.	"Sfogava con le stelle" (Fourth Book, 1603).	172
8.9.	(a) "Ch'io t'ami, e t'ami più de la mia vita" (Fifth Book, 1605); (b) "Cruda Amarilli, che col nome ancora" (Fifth Book).	173
8.10.	"Ma te raccoglie, o Ninfa, in grembo 'l cielo" (Sixth Book, 1614).	174
8.11.	"Così sol d'una chiara fonte viva" (Eighth Book, 1638).	176
8.12.	"Anima dolorosa, che vivendo" (Fourth Book, 1603).	179
8.13.	*Combattimento di Tancredi e Clorinda* (1624/Eighth Book, 1638).	181
8.14.	"Or che 'l ciel e la terra e 'l vento tace" (Eighth Book, 1638).	183
9.1.	*Combattimento di Tancredi e Clorinda* (1624/Eighth Book, 1638).	194
9.2.	"Batto, qui pianse Ergasto. Ecco la riva" (Sixth Book, 1614).	198

Figures

3.1	(a) Monteverdi, Second Book, first edition (Venice: Angelo Gardano, 1590), Quinto partbook; (b) Second Book, second edition (Venice: Alessandro Raverii, 1607), Quinto partbook.	35
8.1	"Batto qui pianse Ergasto. Ecco la riva" (Sixth Book, 1614), Basso Continuo partbook.	180
8.2	*Combattimento di Tancredi e Clorinda* (Eighth Book, 1638), Basso Continuo partbook.	182

Tables

1.1	Poets with three or more settings in Monteverdi's first eight madrigal books.	10
3.1	Monteverdi's madrigal books and subsequent editions.	30
4.1	Clef distribution in Monteverdi's First to Fourth Books of madrigals.	54
4.2	Musicians in Venice with personal connections to Monteverdi.	70
5.1	Predominant voice groupings in "Dolcemente dormiva la mia Clori."	84
5.2	Text and scoring in "Troppo ben può questo tiranno Amore."	119
6.1	Monteverdi madrigal books with texts mentioning birds.	128

Acknowledgments

My book is the result of some forty years of thinking about the music of Claudio Monteverdi, whether his operas or, and increasingly, his other secular vocal music. It has been strongly influenced by frequent conversations over that time with many colleagues and friends working in my field, particularly within the Society for Seventeenth Century Music. Both Seth Coluzzi and Roseen Giles were kind enough to share the manuscripts of their own new books on matters concerning Monteverdi, and our exchanges as a result bore further fruit here. I owe a particular debt to John Eliot Gardiner (Monteverdi Choir and English Baroque Soloists) for his close engagement with my text, and for our ongoing discussions about a composer we each love. I am also grateful to Gregory Barnett, Michael Carlson, Roseen Giles, Emiliano Ricciardi, and two anonymous reviewers for reading my draft, offering valuable suggestions along the way.

My thoughts on Monteverdi and performance have benefited from discussions with Robert Hollingworth (I Fagiolini) and Anne Marie Dragosits (Accademia degli Stravaganti; Vivante), and on matters concerning the theorbo/chitarrone, with Paula Chateauneuf and Elizabeth Kenny. My ears and eyes were also opened by the Monteverdi cycle created by various ensembles at the Utrecht Early Music Festival in 1993, and more recently, the one by Les Arts Florissants (directed by Paul Agnew), culminating with their rendering of the Eighth Book in 2015.

I gladly acknowledge the American Musicological Society for an individual publication subvention from its General Fund, supported in part by the National Endowment for the Humanities and the Andrew W. Mellon Foundation.

My beloved wife, Annegret Fauser, remains my closest collaborator and sternest critic: without her this book could not have been written.

Editorial (etc.) Principles

There are three complete editions of Monteverdi's madrigals, including the volumes in Gian Francesco Malipiero's *Claudio Monteverdi: Tutte le opere* (Asolo, 1926–42; 2nd ed., Vienna, 1954–68) and in the Fondazione Claudio Monteverdi's *Claudio Monteverdi: Opera omnia* (Cremona, 1970–), plus the nine madrigal books in the "Ut Orpheus" series (Bologna, 1998–2008) edited by Andrea Bornstein (Books I–VI, VIII) and Michelangelo Gabbrielli (VII, IX). Some leftover items were included in *C. Monteverdi: 12 composizioni vocali profane e sacre (inedite), con e senza basso continuo* edited by Wolfgang Osthoff (Milan: Ricordi, 1958). Malipiero's series was certainly pioneering for its time, but it was not at all "critical" in terms of its approach to its sources: he often took whatever edition of a given madrigal book was closest to hand, meaning that his readings of individual madrigals follow any errors that might have been introduced therein, some of which are quite drastic. Nor will Malipiero's editorial interventions (dynamics, etc.) find favor nowadays. The Fondazione Claudio Monteverdi (henceforth FCM) edition is certainly the most comprehensive in terms of its documentation and its treatment of the musical sources, although it has its blind spots, plus some notational quirks (e.g., in the handling of triple times) that make it difficult to use in any practical sense. The "Ut Orpheus" editions are the most user-friendly, although their critical apparatus is not always complete. None of those editions pays sufficient attention to Monteverdi's poetic texts, although that defect has now been remedied by Christophe Georis's *Claudio Monteverdi "letterato" ou les métamorphoses du texte* (2013), which is fundamental for its information on the sources of Monteverdi's poetry, and on his deviations from them.

The titles of madrigals adopted in this book, which usually consist of first-line incipits, follow those in the FCM volumes for convenience—even though they tend to modernize the Italian—unless they are illogical or inconsistent. For any quotations from poetry as set by Monteverdi, I prefer to follow Georis, who pays closer attention to his stylings. A madrigal's title given here might therefore differ from any quotation of its first line. In either case, however, some silent editing of punctuation, accents, *et* or *e* for &, and other such matters has occurred to create consistency, while direct speech within a poem has been placed in quotation marks for the sake of clarity even though that was not the practice at the time, nor is it now.

Monteverdi's madrigals were printed in separate partbooks each containing a single vocal or instrumental part, although some could also be set in some kind of score when a performer, usually the continuo player, needed to see the parts aligned vertically (see Chapter 3). Thus, a five-voice collection will have individual books for the Canto (C), Alto (A), Tenore (T), Basso (B), and Quinto ("Fifth"; Q) parts. Any Basso Continuo partbook (B.c.) is identified as such. Additional parts may be assigned to further partbooks—Sesto (6), Settimo (7), Tenore Secondo (T^2), etc.— or may be incorporated into the others. These labels reflect a top-down approach to the texture and do not necessarily identify the type of voice needed: Monteverdi's 1584 collection of three-voice canzonettas has partbooks labeled Canto, Tenore, and Basso, but it does not have music in any tenor or bass range.

All these parts use clefs according to the outer limits of the span of pitches to be presented on a five-line stave with a single leger line above or below (two leger lines are rare). These clefs can be identified according to the pitch indicated on a given line of the stave counting up from the bottom, with C as "middle" C: G2 (treble clef), C1 (soprano clef), C2 (mezzo-soprano clef), C3 (alto clef), C4 (tenor clef), C5 or F3 (baritone clef), F4 (bass clef). Only the treble (G2) and bass (F4) clefs remain in modern use save C3 for the viola, and C4 for the higher regions of the bassoon, trombone, or violoncello. The clefs tend to be grouped as so-called *chiavi naturali* (C1, C3, C4, F4) and higher *chiavette* (G2, C2, C3, F3), with a fifth voice usually doubling either the top one (C1 in *chiavi naturali*; G2 in *chiavette*) or the third one down (C4; C3). For convenience, in my discussion I treat the voices as soprano, alto, tenor, and bass (SATB) whether in *chiavi naturali* or in *chiavette*, so a typical five-voice ensemble will be SSATB—which is Monteverdi's preferred combination—or SATTB, with or without a basso continuo (bc). It is important to note, however, that these labels do not necessarily match modern notions of the ranges, or genders, of the modern soprano, alto, tenor, and bass voices. For example, a "tenor" part in C3 clef may have been sung by a male or female alto; an SATB setting could be sung by all male voices, with castratos and/or falsettists for the upper parts; and there are well-known examples of all-female ensembles that were able to sing pieces for that same scoring. Moreover, although for present purposes I treat all these clefs as notating sounding pitches, it is clear that transposition could have occurred in performance, especially, but not only, in the case of *chiavette*.

The music examples here are largely modeled on the modern editions, using original note values but modern clefs and barring at the *semibrevis*. The mensuration is duple at the *semibrevis* save where noted; the clefs are *chiavi naturali* save ditto, with parts in C3 clef transcribed in the modern treble clef or transposed treble clef, depending on their range. Accidentals are standardized to the extent that repetitions within a measure are ignored. Final *longae* have been converted to whatever note value is needed to fill out a measure.

In my text, all references to specific pitches use the Helmholtz system, in which *c'* is "middle" C; pitches not in italic are not octave-specific. I am willing to use the terms "major" and "minor" in relation to musical triads (as in "a major triad on D," with a major third above the root), although I fully realize that they are anachronistic, and I tend to resist any tonal implication (as in a "D-major triad"). Likewise—and again, despite the anachronism—I sometimes adopt the system unknown to Monteverdi of labeling chords by roman numerals where the numeral itself represents the degree of the scale (with I as the first degree in a given scale and V as the fifth): "major" and "minor" triads are distinguished by upper and lower case (I/i), and "first-inversion" triads (with the third as the lowest sounding note) are indicated by superscript "6" (e.g., IV^6; and by extension, F^6 for a triad on F with its third, A, at the bottom of the texture). For the modes of Renaissance vocal polyphony, I assume that Monteverdi was working within a twelve-mode system rather than an eight-mode one, and I identify them by way of the pseudo-Greek names widely adopted today (Dorian, Hypodorian . . .) even though theorists such as Gioseffo Zarlino declared the usage fraudulent and preferred a numerical system (Mode 1, Mode 2 . . .). I combine these labels with pitches when it is useful to note a mode's first degree (D-dorian) or when a mode is transposed (D-dorian transposed down a fifth to G-dorian with a flat in the signature). Modes each have a "final" and a "co-final" (the fifth degree of the scale save in the Phrygian mode); I avoid such terms as "tonic" and "dominant," even if a cadence created by a major triad built on the co-final of a mode followed by a major or minor one on its final (V–I; V–i) will sound, and even appear to function, like a typical authentic cadence (perfect cadence) in tonal terms.

To trace other composers' settings of texts present in Monteverdi's output, I have relied on Angelo Pompilio's enormously useful *Repertorio della poesia italiana in musica, 1500–1700* (https://repim.itatti.harvard.edu), and on Emiliano Ricciardi's ongoing *Tasso in Music Project: Digital Edition of the Settings of Torquato Tasso's Poetry, c. 1570–1640* (https://www.tassomusic.org). In my transcriptions of primary documents, title pages, and so forth, some silent editing has occurred, including the expansion of standard abbreviations, the standardization of upper/lower case and some orthographies, the addition of accents, and ampersands resolved as "e" or "et" (or sometimes "ed") save in company names. In general, however, I prefer to retain the original. References to Monteverdi's letters are by date: the originals can be found in the modern edition by Éva Lax, though for the most part I follow the translations by Denis Stevens save where modification is needed (which I indicate accordingly). Other references in the footnotes use short-form citations, with full details given in the Bibliography.

1
Introduction

On a verdant mountain in ancient Greece lived the nine Muses, with Apollo at their head. Each was dedicated to a specific discipline, although their roles varied in different Classical sources. Erato and her kithara (love poetry and music) jostled with Euterpe and the aulos (music and lyric poetry) but submitted to Calliope (epic poetry and music), the eldest and most eloquent of the Muses, by virtue of her preeminence in any literary ranking and her close relationship to Clio (history). It hardly mattered in a world where song was poetry, and poetry, song. But as poetry and music moved down separate paths, restoring their mythical union gained some urgency in the Renaissance and early Baroque periods, inspired by Humanist ideals on the one hand, and (Counter-)Reformation pragmatism on the other. Music might represent the celestial harmony of the spheres, but poetry was needed to give it purpose for mortal ears.

A number of Claudio Monteverdi's contemporaries in early-seventeenth-century Italy claimed that just the two components of his surname guaranteed his future rise to musical heights worthy of Parnassus.[1] They used his settings of lyric, epic, and dramatic poetry to prove their point, and his opponents did the same to opposite effect. In particular, Monteverdi's secular vocal chamber works—what for the most part he called his madrigals—became a proving ground to explore multiple ways of thinking about music, poetry, and the relationship between the two. These small-scale vignettes, each lasting but a few minutes in performance, had large-scale consequences for the formation of a poetics of music that changed how composers and performers went about their art, and how listeners responded to its newfound rhetorical powers. He published just under 150 such settings in eight books of madrigals during his lifetime, and others appeared in anthologies and in a posthumous volume. Many of them are often performed today, and rightly so: they are astonishing works that demand constant exploration of just what makes them so.

Cremona, Mantua, Venice

Monteverdi was born in Cremona on or just before 15 May 1567 (when he was baptized). He was the son of a barber-surgeon, and typically, his family treated

---

[1] He was consistently styled "Monteverde" on the title pages of his publications, providing the correct adjectival agreement. However, he tended to sign his letters as "Monteverdi."

music as a means of gaining professional security and even social uplift: his younger brother, Giulio Cesare, became a composer, too. Claudio received his musical training there under Marc'Antonio Ingegneri, *maestro di cappella* of the Duomo.[2] In late 1590 or early 1591, Monteverdi moved from Lombardy to the next-door Duchy of Mantua, joining the household musicians employed by Duke Vincenzo Gonzaga, initially as a player of bowed string instruments. He worked his way up the ranks to become the duke's *maestro della musica* in 1601, composing for, and directing, a highly proficient group of singers and instrumentalists in music for the chamber, for the chapel, and for entertainments.[3] Duke Vincenzo died in February 1612 and was succeeded by his eldest son, Francesco, who reorganized his musical forces. This was not untypical for such transitions, but as a result, Monteverdi and others were dismissed from service under still hazy circumstances, leaving his career in some disarray. Duke Francesco died in December 1612, succeeded by his younger brother, Ferdinando (previously a cardinal), who later seems to have regretted his brother's decision to release Monteverdi. However, he did not move quickly enough to remedy it, for in August 1613, the composer was appointed *maestro di cappella* at St. Mark's Basilica in Venice, the first non-Venetian to hold that post for almost half a century. He stayed there for thirty years, until his death on 29 November 1643.

Monteverdi had been dissatisfied for a fair while with his position in Mantua, and he claimed that Venice offered a much more conducive and lucrative environment for those of his profession. But there are signs that he would have left St. Mark's had the terms been right: in 1616 or thereabouts, the poet Ottavio Rinuccini was trying to tempt him to Florence; in 1623, Monteverdi at least considered a move to the court of the King of Poland; in 1627, he spent significant amounts of time in Parma while he was working on music for the festivities celebrating the marriage of Odoardo Farnese and Margherita de' Medici; and by the 1630s, if not before, he was sending music to the Habsburg court in Vienna, where there was a strong Mantuan musical presence by virtue of the second wife of Emperor Ferdinand II, Eleonora Gonzaga, daughter of Monteverdi's former employer. Monteverdi also remained tied to Mantua by way of citizenship, by family connections, and last but not least, by the annual pension granted him by Duke Vincenzo in early 1609 but often left unpaid. He fretted over the issue for the rest of his life and tried various strategies to fix it. This is one reason that he kept writing music for Mantua, even though he sometimes did his best to resist such commissions. It also explains his later connections with the Habsburgs as a means of exerting pressure on their feudal domain.

---

[2] A useful chronology is in Carter, "Monteverdi and Some Problems of Biography."
[3] On the title pages of his Fourth and Fifth Books of madrigals, Monteverdi was styled "maestro della musica del Serenissimo Signor Duca di Mantova." When petitioning to replace Benedetto Pallavicino in his letter to the duke of 28 November 1601, he requested the title of "mastro et de la camera et de la chiesa sopra la musica." This was probably the title given to Giaches de Wert after Giovanni Giacomo Gastoldi replaced him as *maestro di cappella* of S. Barbara in 1588. Monteverdi himself never had the title of *maestro di cappella* in Mantua.

Monteverdi's move to Venice has often been read as a sign that times were changing, and that princely courts were losing their sway in the musical marketplace in early-seventeenth-century Italy, as they were in other political and economic spheres. The fact that Venice was a republic plays into this argument in obvious ways, as does the contrast between a work such as Monteverdi's opera *Orfeo* (Mantua, 1607) and his much later operas written for the "public" theaters of Venice: *Il ritorno d'Ulisse in patria* (1640), *Le nozze d'Enea con Lavinia* (1641; the music is lost), and *L'incoronazione di Poppea* (1643). But the issue extends to how the composer gets positioned nowadays in terms of music-historical periods. For Leo Schrade, writing in 1950, Monteverdi was "the creator of modern music," and even if that is far too extravagant a claim, most textbooks continue to situate him at the beginning of the musical "Baroque." In 1987, however, Gary Tomlinson made a case for Monteverdi being at "the end of the Renaissance." It may be revealing that his switch was made in a monograph largely concerned with Monteverdi's madrigals rather than his operas or sacred music in which "modern" styles were more straightforwardly applied (as, too, was any *stile antico* in the sacred music). Tomlinson certainly acknowledged the presence of modern(ist) trends in the poetry and the music of Monteverdi's later madrigals, but he did so with a sense of regret that he transferred to a composer resisting the musical fashions of the day, giving some of his last works an air of nostalgia for times gone by.

There is enough archival information to map out Monteverdi's professional career in quite some detail. Various documents also give us some sense of his personality. At least 127 letters from him survive, most to officials in Mantua and the majority of those to Alessandro Striggio (the librettist of *Orfeo*), who rose high up the Gonzaga administration. Even though Monteverdi tended to write in fairly formal terms, as etiquette required, one can often detect a rather sly sense of humor that also plays out in his madrigals. The letters reveal that Monteverdi did not always play the courtly game very well—indeed, he sometimes made some serious gaffes—and he often let his emotions get the better of him. He also had a sense of self-worth that some felt took him above his station, and when he was under stress, he could cross the bounds of propriety. Moreover, he was not always as willing to exert himself as others might have wished, and he became adept at procrastination. Thus, his collaborator during the preparations for the wedding festivities in Parma, Antonio Goretti, complained about Monteverdi's tendency to take afternoons off (he "composes only in the morning and in the evening"), and also about the fact that "he is a man who likes to talk things over in company at great length."[4] Monteverdi's own letters give a similar impression in terms both of his ability to come up with an imaginative range of excuses for not having completed a particular musical task, and of his need to put into words, sometimes at great length, his plans for a particular musical work. Mapping things out in his head also

---

[4] Fabbri, *Monteverdi*, trans. Carter, 213.

seems to have been part of Monteverdi's way of composing. When he was asked to send two sonnet settings to Duke Vincenzo Gonzaga, who was staying near Genoa in the summer of 1607, he spent six days in composing one of them, plus another two in trying it out and copying it ("tra provarlo e riscriverlo").[5] As for the other one, he planned on sending it as soon as possible, "since it is already clearly shaped in my mind" ("poiché nella mente mia nella sua orditura è da me fatto"), although, and typically, he asked for extra time to bring it to completion. It is a provocative remark: one might wonder what he means by "orditura"—whether an outline or a finished work—and therefore what might have happened when Monteverdi eventually put pen to paper.

Charting his musical development is harder because of the evident gaps in his surviving output. His operas *Orfeo* (1607) and *Arianna* (1608)—the latter now lost apart from its lament for the protagonist—occupy a time and place quite different from those of his Venetian works for the stage, and almost nothing survives of the theatrical music that we know he wrote in the gap of thirty-some years between them. A similar interval exists between his two sacred volumes, the *Sanctissimae Virgini Missa . . . ac Vespere* (1610) and his *Selva morale e spirituale* (1640–41), the latter a large collection of sacred and devotional music that presumably reflects Monteverdi's work at St. Mark's and elsewhere in Venice over a significant period of time, although it is hard to discern any clear chronology for the pieces it contains. His madrigals might seem to place matters on a more secure footing, at least for the first half of his career. The First (1587) and Second (1590) Books of five-voice madrigals reflect his studies in Cremona, and his Third (1592), Fourth (1603), and Fifth (1605) are closely tied to his work in Mantua, as is his Sixth (1614), even though he had just moved to Venice. The Seventh Book came out in 1619 (it, too, has a Mantuan connection), but his Eighth only in 1638, although it contains older works such as the *Ballo delle ingrate* going back to 1608. The Ninth Book (1651) was a posthumous collection—like the *Messa a quattro voci, et salmi* (1650)—created by Monteverdi's last printer, Alessandro Vincenti, who it seems, added to music already published a few things out of the deceased composer's bottom drawer.[6] A few madrigals and motets by Monteverdi were included in anthologies published during his Venetian years, but on the whole, they are not sufficient to plug the holes in any narrative one might wish to create about how the composer navigated changing musical worlds. Yet there is a constant presence in all of these settings: a musical mind that seems to have worked in very particular ways.

---

[5] Monteverdi to Annibale Iberti, 28 July 1607.
[6] Very little of Monteverdi's secular music for the chamber survives just in manuscript, including a few earlier three-voice canzonettas plus the *Lamento d'Olimpia* ("Voglio, voglio morir, voglio morire"; S, bc) and the setting over the *ciaccona* (and then a descending tetrachord ostinato) of "Voglio di vita uscir, voglio che cadano" (S, bc). The attribution of these last two pieces is not entirely secure.

The *seconda pratica*

A work's date of publication does not indicate when it was composed. Once Monteverdi had established his presence in Mantua with his Third Book, he had no strong reason to spend time and money on printing books of madrigals; indeed, his employer might have discouraged it as a way of reserving this music for private use, thereby maintaining its exclusivity. This seems to be particularly the case with the Sixth Book: by the time of its publication in 1614, much of its contents dated back several years, Monteverdi was no longer in Mantua, and Duke Vincenzo Gonzaga was dead. But there is another likely reason for the gap of almost eleven years between the Third Book and the Fourth. In late 1598, some of Monteverdi's madrigals came to the attention of the Bolognese music theorist Giovanni Maria Artusi by way of his hearing them performed at a musical evening in Ferrara (on Monday 16 November) hosted by the patron, connoisseur, and sometime composer, Antonio Goretti (later associated with Monteverdi in Parma). This was during the visit of Margaret of Austria, whose marriage to King Philip III of Spain was celebrated by proxy there. Monteverdi probably was not present, given the frantic preparations to receive Margaret in Mantua the following week, with a mammoth performance of Battista Guarini's *Il pastor fido* on the 22nd. Artusi was some thirty years older than Monteverdi and trained in the old school. He criticized those madrigals (without naming their composer) for their irregular dissonance treatment and other improprieties in two treatises, *L'Artusi, overo Delle imperfettioni della moderna musica* (1600) and the *Seconda parte dell'Artusi . . .* (1603). In identifying the "imperfections of modern music," Artusi had other figures in his sights as well, not least the Bolognese theorist Ercole Bottrigari, with whom he disagreed over matters of tuning and temperament. But the fact that the madrigals by Monteverdi that Artusi heard, and sometimes quoted, appeared in print only later, in his Fourth and Fifth Books, suggests how his music first circulated in close-knit circles.[7]

As was typical of such controversies, the one between Artusi and Monteverdi brought proxies into play; Monteverdi was defended by a still unidentified composer who adopted the academic name "L'Ottuso," and also by others writing in his support, including the Mantuan court theologian Cherubino Ferrari, who provided two laudatory poems (included in Monteverdi's Fifth Book of madrigals) that extolled the composer's musical virtues and dismissed the yappings of any Cerberus that might seek to deny them.[8] Artusi himself had already dedicated his first treatise to Cardinal Pompeo Arrigoni, a leading figure in the Supreme Sacred Congregation of the Roman and Universal Inquisition, therefore raising the specter of Monteverdi being a musical heretic.[9] The publication of the composer's Fourth Book in 1603 was presumably some kind of response: it includes one of

[7] For the chronology and the other participants in the controversy, see Carter, "Artusi, Monteverdi, and the Poetics of Modern Music."
[8] Carter, "Cerberus Barks in Vain."
[9] Siegele, "*Seconda pratica*."

the madrigals attacked by Artusi ("Anima mia, perdona" and its *seconda parte*), and the virtuosic display of compositional artifice in its final madrigal, "Piagn'e sospira; e quand'i caldi raggi" (a setting from Tasso's *Gerusalemme conquistata* of 1593), seems designed as direct proof of the composer's abilities.[10] Monteverdi also claimed extra credit by dedicating the book to the Accademia degli Intrepidi of Ferrara, of which Antonio Goretti was a member, as was Duke Vincenzo Gonzaga, at least from a distance.[11]

Two years later, Monteverdi made a more aggressive response in his Fifth Book, which he dedicated directly to the duke himself. This includes at its head the other four madrigals criticized directly by Artusi, in the precise order in which he names them:[12] "Cruda Amarilli, che col nome ancora" (Artusi took issue with its dissonances), "O Mirtillo, Mirtill'anima mia" (modal impropriety), and then "Era l'anima mia" and "Ma se con la pietà non è in te spenta" (openings based on the repetition of a single chord that therefore did not contain the harmonic motion necessary for music to be music). Monteverdi also included at the end of the book a brief statement to the readers wherein he promised to write a treatise in his defense to be titled *Seconda pratica, overo Perfettione della moderna musica*, with the "perfection of modern music" making an obvious play on Artusi's title. He was reportedly still planning that treatise toward the end of his life, but it was never written, it seems. However, his brother, Giulio Cesare, presented a line-by-line commentary on that statement in a "Dichiaratione della lettera stampata nel Quinto libro de suoi madregali" appended to Monteverdi's collection of seemingly light canzonettas, the *Scherzi musicali a tre voci* (1607), issued, somewhat unusually, in a luxurious folio format and dedicated to Prince Francesco Gonzaga.[13] Artusi had already continued his attack by way of a treatise (now lost) written under the pseudonym "Antonio Braccino da Todi," which appeared in 1605 or 1606—to which Giulio Cesare refers in the "Dichiaratione"—and another was published in 1608.[14] Here the notion of "heresy" was made explicit.[15] Amadino's editions of the Fifth Book issued in 1606 and 1608 continued to include Monteverdi's statement (although they more typically dropped the dedication), and the second edition of the *Scherzi musicali* (1609)

---

[10] Tomlinson (*Monteverdi and the End of the Renaissance*, 100) and Privitera ("*Piagn'e sospira*") place the madrigal in the early 1590s because of its apparent archaicisms, but their thinking seems flawed: there is no reason that Monteverdi could not revert to an "earlier" style for later purposes.

[11] Carter, "E in rileggendo poi le proprie note," 145–48. It is striking that Amadino also included the dedication in his second and third editions of the Fourth Book (1605, 1607)—but not his later ones—given that such matter tended to be dropped after the first.

[12] Coluzzi, *Guarini's "Il pastor fido" and the Madrigal*, 311.

[13] The fact that Giulio Cesare Monteverdi dedicated the 1607 *Scherzi musicali* to Prince Francesco Gonzaga might suggest that the volume was in lieu of a score of *Orfeo*; the prince had supported the performance of that opera earlier in the year, but its score (also dedicated to him) was printed only in 1609.

[14] Ossi (*Divining the Oracle*, 35) notes that the "Dichiaratione" refers to the postface to the Fifth Book having been published "a few months before" ("alcuni mesi dietro"), and to Antonio Braccino da Todi's fairly immediate response. This locates the writing of the "Dichiaratione" to a year or more before its publication.

[15] Antonio Braccino da Todi, *Discorso secondo musicale* (Venice: Giacomo Vincenti, 1608), 7: Artusi was justified in criticizing Monteverdi "acciò li studiosi che non conoscono così bene il vero dal falso, non si infilzano nelle cose malfatte, e ne' barbarismi, e per modo di dire nelle heresie in Musica, e nell'Armonia parte principale della Melodia."

included both the "Dichiaratione" and the original dedication. Matters still rankled in 1610, it seems, to judge by a comment Monteverdi made in the dedication (to Pope Paul V) of his *Sanctissimae Virgini Missa ... ac Vespere*. Artusi's death on 18 August 1613 removed him from the equation: Monteverdi's Sixth Book lacks a dedication or any other material that might relate to an ongoing debate, although other theorists continued to refer to it. But the composer's claim made to the music theorist Giovanni Battista Doni in a letter of 22 October 1633 that Artusi had softened his stance and had even come to admire Monteverdi probably contained a degree of wishful thinking.

Artusi's attack on modern music may also have been an attack on modern musical practices adopted in the now defunct Estense court in Ferrara, a city newly brought under the dominion of the Papal States following the death of Duke Alfonso II d'Este in October 1597. If so, it is not surprising that the controversy does not seem to have damaged Monteverdi's position in Mantua; indeed, Duke Vincenzo Gonzaga may have approved of the attention being garnered by his now notorious *maestro della musica*, given the duke's own desire to pick up where Ferrara had left off. Artusi's treatises also fit into a context of fault-finding musical controversies, such as those between Giovanni Spataro and Franchinus Gaffurius around 1500, or Vincenzo Galilei and Gioseffo Zarlino in the 1580s. However, Monteverdi's response was not entirely straightforward. It involved creating a distinction between a "second practice" (*seconda pratica*) and the "first," which was Artusi's domain. Monteverdi used the term in the postface to his Fifth Book (1605) within the title of the treatise that he intended to write about his method of composing.[16] It returned much later in the more ambitious version of that title as *Melodia, overo Seconda pratica musicale* that he communicated to Doni in October 1633. However, the only definition of it was provided by Giulio Cesare Monteverdi in the 1607 "Dichiaratione," where he traced the musical *seconda pratica* back to Cipriano de Rore, who had died in 1565 (two years before Monteverdi was born), and strongly associated it with a "noble" style of composition. It was a matter, he said, of the relationship between *armonia* and *oratione*: the former had charge over the latter in the *prima pratica*, but that was reversed in the *seconda*.[17]

That reversed relationship was justified by reference to Plato's *Republic* (3: 398d), using the Latin translation by Marsilio Ficino. Here the three components of *melodia* (i.e., *melos*; song) are identified as oration, harmony (for Plato, meaning "mode"), and rhythm, with oration taking the lead.[18] It was a familiar dictum commonly adopted by Renaissance Humanists to promote a clarity of text delivery (meaning

---

[16] However, it was previously used by L'Ottuso in his second letter to Artusi quoted in the *Seconda parte dell'Artusi* (1603), 16. Artusi then seeks to demonstrate the absurdity of the term.

[17] Giulio Cesare Monteverdi treats the relationship as one between "serva" and "padrona" (he also adopts the hypercorrect "prattica," although Monteverdi himself consistently used "pratica"). The common translation by way of the gendered "(maid)servant" and "mistress" is a red herring; Monteverdi refers to Duke Vincenzo Gonzaga as his "padrona" in grammatical agreement with "Vostra Altezza."

[18] As Ficino puts it, "melodiam ex tribus constare, oratione, harmonia, rythmo." Giulio Cesare Monteverdi quotes it (but with "rithmo"), as he does other following passages of the text.

more than just "the words") in musical circumstances, chiefly in response to overly complex polyphony. Artusi's argument, however, was that modern composers went too far in allowing the content of a text to justify musical solecism. Monteverdi, in turn, rather craftily used the notion of two "practices" to accuse Artusi in effect of failing to distinguish apples from oranges: the composer might not adhere to *prima pratica* rules of counterpoint and dissonance treatment, but his music was based on, and justified by, different principles. Thus, both sides in the dispute were correct each on their own terms, but those terms were narrowly defined, and in the case of the *seconda pratica*, in not very helpful ways.

Still more confusions are created by the relationship between the *seconda pratica* and the new styles and performance mediums that were emerging in Italy in the decades around 1600. The madrigals that Artusi heard in 1598 and criticized thereafter were all written for the typical combination of five unaccompanied voices. By now, however, the repertory was expanding to include settings for fewer voices with instrumental accompaniment, the latter derived from a "basso continuo," a bassline with figures and other annotations that a player of the harpsichord, theorbo/chitarrone, or some such "foundation" instrument could flesh out to provide the harmonies supporting the voice(s). The solo songs for voice and continuo emerging in Florence and elsewhere from the mid-1580s on—a medium then adapted for early operas there—were an obvious case in point, although save in his theatrical music, Monteverdi tended to avoid them. However, the six continuo madrigals placed at the end of his Fifth Book are quite different from the others. The voices themselves no longer have to sustain the musical flow on their own (which becomes the job of the accompaniment instead), and they can be used in a wider variety of combinations ranging from just a single part through various vocal combinations up to and including the full ensemble. This also allowed Monteverdi to parse and deliver his poetry in a quite different manner.

Those of Monteverdi's contemporaries who praised his music were clear that it had an uncanny power to transform the spoken or written word such as to arouse powerful emotions in the listener. The Bolognese music theorist Adriano Banchieri was wholly on Monteverdi's side as regards the aesthetic basis of the *seconda pratica*, which he formulated in a somewhat more direct way as having the harmony subject to the words ("la musica in quanto all'armonia deve essere soggetta alle parole"). He also thought that Monteverdi's music was worthy of total commendation precisely because it revealed "every emotional part of perfect oration" ("ogni affettuosa parte di perfetta oratione"). Here Banchieri seems to be using "oratione" in the more general, and proper, sense of "delivery."[19] The poet Angelo Grillo was ravished by Monteverdi's settings of his spiritual verse, and another poet with whom the composer worked closely, Ottavio Rinuccini, professed himself a great admirer of his musical abilities.[20] And when Pellegrino Possenti published his own *Lamento*

---

[19] Calcagno, *From Madrigal to Opera*, 48.
[20] Fabbri, *Monteverdi*, trans. Carter, 106 (Banchieri; from his *Conclusioni nel suono dell'organo*), 118–19, 141–44 (Grillo); Carter, "Ottavio Rinuccini's *Narciso*."

d'Arianna (to a text by Marino) in 1623—the same year in which Monteverdi's solo-voice setting appeared in print—he fulsomely acknowledged that Monteverdi had learned harmonious song from the angels, his works filling the world with celestial harmony.[21]

Poets, poetry, and poetics

Monteverdi's large output spans works for the theater, the church, and the chamber; he wrote almost no independent instrumental music, although instruments do start to play a significant role in his music in general. There are crossovers between these various genres: the continuo madrigals in the Fifth Book made their influence felt in Monteverdi's first opera, *Orfeo* (1607), just as the duets given a prominent role in that work had a significant impact on his use of the same medium from the Seventh Book on.[22] The Seventh Book also contains a canzonetta, "Chioma d'oro," which either drew on, or was a source for, the first of the two "Beatus vir" settings published much later in the *Selva morale e spirituale*.[23] Some of the formal features one finds in *Orfeo* and in the 1610 "Vespers" influenced his larger-scale madrigals, particularly in the Eighth Book, and Monteverdi could rearrange sacred texts in the same way as he did some of his secular ones so as to create refrains or sectional divisions. Moreover, the fact that the title page of 1610 edition of the *Sanctissimae Virgini Missa . . . ac Vespere* said that the volume included "some motets suitable for the small chapels and apartments of princes" suggests that boundaries could be fluid in terms of performance venues as well. Treating his madrigals as a separate corpus risks missing out on other important aspects of his music. The advantage, however, is that the genre posed a consistent set of problems that Monteverdi needed to solve each time he started to compose with regard to handling a poem on the one hand, and his musical resources on the other.

The exact nature of the relationships between text and music in Monteverdi's madrigals demands careful thought. Clearly, I am not the first to consider them in this light. Nino Pirrotta's remarkable study of the composer's "poetic choices" and their musical consequences, first published in 1968, provided the foundation for subsequent scholars to consider this repertory in terms of style and structure, "modal" or "tonal" principles, and more recently, issues of gender and of narrative theory. He also tended to take the view that Monteverdi worked best when dealing with texts by demonstrably "great" Italian poets (Petrarch, Torquato Tasso, Battista

---

[21] Pellegrino Possenti, *Canora sampogna . . .* (Venice: Bartolomeo Magni, 1623), dedication to Virginio Dina. Possenti excuses publishing his music "mentre si mirano tante belle compositioni di tanti segnalati huomini, e in particolare quelle del signor Monteverde; che per sua altezza essendosi avicinato al Cielo, da gl'Angioli havendo appreso l'armonioso canto, hanno riempito il Mondo di Celeste armonia."

[22] Whenham, *Duet and Dialogue in the Age of Monteverdi*, 1: 101–3.

[23] For "Chioma d'oro" rather than "Chiome d'oro" (often given as the first line of the setting), see Georis, *Claudio Monteverdi*, 576 n. 82. The singular form appears only in the Quinto partbook (but not in its *tavola*)—everywhere else has the plural—although it is grammatically more correct.

Table 1.1 Poets with three or more settings in Monteverdi's first eight madrigal books.

Battista Guarini	48
Torquato Tasso	17
Giambattista Marino	12
Ottavio Rinuccini	6
Girolamo Casoni	4
Petrarch	4
Giovanni Maria Bonardo	3
Total	94 (out of 148)

Guarini), and Pirrotta had a prejudice typical for his time against the mannerist wit of Giambattista Marino and his imitators that had become the fashion in the early seventeenth century. Given that Monteverdi sets a significant amount of Marino's poetry in his Sixth Book—and occasionally thereafter—this forced Pirrotta into various contortions in dealing with the composer's later madrigals save where reappearances of the great poets, and particularly Petrarch, could be cast in some nostalgic frame.

Pirrotta was right, up to a point. The poets set most frequently by Monteverdi did indeed include the most distinguished of his day, with Guarini at their head, then Tasso and Marino, although Petrarch appears less frequently than one might expect (Table 1.1). Many of these texts were popular enough among madrigal composers, although a surprising number were not. Moreover, some pause for thought is prompted by the fact that over a third of Monteverdi settings fall outside the list, whether of texts by relatively minor figures or a quite large number (twenty-eight) with authors still to be identified. Some of those may not have been Monteverdi's "poetic choice." For the most part, he tended not to write—or at least, publish—the "occasional" pieces marking specific events that are quite often found in the madrigal books of his predecessors and contemporaries. But there must have been times when he was given a text to set to music, or when he tackled a poem to suit some other purpose. The Sestina in the Sixth Book ("Incenerite spoglie, avara tomba") is an obvious case in point, given that it was a lament commissioned by Duke Vincenzo Gonzaga on the death (in early 1608) of the young soprano Caterina Martinelli.[24] The text by Scipione Agnelli, a young Mantuan nobleman, is clumsy, to say the least, and Monteverdi was careless over it. In the Eighth Book, he himself seems to have enlisted some versifier to write "Altri canti d'Amor, tenero arciero," the first of the "Canti guerrieri," to match Marino's much better sonnet at the beginning of the "Canti amorosi," "Altri canti di Marte e di sua schiera." But it has few redeeming qualities, plus a repeated rhyme word ("fiero ... fiero") that would never have been allowed by any serious poet. In these cases, at least, Monteverdi seems

[24] Strainchamps, "The Life and Death of Caterina Martinelli."

to have been willing to turn a blind eye to literary merit, if that factored at all in his reasons for selecting a poem for musical setting in the first place. Indeed, one starts to wonder whether he was quite the "literary" composer one might assume from the frequent discussion of just a select few of his madrigals, or in the context of a *seconda pratica* that prioritized the effective delivery of a text that presumably needed to be worthy of it. He often seems, instead, to have looked for other things in his poetry, whether a crucial word, a neat turn of phrase, a potential paradox, or just something that tempted his musical invention.

There are other prejudices apparent in many discussions of this repertory. Current views of Monteverdi's madrigals still tend to build on the premise that he managed to find some perfect synthesis between music and poetry that explains their undeniable expressive force. A common subtext is that Monteverdi was heading toward some form of musical drama, with the madrigal reaching fruition in the genre to which he also made a major contribution in the early seventeenth century: opera. Thus, as the madrigal declined, something else was needed to take its place. But the tendency to read Monteverdi's madrigals as (proto)dramatic is pernicious because of its mixing of poetic and musical genres. It also loses sight of a far broader range of rhetorical and emotional nuances within the madrigals themselves.

Revealing those nuances is one of the aims of this book. I am less interested in what texts by which poets appear in Monteverdi's madrigal books than in how he chose to deliver, enliven, or even reimagine them. My chief concern is what one might call the nuts and bolts of Monteverdi's text setting rather than any higher-flying ideas concerning the union of words and music. Poetry was something to be grasped and grappled with, and it compelled the composer to wrestle with musical choices and their better or worse consequences. Any poem forced a series of strategic decisions in light of its narrative mode (who was, or is, speaking when, to whom, and about what), its rhetorical organization (statements, questions, exclamations), its syntax (where the main verbs come), and its lexical choices: that is, words that might seem particularly amenable to musical (re)presentation. Some of those decisions would, or should, have been clear-cut; others involved choosing from a number of options that might, in turn, have become defined only as composing was underway. Viewing Monteverdi's madrigals in this manner also requires acceptance of the fact that he was not infallible. He was right to claim, in his postface to the Fifth Book, that "I do not do things by chance" ("non faccio le mie cose a caso"). But the choices that he made, or that were imposed on him by musical or other circumstance, were not necessarily the best.

The Monteverdi with whom I am in conversation is more down-to-earth in other ways as well. His letters reveal him to be witty, playful, and inventive, but also impatient, intransigent, and exasperating. His music is no different. I show him learning his craft in Cremona and honing it in the vibrant cultural world of Mantua in the last decade of the sixteenth century and the first of the seventeenth. I situate his madrigals in the broader context of print cultures in his period. I demonstrate how he benefited from collaboration with specific performers in Mantua and then in

Venice. I analyze his treatment of different poetic and musical genres, of narrative structures, and of texture, harmony, rhythm, and mode. I also dare to suggest that understanding what Monteverdi does in his madrigals can have a significant impact on what we might do to, with, and for them today on or off the concert platform. All this stems from my view of the madrigal as a performative act on the part of its composer, its musicians, or its listeners, and still more, a playful one in terms of manipulating expectations on the one hand, and temporal experience on the other. All these issues come together in what I call a "poetics of the madrigal": that is, how it works in theory and in practice. In Monteverdi's case, they also reveal an astounding musical mind.

2
The Apprentice Composer

Cremona was a musical center of some significance, especially after the appointment of Marc'Antonio Ingegneri as *maestro di cappella* of the Duomo in the mid-1570s.[1] He was born in 1535 or 1536 and died in 1592, so was in his mid-forties when he became Monteverdi's teacher. He gained a precocious student. Monteverdi published his first musical collection at the age of fifteen: a set of three-voice motets, the *Sacrae cantiunculae tribus vocibus*, dedicated to a Cremonese cleric, Stefano Canini Valcarenghi, on 1 August 1582. This was followed by a book of four-voice "spiritual" madrigals on devotional texts in the vernacular, dedicated to Alessandro Fraganesco on 31 July 1583, of which only the Basso partbook survives. Next came one of three-voice canzonettas, dedicated to Pietro Ambrosini, a Cremonese patrician, on 31 October 1584. But Ingegneri also seems to have kept a tight rein on Monteverdi's ambitions, taking him through a carefully curated curriculum. Thus, the subsequent gap of two years and three months prior to the appearance of Monteverdi's *Madrigali a cinque voci . . . libro primo* seems to reflect a further period of in-depth study that then led to what one might deem to be a typical "graduation" exercise, a "first book" of five-voice madrigals that Monteverdi felt able to dedicate to the prominent Veronese patron, Marco Verità, on 27 January 1587. By the time of his Second Book *a5*, Monteverdi was setting his sights on a possible appointment in Milan by dedicating it to Giacomo Ricardi, a high-ranking official there, on 1 January 1590. This was the last of his publications to acknowledge his position as a student ("discepolo") of Ingegneri. In his Third Book (1592) Monteverdi was able, instead, to celebrate his new appointment in Mantua. His dedication to Duke Vincenzo Gonzaga (27 June) also made the situation clear: he compares himself to a plant that brings forth flowers but should then produce fruit—the "flowers" are his performances for the duke as a *suonatore di vivuola*, but these printed madrigals are the "fruit" that will provide more lasting evidence of the fertile ground in which he now finds himself. The image also finds an echo in the first madrigal of the collection, a setting of Tasso's "La giovinetta pianta," where the careful tendering of a plant under the gentle rays of the sun is compared to the cultivation of love in a fair maiden.

Plenty of treatises from the last quarter of the sixteenth century demonstrate the lessons a student needed to learn with regard to the basics of music theory (pitch, rhythm, counterpoint, and mode) and performance, whether as a singer or also,

---

[1] Tibaldi, "La musica a Cremona all'epoca di Monteverdi."

in Monteverdi's case, an instrumentalist. However, the treatises tend to be less clear on how to make the transition to composition. Counterpoint determined the means of combining two or more voice parts by way of consonant intervals (thirds, fifths, sixths, and octaves) and dissonant ones (seconds, fourths, and sevenths), the latter subject to various constraints. It could be taught, even created, by way of improvising over a cantus firmus or in canon (so-called *contrappunto alla mente*), but at some point, the shift needed to be made to working things out in written form. Ingegneri probably did the same as other teachers of the time. He would start with simple contrapuntal exercises of writing one or more parts against a long-note cantus firmus, first note-against-note, then in diminution, with two or more notes against the cantus firmus, therefore allowing the introduction of dissonances by way of passing notes and then suspensions. The opening of Monteverdi's "Non si levava ancor l'alba novella" in his Second Book provides a trace of this process. The move to "free" composition could be initiated by giving the student an opening idea to be developed by way of contrapuntal imitation. Anything on a more extended scale, however, required understanding the different musical modes governing the linear motions of individual voice parts, the ranges in which they operated, the notes on which regular or irregular cadences could be formed, and so forth. This could be developed by identifying a model to be followed or adapted in some kind of way. As Monteverdi became more proficient, Ingegneri probably gave less of any model, or crafted a different kind of assignment; ambitious students would also seek to outdo the model in ways that might or might not exceed their capabilities. We see all this in operation in Monteverdi's "student" collections up to and including his Second Book.

Ingegneri was not the most progressive composer of his generation, but he certainly was solidly grounded in terms of both technique and tradition. Some of the models he gave Monteverdi for the *Sacrae cantiunculae* appear to have been drawn from an old collection, the *Motetta trium vocum ab pluribus authoribus composita* (Venice: Antonio Gardano, 1543), with works by Costanzo Festa, Jacquet of Mantua, Cristóbal de Morales, and Adrian Willaert.[2] For the 1584 canzonettas, Ingegneri seems to have steered his student chiefly to texts previously set in Gasparo Fiorino's Second Book of three- and four-voice canzonettas (1574) and Orazio Vecchi's First Book of four-voice ones (1580), although Monteverdi tended to subject them to more complicated treatment than those composers did. One of Monteverdi's canzonettas, "Chi vuol veder un bosco folto e spesso," also reveals how a student might move from a three-voice setting to a five-voice one: "Se nel partir da voi, vita mia, sento" in his First Book has more or less the same three-voice opening (switching the upper voices). But Monteverdi then brings in the tenor to thicken the texture for the lover's "grave torment," and the bass enters only later for the exclamation, "Deh" (Ex. 2.1).[3]

---

[2] See Anthony Pryer's critical commentary to the FCM edition of the *Sacrae cantiunculae*.
[3] Tomlinson (*Monteverdi and the End of the Renaissance*, 34) makes the point about the opening but cites the wrong canzonetta ("Chi vuol veder d'inverno un dolce aprile").

Ex. 2.1 (a) "Chi vuol veder un bosco folto e spesso" (*Canzonette a tre voci*, 1584; G2, G2, C2); (b) "Se nel partir da voi, vita mia, sento" (First Book, 1587; G2, G2, C2, C3; B [F3] is silent).

This type of textural expansion of a standard canzonetta structure becomes typical of Monteverdi. One further consequence, however, is its impact on his harmonic thinking. Canzonettas tended to be largely homophonic, with clear-cut musical phrases determined by each line of the poetry, and strong motion to cadential goals that might, in turn, be ordered hierarchically in a move from the modal final to its co-final (in most cases, the fifth degree of the scale).[4] The first line of "Chi vuol veder un bosco" moves from a major triad on G through a cadence on B♭ ("bosco") to one on D ("spesso"): its second half (the last two lines of the text) works its way back to a final cadence on G. In "Se nel partir da voi," that G–B♭–D motion also takes up the first line of the text, while the second makes the move back to the cadence on G, but in slower motion with drawn-out dissonances for the "deep torment" ("grave tormento") felt by the lover. The change of pace is striking—as is its impact on our perception of musical time—even as the harmonic goal is the same.[5]

For the First Book more broadly, Ingegneri seems to have required Monteverdi to look at the work of a number of madrigalists publishing in the mid-1580s, including Luca Marenzio and Philippe de Monte, as well as his own most recent works. There are significant similarities between the openings of Monteverdi's setting of "Poiché del mio dolore" and Monte's "Poi che 'l mio largo pianto."[6] Nevertheless, this book already demonstrates the presence of a distinctive musical personality, with a number of fingerprints that become typical of Monteverdi: homophonic exclamations ("Baci soavi e cari"), usually cued by a vocative or exclamatory "o" or some other trigger such as "ahi" or "deh"; two sopranos in close canon overlapping in pitch ("Baci soavi e cari" again); *contrapposti*, sometimes of antithetical poetic ideas (the end of "Ch'ami la vita mia nel tuo bel nome," superimposing "Ch'ami la morte" and "e non la vita mia"); sudden contrasts of texture to match the rhetoric; cheeky text setting (the preemptive entry of the tenor in "Filli cara et amata" with a question that comes only later in the text);[7] and a turn to contrapuntal writing when he loses interest in the words ("Amor, s'il tuo ferire"). Sometimes, like any student, he tries too hard. Ingegneri probably should not have let stand the final cadence of "Amor, per tua mercé, vattene a quella" (Ex. 2.2), even if he were amused by his pupil's attempt to find a way of setting a poem that ends with a painful question ("how, lady, can you make someone who loves you so much die?"). The lover's anger in the setting of Guarini's "Ardo sì, ma non t'amo," on the other hand, gets represented by piling text fragments one on top of the other such that the words can hardly be understood. That may not matter, however: the poem was known well enough, both on its own, and through multiple musical settings.

At this stage, Monteverdi's poetic choices may not always have been his. For the First Book, Ingegneri seems to have guided him toward relatively short texts with

---

[4] Long, *Hearing Homophony*, chap. 4.

[5] I will discuss (in Chapter 8) how this relates to incomplete and complete descents through the melodic fifth (the *diapente*) that defines a given mode, in this case $d''-a'$, then $d''-g'$.

[6] Watkins and La May, "Changing Concepts of Originality in the Madrigals of Gesualdo and Monteverdi," 475–76. Monte's madrigal was first published in his First Book *a6* printed before 1569 (we have only a "reprint" of that year; the first edition is lost). There were further editions of Monte's volume in 1570, 1574, and 1582. This kind of modeling is also discussed in La May, "Imitazione in Monteverdi's Canzonettas and the Madrigals," and Chew, "A Model Musical Education."

[7] The FCM edition styles the original "Filli cara & amata" as "Filli cara e amata." This is correct for modern Italian, where *e* (and) is modified only prior to the same vowel, but not if one wishes to preserve the poetic meter. The FCM editions are generally inconsistent on this issue.

Ex. 2.2 "Amor, per tua mercé, vattene a quella" (First Book, 1587; G2, G2, C2, C3, C4).

[Musical example: five vocal parts (C, Q, A, T, B) with text "far, Don - na, mo - ri - re?"]

between five and eight lines of verse: the exceptions are "Usciam, Ninfe, omai fuor di questi boschi" (nine lines) and "Baci soavi e cari" (thirteen).[8] Those in the Second Book are noticeably longer: between seven lines ("Non giacinti o narcisi," "Crudel, perché mi fuggi") and a mammoth seventeen ("Intorno a due vermiglie e vaghe labra"). Inevitably, this increases the length of the Second Book by some fifty percent over the first, and his printer, Angelo Gardano, had a hard time in squeezing it into the standard format of printed partbooks. The Third is longer still, creating similar problems for its printer, now Ricciardo Amadino (see Chapter 3).

The more ambitious nature of the texts in the Second Book is clear from its opening setting, of Tasso's "Non si levava ancor l'alba novella," a very long *ballata* that Monteverdi divided into two *parti* (fourteen lines each).[9] This, too, may have been an exercise set by Ingegneri: Monteverdi's attention is directed to Luca Marenzio's setting of Petrarch's "Non vidi mai dopo notturna pioggia" (the first nine lines of stanza 5 of *Rerum vulgarium fragmenta* [*RVF*] 127) in his First Book *a4* (1585), on which he draws for a significant number of melodic ideas and contrapuntal combinations.[10] The challenges here, however, were not just the length of Tasso's text, but also the fact that it begins with an extended narration (in the *prima parte*) establishing the typical scene of two lovers at dawn, before moving (*seconda parte*)

---

[8] The texts in three *parti*, including the canzone "Fumia la pastorella" and the "Ardo sì, ma non t'amo" sequence, have eight- and seven-line units respectively.

[9] Newcomb, "The Ballata and the 'Free' Madrigal in the Second Half of the Sixteenth Century," 487–88. One can read this text in two ways. It has a four-line *ripresa* and one ten-line *piede* (Monteverdi's *prima parte*), then a second ten-line *piede* (matching the first in meter and rhyme) and a final four-line *volta* (matching the *ripresa* in meter and rhyme). However, each ten-line *piede* has two *piedi* and a *volta* (3 + 3 + 4 lines), which is why Newcomb considers it a "two-stanza ballata." I am grateful to Emiliano Ricciardi for his advice on this.

[10] Tomlinson, *Monteverdi and the End of the Renaissance*, 41–44. The fact that when Monteverdi "borrows" from Marenzio he takes a madrigal with a different scoring may be suggestive of a training exercise. For a corollary, when Monteverdi matches Marenzio's scoring, the connections are less clear, *pace* Tomlinson's (37–38) argument that "A che tormi il ben mio" (First Book) refers to Marenzio's setting in his Fourth Book *a5* (1584).

to the words they speak as one "leaves" the other: the erotic meaning is clear and is entirely typical of the hyper-sensuality found across all the arts in Monteverdi's period. Such longer texts tend also to create problems by virtue of their more complex syntax, and their tendency to employ subordinate clauses parenthetical to the main argument. For example, in "Intorno a due vermiglie e vaghe labra"—the poet has not yet been identified—Monteverdi had to decide whether the eighth line of the poem ("motti sonori od amorosi o casti") was the end of the first sentence or the beginning of the second. He chose the latter, contrary to the more likely reading of the poem, perhaps because he was distracted by the musical possibilities of kisses as sonic phenomena.[11] This is an early case of what becomes a Monteverdian habit of making idiosyncratic choices in text setting that might or might not be "correct" in poetic terms.

No other composer set "Intorno a due vermiglie e vaghe labra" and only one, Vincenzo Gallo, broached "Non si levava ancor l'alba novella" (in the 1598 anthology *Le risa a vicenda*), here in a drastically reduced form.[12] Ingegneri may have wanted to discourage his student from exposing himself to too much direct competition as he became more secure in his compositional practice. Five of the nineteen madrigals in the First Book had no prior musical settings in print.[13] That number increased to eight (out of twenty) in the Second, of which four were "first" settings of relatively new poetry by Torquato Tasso (the other five Tasso texts had previously been set by at least one composer).[14] This also suggests that Ingegneri was nudging Monteverdi in favor of "modern" verse—in particular by Tasso—but not always the better-known texts. It made sense to protect a relatively young composer from obvious comparisons, given the inherent risks in critical assessments of technique or originality. Sometimes, however, Monteverdi could not resist a challenge.

His response to Ingegneri's own music seems to shift between the First and Second Books. The setting of "Ardo sì, ma non t'amo" in the First owes some debt to Ingegneri's in his Fifth Book *a5* of 1587 (the same mode, although in different clefs); however, it is significantly shorter (thirty-nine measures rather than seventy-three), largely because Monteverdi superimposes phrases of the text and tends to avoid extended repetitions save for the last line.[15] His "Mentr'io mirava

---

[11] Compare the punctuation in Georis, *Claudio Monteverdi*, 382. The FCM edition follows. But to be fair to Monteverdi, one can see why he might have read it differently, which raises an intriguing methodological question concerning the editing of anonymous poetry that survives only in a single musical setting.

[12] https://www.tassomusic.org/work/?id=Trm0379b.

[13] "Se per avervi, oimè, donato il core" (Giovanni Maria Bonardo), "Se nel partir da voi, vita mia, sento" (Bonardo), "Poiché del mio dolore" (related to, but different from, "Poiché 'l mio largo pianto" as set by Philippe de Monte in his First Book *a6* [1569] and others), "Amor, s'il tuo ferire" (anon.), and "Donna, s'io miro voi, ghiaccio divengo" (anon.). "Se pur non mi consenti" might seem to be another case, but Monteverdi got the wrong first line for Luigi Groto's poem: other composers set the correct "Se pur non ti contenti," with "mi consenti" coming as the rhyme in line 3, where Monteverdi has it as well.

[14] The four "new" Tasso settings are "Non si levava ancor l'alba novella," "Dolcissimi legami," "Donna, nel mio ritorno," and "S'andasse Amor a caccia."

[15] Ingegneri, *V libro di madrigali a 5 voci*, ed. Joriini and Mangani. Compare the (rather loose) connections noted by Anthony Newcomb ("The Ballata and the 'Free' Madrigal in the Second Half of the Sixteenth Century," 489–90) between Monteverdi's "Quell'ombra esser vorrei" (Second Book) and Ingegneri's "Quell'acqua esser vorrei" (again in his Fifth Book).

Ex. 2.3 (a) Marc'Antonio Ingegneri, "Mentre io mirava fiso" (Fifth Book *a5*, 1587), Canto (G2); (b) Monteverdi, "Mentr'io mirava fiso" (Second Book, 1590), Canto.

fiso" (Second Book)—another relatively new Tasso text—is entirely the opposite, however. Ingegneri's setting in his Fifth Book is in *chiavette* in the D-hypoaeolian mode. Monteverdi chooses *chiavi naturali* and F-ionian, and he produces a much longer setting (eighty-seven measures rather than fifty-nine) by now engaging in significant textual repetition and development, also with a number of his musical fingerprints (complex *contrapposti*, "villanella"-style harmonic progressions, and so forth). His setting of one of its lines, "facendo mille scherzi e mille giri," might have borrowed Ingegneri's falling-third pattern in sequence for the thousand upon thousand playful turns made by two little spirits emerging from the beloved's eyes (Ex. 2.3). But Monteverdi treats it more straightforwardly in rhythmic terms, makes the counterpoint clearer, adds a nice repetition of "mille," and has no compunction about placing it over a bassline descending by step in half notes (minims) in ways that only barely avoid consecutive fifths. He gives the impression of doing everything he can not to sound like his teacher, while also showing off substantial musical dexterity.

In the Second Book, Monteverdi also starts to engage directly with the competition. His setting of Guarini's "Crudel, perché mi fuggi" sets its sights on both Benedetto Pallavicino and Luca Marenzio. The connection with the setting in Marenzio's Fourth Book *a6* (1587) involves a direct and unmistakable borrowing (Ex. 2.4).[16] This is either homage or plagiarism. Pallavicino presents a more complex case, however, with influences going both ways, especially when he and Monteverdi set the same texts. He, too, was from Cremona, and he probably also studied with Ingegneri. He waited until the age of twenty-eight or so to publish his first book (containing four-voice madrigals) in 1579, followed by four books *a5* (the First appeared in 1581), and one *a6* (1587). He was far less precocious than Monteverdi, although Pallavicino did not have much to fear from him, given that the older composer was firmly in Mantuan service from 1583 on, first under Duke Guglielmo Gonzaga and then Duke Vincenzo. Yet clearly there was some rivalry between the two composers, perhaps because they came from the same stable. Pallavicino's

---

[16] La May ("Imitazione in Monteverdi's Canzonettas and the Madrigals," 179–81) notes the Pallavicino connection, but not the Marenzio one.

Ex 2.4 (a) Luca Marenzio, "Crudel, perché mi fuggi" (Fourth Book *a6*, 1587; G2, G2, C2 C3, C3, F3); (b) Monteverdi, "Crudel, perché mi fuggi" (Second Book, 1590).

Fourth Book *a5* (1588) has a setting of Alberto da Parma's "Filli cara et amata," a poem that Monteverdi had included in his First Book the year before: Pallavicino's madrigal makes passing references to Monteverdi's, but more to the point, it is significantly longer (seventy-three measures in contrast to Monteverdi's fifty) by virtue of its contrapuntal working out, contrasted voice groupings, and text repetition. This, Pallavicino seems to say, is what a mature madrigalist would do with the text. He caps his argument by also setting Parma's *risposta* of the nymph in answer to the lover's complaint ("Dunque, Aminta mio caro"), suggesting that "Filli cara et amata" is incomplete without its companion text.

Monteverdi seems to have used "Crudel, perché mi fuggi" to rise to the challenge. While the Marenzio quotation comes in the middle of the madrigal, its opening is a deliberate reworking of Pallavicino's six-voice setting in his First Book *a6* of 1587. Monteverdi switches Pallavicino's upper voices (SSAT in *chiavette*) to lower ones (ATB in *chiavi naturali*) but gives them almost exactly the same music. Beginning with a trio rather than the full ensemble also creates the potential for some future dialogue between lower- and upper-voice groupings (see Chapter 5). In further contrast to Pallavicino, Monteverdi moves quickly to the "if" part of the lover's initial question ("Cruel one, why do you flee me / if you so much desire my death?"). This makes for greater rhetorical urgency: Pallavicino instead sticks with the "why," with four statements of "perché mi fuggi" in various voice combinations.

Pallavicino (prompted by Ingegneri?) may have aided Monteverdi's move to the Gonzaga household in late 1590 or early 1591, but they seem to have had an uneasy relationship thereafter. When Duke Vincenzo Gonzaga's *maestro* of the household musicians, Giaches de Wert, died in 1596, Monteverdi sought to take over the position, although it went, rightly enough, to the more senior composer. Monteverdi renewed his petition on the death of Pallavicino in November 1601, with indecorous haste and writing somewhat dismissively about him.[17] He also included in his Fifth Book (1605) four madrigals to texts that had been set by Pallavicino (and others). Two of them are continuo madrigals—therefore exploiting vocal textures in a quite different way—but in one of those, "Ahi come a un vago sol cortese giro," Monteverdi deliberately quotes the upper two vocal parts of Pallavicino's setting (1600) of the final line ("Ah che piaga d'Amor non sana mai"), although in a different harmonic context.[18] That line concerns Love's wound that never heals, and one wonders whether Monteverdi's handling of it reflects some grudge against the older composer.

It is also clear, however, that Monteverdi drew on ideas from a wide range of musical works by way of textual association rather than direct imitation. Some of them were contained in single-composer prints: many have noted how in the Second Book, Monteverdi was expanding his musical horizons—a comparison is often made between Wert's "Vezzosi augelli in fra le verdi frondi" (1586) and Monteverdi's own evocation of pastoral delights in "Ecco mormorar l'onde" (both poems are by Tasso).[19] Other models, however, may have come from anthologies, which were a far more efficient way of gaining a representative sample of current styles. The fact that five of the texts in Monteverdi's First and Second Books also have settings in the three volumes of five-voice madrigals *De floridi virtuosi d'Italia* issued by Giacomo Vincenti and Ricciardo Amadino (1583, 1585, 1586) may give some pause for thought, not so much for the purpose of direct comparison as for

---

[17] Pallavicino died on 26 November 1601; Monteverdi's letter to Duke Vincenzo requesting the position in place of the "competent" ("soffiziente") composer was written on the 28th. Given that the duke was currently once more on the battlefield in Hungary, he would probably have received the news of his *maestro*'s death and Monteverdi's letter in the same dispatches.
[18] Tomlinson, *Monteverdi and the End of the Renaissance*, 152.
[19] Ibid., 49–51.

broadening the list of usual suspects from whom the young Monteverdi might have received some influence.[20]

One anthology almost certainly had some connection with the Second Book: the *Spoglia amorosa: madrigali a cinque voci* (Venice: Heirs of Girolamo Scotto, 1584). In addition to composers typical of such collections such as Giovanni Domenico da Nola, Lassus, Marenzio (including "Tirsi morir volea"), Merulo, Monte, Striggio, and Wert, it had settings by those moving in Roman circles, including Palestrina, Giovanni Maria Nanino, and Ruggiero Giovannelli (the last some six years younger than Monteverdi). Both Nanino and Giovannelli often appeared in anthologies as well, and they were adept at the "lighter" style of madrigal (incorporating bouncing canzonetta rhythms, close imitations, and the juxtaposition of different voice groupings) that has a bearing on Monteverdi's own early works. But *Spoglia amorosa* also included two much older madrigals by Cipriano de Rore (who died in 1565): his "Cantai mentre ch'i arsi del mio foco" (a *ballata* by Giovanni Brevio), first published in 1542, and "Alma Susanna, ben felic'il core" (1565).

Although Ingegneri was born and trained in Verona, he wrote eloquently in the dedication of his First Book *a6* (1586) to Duke Ottavio Farnese of Parma on how he had been one of many composers able to spend time at his court, to be in friendly relations with Rore (so, in the early 1560s), and to receive instruction from him. Although Rore had long continued to be held in high musical regard, this was an unusual testimonial for a composer now dead for almost twenty-one years. By virtue of having been taught by Ingegneri, Monteverdi evidently saw himself connected to Rore, who he claimed was the founder of the *seconda pratica*.

If the final setting in any madrigal book was somehow meant to make a statement no less impressive than the first one, Monteverdi's decision to end his Second Book with the first half of Pietro Bembo's (1470–1547) old sonnet "Cantai un tempo, e se fu dolce il canto," fit the bill. The issue is not so much the text itself, which had received a decent number of musical settings following Baldassare Donato's in 1553, including an impressive six-voice one in Philippe de Monte's Second Book *a6* of 1569. Rather, it is the fact that Monteverdi (or Ingegneri) decided that the setting should be modeled on Rore's "Cantai mentre ch'i arsi del mio foco," which had opened his First Book *a5* (1542). The connection is clear by way of mode, cleffing, and a similar opening, and with decidedly archaic results, if not

---

[20] For example, Monteverdi set three texts presented one after the other in the first of the *De floridi virtuosi d'Italia* series (1583): no. 3 ("Ch'ami la vita mia nel tuo bel nome"; music by Lelio Bertani), no. 4 ("Tra mille fiamme e tra mille catene"; Orazio Vecchi)—both in Monteverdi's First Book—and no. 2 ("Se tu mi lasci, perfido, tuo danno"; Marenzio) in his Second. Monteverdi sets that last text as "Se tu mi lassi, perfida, tuo danno!" The poem is problematic, and the attribution to Tasso is not entirely secure. Early printed sources of the text have the first line in the male voice (addressing "perfida") but with an apparent switch to a female one in the middle ("misera ben sarei"). The version set by Marenzio resolves the contradiction by putting the text in the female voice ("perfido . . . misera"). The other solution, adopted by Francesco Stivori in 1588 and Monteverdi in 1590, is to keep "perfida" but switch "misera" to "misero," putting the poem firmly in the male voice. These different readings variously enter the literary tradition.

Ex. 2.5 (a) Cipriano de Rore, "Cantai mentre ch'i arsi del mio foco" (First Book *a5*, 1542; G2, C2, C3, C3, F3); (b) Monteverdi, "Cantai un tempo, e se fu dolce il canto" (Second Book, 1590; G2, C2, C3, C3, F3).

quite the strict counterpoint that Ingegneri might have expected (Ex. 2.5).[21] No less striking, however, is Monteverdi's decision just to set the first two quatrains of the text. Bembo's sonnet is in the typical Petrarchan vein: the poet sang—whether sweetly not he will leave others to judge—but he can do so no more, given that he is deprived of rest and peace: so it goes for one who has placed too much trust

---

[21] Tomlinson (*Monteverdi and the End of the Renaissance*, 55–56) notes the connection. Monteverdi clearly knew a number of madrigals by Rore: in the "Dichiaratione della lettera stampata nel Quinto libro de suoi madregali" appended to Monteverdi's 1607 *Scherzi musicali*, Giulio Cesare Monteverdi offered as precedents for the *seconda pratica* Rore's "Da le belle contrade d'oriente," "Se ben il duol che per voi, Donna, sento," "Poi che m'invita Amore" (and its *seconda parte*, "E se pur mi mantieni"), "Crudele, acerba, inesorabil morte," and "Un'altra volta la Germania strida."

in another ("così va, ch'in altrui pon fede tanto"). It becomes clear in the sonnet's two tercets that the fault lies, typically, with the recalcitrant beloved, the "enemy" of pity, love, and the poet himself. Without that part of the poem, however, the text reads like some expression of concern for a life, or a musical career, somehow going astray.

Monteverdi may have viewed his archaicizing "Cantai un tempo" as a useful way of marking the end of his studies with Ingegneri—the past-tense "cantai" is revealing—paying homage both to Rore, the teacher of his teacher, and to the contrapuntal exercises that had formed part of Monteverdi's own instruction. But he was now heading toward his twenty-third birthday and therefore in search of a job. The dedication of the First Book to Marco Verità, a prominent music patron in Verona (Ingegneri's hometown), and of the Second to Giacomo Ricardi, president of the Milanese senate, suggests that he was looking for something either in the Veneto or in Milan. But any dashed hopes there were soon remedied by his move to join the household musicians of Duke Vincenzo Gonzaga in Mantua in late 1590 or early 1591. His initial appointment as a string player led to a connection with Giacomo Cattaneo (another string player) as Monteverdi entered into what was in effect a second apprenticeship to learn the trade of the court musician: he eventually married Cattaneo's daughter, Claudia, who was a singer—it was a common practice to arrange marriages between musicians, in part so as to allow the wife to continue to perform, given that marrying outside the profession tended to shut down a woman's career.

Monteverdi's dedicating his Third Book (1592) to Vincenzo Gonzaga was a standard response to such an appointment. However, its contents also demonstrate the near-immediate impact of entering a quite different musical and cultural world: Mantua was a magnet for some of the finest musicians, poets, and artists of the period. Monteverdi may still have been keeping an eye out for potential rivals: there are some crossovers with texts set by a composer he could have encountered in Cremona, Flaminio Tresti, who had dedicated his Third Book *a*5 (1590) to the duke.[22] But Monteverdi was now working alongside, and at times competing with, some of the most capable madrigalists of the time, including Giaches de Wert, Benedetto Pallavicino, Giovanni Giacomo Gastoldi, and Salamone Rossi. He also moved into different poetic spheres: Torquato Tasso's lyric poetry had been quite prominent in the Second Book, but in his Third, Monteverdi turned

---

[22] Tresti had set in his Second Book *a*5 (1587) "Dolcemente dormiva la mia Clori" (in Monteverdi's Second Book) and "O come è gran martire" (Third). The latter has textual readings in part followed by Monteverdi; see Georis, *Claudio Monteverdi*, 406, although *pace* Georis, Tresti's Second Book was dedicated to Giovanni Carlo Lercar. Tresti's Third Book has settings of "Stracciami pur il core" and a different "O come è gran martire" text by Guarini, as well as a different passage from Tasso's "Aretia" eclogue ("Come tenera rosa") that was the source for Monteverdi's "La giovinetta pianta." In its dedication, Tresti, now in Casale Monferrato, said that the duke had much enjoyed these madrigals prior to their being printed.

to his eclogues and still more his epic poetry. Tasso (three settings) is also joined by Battista Guarini (eight)—both poets were in high fashion in Mantua.[23] Moreover, Monteverdi encountered a very fine group of singers and instrumentalists who nudged his compositions in striking directions. He may still have had things to learn, but he was no longer a "discepolo" subject to his master.

---

[23] Guarini did not publish his collected *Rime* until 1598. However, more than half of the texts in Monteverdi's Third Book are taken from Giovanni Battista Licino's *Rime di diversi celebri poeti dell'età nostra: nuovamente raccolte e poste in luce* (Bergamo: Comino Ventura, 1587), a source often used by Mantuan (and other) composers.

3
The Madrigal "Book"

The musical "madrigal" embraced settings of a wide range of lyric or epic poetic forms, including canzones, sonnets, and *ottava rima* stanzas or *terza rima* ones, as well as madrigals proper. Poetic madrigals ranged quite widely in formal structure: they could be shorter lyric statements in loosely organized verse, or constructed more regularly on the older model of the Trecento madrigal (often two tercets and a concluding couplet) or *ballata*. All this poetry was cast in the typical meter of "high" Italian verse, the eleven-syllable line (*endecasillabo*), although its close cousin, the seven-syllable one (*settenario*), could also appear in canzones and in poetic madrigals. The length and structure of poem would determine whether it would be set as a single work or divided into a *prima* and a *seconda parte* (e.g., the octave and sestet of a sonnet) or more (for successive stanzas of a canzone, sestina, or verse in *ottava rima*). But the hallmark of all these settings was that they were usually through-composed from beginning to end save for any conventional repetition of the final line(s). In other performance contexts, *ottava* and *terza rima* stanzas could be set strophically (the same music for repetitive groups of lines), as could sonnets (for each quatrain and tercet), but this was more typical of quasi-improvised solo singing to the lute. Excluded from the "madrigal," however, were "lighter" forms such as the strophic villanella and canzonetta, which tended to use short, repetitive stanzas and, in the case of the canzonetta as it developed at the hand of the poet Gabriello Chiabrera, different line lengths (of four, five, or eight syllables, etc.). They also tended to be set for fewer voices: three or four rather than the four, five, or six typical of the madrigal. Thus, Monteverdi's first "secular" publication, the *Canzonette a tre voci* (1584), contains three-voice settings mainly of texts in three or more stanzas for which music is provided only for the first, with the rest of the text printed underneath.[1] Likewise, when Giulio Cesare Monteverdi published in 1607 his brother's settings for three voices plus instruments of strophic canzonettas by Chiabrera and his imitators, he titled the collection *Scherzi musicali* (meaning something like "musical fancies").

Monteverdi trod carefully in his First Book *a5* (1587). It contains seventeen settings of relatively short poetic madrigals—most in the verbal present tense—plus one of the first stanza of a canzone (Guarini's "Baci soavi e cari"), and one of a three-stanza canzone (Antonio Allegretti's rather old "Fumia la pastorella"). Monteverdi's

---

[1] One of the settings ("Tu ridi sempre mai") has just a single stanza. All the texts are in *endecasillabi* and/or *settenari*.

Second Book (1590) expands the poetic range with some longer madrigal texts, plus an ambitious *ballata* at the head of the volume (Tasso's "Non si levava ancor l'alba novella"), an *ottava rima* stanza (Ercole Bentivoglio's "La bocca onde l'asprissime parole"), and at the end, the two quatrains of a sonnet (Pietro Bembo's "Cantai un tempo, e se fu dolce il canto"). The Third Book (1592) goes further still in terms of range and length, bringing in two settings of *ottava rima* stanzas (three each) from Tasso's epic poem *Gerusalemme liberata*, and then a full sonnet at the end. In the Third Book and the Fourth (1603), Monteverdi also adopts the *versi sciolti* (free verse) of the spoken play (Battista Guarini's pastoral *tragicommedia*, Il pastor fido), although not in entirely straightforward ways. But for the purpose of his title pages up to and including the Sixth Book of 1614, these collections all contain "madrigals," regardless of their different poetic contents.

Monteverdi's Seventh Book (1619) breaks the pattern: it has a different form of title (*Concerto. Settimo libro de madrigali a 1. 2. 3. 4. e sei voci, con altri generi de canti*); it avoids the standard five-voice scoring save in the final *ballo*, *Tirsi e Clori*; and it separates the contents by way of that distinction between "madrigali" and "altri generi de canti." Those "other types of songs" include an *ottava rima* stanza set as four strophic variations (two poetic lines each) over a Romanesca bass, a solo-voice *lettera amorosa* and *partenza amorosa*, two canzonettas, and a *ballo*. The *lettera* and *partenza amorosa* are both identified as being "in genere rapresentativo" and use a musical style often now identified as "recitative" (see Chapter 9). But Monteverdi is quite correct: these "other" songs are not madrigals by any traditional definition of the term. Such nuances of genre are further apparent in the title of Monteverdi's *Scherzi musicali, cioè arie, e madrigali in stil recitativo, con una ciaccona a 1. e 2. voci* issued (and also edited?) by the Venetian printer Bartolomeo Magni in 1632. However, matters are starting to become muddled. Here the "arias" are mostly strophic canzonettas; and the *ciaccona* is a setting of a sonnet ("Zefiro torna e di soavi accenti"). One of the "madrigals" is the final setting in the book, "Armato il cor d'adamantina fede," but despite the wording of the title page, this duet for two tenors and continuo is not "in recitative style." Instead, recitative appears only in the beginning of the second stanza of the solo-voice setting of a text in *ottava rima* ("Ecco di dolci raggi il sol armato").[2] Even Magni appears to have been confused by that stanza ("Io ch'armato sin hor d'un duro gelo"): he printed it in the wrong place.

By the Eighth Book (1638), the *Madrigali guerrieri, et amorosi*, Monteverdi seems to be struggling still more with labels. According to the title page, this book of "madrigals of war and love" also contains "alcuni opuscoli in genere rappresentativo" (some little works in [the] representative genre), but the diminutive may have been a marketing strategy to avoid putting off the prospective buyer: the pieces *in genere rappresentativo* include the *Combattimento di Tancredi e Clorinda* and the *Ballo*

---

[2] The two stanzas of "Ecco di dolci raggi" follow the *ottava rima* pattern, although its even-numbered lines are *versi sdruccioli*: i.e., with the accent on the antepenultimate syllable.

delle ingrate, which are hardly "little works." The title page further notes that these *opuscoli* "will serve as short episodes between the songs without action" ("saranno per brevi Episodii frà i canti senza gesto").[3] This suggests a programming strategy that clearly pertained on the evening of the first performance of the *Combattimento* in the Venetian residence of Girolamo Mocenigo in Carnival 1624, when it interrupted a sequence of madrigals "senza gesto" to surprising effect.[4] But the division of the volume itself into two halves labeled "Canti guerrieri" and "Canti amorosi," each containing two *opuscoli in genere rappresentativo* as well as *canti senza gesto*, suggests that its entire content consists of *canti* (songs), the only distinction being whether they are *con* or *senza gesto*. And as for the *canti senza gesto*, they include not just sonnets, an *ottava rima* stanza, and madrigals, but also canzonettas and a very long ode (Rinuccini's "Ogni amante è guerrier: nel suo gran regno").

This shift from books containing madrigals (the First through Sixth) through a "concerto" of pieces mixing them with "altri generi di canti" (the Seventh) to one containing *canti* of a multitude of kinds (the Eighth) raises broader issues. First, the typical madrigal book that retained a sense of consistency, whether or not it was structured internally by way of poetic or musical content, takes on the air of a miscellany. This is not so unusual in the repertory as a whole. Nor is it to say that such a book could not still be organized quite carefully: indeed, what seems to be most like a "miscellany" among Monteverdi's madrigal books, the Seventh, is nothing of the kind. However, the Eighth Book is revealing. It came eighteen years after the Seventh and contains at least some "old" music: indeed, the *Ballo delle ingrate* goes back to 1608, albeit revised for use in Vienna sometime in the 1630s.[5] But if Monteverdi was gathering together pieces composed over a number of years—in what order we cannot tell—his (or his editor's) design for the Eighth Book does not stem from any original compositional plan, even if some later one emerged instead.

Second, the musical expansion of the term "madrigal" was driven at least in part by poetic developments in the early seventeenth century. Poetic genres were ranked according to their literary elevation: epic poetry tended to count for more, given its Classical roots, and within lyric genres, sonnets and canzones carried greater weight (because of Dante and Petrarch) than madrigals, with the canzonetta or its offshoots at the bottom of the scale. Each placed different demands upon the composer in terms of structure, content, expressive potency, and the listener's expectations. Monteverdi's retention of sonnets and *ottava rima* stanzas in the Seventh

---

[3] Monteverdi used a similar wording in relation to the *Combattimento* and a second similar work, *Armida abbandonata*, in his letter to Alessandro Striggio of 1 May 1627, noting that placing such "little episodes" between other musical works does not work out badly ("e tali e simili cose ponno servire come per episodietti fra altre musiche, ché non riescono male").

[4] In the preface to the Eighth Book, Monteverdi notes that the *Combattimento* was done in 1624, and in the prefatory remarks to the piece itself, he says that it was part of an evening's entertainment during Carnival ("In tempo però di Carnevale per passatempo di veglia"). Putting both elements together suggests early 1624, but by virtue of the Venetian calendar (where the new year began on 1 March), it might be early 1625.

[5] The *Ballo delle ingrate* was performed during the festivities in Mantua in May–June 1608 in celebration of the marriage of Prince Francesco Gonzaga and Margherita of Savoy. The text was later altered to suit Viennese circumstances. For the arguments in favor of musical revision (chiefly in the writing for Venere and Plutone), see Tomlinson, *Monteverdi and the End of the Renaissance*, 206.

and Eighth Books has been viewed as a sign of conservatism—although what he does with them is not at all conservative—but he also seems to have liked well-structured poetry as something to build upon in his musical settings, or more often, to react against for the purpose of rhetorical deconstruction.[6] However, the tendency from the late sixteenth century on to elevate the lowly canzonetta—another form of well-structured poetry—into the ambit of the "madrigal" expanded the musical possibilities even as it diluted the poetic ones. This is, in part, what creates the ambiguities of a setting such as "Non avea Febo ancora" with its central *Lamento della ninfa* in the Eighth Book: the text (by Ottavio Rinuccini) is a canzonetta with a refrain, but Monteverdi seems to treat it as something much weightier.

Third, this expansion reflects the impact of the "new" musical styles that emerged around 1600 by way of the instrumental basso continuo. A book of madrigals presented for five unaccompanied voices is one thing; a book with settings for anything from one to eight or more voices plus continuo and perhaps obbligato instruments—as with Monteverdi's *Madrigali guerrieri, et amorosi*—is something else. A traditional polyphonic madrigal relies on the voices alone to sustain the musical texture and flow, regardless of any performance practice that added instruments to support or replace them. In the continuo madrigal, the instrumental bass provides the foundation, meaning that the voices are freer to drop out or in, and they can be exploited in a wider variety of combinations. The impact is obvious in the last six madrigals in the Fifth Book, the first in Monteverdi's case for which the continuo is necessary rather than optional; they are quite different in musical style and structure from the first seven madrigals there. The Sixth Book also makes a clear distinction between six madrigals indicated as "concertato," with an independent continuo line, and four wherein the continuo almost entirely follows the lowest-sounding voice (as a "basso seguente"). None of the settings in the Seventh and Eighth Books can be done without continuo. Monteverdi may have resisted some of the trends of the so-called new music: scholars have often noted how he seems to have preferred duets to solo songs, given the greater musical possibilities afforded by two voices compared with one. But he exploited others to the full.

Fourth and last, these changes had a significant impact on the ways in which Monteverdi's madrigals could best be presented in print, which, in turn, had a demonstrable influence on the changes themselves. This is something less considered in the literature so far, but it turns out to be a matter of some importance.

Printing and publishing

Monteverdi was among the more successful composers of his time in terms of entering the musical marketplace (Table 3.1). Once Ingegneri had allowed him to

---

[6] Compare Giles, *Monteverdi and the Marvellous*, 71–72, on deconstructed sonnets.

Table 3.1 Monteverdi's madrigal books and subsequent editions (all in Venice save where noted).

	First edition (dedicatee)	Subsequent editions
First	Angelo Gardano, 1587 (Marco Verità, 27 Jan.)	Alessandro Raverii, 1607; Bartolomeo Magni, 1621
Second	Angelo Gardano, 1590 (Giacomo Ricardi, 1 Jan.)	Alessandro Raverii, 1607; Bartolomeo Magni, 1621
Third	Ricciardo Amadino, 1592 (Vincenzo Gonzaga, 27 June)	Amadino, 1594, 1600, 1604, 1607, 1611; Antwerp, Pierre Phalèse, 1615; Bartolomeo Magni, 1621
Fourth	Ricciardo Amadino, 1603 (Accademia degli Intrepidi [Ferrara], 1 Mar.)	Amadino, 1605, 1607, 1611, 1615; Antwerp, Pierre Phalèse, 1615; Bartolomeo Magni, 1622; Antwerp, Heirs of Pierre Phalèse, 1644
Fifth	Ricciardo Amadino, 1605 (Vincenzo Gonzaga, 30 July)	Amadino, 1606, 1608, 1610, 1611, 1613,[a] 1615; Antwerp, Pierre Phalèse, 1615; Bartolomeo Magni, 1620; Antwerp, Heirs of Pierre Phalèse, 1643
Scherzi musicali	Ricciardo Amadino 1607 (Giulio Cesare Monteverdi to Francesco Gonzaga, 21 July)	Amadino, 1609, 1615; Bartolomeo Magni, 1628
Sixth	Ricciardo Amadino, 1614	Amadino, 1615; Bartolomeo Magni, 1620; Antwerp, Heirs of Pierre Phalèse, 1639
Seventh	Bartolomeo Magni, 1619 (Caterina de' Medici, 13 Dec.)	Magni, 1622, 1623, 1628, 1641
Scherzi musicali	Bartolomeo Magni, 1632 (Magni to Pietro Capello, 20 June)	—
Eighth	Alessandro Vincenti, 1638 (Emperor Ferdinand III, 1 Sept.)	—
Ninth	Alessandro Vincenti, 1651 (Vincenti to Gerolamo Orologio, 17 June)	

[a] The 1613 edition of the Fifth Book still notes on its title page that Monteverdi is "Maestro della Musica del Serenissimo Signor Duca di Mantova."

progress to the five-voice madrigal, he published six books of them, plus a Seventh and Eighth designed in different ways (and a Ninth appeared posthumously). Add two books of lighter *Scherzi musicali* (1607, 1632), one opera (*Orfeo*), and two substantial volumes of sacred music (plus a posthumous third). In terms of books of secular madrigals, Luca Marenzio published more (two *a4*, nine *a5*, and six *a6*), as did Giaches de Wert (one *a4* and eleven *a5*, plus a posthumous volume). But Marenzio's freelance career was less stable, and Wert slowed down in his later years, in part because of age and ill health, but also, it seems, given the various scandals in which he was involved. Nor was their later music as popular in Italy as Monteverdi's: Wert's Tenth Book of 1591 had only one edition, as did Marenzio's Sixth *a5* of 1594. Monteverdi's Third Book of 1592, on the other hand, was far more successful at least in terms of its appearing in multiple editions, given that five were issued after the first by its original printer, Ricciardo Amadino, between 1594 and 1611.[7]

Monteverdi's first publication, the *Sacrae cantiunculae tribus vocibus* (1582), was printed by Angelo Gardano in Venice; his second, the *Madrigali spirituali a quattro voci* (1583), in Brescia by Vincenzo Sabbio at the commission of a Cremonese bookseller, Pietro Bozzola; and his third, the *Canzonette a tre voci ... libro primo* (1584) by Ricciardo Amadino and his then business partner Giacomo Vincenti. In none of these cases did the printer likely have any commercial interest in them: instead the printing costs would have been Monteverdi's responsibility, whether or not funded by third parties who may have included their dedicatees. For his First Book a5, Monteverdi went back to Angelo Gardano, as he did for his Second: it was a typical move, given the prestige attached to that press. For the Third, however, Monteverdi switched to Ricciardo Amadino, who had split from Vincenti in 1586; although Amadino and Vincenti had gone their separate ways, they each tried to corner the more progressive niches of the market. That shift to Amadino may have been prompted by some Mantuan colleagues, or perhaps the printer was being particularly aggressive about luring composers into his stable.[8] But Monteverdi then stayed with Amadino through his Sixth Book (including his other publications): that is, until Amadino ceased publishing sometime in 1617. For the Seventh Book, Monteverdi turned back to the Gardano press (now run by Bartolomeo Magni, Angelo Gardano's son-in-law), but for the Eighth, he switched to another Venetian printer, Alessandro Vincenti (son of Giacomo)—although Magni printed the *Selva morale e spirituale* of 1640–41—and Vincenti had some leftover pieces to include in the posthumous Ninth Book.

The First and Second Books did not make much of a splash; nor, probably, did Monteverdi expect them to.[9] They were reissued in 1607 by Alessandro Raverii, a rather opportunistic Venetian printer, and Magni included them in his series of editions of all of Monteverdi's madrigal books to date in 1620–22. Two madrigals from the Second Book were also included in a musical anthology issued in 1597 by the Nuremberg printer Paul Kauffmann: the *Fiori del giardino di diversi eccellentissimi autori*.[10] But the rest of the First and Second Books did not enter the marketplace in

---

[7] I use the term "multiple editions" deliberately. In the case of typeset music printing, a volume identified as "nuovamente ristampato" (newly reprinted) is not, strictly speaking, a "reprint," given that each time it had to be reset from scratch, however closely it might follow a previous edition in terms of content and layout. Engraved editions are a different case, given that the original plates could be kept and reused, with or without further changes being made to them.

[8] Wert largely published with the Gardano press; Pallavicino switched between Angelo Gardano and Giacomo Vincenti (Amadino's former partner); Gastoldi and Salamone Rossi were strongly in the Amadino camp. One suspects that Gardano was selective in what he took on, save in the case of "vanity" editions in which he had no subsequent financial interest. Amadino was certainly more aggressive in issuing "reprints" of volumes published by him. But in the absence of contracts signed between composers and printers, or other documentary evidence of their relationships, it is hard to draw conclusions about who printed what and why.

[9] For example, they are not included in the catalogue of books available for sale from the Giunti bookshop in Florence printed in early 1605 (it is dated 1604 *stile fiorentino*), which does, however, list Monteverdi's Third Book; see Mischiati, *Indici, cataloghi e avvisi degli editori e librai musicali italiani*, 118.

[10] Kauffmann included six madrigals by Monteverdi in the order they originally appeared: "Non si levava ancor l'alba novella" and "Dolcemente dormiva la mia Clori" (Second Book); "La giovinetta pianta," "Sovra tenere erbette e bianchi fiori," and "Stracciami pur il core" (Third); and "Ah, dolente partita!" (Fourth; i.e.,

any similar way: Monteverdi quite properly identified himself on their title page as Ingegneri's "discepolo," but this was not likely to attract anyone browsing the shelves of a music-seller's shop. We do not know what financial arrangements were made with Amadino for the Third Book, but the printer must quickly have realized that he had a hot commodity on his hands, given those subsequent editions that would almost certainly have been done at his own expense. This established a pattern for the subsequent madrigal books as well save for the Eighth, a very large and rather cumbersome collection that could never realistically have been expected to sell well.[11]

Those subsequent editions of the Third Book certainly kept Monteverdi's name in the public eye, and also covered a twelve-year gap in his published output prior to the appearance of the Fourth Book in 1603.[12] Given his position in Mantua, he had no strong reason to issue madrigals containing works that in some sense now "belonged" to his employer; he was busy doing other things; and he may also have needed time to absorb the "late" madrigal books issued in the mid-1590s by Wert and Marenzio, as well as those emerging in Ferrarese circles by Alfonso Fontanelli, Carlo Gesualdo, and Luzzasco Luzzaschi. What prompted the Fourth Book and then the Fifth (1605), however, was almost certainly the attack launched by Giovanni Maria Artusi in 1600 and renewed in 1603. Their prefatory materials call these madrigals Monteverdi's "creations" ("parti" in the Fourth and the singular "parto" in the Fifth); they are no longer just "fruits" or the like, but the product of some labor.[13] But the dedications of those two books, plus the celebratory poems and other paratextual elements in the Fifth, suggest that Monteverdi was now adept at using the medium of print to further his cause.[14]

Formats

Music printing was subject to various constraints determined by the available technologies on the one hand, and conventional practice on the other. To state the

before Monteverdi published it himself). This was a mammoth collection that included works by a number of Monteverdi's immediate colleagues in Mantua (Gastoldi, Pallavicino, Rovigo, Wert)—although Monteverdi is the most prominent of them—plus many others (including Andrea and Giovanni Gabrieli, Marenzio, Merulo, Monte, Nanino, Vecchi, etc.). Its preface is undated, so it is not clear precisely when the volume appeared.

[11] Monteverdi's Eighth Book was still listed for sale in Alessandro Vincenti's catalogue of his holdings printed in 1662 (Mischiati, *Indici, cataloghi e avvisi degli editori e librai musicali italiani*, 215), but so, too, was a great deal of music that would count as old. It was expensive (£16.10s., increased from £16 in Vincenti's 1649 and 1658 catalogues), but that was largely due to its size, given that prices were strongly influenced by the amount of paper involved in a given book.

[12] So did the inclusion of four canzonettas in Antonio Morsolino's *Il primo libro delle canzonette a tre voc . . . con alcune altre de diversi eccellenti musici* (Venice: Ricciardo Amadino, 1594). This is a rather odd collection: Monteverdi's settings are nos. 2, 6, 10, and 14, i.e., each at the head of regular subsections of the book, which gives him more prominence than one might expect. There is some Cremonese connection here, given that Morsolino also includes pieces by his apparent relative, Uomobuono Morsolino, who was organist at Cremona cathedral from 1591 to 1611. Its dedicatee, Conte Bernadino da Porto, was presumably a member of the prominent family in Vicenza.

[13] Georis, *Claudio Monteverdi*, 209–10. The Italian term can be used metaphorically, but it still has connotations of giving birth or producing offspring.

[14] Carter, "Cerberus Barks in Vain."

obvious, print determined what could or could not be printed, and how it would appear on the page. While such material matters might seem worthy of consideration merely to satisfy bibliographical curiosity, in fact they have a significant impact on how Monteverdi's madrigals came to light, and on how we should view them today.

A typical book of five-voice madrigals was presented in five partbooks in quarto format labeled Canto, Alto, Tenore, Basso, and Quinto (Fifth); one of six-voice madrigals would also have a Sesto (Sixth) partbook. In the case of any set of five partbooks that included one or more pieces for a greater number of voices, the additional parts would need to be placed on an opening face to face with one of the other voices, with coordinated page turns, so that two singers could sing from the same book. Those partbook labels were generic rather than voice-specific: the Basso would contain the lowest sounding voice, but depending on the clef it might not be for a "bass" singer; likewise, the Quinto could contain parts matching the voices in the Canto one (so, an SSATB setting) or the Tenore (SATTB), or in some other range. Each part would be printed as a succession of notes without bar lines: singers had to keep time themselves, and if they miscounted when sight-reading a piece, or if the ensemble fell apart for other reasons, there was scant choice but to go back to the beginning. But there was no need for these madrigals to be issued in score for performance purposes, just as there was none in the case of a string quartet by Haydn or Mozart. When Artusi took Monteverdi to task over his irregular dissonance treatment in 1600, however, he needed scored-up versions of the relevant passages in order to illustrate his points, although given that the relevant madrigals from the Fourth and Fifth Books had not yet been printed, we do not know what sources he used.[15]

In the standard quarto format, each partbook would usually consist of three printed sheets each containing four pages on either side (so, twelve folios or twenty-four pages). The correct manner of folding and collating these sheets—something that could be done by a bookbinder rather than the printer—would be aided by "signatures" (A, A2, etc.) at the foot of specific pages. The first folio would contain the title page and on its reverse, the dedication; the printed music would usually begin on fol. 2r, which would be paginated as "1"; the book would then run to page 22 (i.e., fol. 12v), which would contain a "tavola" (table of contents). Having each madrigal or its sectional subdivisions (labeled *prima parte*, *seconda parte*, etc.) take up a single printed page was the most visually elegant strategy: this allowed for twenty-one madrigals (or parts thereof), which explains the number of settings in Monteverdi's First and Second Books.

Those first two books were printed by Angelo Gardano in oblong quarto format (with six staves per page); on the other hand, Ricciardo Amadino and others consistently preferred upright quarto (eight staves per page). The choice for one or the

---

[15] There is a broader, as yet insoluble, problem in terms of whether Monteverdi first wrote out his madrigals in scores from which parts were later extracted (whether by the composer or the printer). In other words, scores may have existed to which Artusi somehow gained access.

other did not affect the overall structure of the partbook (three printed sheets), but it could have an impact on how individual madrigals would fit on a single page, or not, depending on how many notes could be printed on six longer staves or eight shorter ones. The Quinto partbook of the Second Book in Gardano's edition (1590) and Alessandro Raverii's (1607) reveals the issues (Fig. 3.1). For reasons of space, Gardano began the first madrigal in the book, the long "Non si levava ancor l'alba novella," on two staves below the dedication. Thereafter, he managed to have each madrigal begin at the top of a page until "Mentr'io mirava fiso" (p. 12), which carried over to page 13 by one stave. The next madrigal, "Ecco mormorar l'onde" was not short, either, forcing a page turn. But Gardano got things back on track by fitting the next two madrigals, "Dolcemente dormiva la mia Clori" and "Se tu mi lassi, perfida, tuo danno!", on the rest of page 14 going over to page 15 (a single opening). Raverii, using the upright format, started "Non si levava ancor l'alba novella" at the top of a page (he had no choice, given the lack of a dedication), but he had mixed success in positioning the other madrigals similarly: he managed it almost entirely in the Basso partbook—the bass part in any madrigal tends to have fewer notes—but less so elsewhere. In his Quinto partbook, "Mentr'io mirava fiso" starts at the top of page 12 but now runs over to the second stave of page 13 (not Gardano's first stave), so Raverii used a different madrigal, "Se tu mi lassi," to fill out the page. "Ecco mormorar l'onde" starts at the top of page 14 running over to the first two staves on page 15, whereupon Raverii chose to fit "La bocca onde l'asprissime parole" on the rest of page 15, prior to "Dolcemente dormiva" at the top of page 16. Thus, the sequence of madrigals is different in the two editions. However, Raverii made the mistake of printing in his Canto, Tenore, and Quinto partbooks the table of contents in the order given in Gardano's edition (his Alto and Basso partbooks are correct). Bartolomeo Magni's 1621 edition followed Raverii's sequence of madrigals, but its tables of contents in the partbooks are now in the proper sequence.[16]

Ricciardo Amadino had to make similar accommodations even in his first editions. In the case of the Third Book, the beginning of the first madrigal, "La giovinetta pianta," is positioned at the foot of the dedication, as Gardano had done for "Non si levava ancor" in the Second. Given the increasing length of the madrigals in this book, there are some mid-piece page turns (not a problem for singers, though in other contexts it becomes so for instrumentalists), and there was room for a *tavola* only in the Alto and Basso partbooks: Monteverdi's soprano and tenor parts generally had more notes and so took up more space. Even so, the Third book has only twenty settings rather than twenty-one. We do not know if a madrigal was rejected at the printing stage because it would not fit: "Ah, dolente partita!" (eventually placed at the beginning of the Fourth Book) may be a possible candidate, given that it appears with other madrigals from the Third Book in Kauffmann's *Fiori del giardino di diversi eccellentissimi autori* (1597), before the composer published it

---

[16] This explains the oddity of Malipiero's edition of the Second Book, which follows the order in the Raverii and Magni editions rather than the original.

THE MADRIGAL "BOOK" 35

(a)

(b)

Fig. 3.1 (a) Second Book, first edition (Angelo Gardano, 1590), Quinto partbook, p. 13 (British Library, London); (b) Second Book, second edition (Alessandro Raverii, 1607), Quinto partbook, p. 13 (Library of Congress, Washington, D.C.). Both pages have the same dimensions, with (b) in upright format.

himself.[17] Monteverdi's Fourth, Fifth, and Sixth Books similarly fall "short" because their individual settings are too long.

There was, in principle, no need for the 1607 *Scherzi musicali* to be in a larger folio format (eleven staves per page) laid out in so-called choirbook form, with the parts for each setting placed separately on the same opening (vocal on the left and instrumental on the right, with the recto also containing subsequent stanzas of the text printed on their own). It could just as well have been printed in partbooks like many other such volumes of the period. But this was clearly intended to be some kind of luxury edition—it was the first of Monteverdi's prints to claim a "privilege" on its title page to assert a form of copyright protection—perhaps because it contained Giulio Cesare Monteverdi's "Dichiaratione," which, also somewhat unusually, was included in subsequent editions of the collection.[18] The rise of the continuo madrigal, however, did force some changes in printing layouts. In the Fifth Book, the Basso Continuo partbook simply presents a single line, but in the Sixth, most of the "concertato" madrigals with an obligatory continuo are presented in what is labeled a "partitura": that is, a short score giving the bass and a principal voice (minus text save for occasional cues) in cases where coordination between singer(s) and instrumentalist(s) would be an issue. The same format (but now also with the text) is adopted for a few of the settings in the Seventh Book, where some kind of score is needed for solo songs in a declamatory style (the setting of Giambattista Marino's sonnet "Tempro la cetra, e per cantar gli honori" at the head of the volume, and the *lettera amorosa* and *partenza amorosa*) and for the canzonetta "Chioma d'oro." The same is true in the Eighth Book, which sometimes extends to providing full scores for the "representative" pieces such as the *Combattimento di Tancredi e Clorinda*. Those full scores force a different format. The Sixth and Seventh Books are still in upright quarto, but in the Eighth, the Basso Continuo partbook (though not the others) is in folio with twelve staves per page.

The more a madrigal book deviated from any standard format, the more it created problems for the printer, adding time and cost (not least in terms of paper), while also leaving greater room for error, or forcing adjustments to suit the pagination. The Seventh Book begins with "Tempro la cetra," and the next piece in the Canto and Quinto partbooks is "A quest'olmo, a quest'ombre et a quest'onde" for six voices plus instruments; this is followed by "Non è di gentil core," a duet for two

---

[17] Fabbri (*Monteverdi*, trans. Carter, 32) suggests that "Ah, dolente partita!" could have been included in some prior, now lost, anthology (presumably Italian), given that the 1597 *Fiori del giardino* does not generally contain unpublished settings. However, Kauffmann's sources in general need closer analysis; his reading of "Ah, dolente partita!" has some less good variants compared with the version published in 1603.

[18] For the "privilegio," see Agee, "The Venetian Privilege and Music-Printing in the Sixteenth Century." Agee notes (42) that in Venice after 1603, privileges were granted automatically on gaining a *licenza* to print a given work (the latter based on a review of its probity). Nevertheless, claiming a privilege on a title page still served a purpose, although it was quite common from the 1620s on. Other Monteverdi editions making such a claim include the Sixth, Eighth, and Ninth Books, plus Bartolomeo Magni's editions of the *Lamento d'Arianna*, etc. (1623), and the 1632 *Scherzi musicali*.

sopranos and continuo. In the Basso Continuo partbook, however, "A quest'olmo" and "Non è di gentil core" are reversed, simply because of the need to avoid a midpiece page turn for the continuo player in the six-voice setting. Thus, "Non è di gentil core" is meant to come third in the book as the first of its fourteen duets (then four settings for three voices and two for four). Likewise, "Non vedrò mai le stelle" in the Seventh Book is shifted out of sequence in the Tenore partbook—before, rather than after, "Ah, che non si conviene"—as a way of maximizing the available space.[19] The Eighth Book has similar oddities: there are nine partbooks in all, and not everything always seems in quite the right place, which may also reflect the fact that at least parts of the volume seem to have been a compilation of various manuscripts copied and sent to Vienna at different times and in different formats.[20]

Although partial or full scores were needed for the continuo players in cases where they could not just follow the beat (e.g., where singers were likely to vary the tempo), such arrangements created additional problems for printers in terms of their complex typesetting, requiring the content of individual staves to be vertically aligned. Continuo parts were no less tricky for printers who lacked the fonts or expertise for elaborate figuring to indicate the harmony (sharps, flats, and numerals). Ricciardo Amadino had difficulties in both regards in the score of *Orfeo* issued in 1609: its continuo line is very sparsely figured, with just a few flats to indicate minor triads and sharps for major ones (including some mistakes), plus very occasional figures for unusual suspensions.[21] This stands in contrast to the quite elaborate (typographically speaking) combinations of accidentals and numerals found in the first opera scores and solo-song collections printed in Florence and Rome. It seems likely, however, that this was Monteverdi's fault, at least in part: other of Amadino's prints around this time do have more comprehensive figuring, so the composer himself seems to have been reluctant to provide it, for whatever reason. This is true of his later editions, as well. But it left his instrumentalist(s) with some tricky issues to negotiate in performance, and modern-day ensembles have inherited them (see Chapter 8).

---

[19] Also odd is the fact that the Tenore partbook contains the T^2 part for "Non vedrò mai le stelle," whereas T^1 is in the Alto partbook (perhaps because it goes quite high, up to a'). This is typical of the Seventh Book, however, which often has what one might identify as T^2 parts in the Tenore partbook, and T^1 in the Quinto, although it is not always clear which part should be T^1, given Monteverdi's tendency to overlap the voices. It is possible, however, that Monteverdi sometimes tried to give some prominence to the singers normally allocated to the "second" roles (S^2 or T^2) in the standard Quinto partbook. Something similar occurs when the "lower" voice (S^2 or T^2) exchanges position with the upper one for a brief but surprising (for the singer) moment.

[20] The nine partbooks are labeled Canto Primo, Alto Primo, Alto Secondo, Tenore Primo, Tenore Secondo, Basso Primo, Basso Secondo, Quinto (in effect, "Canto Secondo"), and Basso Continuo. As an example of odd layouts, the TTB parts for the central section of "Non avea Febo ancora" (the *Lamento della ninfa*) are not in the tenor and bass partbooks (which have the outer sections, with the central one marked "tacet") but are in score format (with S) in the Alto Primo partbook. Monteverdi explains his use of a score here (see Chapter 9), but its location is still odd unless it was just for reasons of space.

[21] Carter, "Some Notes on the First Edition of Monteverdi's *Orfeo*," 505.

Production issues

We do not know how closely Monteverdi oversaw the printing of his madrigal books, or whether and how others might have intervened in the editorial process. All the dedications in those which have them—the Sixth does not—were signed in the place where Monteverdi currently lived (Cremona for the First and Second Books; Mantua for the Third to Fifth; Venice for the Seventh and Eighth). Thus, one can reasonably assume for the first five books that he mailed the materials for them to his printer—or had someone transport them—and relied on others to usher them through the press.[22]

He was not always well served by his printers. Ricciardo Amadino's second (1606) edition of the Fifth Book was "newly corrected and reprinted" according to the title page ("Di nuovo ricorretto, e ristampato"), and it contains some significant differences from the first issued the year before.[23] They go well beyond the correction of straightforward typographical errors, and Monteverdi must have somehow communicated them to Amadino. However, subsequent editions of the same book do not always take these differences into account, and they can themselves contain additional variants that might or might not have been sanctioned by the composer.[24] Even when Monteverdi was himself in Venice, he does not always seem to have engaged directly with the printer. The Sixth Book has some exasperating musical errors suggesting that any proof was not well read; Amadino's second edition of 1615 noted on the title page that its madrigals, too, were "newly corrected and reprinted" ("Di nuovo corretti, e ristampati"). This fixed the most egregious errors but introduced others. Bartolomeo Magni made a complete hash of the 1632 *Scherzi musicali*, printing one page twice, and one piece in the wrong place. Alessandro Vincenti also did a poor job with the 1634 anthology, *Arie de diversi*, which included two settings by Monteverdi. Both printers, it seems, were now suffering from the aftermath of the plague in Venice (1630–31), which could have left them short of competent staff.

Monteverdi may not have helped matters, given that the manuscript materials he delivered to the printer seem not always to have been in the best order. Antonio Goretti was driven to despair when working with the composer on the music for the wedding festivities in Parma in 1627–28 because he had to make fair copies of musical bits and pieces given to him in complete disarray.[25] Nothing of what

---

[22] Monteverdi himself did precisely this for Francesco Petratti's *Il primo libro d'arie a una e due voci* (Venice: Alessandro Vincenti, 1620); see his various letters to Paolo Giordano II Orsini, Duke of Bracciano (Petratti's patron), from late 1619 and early 1620. Petratti was Cremonese, which may be one reason for the favor being asked of Monteverdi.

[23] Jacobsen and Jacobsen (eds.), *Claudio Monteverdi: Il quinto libro de madrigali*, viii–x. By this reckoning, the decision by the FCM edition to treat the 1605 print as its primary source was probably a mistake.

[24] This means that editing Monteverdi's madrigals can involve some tricky decisions based on comparison of all the surviving editions, and ideally, all surviving copies of each one in case of so-called stop-press corrections. Malipiero tended to rely on whichever edition was most easily available to him in convenient libraries. The new FCM edition is more scrupulous but still tends to assume that all copies of a given edition will be the same, which is not true; compare Carter, "Some Notes on the First Edition of Monteverdi's *Orfeo*," 499–500.

[25] Fabbri, *Monteverdi*, trans. Carter, 212–13.

Monteverdi sent to his printers survives save as ghostly echoes in the prints themselves. But if we can fairly assume that typesetters were paid to print what was put in front of them—and did not have time to make significant editorial decisions—then save for straightforward typographical errors, any problems in a printed edition will likely derive from its source(s).[26] It follows that prior to correcting an apparent error in a Monteverdi print (or any other), one must first consider how it could have come about (see Chapter 7).

Paying careful attention to such matters brings dividends. For example, the *Combattimento di Tancredi e Clorinda* is presented in various ways in the Eighth Book in terms of its vocal and instrumental parts, including a short score in the Tenore Primo partbook (for the character named Testo) and a full score in the Basso Continuo one. There are significant differences between those two scores: the one for Testo has better musical readings, whereas the continuo score is more correct so far as the poetic text is concerned (taken largely from Tasso's *Gerusalemme liberata*). The spelling of words in the text underlay is also quite different, with Testo's score conforming quite closely to what we can identify from Monteverdi's letters as his own orthographical mannerisms. One might plausibly suggest that the Testo score was prepared by Monteverdi himself and then modified during rehearsal (hence the better musical readings), whereas the continuo score was created by someone else, who also tried to clean up some of the composer's misreadings of Tasso. That "someone" may have been his printer, Alessandro Vincenti.[27] But whatever that case, the various presentations of the *Combattimento* in the Eighth Book must come from different branches of any *stemma* generated by the sources prior to their being submitted for typesetting. Thus, any edition of the work needs to evaluate its materials quite carefully, probably conflating them to produce a "best" text even if that never existed in written form. This is typical of the Eighth Book as a whole, which is deeply problematic in terms of the sources from which the printer worked, and there is not yet a proper critical account of all these issues and their likely consequences.

These processes also have a bearing on the extent to which Monteverdi's madrigal books might be considered as coherent entities reflecting some deliberate design on the composer's part. The only evidence we have of Monteverdi creating a "collection" of madrigals—outside of the books themselves—comes from a letter by Don Bassano Casola (or Cassola), the composer's vice-*maestro* in Mantua, to Cardinal Ferdinando Gonzaga on 16 July 1610.[28] Casola notes the imminent appearance in

---

[26] As an intriguing case in point, the Tenore partbook of the Third Book gives the text incipit for "Vattene pur, crudel, con quella pace" as "Vivrò," confusing it with "Vivrò fra i miei tormenti e le mie cure." This could have happened in any number of ways, but it does not appear to be a printing error.

[27] The orthographies in the continuo match quite closely those used in Vincenti's edition of Martino Pesenti's *Arie a voce sola . . . libro terzo* (1636). Pesenti was blind from birth, and Vincenti says in the dedication to this volume that he had in effect acted as the composer's amanuensis ("Io mi sono sforzato in tutti i tempi di servire à questo amoroso Tiresia con gl'occhi de' miei caratteri"), so one can plausibly assume that the orthographies there are Vincenti's.

[28] Some secondary sources date the letter 26 July 1610; see Kurtzman, *The Monteverdi Vespers of 1610*, 40 n. 136.

print of a sacred collection containing a Mass and Vespers (the *Sanctissimae Virgini Missa . . . ac Vespere*), and says that Monteverdi is also preparing "una muta di madrigali a cinque voci" (a set of five-voice madrigals) to contain three laments ("pianti"): the *Lamento d'Arianna* ("with the usual melody [*canto*] throughout"); a lament of Hero and Leander by Marino (usually assumed to be canzone no. 9 of his 1602 *Rime . . . parte seconda*); and a third of a shepherd on the death of his nymph (the Sestina "Incenerite spoglie, avara tomba") to a text written by Scipione Agnelli and comissioned by Duke Vincenzo Gonzaga on the death of the young singer Caterina Martinelli.[29] No setting related to Hero and Leander by Monteverdi survives, but he did have other madrigals in his portfolio that could go in the Sixth Book: a spiritual contrafact of "Una donna fra l'altre onesta e bella" (as "Una es, o Maria, o speciosa") was published by Aquilino Coppini in 1609, and "Misero Alceo, del caro albergo fore" and "Presso un fiume tranquillo" were known in the circles of Heinrich Schütz perhaps by 1612.[30] The two Petrarch settings "Zefiro torna e 'l bel tempo rimena" and "Oimè il bel viso, oimè 'l soave sguardo" may have been the sonnets that Monteverdi mentioned in his letter to Annibale Iberti of 28 July 1607, intended for the "gentlemen singers" who had accompanied Vincenzo Gonzaga on the duke's typical summer visit to Sampierdarena (near Genoa).[31] Monteverdi further promised Prince Francesco Gonzaga on 26 March 1611 to send "a couple of madrigals, and anything else that I might understand may be to Your Highness's taste" (in a letter that had enclosed a "Dixit Dominus" for eight voices, plus a motet for two for the Elevation and one for five for the Blessed Virgin). But if Monteverdi did originally have a plan for the Sixth Book, it did not quite work out that way in the end.

Moreover, while it might be tempting to imagine that Monteverdi submitted a sequence of madrigals as he wanted them to appear in press, it is usually impossible to tell whether the printer followed that order, or deviated from it because of layout or other such issues. Thus, it can be risky to assume that the overall sequence of settings in a given book represents any coherent overall design on the part of the composer unless other evidence can be brought to bear on the matter. None of Monteverdi's madrigal books adopts a common ordering principle by way of one or more modal cycles, identified by clef, system, and final. For that matter, any narrative threads running through a series of madrigals could probably be woven in other ways as well.[32] There are some signs of like being matched with like in smaller

---

[29] Fabbri, *Monteverdi*, trans. Carter, 109. Tomlinson (*Monteverdi and the End of the Renaissance*, 157) associates Monteverdi's interest in Marino (who is prominent in the Sixth Book) with the arrival in Mantua of the Neapolitan soprano Adriana Basile in July 1610. The poet's canzone (no. 9) headed "Leandro," "Stese la notte havea," is not quite a lament, and it turns out at the end to be narrated by one Licone to a group of fishermen, meaning that it is not fully mimetic in the sense of the *Lamento d'Arianna* or the Sestina. It is not clear how Monteverdi would have set it if he ever did.

[30] Watty, "Zwei Stücke aus Claudio Monteverdis 6. Madrigalbuch in handschriftlichen Frühfassungen," discussing Kassel, Landesbibliothek und Murhardsche Bibliothek, 2° Ms. Mus. 57f. However, the precise date and origin of this manuscript remain unclear.

[31] Pryer, "Monteverdi, Two Sonnets and a Letter."

[32] Two examples concerning the Fourth Book are revealing. Chafe (*Monteverdi's Tonal Language*, 77) identifies broader groupings in it by way of system (natural versus flat), although typically, he does not take

subsets of a collection, whether in textual or musical terms.[33] Monteverdi probably also had greater influence over which pieces would come first or last in a given book. The first setting in the 1584 *Canzonette a tre voci*, "Qual si può dir maggiore," pays homage to its dedicatee, Pietro Ambrosini.[34] The last, "Or, care canzonette," is a conventional envoi instructing these pieces to be grateful to those who listen to them, to be pleasing to those who sing them, and to request forgiveness for any errors they might contain. Likewise, Monteverdi's First Book begins with "Ch'ami la vita mia nel tuo bel nome," which plays on the name "Camilla," the daughter (it seems) of the dedicatee, Marco Verità.[35] The first madrigal of the Second Book, setting Tasso's "Non si levava ancor l'alba novella," was presumably placed there because of its poetic heft, while the opening one of the Fifth, "Cruda Amarilli, che col nome ancora," is the first of the madrigals to which Artusi took such exception in his 1600 treatise. Final madrigals also bore some weight by virtue of their musical content—as with "Piagn'e sospira; e quand'i caldi raggi" (another Tasso setting, and another barb against Artusi) in the Fourth Book—or scoring, as with the last two madrigals of the Fifth Book (for six and nine voices respectively, the latter also with instruments), or the seven-voice "Presso un fiume tranquillo" at the end of the Sixth.

There can be no doubt that Monteverdi's Eighth Book of 1638, the *Madrigali guerrieri, et amorosi*, was conceived in some sense as a "book." He had strong reasons to dedicate it to a Habsburg emperor, given Monteverdi's campaign to gain an ecclesiastical benefice to provide a regular income equivalent to the lifetime pension that was granted him by Duke Vincenzo Gonzaga in 1609 but that was not always paid on time.[36] The fact that its intended dedicatee, Emperor Ferdinand II, died in 1637 forced Monteverdi to switch to his successor, Emperor Ferdinand III, which he did without too much difficulty, given the shared name. He had already been sending music quite regularly to Vienna, some of which reappears here. And presumably it was Monteverdi's idea to divide the book into two halves containing "Canti guerrieri" and "Canti amorosi." The general themes of "war" and "love"—sometimes as two sides of the same coin—also matched the famous Habsburg motto, "Bella gerant alii, tu felix Austria nube" (Let others wage wars: you, happy

---

clefs into account, which would modify, and perhaps nullify, his scheme. Ossi (*Divining the Oracle*, 96–110) makes broader connections by way of internal cross-references within the book's texts, as well as on affective grounds, although he then has to worry about settings that appear "out of place" (*Divining the Oracle*, 102).

[33] Again in the Fourth Book, the two settings beginning "Cor mio" are side by side, as are the two "Anima" ones (while the second of the latter, "Anima del cor mio," is followed by "Longe da te, cor mio"). Similarly, "Io mi son giovinetta" and the following "Quell'augellin che canta" are musically related; see Ossi, *Divining the Oracle*, 103–8.

[34] Pirrotta, "Monteverdi's Poetic Choices," 272.

[35] But obviously, the text works for any "Camilla": the first setting of it, by Lelio Bertani, was included in the anthology *De floridi virtuosi d'Italia: Il primo libro de madrigali a cinque voci* (Venice: Giacomo Vincenti and Ricciardo Amadino, 1583).

[36] Saunders, "New Light on the Genesis of Monteverdi's Eighth Book of Madrigals." For the saga of the pension, see also Besutti, "Claudio Monteverdi cittadino mantovano." Monteverdi initiated the process of entering the priesthood in May 1629 and was ordained on 16 April 1632; see Fabbri, *Monteverdi*, trans. Carter, 226.

Austria, marry).[37] It was timely. The lull in the Thirty Years' War following the Battle of Nördlingen (1634) and Ferdinand II's agreement to the Peace of Prague (1635) would have encouraged the notion that songs of war could turn to love, although it was not to last. Monteverdi's plan behind the Eighth Book was convenient in other ways as well, given that it enabled him to pull together a collection of older and newer settings, some better fitting its theme than others. As a result, however, the volume is so specific to its purpose that it is not surprising that it was never reissued.

The Seventh Book

The purpose and planning of the Seventh Book (1619) is less transparent but still quite carefully thought out. Given Monteverdi's secure position at St. Mark's, Venice, from 1613 on, he had no pressing professional reasons to publish his secular or sacred music; indeed, he seems to have steered relatively clear of the printing presses save when he was asked to contribute items to anthologies of either kind. The Sixth Book, published the year after Monteverdi's move, is often read as a gesture of newfound independence from patronal constraints, given its absence of a dedicatee: the *tavola* is instead placed at the beginning of each partbook, as if it were the contents of the book, rather than any noble endorsement, that would serve to advertise its merits.[38] That the Seventh Book (1619) does have a dedicatee, however, stems from the fact that it had similar ulterior motives to the Eighth.[39] Monteverdi managed to disguise them better—the book was reprinted several times—which means that it requires some effort and even imagination to discern exactly what he intended by, with, and for it. The book's title, "Concerto," is vague enough, although the subtitle explains that it contains madrigals and "other types of songs." After the first two settings, the "madrigals" are organized by scoring, with duets for SS (4), AA (1), TT (8) and TB (1).[40] Then come pieces for three voices (4), then four (2), culminating in "Con che soavità, labra odorate," for solo soprano and an instrumental ensemble. The "other types of songs" follow. This is logical enough, but the wholly unusual "Con che soavità" helps reveal the other agendas at work here.

As with the Eighth Book, the Seventh was connected to Monteverdi's campaign for his pension (so his letters make clear). But here he directed his attention to the

---

[37] Carter, "The Venetian Madrigals," 186.

[38] The Basso Continuo partbook has no *tavola*: its place at the end is taken, instead, by a sonnet praising the composer. But having the *tavola* at the beginning of the other partbooks also saved space by not leaving the verso of the title page blank.

[39] The dedication is dated 13 December 1619, although Monteverdi complained in his letter to Alessandro Striggio of 19 October 1619 that he had intended it to come out by the time of writing. He then was unclear whether he should come to Mantua himself to present the volume to its dedicatee, Caterina de' Medici, Duchess of Mantua, but he ended up sending it there around 22 February 1620 so that Striggio could do the honors.

[40] There is no obvious reason that the TB duet, "Se 'l vostro cor, Madonna," is placed before the final TT duet "Interrotte speranze, eterna fede," unless the point was to end this part of the sequence with the most painful text of all.

new Duchess of Mantua, Caterina de' Medici, who had married Duke Ferdinando Gonzaga in February 1617. Ferdinando regretted his predecessor's decision to discharge Monteverdi from Mantuan service, and the death of Monteverdi's successor as *maestro della musica*, Santi Orlandi, in July 1619, prompted repeated efforts to lure the composer back from Venice. All of them failed because, Monteverdi said, his professional situation was far too favorable to warrant any such move. Nevertheless, he seems to have been out to show what Mantua had lost. The distinctly nostalgic tone of the second setting in the book, the stunningly beautiful "A quest'olmo, a quest'ombre et a quest'onde" for six voices and instruments, also suggests that Monteverdi may now have been looking back to Mantua with rose-tinted spectacles: Giambattista Marino gave the sonnet the caption "Rimembranza di antichi piaceri" (Remembrance of old pleasures) as the lover invokes the memory of happier days. However, "A quest'olmo" also plays a significant part in a broader program presented by the Seventh Book as a whole.

Monteverdi's model for the Seventh Book was probably a collection of settings by a former Mantuan colleague and still a friend, the tenor Francesco Dognazzi's *Il primo libro de varii concenti a una et à due voci, per cantar nel chitarone o altri simili istrumenti* (Venice: Bartolomeo Magni, 1614). Dognazzi's "varii concenti" for voice(s) and continuo are made up of what are labeled "concerti" at the head of the *tavola*: a sequence of solo songs variously in the soprano and tenor clefs (madrigals, sonnets, an *ottava rima* set to the *aria di Romanesca*, canzonettas) and then duets: a madrigal (SS), a sonnet to the *aria di Ruggiero* (ST), a dialogue (ST), and two canzonettas (SS)—those last three pieces have instrumental ritornellos. For his own "concerto," Monteverdi constructs a more elaborate scheme, although he was drawing on similar elements. The Seventh Book begins with a setting of Marino's "Tempro la cetra, e per cantar gli honori," the sonnet opening the "third part" of Marino's *Rime* added when the poet republished the first and second parts under the collective title *La lira* in 1614. Monteverdi treats it in the manner of an operatic prologue, and therefore as a musical preface to the book as a whole. Then comes "A quest'olmo," followed by that sequence of duets, trios, and quartets culminating in "Con che soavità" prior to those "other types of songs" ending with the *ballo*, *Tirsi e Clori*, that Monteverdi had composed in 1615 for performance in Mantua.[41]

In the opening "Tempro la cetra," the poet tries to tune his lyre to sing of Mars but finds that it resists the effort; as he stands by the shore surrounded by flowers, Love dictates amorous notes to him ("Così pur, tra l'arene e pur tra' fiori, / note amorose Amor torna a dettarmi"). He therefore asks his Muse to return to tender conceits ("teneri scherzi") while Mars, tempering his harshness, sleeps on Venus's bosom. Monteverdi's choice was timely, given the end of the Mantuan War of Monferrato with Savoy after the final signing of the Peace of Asti in 1617. Duke Ferdinando

---

[41] Carter, "Winds, Cupids, Little Zephyrs and Sirens," 494. Monteverdi said that he intended to present *Tirsi e Clori* to Duke Ferdinando Gonzaga in the summer of 1615, although it was sent to Mantua in November, probably with the intention of a performance in Carnival 1616.

Gonzaga no longer needed to be the warrior but could instead engage in more amorous pursuits with his new bride, Caterina de' Medici, who herself came from the "city of flowers," Florence. Indeed, the poetry set in the Seventh Book is full of references to flowers, clearly with its dedicatee in mind.[42]

Monteverdi's dedication to the book establishes another strategy. It begins with what seems to be a conventional self-deprecatory trope: he would not have dared present this new *concerto* of madrigals to Caterina if he were not certain that although she takes delight in the concerts of muses directed by Apollo himself, nevertheless she would not disdain hearing some rough sound from the composer's humble pipe because from the cradle her parents (Grand Duke Ferdinando I de' Medici and Christine of Lorraine) had taught her to appreciate rare things but also not to dismiss lowly ones.[43] Monteverdi embeds the idea within the collection itself: in "A quest'olmo," the two obbligato instrumental parts shift from two violins to two parts each labeled "flautino o fifara" (recorder or transverse flute) precisely when a solo bass voice refers directly to "la mia Clori" giving herself completely to the speaker. But if those recorders or flutes invoked Monteverdi's "humble pipe," he also needed to cater for the "concerts of muses" —hence the following sequence of madrigals that culminates in "Con che soavità," which according to the *tavola* is for solo voice and nine instruments ("concertato a una voce e 9 istrum[enti]"). Matters are a bit more complicated, in fact: this setting has a "primo choro" for a soprano and continuo, a "secondo choro" for three high string instruments and continuo, and a "terzo choro" for three low string instruments and continuo.[44] But Monteverdi's "nine" seems deliberately chosen with the nine Muses in mind, most playing the string instruments conventionally associated with Apollo's lyre.[45]

Not everything in the Seventh Book is quite so rosy. In one of the SS duets, "Io son pur vezzosetta pastorella," the speaker is a fair shepherdess with cheeks of roses and jasmine who claims that "here" there is no noble maid of Flora who does not claim her to be most beautiful of all ("Di Flora non vi è qui nobil Donzella / . . . / il titol non mi dian de la più bella").[46] When she goes to the ballroom, every shepherd brings

---

[42] Georis, *Claudio Monteverdi*, 532 n. 4. The repeated references are clear: "fiori" (or the singular, "fiore")—often with an upper-case beginning—appears in "Tempro la cetra," "A quest'olmo," "Io son pur vezzosetta pastorella," "O viva fiamma, o miei sospiri ardenti" (by virtue of a change to the original text; *Claudio Monteverdi*, 540 n. 22), "Interrotte speranze, eterna fede," "Vaga su spina ascosa," and *Tirsi e Clori*. "Rose" (roses) appears in "Perché fuggi tra' salci," "Vaga su spina ascosa," and "Chioma d'oro."

[43] "Non ardirei d'appresentare questo mio nuovo Concerto de Madrigali all'Altezza Vostra Serenissima s'io non fossi sicuro, ch'ella benché sia avezza à Concerti di Muse Concertati dallo stesso Apollo, non si sdegna però d'udire tal'hora qualche rozzo suono d'humil Sampogna, perché apparò sino nelle fasce, da suoi Gran Gentori à pregiare le cose rare, et non dispregiare le vili."

[44] Welker, "Con che soavità." The continuo scoring is specified as (Choir 1) two chitarroni, harpsichord, and spinet; (Choir 2) harpsichord; and (Choir 3) organ. The string instruments in Choir 2 are *viole da braccio*, and those in Choir 3, *da gamba*. Those continuo instruments need considering carefully in terms of their range of pitches and also tuning (see Chapter 8). It is worth noting that by this reckoning, there is no bowed string instrument doubling the continuo line; indeed, Monteverdi makes a point of that by not having the contrabass gamba in Choir 3 play continuously.

[45] Haramaki ("Beyond the *Seconda prattica*," 308 n. 20) makes the connection with the Muses but not with Monteverdi's dedication. Another "Apollo" reference occurs in "Tempro la cetra" where the tenor invokes a "lira sublime," although the Basso Continuo partbook has Marino's "tromba sublime."

[46] The sonnet is included in the *Mostre poetiche del Incolto Academico Immaturo* (Venice: Evangelista Deuchino, 1620), 21. The member of the Venetian Accademia degl'Immaturi with the academic name

her gifts so that she might dance with them. But she then goes on to complain that "Lidio" ignores her glances and pleas for comfort. The caption given to the poem when it was published separately (in 1620) makes the point even clearer: "Pastorella ad un Pastor che non l'ama" (A shepherdess to a shepherd who does not love her). Here the unyielding shepherd is "Floro," not "Lidio," but it would not have fitted Monteverdi's apparent intention if the reluctant lover were Florentine as well.

Caterina de' Medici's marriage to Ferdinando Gonzaga was not always a happy one. While most such dynastic relationships were dictated by political expediency, their wedding in February 1617 had less of the typically lengthy pomp and circumstance both in Florence—in part because the ceremony took place, unusually, directly before Lent—and then in Mantua. There was also some embarrassment over the fact that Ferdinando had been forced to dissolve his prior secret marriage to Camilla Faà di Bruno, by whom he had a son. The duke and duchess were affectionate enough in public, according to contemporary reports, but otherwise their relationship sometimes appears to have been fraught. Caterina had also suffered two miscarriages, one some four months after the marriage and another in October 1618, and it is clear that in the latter half of 1619 she was hoping to become pregnant again.[47] In that light, at least some of the settings in Monteverdi's Seventh Book appear to give voice to a duke and duchess whose relationship needed lubrication so as to bear proper fruit. Music's erotic powers on the one hand, and therapeutic ones on the other, were commonly accepted in this period.[48] But here they seem to be put to a quite specific purpose.

The setting immediately after "Io son pur vezzosetta pastorella," another soprano duet, continues the theme. "O viva fiamma, o miei sospiri ardenti" is an old sonnet by Giovanni Andrea Gesualdo da Traetto, first published in 1545, constructed by way of a series of vocatives as the lover seeks an audience for a typical Petrarchan plaint. While such matters are generally voiced by a male poetic "I," the text here is gender-neutral, meaning that it lacks pronouns or adjectival agreements that indicate a male or female speaker. For the purposes of the Seventh Book, it also carries a certain edge. The first tercet originally addressed the glorious laurels, green myrtles, and the sweet and pleasant place where "I" once scattered delightful song(s):

"Incolto" is Giovan(ni) Francesco Ferranti; Georis, *Claudio Monteverdi*, 538. Although Ferranti's volume is dedicated to the Venetian *letterato*, Nicolò Crasso, the poet certainly had some Florentine connections; he wrote a eulogy on Prince Francesco de' Medici (son of Grand Duke Ferdinando I), who died in 1614. He also wrote verse in praise of Adriana Basile; see Bosi, "Adriana's Harp," 92.

[47] On 12 December 1619 (coincidentally, the day before Monteverdi signed the dedication to the Seventh Book), the Mantuan court secretary, Antonio Costantini (in Casale Monferrato), reported to Caterina his conversation with Margherita Camonzoli (a nun, it seems) about the duchess's hopes to bear a son: Camonzoli advised that Caterina not seek human remedies (potions, talismans, etc.) but should pray continuously, wait for divine favor, and dress in a humble manner; Florence, Archivio di Stato, Mediceo del Principato 6113, fol. 206. For other attempts to aid Caterina in this regard, see Strocchia, *Forgotten Healers*, 74–77.

[48] See, for example, the essays in Blackburn and Stras (eds.), *Eroticism in Early Modern Music*; Horden (ed.), *Music as Medicine*. For musical performances as a therapeutic aid during pregnancy, see also Carter and Goldthwaite, *Orpheus in the Marketplace*, 215, 252–53, 261.

o gloriosi allori, o verdi mirti,
o luogo un tempo e me dolce e giocondo,
ove io già sparsi dilettoso canto;
...

In Monteverdi's setting, however, the opening line of this tercet is changed to include another reference to flowers: "o vaghe herbette, o fiori, o verdi mirti" (o charming meadows, o flowers, o green myrtles). A revised possessive pronoun in the last line of the second quatrain also seems significant: "o sola mia cagion d'aspri tormenti" is slightly less accusatory than "o spietata cagion de' miei tormenti" ("my sole cause of harsh torments" instead of the "bitter cause of my torments"). But placing "O viva fiamma" alongside "Io son pur vezzosetta pastorella" would seem to put musical words in the mouth of a Duchess of Mantua who had once been able to sing delightful songs in flowery meadows but could do so no more. The Romanesca setting of Bernardo Tasso's *stanza di lontananza* (on the beloved's absence), "Ohimè, dov'è 'l mio ben, dov'è 'l mio core?"—another soprano duet—also suggests a painful moment in a shaky relationship: the text is again grammatically neutral despite its adoption of seemingly male-voice tropes. Yet if "Con che soavità" is to be read in the same light, Caterina de' Medici still hopes for something better: a "sweet harmony" of kisses as words, and words, kisses.

The texts set in the Seventh Book cover all aspects of love, but in this new context, they present more than just a conventional series of complaints or desires from the male or female side of things. The collection takes the typical narrative elements of a sequential *canzoniere* but adjusts them, first, because the lady is attainable (her love is more unrequited than his), and second, because she is given a voice.[49] Its texts are also often delivered by, or to, characters with generic male and female pastoral names: Ergasto, Lidio, Filli, Licori, and the like. The most prominent ones to emerge, however, are Tirsi and Clori.[50] In the first tercet of "A quest'olmo," the unnamed speaker, here voiced by a solo bass, remembers the happy day when "la mia Clori" (subsequently rhymed by "fiori") fully gave her heart to him ("tutta in dono se stessa e 'l cor mi diede").[51] Monteverdi places two unnamed lovers in dialogue in the penultimate setting of the book, the canzonetta "Amor, che deggio far": here the music alternates "female" and "male" voices for its first four stanzas (S, T, SS, TB)—also plausibly in terms of the text—before bringing them together for the fifth (SSB) and sixth (SSTB).[52] He has already done something similar in the setting of

---

[49] For one "typical" narrative sequence in a *canzoniere*, see Calcagno, *From Madrigal to Opera*, 155–56, which also notes the role of *partenze*.

[50] Marenzio had associated "Tirsi" and "Clori" with a different noble couple, the Duke and Duchess of Bracciano, in his Sixth Book *a5* (1594); see Calcagno, *From Madrigal to Opera*, 171.

[51] In Marino's *Rime boscherecce*, "A quest'olmo" forms part of a rather complex sequence that includes exchanges between Ergasto, Tirsi, Batto, and others; see Chapter 9. Although its speaker is implied to be Ergasto, it could just as well be Tirsi for Monteverdi's purpose. For these kinds of "identity shifts" more broadly, see Calcagno, *From Madrigal to Opera*, 161–63 (discussing Marenzio).

[52] Thus, in stanza 2 (set for T) the poetic voice describes himself as a "fido amator" (faithful lover). This text was printed anonymously in Remigio Romano's *Prima raccolta di bellissime canzonette musicali e moderne* (Vicenza/Venice: Angelo Salvadori, 1618), 4–5, headed "Bellissima canzone musicale, e moderna."

Guarini's "Parlo, misero, o taccio?" earlier in the volume, as a trio for two sopranos and bass plus the basso continuo. The poet (in the male voice) debates the merits of speaking or staying silent about his love, but in the final line, he imagines what the beloved's fair face might say to her obdurate heart: "Chi può mirarmi, e non languir d'amore?" (Who cannot gaze upon me and not languish for love?). That line should, in principle, be in the female voice (or at least, the voice of a female face): Monteverdi responds by allocating "Chi può mirarmi" to the second soprano, but then—oddly enough—the bass interrupts to repeat the beginning of the line and take it to its end. The two sopranos then have the beginning of the line, joined by the bass to complete it in a three-part statement that could easily have led to a final cadence for the setting. Monteverdi is not yet done, however: the bass picks up the beginning of the line once more, with embellished writing, and continues to take the lead as the piece heads to its proper conclusion. The poem is a monologue, but Monteverdi seems to have turned it into some kind of musical dialogue between the male and female lovers who are so much at odds in the Seventh Book until they find reconciliation in the final *ballo*, *Tirsi e Clori*. Here the pastoral names return as Tirsi (T) and Clori (S) alternate stanzas prior to one where they join together, leading to a five-part ensemble (SSATB) for the *ballo* itself. Now their affections are renewed in harmonious lockstep. But they have taken a rocky road to reach that point.

The fact that *Tirsi e Clori* was written for Mantua when Duke Ferdinando Gonzaga was in a very different romantic relationship is only a slight inconvenience so far as its purpose in the Seventh Book is concerned. But given the explicit content of the Seventh Book, including that remarkable statement in "Io son pur vezzosetta pastorella," it is hard to imagine that Caterina de' Medici or her advisors had not somehow approved its design in advance, and perhaps had even requested the inclusion of some of its texts. Monteverdi was in close enough contact with a number of Mantuan officials who could have played a role, including Alessandro Striggio (whom Monteverdi asked to present the volume to the duchess) and Ercole Marliani (with whom the composer was currently collaborating on the opera *Andromeda*).[53] The volume may reflect his bowing to new poetic fashion in the witty, image-laden madrigals of Marino and his imitators.[54] But he did so with an ulterior motive in mind. The duchess also seems to have appreciated the volume: she sent Monteverdi a gold chain worth at least 100 ducats, which was a standard means of rewarding service done by someone living outside the state, given that it could be sold or

---

[53] In his letter to Alessandro Striggio of 19 October 1619, Monteverdi referred to the Seventh Book ("la mia operetta stanpata") in a rather casual way such as to suggest that Striggio already knew about it, although there is no prior reference to it in their surviving correspondence. For Marliani, see Carter, "Monteverdi, Early Opera and a Question of Genre."

[54] So Tomlinson (*Monteverdi and the End of the Renaissance*, 172–73) reads it. His tinge of disapproval matches Pirrotta ("Monteverdi's Poetic Choices," 304), who, however, is a bit more sympathetic both to the poet and to the composer. Schneider ("Rethinking Claudio Monteverdi's Seventh Book of Madrigals") tries to redress the balance.

pawned in the currency of the recipient's choice.[55] A one-time gift worth a quarter of the composer's annual salary was no small matter.

Work and "work"

One might well ask what Caterina de' Medici was getting in return for those 100 ducats. Monteverdi's Seventh Book of madrigals is certainly a physical object, or a collection of them: six partbooks in upright quarto format. It is not particularly beautiful to look at, however: Monteverdi (or his printer) did not spend money on an elaborate title page bearing the Gonzaga coat of arms, although he did include in all the partbooks an anonymous sonnet extolling his musical abilities. And while the duchess could turn their pages, she could not "read" the book in any coherent fashion: Monteverdi's text setting, with its repetitions on the one hand, and its fragmentation across the voices on the other, meant that almost none of its poetry is presented in a visually coherent way. To state the obvious, the Seventh Book, or its separate pieces, could be experienced only in live performance by whatever singers and instrumentalists the duchess had to hand, perhaps including herself in the case of the more straightforward pieces.[56] And while those performers would each concentrate on delivering their individual parts, they, too, might not have had much idea of how their work might cohere into what we would nowadays call a musical "work."[57]

Music prints tended to give a redacted reading of their contents, in part for typographical reasons, but also so as not to limit their marketability. Pitches and rhythms were notated straightforwardly enough, and dynamics and tempo markings were starting to make an appearance. But much still needed to be done to put what was on the page to sonic effect. Monteverdi was more fastidious than many in notating ornamentation when it was embedded in his compositional fabric, and he was also clear when it should not be applied (e.g., in the *Combattimento di Tancredi e Clorinda*). But other information was reduced or omitted. For example, the composer had sent the Mantuan court secretary, Annibale Iberti, instructions for performing *Tirsi e Clori* on 21 November 1615. He wanted Tirsi to be accompanied by a harpsichord and Clori by a chitarrone or, even better, a harp, with each of those singers playing a chitarrone themselves;[58] there should be eight voices (including

---

[55] Denis Stevens slightly misses the point in his "Monteverdi's Necklace" by reading the chain as, precisely, a "necklace" and ignoring the currency issue. But as Stevens notes, the composer did indeed use the chain as security for a loan of the money he needed to bail his son Massimiliano from arrest by the Inquisition in Mantua in September 1627. This also means that he had not liquidated the gift earlier to cover any printing costs for the Seventh Book.

[56] Like all the Medici princesses of this period, Caterina was taught singing by Jacopo Peri in Florence; see Carter and Goldthwaite, *Orpheus in the Marketplace*, 212–13, 259–60.

[57] Compare the discussion of "the work of opera" in Calcagno, *From Madrigal to Opera*, 26–31.

[58] Tirsi's and Clori's parts (in the Tenore and Canto partbooks) are not provided with a bassline to enable them to accompany themselves. However, an early manuscript of "Presso un fiume tranquillo" (Kassel, Landesbibliothek und Murhardsche Bibliothek, 2° Ms. Mus. 57f) shows how additional continuo lines could be copied out to enable this kind of performance practice; see Watty, "Zwei Stücke aus Claudio Monteverdis 6. Madrigalbuch in handschriftlichen Frühfassungen."

Tirsi and Clori) singing the *ballo* itself (although it is in five vocal parts), plus eight string instruments (*viole da braccio*) and a *contrabasso*, a *spinetta arpata*, and, if possible, two small lutes ("leutini"). None of this is apparent in the Seventh Book, which notes only that Clorì is to be accompanied by "another chitarrone or spinet" ("un altro Chitarone o Spinetta") meaning that Tirsi was to be accompanied by a different chitarrone. The table of contents says that *Tirsi e Clori* is "Concertato con Voci et Istrumenti à 5," but in the Tenore partbook, the *ballo* itself is headed "Con voce [sic] et Istromenti se piace," meaning that save for the continuo, any instruments doubling the voices are optional (there is no separate music for them).

When Aquilino Coppini produced three volumes of sacred contrafacts of madrigals by Monteverdi (mostly) and others in 1607–9, he first needed to create scores of them to be sure that his new words were placed appropriately in different voices. By also printing the five-voice settings in "partitura," he provided the first opportunity to see, rather than just hear, Monteverdi's music in the round. But if Monteverdi's own partbooks presenting his madrigals were essentially scripts for performance in a given time and place, we might also ask what singers and instrumentalists were expected to bring to the event other than delivering the right notes at the right time. What elements of their performance practice were determined by what was on the printed page, what were enacted by way of common conventions of the time, and what could happen just by chance in the moment? As a corollary, our modern ability to read Monteverdi's madrigals in score—whether singly or grouped in their "books"—is certainly a boon for analysis, but it focuses the attention on a fixed musical object that was not, in fact, so fixed. We lose the element of surprise inherent in any musical experience, whether as performers or as listeners. We become blasé over musical moments that should generate wonder. Monteverdi's work as a composer, the performers' work as performers, and our work as listeners should do more than just create a work to be contemplated from afar.

4
Monteverdi's Performers

The multiple editions of Monteverdi's madrigal books issued during his lifetime suggest that his music was well able to enter the musical marketplace and appeal to a broad range of consumers. However, these works were not composed in a vacuum. When he became Duke Vincenzo Gonzaga's *maestro della musica* in late 1601, he had very specific duties to fulfill. In the "Dichiaratione" appended to Monteverdi's 1607 *Scherzi musicali*, Giulio Cesare Monteverdi explained his brother's comment in the statement at the end of the Fifth Book of madrigals that no one should be surprised at the lack of his response to the criticisms made of his music by Giovanni Maria Artusi, given that his service to the duke left him little time for anything else. Giulio Cesare explained exactly what that service entailed: Monteverdi was not only in charge of providing sacred and chamber music for the duke ("tanto da chiesa quanto da camera"), but also other one-off obligations ("altri servitii non ordinarii") that took up the greater part of his time, including music for tournaments, court ballets, comedies, and various *concerti* (performances or ensembles), in addition to his role as one of two players of the *viola bastarda*.[1] The dedications of other Monteverdi editions reveal that this "chamber music" was done in the "regie camere" of the duke (the Fifth Book madrigals) and of Prince Francesco Gonzaga (the 1607 *Scherzi musicali*), and no doubt elsewhere in the ducal palace. By late 1610, if not before, there were also regular Friday evening musical performances in the palace's Sala degli Specchi.[2] In Venice, Monteverdi was head of a large group of musicians who performed not just in St. Mark's but also in other churches and related institutions in the city, as well as on secular occasions and for private patrons. This was one of the advantages of working there, so Monteverdi often said in his letters, given the artistic and also financial opportunities of a lively musical city.

He had some fine singers and instrumentalists available to him in both his places of work. As *maestro* he was rigorous in auditioning them for service and identifying their strengths and weaknesses.[3] He also made significant demands of them, exploiting their individual and collective abilities to the full. His responsibilities as a composer and as an ensemble director were closely intertwined. It was the job of any *maestro* to produce music for, and direct, a group of performers in ways to show them off to their best abilities. Monteverdi also played the typical games to keep on

---

[1] Bates, "Monteverdi, the Viola Bastarda Player."
[2] Monteverdi refers to these Friday concerts in his letters to Cardinal Ferdinando Gonzaga of 28 December 1610 and 22 January 1611. For the location, see Besutti, "The 'Sala degli Specchi' Uncovered."
[3] For singers, see Wistreich, "La voce è grata assai."

his side musicians who might otherwise become jaded by the tedium that inevitably burdened their professional lives, with in-jokes (e.g., suspensions resolving irregularly), surprises (an inner voice suddenly exposed within the texture), and captivating musical moments. But just who sang and played Monteverdi's madrigals remains a complex question. We have scant documentary evidence for it, although a close reading of the music offers important clues.

Cleffing and ranges and modes

The standard nomenclature for musical partbooks—Canto, Alto, Tenore, Basso—simply reflects the order of voices from top to bottom, with any Quinto and Sesto (etc.) partbooks containing parts for whatever others were added to the texture. Thus, Monteverdi's *Canzonette a tre voci... libro primo* (1584) was printed in three partbooks labeled Canto, Tenore, and Basso, but the second and third of them do not contain music notated for tenor and bass voices; rather, these canzonettas are all for some combination of three high voices (SSA).

Any would-be purchaser of a book of madrigals therefore needed to inspect the contents to determine what voices were needed to sing them. That information would be provided, in the first instance, by the clefs used at the beginning of the stave for each vocal part. There were two standard options for SATB voices: so-called *chiavi naturali* (C1, C3, C4, F4 clefs) and "high" *chiavette* (G2, C2, C3, F3).[4] The clef determined the outer limits of each voice in terms of its notated range: normally from the space below the bottom line of the five-line stave to the space above the top line (so for the C1 clef: $b-e''$), with a possible extension by a step either way via one leger line ($a-f''$).[5] In terms of range, *chiavette* sat a third higher than *chiavi naturali*, but in either case, the total ranges of S and A sat a fifth apart, of A and T a third apart, and of T and B a fifth apart; with S and T sharing almost the same range an octave apart, and likewise A and B.

Musical modes then come into play. A piece, say, in the Dorian mode will be based on the octave species D–D (treating D as the "final"), with a different sequence of tones and semitones compared to the Phrygian mode (E–E) or the Mixolydian (G–G).[6] A given mode can also be transposed down a fifth (or up a fourth) by way of adding a B♭ to the signature, therefore preserving the same sequence of tones and

---

[4] For this manner of identifying clefs, see my initial statement of "Editorial (etc.) Principles."

[5] This was the norm, although by the early seventeenth century, increased vocal ranges, and the demands of instrumental ones, prompted an increased use of additional leger lines. For example, if the top string of the violin was tuned to e'', music for the violin notated in the C1 clef (with a single leger line above) could reach only f'', and in the G2 clef, a''. This is one reason that the "violin" clef, G1 (going up to c'''), appeared later in the Baroque period, although any writing for the lower two strings of the violin (tuned to g and d') then forced more leger lines below the stave.

[6] I leave the Lydian mode (F–F) out of the reckoning for the moment because the fourth note of its octave, B♮ (a tritone above the final), created melodic and harmonic problems that were often avoided by changing it to B♭, therefore modifying the "pure" form of the mode.

semitones.[7] Each of these octave species consists of separate species of fifths and fourths, themselves distinct in terms of their sequence of tones and semitones (see Chapter 8).[8]

Now clefs and modes come together. In principle, a given piece should adhere to a given mode. But the modal system evolved from one created as a means of classifying monophonic music (plainchant) rather than polyphony. So while the D–D octave species will fit neatly within the upper and lower boundaries of the C1 and C4 clef, that is not the case for the C3 or F4 one. In order to maintain the mode in all voices, a theoretical fudge was needed, and it was largely acknowledged as such. If the D–D octave comprises a fifth plus a fourth (D–A–D), the fourth can be placed beneath the fifth (A–D–A) while still keeping the D "final": hence the distinction between the "authentic" Dorian mode (a fifth plus a fourth) and a "plagal" one (a fourth plus a fifth). And just as the authentic Dorian octave will fit within the C1 and C4 clefs, the plagal one will work for the C3 and F4 clefs, meaning that parts for SATB can all be in one or other version of the Dorian mode.

Thus, *chiavi naturali* will suit some modes but not others, and likewise *chiavette*. For example, a "soprano" part using the full octave in the authentic G-mixolydian mode (*g′–g″* with B naturals), or the authentic transposed Dorian mode (*g′–g″* with B flats), needed to be notated in the G2 clef (and likewise, its authentic or plagal counterparts in *chiavette*). Given that modes also had standard cadence points— normally the final and the co-final (the fifth degree of the scale save in the Phrygian mode)—and had different potentials in terms of the ability to move outside them (whether sharpward or flatward), madrigals in *chiavi naturali* and in *chiavette* will tend also to have a different range of harmonic possibilities. However, composers tended to use *chiavi naturali* for a wider range of modes than *chiavette*.

For present purposes, I assume that Monteverdi notated pitches as they sound. It is important to realize, however, that modes are intervallic constructs (sequences of tones and semitones) and are not pitch specific. Indeed, within a purely vocal performance, the D that forms the final of the Dorian mode need not be a sounding D by any nominal pitch standard: the singer who begins must select a starting pitch that does not take any of the following singers out of their range, but that starting pitch need not sound as notated. Likewise, if the D-final is, say, a sounding C, the piece will still sound in the Dorian mode by virtue of its intervallic content. (This is one significant difference between modern major/minor scales, wherein the

---

[7] One common such transposition is the Dorian mode (with a final on D) to G-dorian with a B♭ signature. This is one reason that J. S. Bach, say, will usually notate a movement in "G minor" with a one-flat signature rather than the modern two-flat one. One might then argue over what that means for any affective reading of such a movement, given that G-dorian and G minor do not necessarily signify the same thing in any emotional terms.

[8] In the eight-mode system (with authentic and plagal versions of the Dorian, Phrygian, Lydian, and Mixolydian modes), the combined species of fifths and fourths are unique to each mode. In the twelve-mode system they are not: thus, the Aeolian mode has the "Dorian" fifth (TSTT) plus the "Phrygian" fourth (STT), and the Ionian has the "Mixolydian" fifth (TTST) plus the "Lydian" fourth (TTS). This is why some music theorists of the time rejected the notion of a twelve-mode system that others were advocating as typical of modern practice.

patterns of tones and semitones are constant regardless of the starting pitch.) The singer is more constrained when instruments come into play, however, given that they are generally tuned to fixed pitches: the key on a harpsichord identified as a D will play some kind of sounding D. In cases in which the continuo begins, this is easy enough: the singer follows the instrument. But to take Monteverdi's "Mentre vaga Angioletta" (Eighth Book) as a counterexample, the sounding pitch of the *a* for the solo tenor at the beginning cannot be chosen at random, given that the continuo subsequently enters (in m. 17) with a minor triad on G. If singers performing with one or more instruments wish to choose a sounding pitch different from the notated one, then the instrumentalist(s) must transpose accordingly. Voices and instruments together therefore rely on a standard pitch. That is not to say that an *a'* on, say, a Mantuan harpsichord necessarily sounded the same pitch as on a Venetian one. But it is striking that with only a very few exceptions, Monteverdi tended to use *chiavi naturali* for his continuo madrigals, which avoids another issue associated with *chiavette*: whether or not they force downward transposition.[9]

The upshot of all this is that in the case of purely vocal performance, the notated pitches of a madrigal within a given set of clefs may not necessarily reflect the vocal ranges, or voice-types, required to perform it depending on what transposition might occur. Similarly, a madrigal in *chiavette* might or might not sound a third or so higher than one in *chiavi naturali*: Monteverdi could have chosen *chiavette* for reasons of mode rather than tessitura. His *Canzonette a tre voci* have the top part in G2 clef for all the pieces where the modal octave is f'–f'' (whatever the mode itself might be), g'–g'', and a'–a'', but in C1 clef when c'–c'' or d'–d''. The lowest voice is in the C2 or C3 clef (mostly the latter) according to similar principles. Moreover, while one might assume that Monteverdi intended these settings for actual SSA voices, this does not prevent them being performed by a vocal ensemble in a lower range, assuming that the singers could read the clefs.

Given the increasing standardization of clef combinations in Monteverdi's continuo madrigals—from the last six in the Fifth Book through the Sixth, Seventh, and Eighth—the more varied ones in his earlier books are potentially more revealing of different performance circumstances (Table 4.1). His choices of clefs in the *Canzonette a tre voci* help explain the rather unusual ones in his First Book of five-voice madrigals, given that he seems often to have conceived those madrigals within a three-voice framework to which he then added two further voices (usually the lower ones). It is striking that only two of the madrigals in the First Book are in standard *chiavi naturali* combinations ("Questa ordì il laccio, questa" with two C1 parts; "Filli cara et amata" with two C4 ones), and while five of the others are in

---

[9] See Barbieri, "'Chiavette' and Modal Transposition in Italian Practice"; Johnstone, "'High Clefs' in Composition and Performance." The argument that all pieces in *chiavette* should automatically be transposed in pitch by a specific degree (down a fourth, a fifth, or a third) is irrelevant for works just for voices. Instrumental accompaniment brings a different set of issues into the equation, depending on the instruments involved, on the repertory (sacred versus secular), and on the pitch standard used in a given place and time. In the case of the madrigals, modern ensembles will often transpose individual settings, particularly when performing a single book in sequence.

Table 4.1 Clef distribution in Monteverdi's First to Fourth Books of madrigals.

First Book (1587)	G2, G2, C2, C3, F3 (5 settings)
	G2, G2, C2, C3, C4 (4)
	G2, C1, C2, C3, C4 (3)
	G2, C1, C2, C3, F3 (2)
	G2, C2, C3, C3, F3 (1)
	C1, C1, C3, C4, F4 (1)
	C1, C3, C4, C4, F4 (1)
Second Book (1590)	G2, G2, C2, C3, F3 (3)
	G2, C2, C3, C3, F3 (3)
	C1, C1, C3, C4, F4 (13)
	C1, C2, C3, C4, F4 (1)
Third Book (1592)	G2, G2, C1, C3, F3 (1)
	G2, G2, C2, C3, C4 (1)
	G2, G2, C2, C3, F3 (3)
	G2, C1, C2, C3, F3 (1)
	C1, C1, C1, C3, F4 (1)
	C1, C1, C2, C3, F4 (2)
	C1, C1, C3, C4, F4 (5)
	C1, C3, C3, C4, F4 (1)
Fourth Book (1603)	G2, G2, C2, C3, F4 (1)
	C1, C1, C3, C4, F4 (11)
	C1, C2, C3, C4, F4 (5)
	C1, C2, C4, C4, F4 (2)

standard *chiavette*, the rest are not quite so. The cleffing in the Second Book is more regular, with a notable shift to *chiavi naturali*; thus, the madrigals here are also in a wider range of modes, and their presentation is more straightforward than in the First Book, which at times is very odd indeed. The Third Book splits between madrigals in *chiavette* (6) and *chiavi naturali* (9), although in either case it has some rather unusual combinations of clefs that demand further explanation. The Fourth Book is entirely in *chiavi naturali* with the sole exception of its opening madrigal, "Ah, dolente partita!"; this is another reason to suggest that it may have originally been intended for the Third Book.[10] In all these cases, however, we can see Monteverdi's very strong preference for textures with paired upper voices, usually equal in range; only three madrigals in the first four books have parts for two tenors.[11]

It seems reasonable to assume that Monteverdi was intending his madrigals largely to be performed with one voice to a part, which is surely true for the more virtuosic passages in the continuo ones. There are exceptions: Monteverdi's instructions for the performance of *Tirsi e Clori* sent to Annibale Iberti in Mantua

---

[10] The Fourth Book is strange for another reason, however. In the six madrigals in *chiavi naturali* where the second voice is in C2 clef, that part is in the Alto partbook for five of them ("Anima del cor mio" is the exception), meaning that the Quinto partbook has some parts in C3 clef. This is very unusual. Assuming that it reflects the original sources (which seems likely), it suggests that the parts in the Alto partbook were intended for two different singers, one with a higher range and one with a much lower one. Using the Alto partbook for some C2 parts may also have a bearing on which "Mantuan" ensemble was meant to sing them, so we will see.

[11] Two of them have texts explicitly in the male poetic voice: "Filli cara et amata" in the First Book, and "Longe da te, cor mio" in the Fourth. The third is the gender-neutral "Cor mio, non mori? E mori!" (Fourth Book).

in November 1615 asked for eight singers in its final *ballo*, even though the music later published in the Seventh Book is scored in five vocal parts (SSATB). There may be other cases in which Monteverdi needed to boost the sound by way of doubling voices. But although "Questi vaghi concenti" at the end of the Fifth Book might appear to be a case in point, with a "primo choro" (SSATB) and a "secondo choro" (SATB), it was almost certainly written for the nine male singers under Monteverdi's control at the Mantuan court. Therefore, its clefs, and the vocal ranges embedded within them, were chosen with not just a particular voice-type or mode in mind, but also a particular singer. Different clef combinations in different madrigals also suggest groups of singers constituted in different ways. This is a tricky argument to pursue: singers could sing in different clefs—Luzzasco Luzzaschi writes for the Ferrarese *concerto delle dame* in both G2 and C1 clefs—and in different parts of their vocal range. Yet there are times when it is possible to get a strong sense of the individual musicians with whom Monteverdi almost always worked so closely.

Musicians in Mantua

While the odd clef combinations in Monteverdi's First Book may be due to their structural origins within the canzonetta tradition, the turn to more normative clef combinations in the Second probably reflects an attempt to create a madrigal book more in the standard mold. The variations in the Third Book, however, would appear prompted specifically by Monteverdi's move to Mantua and therefore his access to a quite different range of performers in what was, for him, a new musical world.

Federico Follino described that world in his account of the festivities celebrating the marriage of Prince Francesco Gonzaga and Margherita of Savoy in May–June 1608 (for which Monteverdi had composed *Arianna* and the *Ballo delle ingrate*). He made three points. First, the male and female musicians who performed in the entertainments were all excellent and all in the duke's service ("tutti servitori del Duca"), except for two who were recruited from elsewhere so as to satisfy others. Second, the duke's household had outstanding experts in all the sciences and arts, including an exquisite musical consort ("musica esquisita") comprising not just men of valor in this profession, but also many women with few to match them in Italy ("molte donne, che per avventura han poche pari in Italia"), as those who heard them in the festivities could testify. Third, it had not otherwise been the duke's custom to have women appear in any theatrical or similar context either in public or in private ("comparire in spettacolo né pubblico, né privato"), but only when he wanted to honor some prince would he have them perform apart and in the presence of a very few, and of his more intimate familiars ("con fargliele udire apartatamente, et alla presenza di pochissimi, e suoi più intimi famigliari").[12]

---

[12] Federico Follino, *Compendio delle sontuose feste fatte l'anno MDCVIII nella città di Mantova per le reali nozze del serenissimo prencipe Don Francesco Gonzaga, con la serenissima infante Margherita di Savoia*

Follino was trying to protect Duke Vincenzo from any opprobrium that might be attached to putting female singers on public display. But his account in general seems to be correct. When Vincenzo ascended the throne in 1587, he significantly expanded his musical forces from the twelve to fifteen performers employed by his father, Duke Guglielmo. The first surviving pay records following his accession, from the years 1589–90, include Wert as *maestro di cappella*, Alessandro Striggio (the elder) and Benedetto Pallavicino, some fourteen singers, one organist, one harpist, and two string players.[13] Such records can be tricky: not every musician in the court roll was necessarily identified as such (e.g., if they were listed in some other capacity); salary payments for them could have come from multiple sources (and therefore were not noted in a single place); and instrumental ensembles such as wind or string bands could be bought in on per-service basis.[14] For example, although three female singers are listed in the 1589–90 record, Duke Vincenzo reportedly took four of them to Ferrara in April 1589.[15] And although the string player Giacomo Cattaneo (Monteverdi's father-in-law) appears only in the pay records from 1603 on, he was presumably in service before that point.

That list of musicians from 1589–90 is close enough to the next available one from 1592–93, save where persons left and were replaced, so it provides a decent overview of what was available to Monteverdi during his first years in Mantua. The singers fall into two groups. One was a mixed ensemble made up of members of the Pellizzari (Pelizzari) family, comprising Antonio, his daughters Lucia and Isabetta, and his sons Annibale and Bartolomeo. They had been recruited from Vicenza in 1588, although the two sisters had sung in Mantua earlier. The other group was made up of male singers—seven (probably) in 1589–90; nine in 1592–93—including two castratos (but only one is listed in 1592–93), with the rest presumably distributed among male altos (falsettists), tenors, and basses. In the 1592–93 list, one of the altos was Giulio Cesare Perla, and one of the basses, Fra Serafino Terzi. Two other singers present in the 1589–90 and 1592–93 lists came from the Jewish community and therefore were paid as "extra-ordinary": Isacchino della Profeta, a falsettist and lutenist, and the renowned Madama Europa, the sister of the string player Salamone Rossi. As for those

---

(Mantua: Aurelio e Lodovico Osanna, 1608), 74. His explanation for the two musicians recruited from elsewhere is a typical excuse: the Mantuan court did not have enough singers for such special occasions so needed to "borrow" them from other courts (often Florence), but that borrowing was explained as a favor to whoever employed them.

[13] Parisi, "Ducal Patronage of Music in Mantua," 28–29. Parisi's subsequent tables provide similar lists in varying degrees of completeness from the years 1592–93, 1603–8, 1606–8, 1615–18, 1621, and 1622.
[14] Ibid., 124.
[15] Ibid., 153. The relevant document is a dispatch from the Medici resident in Ferrara, Orazio della Rena, dated 14 April 1589, given in Newcomb, *The Madrigal at Ferrara*, 1: 273 (doc. 78). However, it is odd because it mentions "four ladies from Vicenza" ("quattro Dame Vicentine"). For another mention of a fourth singer in 1594, see Parisi, "Ducal Patronage of Music in Mantua," 474. Newcomb (*The Madrigal at Ferrara*, 1: 99–100) is incorrect to identify these four singers as the Pellizzari sisters, Lucrezia Urbana, and "Catterina Romana" (Caterina Martinelli). The paylist he notes as coming from 1591 is the one given in Parisi, "Ducal Patronage of Music in Mantua," 30, compiled in or after 1603; for the incorrect date, see "Ducal Patronage," 56 n. 81. Lucrezia Urbana was in Mantuan service from 1603 to 1608 ("Ducal Patronage," 509); Caterina Martinelli was recruited from Rome in mid-1603 ("Ducal Patronage," 457–59).

male singers, some were doing double duty from the *cappella* of S. Barbara, even though it was now officially a separate body (with Giovanni Giacomo Gastoldi at its head). However, if they were in orders and/or tied to a monastery, permission could be needed for them to perform in secular clothing, and also to participate in particular types of musical events.[16]

The Pellizzari sisters were particularly versatile, not just vocally but also given that they played instruments that included the cornett and trombone—surprisingly for their gender—and probably plucked string instruments as well. But they came as a five-voice package: their father and two brothers presumably were an alto, a tenor, and a bass, although we do not know who was which. Duke Vincenzo lent three members of the family to Florence for the festivities celebrating the wedding of Grand Duke Ferdinando de' Medici and Christine of Lorraine in April–May 1589: in the second of the grandiose *intermedi* accompanying the performance of Girolamo Bargagli's comedy, *La pellegrina*, the three-voice setting by Luca Marenzio, "Belle ne fe' natura," was sung "with exquisite manner and art" by "two young women who serve the Most Serene Duke of Mantua to no little envy of those who love such noble skill, and by a *putto*, their brother, accompanied by the sound of a harp and two *lire* [*da braccio*]."[17] The term "putto" can mean a boy, but it was also used for a castrato.[18] Either way, in "Belle ne fe' natura" the two sisters presumably sang the upper two parts (both in G2 clef), and their brother, the bottom one (in C1). And although Marenzio's setting was relatively simple as required by something done on a very large stage, it seems to have captured Lucia and Isabetta's competitive delight in overlapping vocal lines. We find similar writing in some of Monteverdi's Third Book madrigals as well (Ex. 4.1).

Thus, it seems reasonable to suggest that the five madrigals in Third Book with two soprano voices (both in G2 clef or the second in C1) and the next lowest in C2 clef (plus two lower voices in C3 and C4/F3) were designed at least for the upper members of the Pellizzari ensemble, if not the entire group: these include "Sovra tenere erbette e bianchi fiori," "O dolce anima mia, dunque è pur vero," "Vattene pur, crudel, con quella pace," "Occhi, un tempo mia vita," and perhaps "Vivrò fra i miei tormenti e le mie cure" (thus, including at least one of the Tasso epic settings, if not both).[19] If so, the Pellizzari brother who sang the C2 parts had developed a quite large range (g–d'' in "Vattene pur, crudel"). The same argument might apply to two other madrigals with the top parts in C1 clef and the third in C2 (with the tenor in C3 and bass in F4): the opening "La giovinetta pianta" and "O rossignuol

---

[16] For the castrato Teodoro (Girolamo) Bacchino, see Parisi, "Ducal Patronage of Music in Mantua," 401–2.

[17] The 1591 edition of the music has the heading "Il seguente Madrigale cantorno con esquita maniera, et arte due giovine, che servono il Serenissimo duca di Mantova con invidia più che mediocre de gl'amatori di così nobil virtù: e da un putto lor fratello accompagnate dal suono di un'Arpa, e due Lire." See Walker (ed.), *Musique des intermèdes de «La pellegrina»*, xli, 37.

[18] For the latter usage, see Parisi, "Ducal Patronage of Music in Mantua," 629 n. 508 (Francesco Rasi proposes bringing to Mantua from Florence a "putto di maggiore età").

[19] The Quinto part (C1) of "Vivrò fra i miei tormenti e le mie cure" (b–f'') does not quite fit the other Quinto parts of the "Pellizzari" madrigals (in G2 clef), but the difference may not be enough to matter.

Ex. 4.1 (a) Luca Marenzio, "Belle ne fe' natura" (*Intermedio II*, 1589; G2, G2, C1);
(b) Monteverdi, "Ch'io non t'ami, cor mio?" (Third Book, 1592; TB are silent).

ch'in queste verdi fronde." There is also no reason that some of the madrigals for SSATB in *chiavi naturali* (but not all of them) could not have worked for the same ensemble.

Hiring the Pellizzari family seems to have been part of Duke Vincenzo's attempt to create a *concerto delle dame* on the Ferrarese model. At least two of the Third Book madrigals also appear to bring in a third soprano (possibly Madama Europa): "O come è gran martire" (G2, G2, C1, C3, F3) and "Lumi, miei cari lumi" (C1, C1, C1, C3, F4). Both texts are gender-neutral and therefore could just as well be in a female poetic voice; their settings have striking SSS openings; and they delay the entrances of the tenor and bass (for twenty-one and fourteen measures respectively). The clear musical reference is to the famed *concerto* of Ferrara that provided "private music" (*musica segreta*) for Duke Alfonso II d'Este, a type of environment that Federico Follino also claimed as more typical for Mantua in his account of women singers there. Duke Alfonso's wife was Margherita Gonzaga—Vincenzo's sister—and when the prince visited Ferrara in the early 1580s, he was as fascinated by the ensemble's musical abilities as he was by the beauty of the performers. Vincenzo Gonzaga as duke clearly wanted to establish a similar *concerto*; so, too, did Grand Duke Ferdinando de' Medici in Florence. Indeed, after Ferrara seceded to the Papal States on the death of Alfonso II without a legitimate heir in late 1597, Vincenzo seems to have viewed Mantua as providing the logical continuation of the duke's achievements in music and perhaps theater, and he made significant efforts to procure the music written specifically for the Ferrarese ensemble by its principal composer, Luzzasco Luzzaschi, which he did in 1606.[20]

Other SSATB settings in *chiavi naturali* in the Third Book, however, do not fit the pattern. The C3-clef parts in the Alto partbook for "Stracciami pur il core" and "Ch'io non t'ami, cor mio?" cover an unusually large range (*e–a′*, and "Se per estremo ardore" and "Perfidissimo volto" take this even further still (*d–b♭′*).[21] Indeed, "Se per estremo ardore" has two such parts in C3 clef, meaning that two of Monteverdi's "alto" singers were capable of covering an octave and a sixth. He also seems to have wanted to highlight one or other of them, given its unusual solo opening, and likewise in "Perfidissimo volto." It is impossible to tell whether these altos were male falsettists or high tenors (in the manner of an *haute-contre*). But the fact that the "tenor" parts in C3 clef in the *chiavette* madrigals in general do not have so wide a range ("Vivrò fra i miei tormenti" is the exception) suggests the presence of two different vocal ensembles within the madrigals of the Third Book: one made up of the Pellizzari family (with or without an additional soprano), and the other of the male singers among the duke's household musicians: that is, two castratos plus one or two altos, one or two tenors, and a bass. The "Pellizzari" madrigals are usually in *chiavette* but not always so (female sopranos can sing in C1 clef). The "all-male" madrigals are always in *chiavi naturali*, given that castratos did not normally sing in G2 clef.[22] Even if these ensembles could be mixed in various ways—with the Pellizzari sisters joining male singers outside their family, the variety of scorings in the Third Book means that it could not, and cannot, be performed in its entirety by the same five singers.

This also raises the question of which ensemble was used on what occasions and in what locations. If Duke Vincenzo generally allowed his female singers to perform only in private—so Follino suggested in 1608—that would not prevent the all-male ensemble from doing the same, although it could also be used on less "private" occasions. This potentially situates the "Pellizzari" madrigals—including two of the Tasso settings, or perhaps all three—in a more intimate context than one might expect. Perhaps surprisingly, however, all the Guarini poems given first-time (or nearly so) settings in the Third Book are for the "all-male" ensemble, or at least, for the standard combination of voices in *chiavi naturali* (all the "Pellizzari" ones had prior settings).

---

[20] Parisi, "Ducal Patronage of Music in Mantua," 136–38; Stras, *Women and Music in Sixteenth-Century Ferrara*, 308.

[21] The C3 part in the Tenore partbook for "Lumi, miei chiari lumi" has a similar range; the same is true for the Tenore partbook's C3 part for "Vivrò fra i miei tormenti" (*e–b♭′*). Salamone Rossi could even take his C3 parts down to *c*, as in "Che non fai, che non pensi" in his First Book *a5* (1600). The same singer, or one like him, appears in some of the madrigals in Monteverdi's Fourth, Fifth, and Sixth Books as well. However, wide-ranging C3 parts can also be found in Monteverdi's Second Book.

[22] This is certainly true of Monteverdi's *Orfeo* (1607), which was first performed by an all-male cast, with castratos taking the female roles. All the soprano parts (including in the choruses) are in C1 clef, generally going up to *e″* (with just one isolated *f″* in "Ecco Orfeo cui pur dianzi" at the end of Act I). The exception is the final chorus of Act V ("Vanne, Orfeo, felice a pieno"; G2, C1, C3, C4, F4), which is known to be a later addition not connected to the premiere.

The Fourth Book of 1603 is somewhat unusual in this light. "Ah, dolente partita!" is the only setting in *chiavette*, and its vocal ranges are close enough to the "Pellizzari" settings in the Third Book (save for the C3 part in the Tenore partbook having that wide-range *e–a'*), which is where, I have suggested, it could have originally belonged. The rest of the Fourth Book is entirely in *chiavi naturali*, which may also reflect the fact that Monteverdi was steering it in a different direction. In the dedication to the Accademia degli Intrepidi of Ferrara, he says that he had wanted to present some of his madrigals in manuscript to Duke Alfonso II d'Este but was prevented by the duke's death (in October 1597), so he was including them in the present edition, plus "other new madrigals."[23] At least some of the contents of the Fourth Book went back several years: "Ah, dolente partita!" was first published in 1597, and "Anima mia, perdona" was criticized by Artusi on the basis of his encountering it in November 1598. As for the madrigals to be presented in manuscript to Alfonso II—and given the duke's interest in female singers—one might speculate that they were those in the Fourth Book that begin with prominent upper-voice trios (C1, C1, C3), such as the three madrigals one after the other in the middle of the book: "Io mi son giovinetta," "Quell'augellin, che canta," and "Non più guerra, pietate." There are prominent upper-voice trios or duets in other madrigals here as well ("A un giro sol de' belli occhi lucenti," "Volgea l'anima mia soavemente," the *seconda parte* of "Anima mia, perdona," and "Anima dolorosa, che vivendo"). Also, some of the C1 parts in the Fourth Book have unusually wide ranges, such as *a–f''* in "Non più guerra, pietate" and "Sì, ch'io vorei morire," and *a–g''* in "Voi pur da me partite, anima dura." They do not quite seem "Mantuan" in intent.

By the time of the publication of the Fourth Book, Monteverdi had been Duke Vincenzo's *maestro della musica* for fifteen months or so. The household musicians were also growing in number, from eighteen or so in 1589–90 to the low thirties in 1606–8. The Pellizzari sisters and their brother Annibale were still on the payroll in 1603, although Antonio (their father) was not—he may have died in 1595—and likewise Bartolomeo.[24] It is not clear whether Madama Europa was still available, but the female contingent had already been increased by way of Claudia Cattaneo (Monteverdi married her in 1599); by August 1603, the young Roman soprano, Caterina Martinelli (b. 1589 or 1590), was lodged in the Monteverdi household for further training; and the Neapolitan harpist Lucrezia Urbana (probably also a singer as well) was recruited that same year. For the other singers, Monteverdi seems to have maintained a similar constitution of castratos—by 1605, Giovanni Battista Sacchi and Giulio Cardi were at their head—and lower male voices. However, he gradually boosted the number of tenors: Francesco Rasi, who had studied with Giulio Caccini in Florence, had already joined the ensemble by November 1598, if

---

[23] Four canzonettas by Monteverdi had already been sent to Alfonso II d'Este's wife, Margherita Gonzaga, in December 1594, possibly the ones included in Antonio Morsolino's *Il primo libro delle canzonette a tre voci* (1594), which had been published earlier in July; see Newcomb, *The Madrigal at Ferrara*, 1: 208.

[24] Parisi, "Ducal Patronage of Music in Mantua," 474.

not before, and he would be followed by Pandolfo Grande, Francesco Campagnolo (another of Monteverdi's students), and Francesco Dognazzi. This new corpus of tenors started to make an impact on Monteverdi's madrigals, particularly in the continuo madrigals in the Fifth and Sixth Books, and also, of course, in *Orfeo* and the 1610 "Vespers." Those last two works also reveal the fruits of another strategy adopted by Monteverdi as *maestro della musica*: he formalized the position of a five-part wind band (headed by the cornettist Giulio Cesare Bianchi, recruited in 1602), and probably in 1603, he brought in two string players from Casale Monferrato— the brothers Giovanni Battista and Orazio Rubini—to build up a string band of some eight players (with Salamone Rossi making a ninth). The instrumentalists were versatile in the ways typical of their profession: the Rubini brothers, for example, also played the theorbo. Some of them, and likewise some of the singers, were also composers.[25] Monteverdi later suggested that some such ability was always useful in performers because they would therefore be able better to understand any music.[26] In Mantua, it also aided him in his duties as *maestro*, given that we start to see a clear division of labor in terms of what Monteverdi was required to compose, and what could be left to others.

The Fifth Book bears witness to all these developments in specific musical ways. In contrast to the Fourth, Monteverdi returns to the mixture of clef combinations found in the Third. Of the *Pastor fido* settings, the long Dorinda/Silvio exchange beginning with "Ecco, Silvio, colei che in odio hai tanto" is in standard *chiavette* (G2, G2, C2, C3, F3), and "Cruda Amarilli" is in an unusual variant of them (G2, C1, C3, C3, F3), and doubly so because it is, in principle, voicing the male shepherd Mirtillo.[27] The rest of the collection is in *chiavi naturali*. The high-clef "Ecco, Silvio" and its subsequent parts fit the "Pellizzari" scoring seen in the Third Book— regardless of whether it was for the same singers—save for the use of high b♭″, which almost certainly forces some manner of downward transposition. But "Cruda Amarilli" does not: the two C3 parts have quite different ranges—the first, in the Tenore partbook, is the typical *g–a′*, but the second (Quinto) is *e–a′*, and therefore suspiciously like the wide-ranging "alto" found in the non-"Pellizzari" madrigals in the Third Book (and in the Fourth). The tendency of its bass part to break into *passaggi* (at "ahi lasso") also suggests a new singer in the ensemble who further

---

[25] Rasi and Dognazzi were not the only ones to issue their own musical collections in print. Salamone Rossi published a wide range of secular music and instrumental music, with a number of settings of texts also treated by Monteverdi; see Harrán, *Salamone Rossi*. In Monteverdi's letter to Alessandro Striggio of 9 December 1616 concerning the ill-fated *Le nozze di Tetide*, he suggested that Adriana Basile, Rasi, and Dognazzi could each compose the music for their roles so as best to suit their voices. The anthology *Motetti a una, due, tre, et quattro voci col basso continuo per l'organo, fatti da diversi musici servitori del Serenissimo Signor Duca di Mantova* (Venice: Giacomo Vincenti, 1618), collected by Federico Malgarini (another Mantuan singer), contains pieces by a large number of Mantuan singers and instrumentalists (the latter including the Rubini brothers), several of whom were there during Monteverdi's time.

[26] So Monteverdi says in his report on the Bolognese bass singer Giovanni Battista Bisucci to Alessandro Striggio on 20 June 1627.

[27] For this text, *chiavette* were adopted by Wert (G2, G2, C2, C3, C4) and Pallavicino (G2, C2, C3, C3, F3), but not Marenzio.

appears in "Amor, se giusto sei" and "Questi vaghi concenti."[28] In other words, Monteverdi now seems to be mixing and matching voices from ensembles that were in some sense previously kept separate. Perhaps this is not surprising, given his new position as *maestro* and his apparent reorganization of the musical establishment in 1602–3. One might still fairly assume that the top parts in the *chiavette* madrigals, and some of the *chiavi naturali* ones, were taken by women singers. But Monteverdi also started to exploit the new tenors whom he had recruited, whether as soloists or in what became a favorite texture of his: duets. It hardly seems coincidental that the first of the continuo madrigals in the Fifth Book, "Ahi come a un vago sol cortese giro," gives such prominence to two tenor voices singing in an ornamented style, even as he used other of the continuo madrigals to showcase different individual singers in turn.[29]

Monteverdi's position in charge of the household music meant that he directed the full ensemble or various subsets thereof, and up to a point, he composed appropriate music in either case. On 26 April 1604, Alessandro I Pico, Principe di Mirandola, wrote to Vincenzo Gonzaga to ask for the favor of having use of "Monteverdi, your musician, with your [or "his"] women to compose and stage [*recitare*] and sing a few things" in the entertainments he was planning to welcome to his city his new bride, Laura d'Este.[30] The "women" presumably now included Claudia Cattaneo and Caterina Martinelli, but if they did indeed form a literal *concerto delle dame* without male singers, one has to ask what music they sang. Monteverdi may at some time have composed for them some version of the *Scherzi musicali* that he published in 1607 (all for SSB, two violins, and continuo). Or perhaps he adapted his five-voice madrigals for reduced forces, as much later did the England-based Italian singer-composer, Angelo Notari (1566–1663), with arrangements of the "Ecco, Silvio, colei che in odio hai tanto" and "Ch'io t'ami, e t'ami più de la mia vita" sequences in the Fifth Book as duets for two sopranos and continuo.[31]

Equally, however, Monteverdi was happy to provide compositions to be performed just by male singers if that is what circumstances required. When he went to the battlefield in Hungary with Duke Vincenzo Gonzaga in 1595, he was head of a small musical contingent that also included a castrato (Teodoro Bacchino)

---

[28] For a slightly different reading of the bass *passaggio* in "Cruda Amarilli" (as a technique drawn from Monteverdi's experience with the *viola bastarda*), see Coluzzi, "Licks, Polemics, and the *Viola bastarda*."

[29] Pirrotta ("Monteverdi's Poetic Choices," 301) notes the composer's increasing recognition of "the individuality of each performer." "Ahi come a un vago sol" also has that wide-ranging C1 part (a–g''; S² in the Alto partbook) found in "Voi pur da me partite, anima dura" in the Fourth Book.

[30] Parisi, "Ducal Patronage of Music in Mantua," 603 n. 398: "il Monteverde suo musico con le sue donne, per comporre et per recitare et cantare alcune cose nella festa ch'io preparo." The wording "per recitare et cantare" is ambiguous, but "recitare" is usually associated with some manner of theatrical performance, and while "cantare" might also apply to the stage, the "alcune cose" suggests multiple musical works. In 1607, Monteverdi wrote (part of) a *ballo* that Alessandro Pico commissioned to celebrate his wife's first pregnancy (it was done on 22 February, two days before the premiere of *Orfeo*); see Patuzzi, "S'a queste d'Este valle."

[31] In British Library, Add. MS 31440 (from the second quarter of the seventeenth century); see Henson, "Foreign Songs for Foreign Kings." Notari also made a similar adaptation of "Cruda Amarilli, che col nome ancora," plus a solo version related to it; "Foreign Songs," 86–93.

and two basses (Giovanni Battista Marinoni and Serafino Terzi), plus a "chaplain," Padre Valerio da Ferrara, who may also have performed within the ensemble.[32] In July 1607, when Monteverdi spent his customary time in Cremona while Vincenzo Gonzaga and his entourage summered in Sampierdarena near Genoa, he received a commission from the duke to set two sonnets to be performed by the "gentlemen singers" who had accompanied the duke there along with the vice-*maestro*, Bassano Casola.[33]

The continuo madrigals in the Fifth Book also give the impression of being composed for a stable ensemble largely comprising male singers. This certainly seems to be the case with the final madrigal in the book, "Questi vaghi concenti," set for nine voices divided into two groups (SSATB/SATB), with an initial sinfonia, part-repeated in the middle, for nine instruments (Monteverdi's new string band) plus continuo.[34] Anything scored for "nine" voices and/or instruments is going to have some connection with the Muses, as also in the case of "Con che soavità, labra odorate" in the Seventh Book. The voice parts in "Questi vaghi concenti" further match in terms of range the singers who were needed to perform the original version of *Orfeo* (with Francesco Rasi, in addition, in its title role), which we know was done with an all-male cast.[35] Likewise, the Sixth Book madrigals are all in *chiavi naturali* and seem largely designed for the same SSATB ensemble, save where Monteverdi uses SSTTB in two of the *concertato* settings ("Una donna fra l'altre onesta e bella" and "Qui rise, o Tirsi, e qui ver' me rivolse"), as he had done with "Ahi come a un vago sol cortese giro" in the Fifth.[36]

Monteverdi used "Questi vaghi concenti" to prove the worth of the duke's musical establishment. That, too, was part of his job. But one gets the sense that

---

[32] For the Hungary trip, see Fabbri, *Monteverdi*, trans. Carter, 30–31. Marinoni and Terzi were definitely "basses," although that is not necessarily to say that they had the same vocal register, and indeed, it would be odd for the constitution of the Hungary ensemble if they did. This Marinoni (born *c.* 1560) is not to be confused with the tenor and theorbist of the same name (1596–1657) who worked with Monteverdi in St. Mark's; see their separate entries in the *Dizionario biografico degli italiani*.

[33] In his letter to Annibale Iberti of 28 July 1607, Monteverdi sent one of the sonnet settings and promised the other. Pryer ("Monteverdi, Two Sonnets and a Letter") suggests that the sonnets were the SSATB settings of Petrarch's "Zefiro torna e 'l bel tempo rimena" and "Oimè il bel viso, oimè 'l soave sguardo" in the Sixth Book, in part because both contain echoes of music in *Orfeo*. But "Una donna fra l'altre onesta e bella" (SSTTB, bc) remains a possibility—despite Pryer's removing it from the reckoning, in light of its need for a continuo instrument—given that Aquilino Coppini published a contrafact of this madrigal in May 1609.

[34] The nine string instruments play in five real parts with doublings. "Questi vaghi concenti" would seem to have served a similar purpose to Gastoldi's "Al suon de' nostri accenti" in his *Concenti musicali, con le sue sinfonie, a otto voci* (Venice: Ricciardo Amadino, 1604). Like about half the pieces in Gastoldi's volume, "Al suon de' nostri accenti" begins with an instrumental sinfonia in two four-part "choirs," and the voices are similarly divided (two groups in G2, C2, C3, C4). The text has the singers presenting their "accents" to exalted spirits, servants of love, and friends of virtue to make winter pass into spring, then summer.

[35] Carter, "Singing *Orfeo*," also summarized in Carter, *Monteverdi's Musical Theatre*, 96–99.

[36] However, Monteverdi appears to write for two different bass voices, one capable of going down to *D* (in "Lasciatemi morire," "A Dio, Florida bella, il cor piagato," and "Presso un fiume tranquillo," in the last case going up to *c'*). Bass parts with a similar range can also found in Salamone Rossi's Fourth Book *a*5 (1610). A similar bass appears in Monteverdi's Seventh Book in a more soloistic context (e.g., in "Parlo, misero, o taccio?" with a range of *D–e'*). The bass Matteo Rossi was in service in Mantua from 1613 to 1622, but Duke Ferdinando Gonzaga was also interested in hiring a bass with a particularly low range in November 1614; see Parisi, "Ducal Patronage of Music in Mantua," 328 n. 34. Another candidate is the Mantuan Giovanni Amigoni (*c.* 1584–1627), who was briefly at St. Mark's in 1619–20 but was in service in Mantua in the early 1620s, as he had perhaps been before; "Ducal Patronage," 400.

Monteverdi's role in Mantua became as much that of a director or administrator as of a composer, save in special circumstances.[37] Just as he could rely on Bassano Casola to rehearse those madrigals in Sampierdarena in the summer of 1607, so did he have others perfectly capable of taking charge of music on their own: for a musical event in Lake Garda in July 1609 (another favorite place for the ducal family to spend the summers), the bulk of the arrangements to get the instrumentalists in place were made by the cornettist Giulio Cesare Bianchi. Although the tenor Francesco Dognazzi sang, and Salamone Rossi and Giulio Cesare Monteverdi were present, the music appears to have been composed by Bianchi himself.[38]

Likewise, the repertory of those regular Friday evening performances in the Sala degli Specchi in the ducal palace was wider than Monteverdi's own publications suggest. These seem to have been surprisingly open events: when Monteverdi wrote to Cardinal Ferdinando Gonzaga about them on 22 January 1611 (a Saturday), he said that the day before, those attending included the "Most Serene Lord Duke and the Most Serene Lady Duchess, the Lady Isabella of San Martino, the Lord Marquis and Marchioness of Solferino, ladies and knights from the entire court, but also more than a hundred other gentlemen from the city too." Indeed, so great was the crush that Monteverdi thought that the duke would need to place guards at the door to control admission. The chief attraction, it seems, was the famous virtuoso singer Adriana Basile, recently recruited from Naples, who had arrived in Mantua in the summer of 1610. In that letter to the cardinal, Monteverdi also acknowledged receipt of two madrigals that he said would be performed on some future Friday evening. One, "Ahi, che morir mi sento," was to be sung by Basile and the castrato Giovanni Battista Sacchi to the accompaniment of two theorbos and an *organo di legno*, while the other (unidentified) just to the organ alone. Both had been composed by Cardinal Ferdinando himself, it seems.[39]

Basile had come to Mantua with her husband, Mutio Baroni, along with her two sisters, Vittoria and Margherita, who were also singers, and her brothers Giovanni Battista (a poet) and Lelio (another musician). This filled a need for women singers created by the deaths of Claudia Cattaneo in 1607 and Caterina Martinelli in early 1608. But it seems clear that the ensemble was no longer a *musica segreta* in the narrowest sense of the term: Adriana Basile was not being paid an exorbitant salary

---

[37] Stras (*Women and Music in Sixteenth-Century Ferrara*, 308) also suggests that the receipt in Mantua of a very large collection of madrigals in manuscript by Luzzasco Luzzaschi in March 1606 may have freed Monteverdi to concentrate on other things.

[38] The documents variously cited by Parisi ("Ducal Patronage of Music in Mantua," 552–53 n. 102, 653 n. 563) are confusing about this event. It appears to have involved some kind of pageant with fireworks devised by Federico Follino ("Ducal Patronage," 214–15 n. 173). But *pace* "Ducal Patronage," 167, Claudio Monteverdi does not seem to have been directly involved. Bianchi refers to "le compositioni ch'io portai meco," which suggests that he was more than just the carrier of them.

[39] "Ahi, che morir mi sento" is presumably the "cantata with the accompaniment for two archlutes" to which Monteverdi referred in his previous letter to the cardinal of 28 December 1610. In his 22 January letter, he styles it "Ahi che morire mi sento," although this does not seem metrically correct. For Cardinal Ferdinando's interests as a poet and composer, see Strainchamps, "New Light on the Accademia degli Elevati of Florence." Ferdinando composed some of the music included in Marco da Gagliano's opera *Dafne*, performed in Mantua in early 1608.

to be hidden away in a private chamber. We know that she participated in five-voice madrigals, and in Mantua, she sang duets with castratos (Giovanni Battista Sacchi) and tenors (Francesco Campagnolo). But she was also famous for having a repertory of some three hundred Italian and Spanish songs known by heart, which she performed to her own accompaniment (she played the Spanish guitar, harp, and *lira da braccio*).[40]

Other virtuoso singers also took center stage. Francesco Rasi is an early case in point, given his printed and manuscript collections of solo songs that brought the Florentine style of singing to Mantua, as well as his role in Mantuan theatrical and similar entertainments, not least as the protagonist of Monteverdi's *Orfeo*. He was joined by the tenor Francesco Campagnolo in the performance of *Il rapimento di Proserpina* (music by Giulio Cesare Monteverdi) in Casale Monferrato on 29 April 1611. Here both singers demonstrated how they were the most outstanding examples of their art, for who could better make heard

> sweeter accents, faster passages, more pitying emotions, more ardent sighs, more lovely fugues, more entwined *groppi*, more charming *tremoli*, more graceful *trilli*, harsher consonances and sweeter dissonances sounding one like the other, as a result of which we enjoy paradise through our ears, and we see brought into practice what was mythically ascribed by ingenious poets to the harmony of Orpheus, Arion, and Amphyon?[41]

On other occasions, Giovanni Battista Sacchi and Francesco Dognazzi sang duets with the same combination of vocal fireworks, one of which appears contained in Dognazzi's *Il primo libro de varii concenti* (1614), a collection that, I have noted, had some influence on Monteverdi's Seventh Book (Ex. 4.2).[42]

Monteverdi was certainly familiar with these vocal techniques, and he could write music to match them, so we see both in *Orfeo* and in the 1610 "Vespers." But the notable shift from the end of the first decade of the seventeenth century into the second in favor of freestanding solo songs and duets did not have as much impact on his "Mantuan" madrigals as one might expect. There may be some "lost" works to take into account here: for example, on 24 June 1610, the Florentine poet Ottavio Rinuccini noted to Cardinal Ferdinando Gonzaga how everyone in Florence—and

---

[40] Parisi, "Ducal Patronage of Music in Mantua," 405–10. For her songs known by heart, see "Ducal Patronage," 181–82 n. 49. That "three hundred" should not be taken literally: it was a standard figure to mean "a great many."

[41] Kirkendale, *The Court Musicians in Florence during the Principate of the Medici*, 580: "Per questa attione furono chiamati i più eccellenti cantanti che oggidì vanta l'Italia, et basta a dire che venne il signor Francesco Rasi et il signor Francesco Campagnolo ambidui musici del Serenissimo Signor Duca di Mantova, i quali sono i due Poli che a' tempi nostri sostengono l'arte del ben cantare, poiché chi ci può far sentire accenti più soavi, passaggi più veloci, affetti più pietosi, sospiri più ardenti, fughe più leggiadre, groppi più annodati, tremoli più vezzosi, trilli più gratiosi, più dure dolcezze e più dolci durezze di quelle che ci fan sentire questi, mercè de' quali godiamo per l'orecchie il paradiso et vediamo realmente operarsi quanto dagli ingegnosi poeti fu favolosamente ascritto all'armonia d'Orfeo, d'Arione e d'Anfione?"

[42] For Sacchi and Dognazzi singing together, see Parisi, "Ducal Patronage of Music in Mantua," 658–59 n. 601. They were also with Rasi in Verona in May 1614; "Ducal Patronage," 660 n. 605.

Ex 4.2 Francesco Dognazzi, "Ite caldi sospir'al freddo core" ("Sopra l'Aria di Ruggiero"); *Il primo libro de varii concenti*, 1614), 21 (end of the *prima parte*).

especially Jacopo Peri—had admired a duet and other arias by Monteverdi that had reached the city.[43] Likewise, Angelo Grillo was effusive in a praise of a spiritual madrigal that Monteverdi had sent him from Mantua (setting one of his poems) that seems to have been for solo voice or duet.[44] But only in the Seventh Book (1619) did he publish settings in the more "modern" style that had been used in Mantua in the years before he left, and he did so for very specific reasons to do with its dedicatee, Caterina de' Medici, the new Duchess of Mantua.

Until that point, Monteverdi appears in general not to have fallen for such fashionable pieces, given that there were others in Mantua who could compose them instead. Rather, he seems to have made something of a sport of taking texts known in musical settings for one, two, or three voices and instrumental accompaniment and demonstrating what could still be done with them with a larger ensemble.[45] His "Sfogava con le stelle" in the Fourth Book is a case in point if Monteverdi knew of Giulio Caccini's solo-voice setting in his *Le nuove musiche* published in 1602,

---

[43] Kirkendale, *The Court Musicians in Florence during the Principate of the Medici*, 219: "Quelle poche cose che sono comparse del Monteverdi, come il duo e altre arie, sono ammirate da tutti universalmente e dal Zazzerino fuor di modo." Jacopo Peri was commonly known as "Zazzerino."

[44] Fabbri, *Monteverdi*, trans. Carter, 118. Grillo's letter is undated but mentions both Francesco Campagnolo and Adriana Basile, so it must have been written after Basile's arrival in Mantua in mid-1610 and before Monteverdi's departure. From 1609 to 1612, Grillo resided in the monastery of S. Benedetto di Polirone (15 km southeast of Mantua), and from 1612 to 1616 (or perhaps later), in S. Nicolò del Lido (Venice).

[45] The reverse seems to have occurred in Mantua as well: Francesco Rasi's *Vaghezze di musica per una voce sola* (Venice: Angelo Gardano & Fratelli, 1608) includes two settings of poems by Guarini that Monteverdi had set in his Fourth Book: "Cor mio, mentre vi miro" and "Voi pur da me partite, anima dura" (as "Voi pur vi dipartite...").

although its contents dated back over more than a decade.[46] Likewise, if the Fourth Book's "Io mi son giovinetta" was one of the madrigals that Monteverdi wanted to present to Duke Alfonso d'Este, he was then willing to accept the competition with Luzzasco Luzzaschi's much more "Ferrarese" setting of the same text for two sopranos in his *Madrigali . . . a uno, e doi, e tre soprani fatti per la musica del già Serenissimo Duca Alfonso d'Este* (Rome: Simone Verovio) published in 1601 but—as its title makes clear—containing music written earlier.[47] However, Monteverdi then countered by including among the continuo madrigals in his Fifth Book, two texts by Guarini set for three sopranos in Luzzaschi's 1601 book: "Troppo ben può questo tiranno Amore" (in a slightly different version) and "«T'amo mia vita!», la mia cara vita." The same impression is created by the two musical versions of Marino's "Presso un fiume tranquillo" published in 1614, one as a duet by Francesco Dognazzi—probably another of the pieces he sang with Giovanni Battista Sacchi—and the other, the seven-voice setting in Monteverdi's Sixth Book. In this case, however, his writing for Eurillo (T) and Filena (S) probably has echoes of Dognazzi and Sacchi's performances in dueling ornamentation.

Venice

The centrifugal forces of music in Mantua may have caused Monteverdi some headaches as *maestro della musica*, given that he later expressed satisfaction over the fact that in Venice he had full control over the selection and administration of the musicians under his purview in St. Mark's.[48] But he did not have unfettered access to them outside of the basilica. The musical *cappella* was far larger than the ensemble Monteverdi had directed in Mantua, with around twenty-four singers in 1616 and thirty-eight in February 1642, plus some eighteen instrumentalists and two organists. Like any group of musicians of that size, it was both fractious and factional. Moreover, both the singers and the instrumentalists arranged themselves into *compagnie* for extramural purposes. In 1617, the *maestro di cappella* was explicitly excluded from any involvement in the singers' *compagnia*, and while Monteverdi regained control over it in 1620, his authority was a matter of dispute: this was one reason for the very public argument with the bass singer

---

[46] Carter, "'Sfogava con le stelle' Reconsidered," which also discusses the apparent influence of Monteverdi's setting on Salamone Rossi's in his Second Book a5 of 1602. The text was also set in Francesco Stivori's *Madrigali et canzoni a otto voci . . . libro terzo de suoi concerti* (Venice: Ricciardo Amadino, 1603), a rather odd collection that needs further examination.

[47] Luzzaschi sent songs ("canti") to Duke Vincenzo Gonzaga in December 1598; see Parisi, "Ducal Patronage of Music in Mantua," 716 n. 18. They may have included those published in 1601; see Stras, *Women and Music in Sixteenth-Century Ferrara*, 333. Luzzaschi was the first to set a version of Guarini's "Io mi son giovinetta," included in his 1601 volume: the text varies from Monteverdi's, although it has the "Son giovinetto anch'io" line lacking in the earliest (1590) source for the poem; see Georis, *Claudio Monteverdi*, 446–47 n. 22.

[48] So Monteverdi wrote to Striggio on 13 March 1620 as yet another reason that he was disinclined to return to Mantua.

Domenico Aldegati in 1637. Some performers at St. Mark's leveraged a clause in their contracts that gave them the freedom to perform elsewhere whenever and wherever they liked so long as it did not interfere with their duties.[49] Others, such as Bartolomeo Barbarino, preferred to be hired on an ad hoc basis. Others still, however, were more tied down.

Aldegati stated that Monteverdi was a "thieving fucking billy-goat" ("quel ladro becco fotuto"), so Monteverdi complained to the procurators on 9 June 1637.[50] The singer, from Cesena, had apparently been a troublemaker from the start of his employment in St. Mark's on 3 January 1612. But Monteverdi did not have all the St. Mark's musicians on his side. His attempts to introduce discipline into the *cappella* in 1615 by establishing fines for unauthorized absences would have pleased some but not others. Not to be discounted, however, was the fact that the composer was, and remained, a foreigner, the first to be appointed *maestro* since Cipriano de Rore. Thus, it was easy for an enemy to denounce him as a traitor to the Republic of Venice by virtue of his loyalties to the Holy Roman Empire (given his Mantuan citizenship), as occurred in 1623.[51] Indeed, a number of the foreigners in the *cappella* appear to have been the victim of prejudice from their Venetian colleagues, prompting them to band together in solidarity.

It seems clear that Monteverdi supported the work of several of his colleagues at St. Mark's. For the collection of *Arie de diversi* that appeared in 1634, the printer Alessandro Vincenti appears to have turned to Monteverdi to help him restore his fortunes following the disastrous impact of the plague in 1630–31: the collection opens with two arias by Monteverdi, and it includes others by St. Mark's musicians (Giovanni Pietro Berti, Francesco Cavalli, Giovanni Felice Sances, and Gerardo Biancosi), plus a singer, Bonivento Boniventi, who acted as Monteverdi's assistant prior to entering the musical *cappella*.[52] Cavalli's aria ("Son ancor pargoletta") was his first printed work, while neither Biancosi nor Boniventi otherwise published any music: their arias here seem to have been written under Monteverdi's influence, if not instruction.

This was a small group, however, and one also reflective to some degree of Monteverdi's immediate social circles in Venice documented by way of his being asked to act as godparent, of those who testified on his or his sons' behalf, and of

---

[49] For the cases of Vito Rovetta (organist), Flaminio Corradi (tenor, theorbo), Francesco Rossi (bass), and Bartolomeo Strambali (alto), see Di Pasquale, "La cappella dogale di San Marco," 41 n. 116.

[50] See Monteverdi's letter to the procurators of St. Mark's, 9 June 1637; the incident is discussed in detail in Di Pasquale, "Le compagnie dei musici marciani," 208–10. For Aldegati's prior history as a rabble-rouser, see "Le compagnie," 192, 198, 203.

[51] Matteo Caberloti had to fudge the issue of Monteverdi's nationality in his funeral oration included in the *Fiori poetici raccolti nel funerale del Molto Illustre e Molto Reverendo Signor Claudio Monteverdi*, edited by Giovanni Battista Marinoni (Venice: Francesco Miloco, 1644), although he did say that he was always loved and revered by the musicians of St. Mark's.

[52] Other composers here included Carlo Milanuzzi, Martino Pesenti, and Orazio Tarditi, who had all previously published with Vincenti, plus the young Olivetan monk Scipione Giovanni, currently residing in Padua. The collection also has two anonymous pieces.

others who clearly expressed their admiration for him in one way or another (Table 4.2). Perhaps inevitably, he associated mostly with musicians connected to St. Mark's.[53] Some of them probably regarded themselves in some sense as Monteverdi's students (Cavalli, Rovetta), although only one formerly identified himself as such: the tenor Giovanni Battista Marinoni.[54] Many, however, were foreigners as well, and while that might sometimes have been a quirk of circumstance—Monteverdi needed Mantuans to bear witness to the fact that his sons were indeed legitimate—it could also reflect the preference to stick together in the way outsiders often do.

Monteverdi certainly drew on his singer friends to perform his secular music: the baritone Giacomo Rapallini (also styled Rapallino) took the role of Ubaldo in *Armida abbandonata* when it was performed in Venice, and he offered to do the same in Mantua.[55] Monteverdi also knew the voice of another bass, Giovanni Amigoni, well enough to feel comfortable writing the role of Peneo (Peneus) for him in the *ballo*, *Apollo*, composed for performance in Mantua in 1620, singing in the virtuoso *alla bastarda* style with wide-ranging ornaments (so he wrote to Alessandro Striggio on 8 and 15 February 1620). The tenors with whom Monteverdi was friends at various points during his time in Venice—Bartolomeo Barbarino, Giovanni Battista Marinoni, Vincenzo Remedio, Stefano Rivieri, and Antonio Vicentini—were also fine singers, as was his own son Francesco. Monteverdi's access to them may well explain the madrigals he wrote with unusual scorings involving three tenors: "Vago augelletto che cantando vai" in the Eighth Book (SSATTTB, bc), "Sì, sì, ch'io v'amo" in the Ninth (TTT, bc), and "Voi ch'ascoltate in rime sparse il suono," one of the "moral" settings in the *Selva morale e spirituale* (STTTB, 2 vln, bc). Add his two alto friends—Bonivento Boniventi and Giovanni Giuliani—and they constitute a plausible group of singers for the bulk of the smaller-scale settings (AA, AAB, ATB, TT, TTB) that dominate Monteverdi's secular output in Venice. Given that at least two of these tenors also played theorbo, and that Monteverdi was also friends with string players (Giovanni Rovetta, plus Carlo Farina for the brief time he was in Venice) and a keyboard player (Cavalli), one starts to get the sense of the performers on which the composer could draw should he be called upon to provide music for an evening's entertainment.

---

[53] Table 4.2 largely draws on information now available in Baroncini and Di Pasquale (eds.) *Monteverdi a San Marco*. It excludes other non-Venetian musicians with whom Monteverdi was in contact, not least his fervent admirer, Bellerofonte Castaldi (see Dolata, "Bellerofonte Castaldi"). Some of the broader issues concerning the composer's immediate circles are discussed in Baroncini, "Monteverdi in Venice." Even Monteverdi's acting as godparent to a child of a paper-seller (including of music-manuscript paper), Zuanne *cartoler*, in 1626 fits the pattern.

[54] In the dedication to the three Procurators of St. Mark's of the *Fiori poetici* (1644), the tenor Giovanni Battista Marinoni, who edited the volume, says that he hopes to have done the duty of a well-disciplined student ("confide, c'haverò corrispos[t]o all'officio di un ben disciplinato scholare").

[55] Monteverdi wrote very favorably of Rapallini to Alessandro Striggio on 7 May 1627 in response to yet more efforts to recruit a bass to Mantua (probably in light of the death of Giovanni Amigoni on the 4th): "he is a priest, but a baritone and not a bass. Nevertheless he lets his words be heard clearly, he has something of a *trillo*, some graces, and he sings boldly." The fact that Monteverdi then thought that another bass from Bologna was a better prospect (so he wrote to Striggio on 20 June) may have been an attempt to extricate Rapallini from an offer that the singer wanted to refuse.

Table 4.2 Musicians in Venice with personal connections to Monteverdi (V1634 = *Arie de diversi*, ed. Alessandro Vincenti [Venice: Alessandro Vincenti, 1634]).

Name	Origin	Employed at St. Mark's	Notes
Giovanni Amigoni (c. 1584–1627): bass	Mantua	1619–20	Returned to Mantua; M. wrote role of Peneo in *Apollo* (Mantua 1620) for him.
Bartolomeo Barbarino (d. after 1640): tenor, theorbo	Fabriano (nr. Ancona)	Numerous ad hoc services	M. is godfather to his son Marin Guglielmo, 23 March 1615.
Bonivento Boniventi (c. 1590–1640): alto	Crema	1638–40	One aria in V1634. M.'s assistant prior to entering the *cappella*.
Francesco Cavalli (1602–76): singer (S, then T), organist, composer	Crema	1616–68	One aria in V1634. Edited M.'s posthumous *Messa . . . et salmi* 1650).
Carlo Farina (c. 1595–1639): violin	Mantua	—	Son of Luigi Farina (member of Mantuan string band). In Venice (S. Stefano), 1622–24. Testified to Massimiliano Monteverdi's legitimacy, 2 April 1622.
Benedetto Ferrari (c. 1603–1681): composer, theorbo	Reggio nell'Emilia	—	Wrote a laudatory sonnet prefacing the libretto of *Arianna* (1640).
Giovanni Giuliani *detto* Arzignan (b. 1573): alto	Arzignano (nr. Vicenza)	1600–1644	Testified to the Inquisition as to M.'s good character, 4 April 1631.
Antonio Grimani "il Turchetto" (c. 1598–1665): castrato	Prevesa (Greece)	1617–c. 1623, ad hoc in 1635	Sang under M. in Parma, 1628.
Francesco Man(n)elli (b. 1595–97; d. before 27 Sept. 1667): bass, composer	Tivoli/Rome	1638–44	M. baptized his son Giovanni Battista, 25 August 1639. M. was associated with him in operatic ventures in Venice.
Giovanni Battista Marinoni *detto* Giove (1596–1657): tenor, theorbo	Venice	1623–52	Owned a portrait of M.; arranged his memorial service. Edited *Fiori poetici* (1644) eulogizing M.; here he identifies himself as M.'s student.
Giacomo Rapallini: baritone/bass	Mantua	1622–47	M.'s "dearest friend" (letter to Striggio, 4 February 1628); had been his neighbor in Mantua. Testified to Francesco Monteverdi's legitimacy on 22 March 1624. Sang Ubaldo in *Armida abbandonata*.

Vincenzo Remedio: tenor; ?theorbo	Mantua	1619–?	Testified to Francesco Monteverdi's legitimacy, 22 March 1624.
Stefano Rivieri (c. 1567–1644): tenor	Ferrara	1598–1644	Testified to the Inquisition as to M.'s good character, 4 April 1631.
Giovanni Rovetta (c. 1596/99–1668): violin, bass	Venice/Veneto	1623–68	Praises M. in his *Salmi concertati a cinque et a sei voci* (1626); directed the music at his funeral; succeeded him as *maestro*.
Antonio Vicentini (b. c. 1584): tenor	Mantua	1620–29	Testified to Massimiliano Monteverdi's legitimacy, 2 April 1622.
Sigismondo Zanetti: singer, copyist			M. was godparent to his child in 1615.

Note: Others may include the following:

1 Additional composers contributing to V1634 employed in St. Mark's: Giovanni Pietro Berti (organist; 1624–39); Giovanni Felice Sances (tenor, ?theorbo; 1626–35); Gerardo Biancosi (tenor, theorbo; 1614–35).

2 "Venetian" editors of collections that include works by Monteverdi: Carlo Milanuzzi (organist at S. Stefano, 1623–29); Leonardo Simonetti (castrato at St. Mark's, 1612–31).

Save for his large-ensemble settings in the Seventh and Eighth Books, or the soprano-led ones in the Seventh, the only secular chamber works in Monteverdi's Venetian output that include vocal lines in the C1 clef (almost never G2) are the *Combattimento di Tancredi e Clorinda* (Clorinda); four of the solo-voice settings in the 1632 *Scherzi musicali*; the version of "Su, su, su, pastorelli" (SSA, bc) and the *Lamento della ninfa* in the Eighth Book; the dialogue-duet "Bel pastor dal cui bel guardo" (ST, bc) and the setting of "Come dolce oggi l'auretta" (SSS, bc) in the Ninth Book, the latter taken from his theatrical *Proserpina rapita* of 1630; and the solo-voice arias and cantatas in two anthologies, Carlo Milanuzzi's *Quarto scherzo delle ariose vaghezze* (1624), and the *Arie de diversi* (1634). However, those last settings are in C1 clef by default: it was the standard clef for such collections, regardless of the intended singer.[56] The same may be true of the pieces in the 1632 *Scherzi musicali*, which are all explicitly and firmly in the male poetic voice, as are the 1624 and 1634 arias.[57] It is also revealing that one of the latter, "Perché se m'odiavi," was modified for a TTB setting in the Ninth Book: it is impossible to tell which version came first. Likewise, the SSA setting of "Su, su, su, pastorelli" in the Eighth Book must have followed the TTB one in the Ninth, given that although the music is different, the text of the SSA version is corrupt, based on a careless misreading of the TTB parts.[58]

During his time in Venice, Monteverdi seems to have had little direct contact with female singers there save when he returned to the field of opera in the very late 1630s, probably with the encouragement of Benedetto Ferrari and Francesco Manelli (both in the Monteverdi circle). One exception was Adriana Basile's visit to Venice in 1623 in the entourage of the Duke and Duchess of Mantua: this may have been what prompted the printer Bartolomeo Magni to issue that year a badly put-together edition of the *Lamento d'Arianna* (the first of the solo-voice version) and the *lettera amorosa* and *partenza amorosa* from the Seventh Book.[59] Another is when Monteverdi went to Parma to compose music for the Farnese-Medici wedding festivities, when he wrote stage music for Settimia Caccini (a daughter of Giulio Caccini who had been in Mantuan service from 1613 to 1619). This is not to say that women did not sing in those musical events in Venice to which Monteverdi

---

[56] Bellerofonte Castaldi complained about this in the postface to his *Primo mazzetto di fiori* (Venice: Alessandro Vincenti, 1623), where he stated that anything amorous in the male poetic voice should be set in the tenor clef, because it was more appropriately masculine than having it sung by any male soprano (falsettist, he says, but presumably castratos would fall under the same objection).

[57] The only possible exception is "Ohimè, ch'io cado, ohimè" in Milanuzzi's 1624 volume, depending on how one reads the text.

[58] For the SSA setting in the Eighth Book, Monteverdi seems to have taken just the text of the bass part of the TTB setting, therefore omitting lines delivered only by the two tenors; see Carter, "Two Monteverdi Problems," 427–32. The versification of "Su, su, su, pastorelli" is often misconstrued in editions of Monteverdi's madrigals: it is made clear by the anonymous setting of the first two stanzas of the canzonetta in the anthology *Arie de diversi* (1634) edited by Alessandro Vincenti.

[59] It may also not be a coincidence that around the same time the *Lamento d'Arianna* was also included at the head of the anthology *Il maggio fiorito: arie, sonetti, e madrigali, à 1.2.3. de diversi autori*, edited by Giovanni Battista Rocchigiani (Orvieto: Michel'Angelo Fei & Rinaldo Ruuli, 1623); the collection was printed in partbooks, with none of its settings attributed to their composers. Neither edition is dated beyond its year, so absent further archival information, it is impossible to tell which came first.

was invited to contribute, but, rather, that he usually did not choose to compose directly for them—again, save in the late operas—or they did not need him to do so. To judge by the small-scale secular settings that survive from Monteverdi's Venetian period, however, he was moving predominantly in male musical circles.

In one of the letters (13 March 1620) he wrote to Alessandro Striggio to explain why he could not contemplate returning to Mantua as *maestro della musica*, he stated that one of the many advantages of Venice was that there was no gentleman there who did not honor him, and that the whole city came running whenever he was asked to make music outside of St. Mark's, whether for the chamber or the church. Strong evidence survives of two such occasions in terms of secular music, although there must have been more. In his letter to Striggio of 1 February 1620, Monteverdi reported on the progress of his work on a musical eclogue, *Apollo*, that was intended for performance in Mantua in the spring. He had already composed a part of it and may have been slightly embarrassed at having broken protocol:

> The *Lamento d'Apollo* has been heard by certain gentlemen here, and since it pleased them in the manner of its invention, poetry, and music, they think—after an hour of concerted music [*dopo un'ora di concerto*] which usually takes place these days at the house of a certain gentleman of the Bembo family, where the most important ladies and gentlemen come to listen—they think (as I say) of having afterwards this fine idea of Your Most Illustrious Lordship put on a small stage [*sopra una senetta*]. If I have to compose the ballet [*ballo*] for this, would Your Most Illustrious Lordship send me the verses as soon as possible? But if not, I shall add something of my own invention so that such a fine work of Your Most Illustrious Lordship can be enjoyed.

The patron here was Gian Matteo Bembo.[60] But these kinds of evening entertainments were presumably common enough in Venetian patrician households. On 16 April 1630, one of Monteverdi's Venetian patrons, Girolamo Mocenigo (1587–1658), celebrated the wedding of his daughter, Giustiniana, to Lorenzo Giustiniani (another Venetian family with which the composer associated) with the customary festivities in his residence (now the Hotel Danieli). Following a banquet and dancing that lasted until sunset ("le 24 ore"), the guests went up one floor into a room prepared for the performance of a dramatic work, *Proserpina rapita*, with music by Monteverdi to a libretto by Giulio Strozzi. That music is lost save for a small portion included as a canzonetta, "Come dolce oggi l'auretta," in

---

[60] Baroncini, "Monteverdi a Venezia," 155–63. Bembo's musical *ridotto* had already been noted by Angelo Grillo ("Monteverdi a Venezia," 157). However, I am suspicious of Baroncini's suggestion (159) that the text set by Monteverdi had some connection with the "Apollo, e Dafne fuggitiva, idilio bellissimo accomodato eccellentemente in stile recitativo" in the 1622 edition of Remigio Romano's *Terza raccolta di bellissime canzoni alla romanesca* (Vicenza/Venice: Angelo Salvadori), 26–29 (it is not present in the 1620 edition). This text begins with narration (Apollo loves Dafne), then Apollo's plea to Dafne (who is still alive), and a final brief narration describing her metamorphosis. Therefore, it does not include any "lament," strictly speaking.

the posthumous Ninth Book, although without knowledge of Strozzi's libretto, one would be hard-pressed to recognize its "theatrical" origins.[61]

As for that evening in Bembo's residence in 1620, the format of an hour's "concert," followed by something "dramatic," was matched by a similar event hosted by Girolamo Mocenigo in Carnival 1624. A *veglia* "in the presence of all the nobility" began with some "madrigali senza gesti" (i.e., not acted) when suddenly three figures appeared, Clorinda and Tancredi in armor, and Testo (the last, the "narrator") to perform the *Combattimento di Tancredi e Clorinda*.[62] It is a powerful scene. The Christian Tancredi loves the Saracen Clorinda, and she him; they meet by accident each in full armor (therefore the one not recognizing the other) and fight. As Tancredi stands victorious, he realizes whom he has mortally wounded. Clorinda, in turn, asks to be baptized and dies with her eyes on heaven. But the intent to surprise the audience with that opening is clear—Testo begins after just a single chord from the continuo—and it must have been a stunning moment, as would have been the entrance of the instruments shortly thereafter to pace the narrative action and provide imitative sonic effects of a trotting horse, the sounds of battle, and so on.[63] As Monteverdi said in his performance instructions in the Eighth Book, this was a distinct novelty for its time ("canto di genere non più visto né udito"). He also enjoyed showing off: "listen to the swords clashing together horribly," says Testo ("Odi le spade horribilmente urtarsi"; stanza 55), and we do in the strings, also admiring just how clever Monteverdi is at producing the effect.[64]

The *Combattimento* was later published toward the end of the "Canti guerrieri" that form the first half of the *Madrigali guerrieri, et amorosi* (1638). In that context, it is indeed preceded by settings "senza gesti," though not necessarily the ones that had been performed in Mocenigo's residence more than a decade earlier. Nor do we know what music by Monteverdi might have been done in Gian Matteo Bembo's *ridotto* in 1620, or what were the two "madrigals" that the composer sent to Prince Alfonso III d'Este in Modena in 1623–24 (plus two more madrigals and some three-voice canzonettas that Monteverdi promised him).[65] Save for the Seventh

---

[61] Carter, *Monteverdi's Musical Theatre*, 226–33. The piece required elaborate scenic effects (cloud machines, the appearance of Mount Etna, an Underworld scene, and three characters transformed into natural objects), making one wonder how it could have been done in a simple room.

[62] So Monteverdi described (and instructed) in the separate preface to the *Combattimento* in the Eighth Book. For the broader context, see Cascelli, "Place, Performance and Identity in Monteverdi's *Combattimento di Tancredi e Clorinda*." Clorinda was on foot and Tancredi on a "cavallo mariano," some kind of wooden horse as used in Venetian carnival processions; see Mantoan, "Prove generali di teatro musicale in laguna," 86–87. Tasso's text (*Gerusalemme liberata*, Canto 12, stanza 53) requires Tancredi to be riding something, given that he gets down from it to deal with Clorinda on equal terms.

[63] We might also wonder where the string instruments, at least, were positioned at this first performance, whether in sight of the audience or, perhaps more intriguingly, not. Ossi (*Divining the Oracle*, 241) says that in the *Combattimento*, "the instruments were supposed to be offstage," but I know of no direct evidence for that. In the preface to the *Combattimento* in the Eighth Book, Monteverdi says that Tancredi and Clorinda enter unexpectedly "from the part of the room in which music will be performed" ("dalla parte dela Camera in cui si farà la Musica"). Given the performance context (including the previous madrigals *senza gesto*), this presumably means that Tancredi and Clorinda move more toward the center of the room rather than entering from a different one.

[64] Carter, *Monteverdi's Musical Theatre*, 191–92.

[65] For Modena, see the documents in Fabbri, "Inediti Monteverdiani," 74–78, summarized in Fabbri, *Monteverdi*, trans. Carter, 187–88 (which identifies the recipient as Duke Cesare I d'Este, probably wrongly).

and Eighth Books of madrigals—each of which is a special case—Monteverdi did not publish much new secular music during his time in Venice: one short volume of *Scherzi musicali* (1632) and eight settings in anthologies. Nor was there a large amount surviving after his death. When the printer Alessandro Vincenti put together two posthumous volumes, there was enough sacred music to create a solid collection for Mass and Vespers (1650), with Francesco Cavalli supplying the Magnificat: only its final *Letanie della Beata Vergine* had previously been published (twice). This is not surprising, given the large number of works Monteverdi must have composed for St. Mark's—many are lost—that he also might not have wanted to make public so that they would remain exclusive to his own use.[66] In the case of the *Madrigali e canzonette a due e tre voci . . . Libro nono* (1651), however, Vincenti could find only ten new settings: of the remaining six, one ("Zefiro torna e di soavi accenti") came from the 1632 *Scherzi musicali*, for which Bartolomeo Magni's copyright privilege had expired, and five from collections that Vincenti had printed himself, including the TTB version of "Perché se m'odiavi" in his *Arie de diversi* (1634) and four duets from the Eighth Book. Save for the initial "Bel pastor dal cui bel guardo" (ST, bc), all of the new pieces are strophic canzonettas set for three voices and continuo, most for TTB.[67]

Of course, for any musical evenings in the residences of Gian Matteo Bembo, Girolamo Mocenigo, or other Venetian patricians, Monteverdi could also have drawn on musical material that was in his Seventh Book, or that was subsequently included in his Eighth. A few of the texts in the Seventh Book may have a Venetian flavor.[68] But the volume was strongly designed for Caterina de' Medici, Duchess of Mantua, and therefore largely for Mantuan singers, whether the women currently there (the Basile sisters and now Settimia Caccini) or the type of male or mixed ensembles with which Monteverdi had once been very familiar. It is hard to imagine the settings for soprano voice(s) of poems directly or implicitly in the female voice not being sung by female singers. "Io son pur vezzosetta pastorella" (SS) is an obvious case in point, but the same applies to other gender-neutral texts that seem to be giving voice to Caterina, such as the duets "O viva fiamma, o miei sospiri ardenti" and "Ohimè, dov'è 'l mio ben, dov'è 'l mio core?" as well as the solo-voice setting of "Con che soavità, labra odorate."[69]

Tomlinson (*Monteverdi and the End of the Renaissance*, 199–200) suggests that the madrigals may have been "Se vittorie sì belle" (Eighth Book), to a text by the Modenese poet Fulvio Testi, and what he views as its companion piece in the book, "Armato il cor d'adamantina fede" (perhaps also by Testi).

[66] Kurtzman, "Monteverdi's Missing Sacred Music." It is worth adding that almost all the sacred music that Monteverdi published in anthologies appeared in collections by editors not based in Venice: the exception is the *Ghirlanda sacra scielta da diversi eccellentissimi compositori de varii motetti à voce sola* (Venice: Bartolomeo Magni, 1625) collected by Leonardo Simonetti, a castrato at St. Mark's.

[67] In one of its poetic sources (Florence, Biblioteca Nazionale Centrale, Magl. VII.902, fols. 102r–103r), "Bel pastor dal cui bel guardo" is styled a "dialogue" between Aminta and Clori. It, too, is in the vein of a canzonetta (with refrain), although it is not entirely regular as such.

[68] Baroncini, "Monteverdi a Venezia," 159–61.

[69] Of the other SS duets, "Chioma d'oro" is neutral, although its subject implies a male speaker. "Non è di gentil core" and "O come sei gentile" are in the male poetic voice, although not so strongly that it might matter.

The Eighth Book is a very different case. Monteverdi had been sending music to Vienna since the early 1630s, if not before, prompted, first, by the fact that Emperor Ferdinand II had married Eleonora Gonzaga, the youngest daughter of Duke Vincenzo and Eleonora de' Medici, in 1622 (in 1621 by proxy in Mantua), and then as part of his strategy to secure payment of the pension that Vincenzo granted the composer in early 1609. Empress Eleonora did much to re-create her Mantuan cultural experiences in Vienna, building on them to develop a distinctive culture at the Habsburg court; she was also the dedicatee of Monteverdi's *Selva morale e spirituale* (1641).[70] Of the Eighth Book madrigals, "Or che 'l ciel e la terra e 'l vento tace" appears to have been known in Vienna by 1635, and likewise at least some of Monteverdi's music in the *concitato genere* and perhaps the *Lamento della ninfa*. That argument hinges on the presence of allusions to a number of the Eighth Book madrigals in Giovanni Giacomo Arrigoni's *Concerti di camera* (Venice: Bartolomeo Magni, 1635); Arrigoni was organist to the Viennese Hofmusikkapelle from 1632 to 1638, and he dedicated his volume to Ferdinand III as King of Hungary and of Bohemia.[71] Monteverdi also noted in the dedication of the Eighth Book to Emperor Ferdinand III that the emperor's father, Ferdinand II, had welcomed and honored "these my musical compositions" in manuscript, prompting the composer to give them to the press.[72]

Monteverdi originally intended to dedicate the Eighth Book to Ferdinand II: in his internal preface to the *Combattimento* (performed in 1624), he notes that it had been done in Mocenigo's residence twelve years before ("già dodici anni"), meaning that the package he sent to his printer (Alessandro Vincenti) contained a text written in 1636. However, Ferdinand II died in February 1637, forcing a quick change of plan. Given the intended dedicatee, Monteverdi chose, or adapted, texts that named the emperor or the Danube, as in the case of the two *balli*, "Volgendo il ciel per l'immortal sentiero" and the *Ballo delle ingrate* (the latter adapting the work staged in Mantua in 1608). In "Ogni amante è guerrier: nel suo gran regno," Rinuccini's paraphrase and long extension of Ovid's "Militat omni amans" (*Amores* I.9), all the references in the original text to Henri IV of France get changed to Emperor Ferdinand III (not II) as "o gran Ferdinando Ernesto."[73] In the opening setting of the

---

[70] Besutti, "'Cose all'italiana' e alla tedesca 'in materia di ricreatione'."

[71] Saunders, "New Light on the Genesis of Monteverdi's Eighth Book of Madrigals." That Monteverdi sent music to Vienna is clear. As for what this music was, Saunders notes that Arrigoni's setting of "Or che l'aria e la terra arde e fiammeggia"—Marino's sonnet echoing the first line (but not the rest) of Petrarch's "Or che 'l ciel"—has some resonances with Monteverdi's Petrarch setting. Saunders also identifies, somewhat less convincingly, the second section of "Ogni amante è guerrier: nel suo gran regno" (the bass solo, "Io, che nell'ozio nacqui e d'ozio vissi") as the source of Arrigoni's *concitato* gestures in his "Arpie del mar, che da l'estreme sponde" (another Marino sonnet). In his edition of Arrigoni's volume, Pyrros Bamichas notes the fact that Arrigoni's "Ferma il passo, o verginella" is a ground-bass setting with the same descending "lament" tetrachord as Monteverdi's *Lamento della ninfa*. There are some musical similarities between those two settings, although they may just reflect the harmonic constraints of the ostinato pattern. Arrigoni also included a *ciaccona* setting with the offset version of the bassline, but not quite the same one as in Monteverdi's "Zefiro torna e di soavi accenti" (in the 1632 *Scherzi musicali*).

[72] In presenting "queste mie compositioni Musicali" to the emperor, Monteverdi notes that "Ferdinando, il gran genitore della Maestà Vostra, degnandosi, per la sua innata bontà, di gradirle scritte, mi ha concesso quasi un autorevole passaporto per sfidarle alla stampa." Of course, this does not establish exactly which of the Eighth Book madrigals had been seen by Ferdinand II in manuscript.

[73] For example, in the *seconda parte*, "Io, che nell'ozio nacqui e d'ozio vissi," Rinuccini's "carco di spoglie, o glorioso Enrico" becomes "carco di spoglie, o gran Fernando Ernesto." This could conceivably have been a late

Eighth Book, "Altri canti d'Amor, tenero arciero," the sonnet also manages to sneak in another reference as well in its sestet, which requests that this "green, still new work" ("il verde ancor novo lavoro") should be welcomed by "gran Fernando."[74]

If, in turn, Monteverdi looked at Arrigoni's 1635 *Concerti di camera*, he would have seen the kind of collection suitable for the Habsburg court: a mixture of madrigals, sonnets, and canzonetta-style texts set for two to six voices and continuo (with one setting for solo tenor), some also with string parts, whether for just two violins or an entire string band. Arrigoni also included two instrumental sonatas. The Eighth Book fits that mold (save for the separate sonatas), although it is much more neatly organized, and it contains texts by a wider range of poets.[75] But Arrigoni's collection also gives some sense of the musical forces available in Vienna to perform whatever music Monteverdi sent there. Eleanora Gonzaga's presence as empress was crucial, not just because of her own cultural interests but also given that she offered sanctuary to a number of musicians previously attached to Mantua but who had left as a result of the crisis created by the death of Duke Vincenzo II Gonzaga and the War of Mantuan Succession (1628–31). At various times they included Margherita Basile (sister of Adriana), Francesco Dognazzi, Bernardo Pasquino Grassi (a tenor), and the string players Orazio and Giovanni Battista Rubini, plus the latter's wife, Lucia (another singer). In 1631, Margherita, Lucia, Dognazzi, and the Rubini brothers (plus an organist) formed the imperial "musica piccola da camera," and at least Lucia and the Rubinis continued in some similar capacity.[76] Arrigoni certainly wrote some fairly virtuosic music for whatever singers were available to him, including three spectacular bass voices, to judge by his setting for them of "Arpie del mar, che da l'estreme sponde."

Monteverdi may have wanted to teach Arrigoni's tenors a thing or two, however. Although some of the tenor writing in the *Concerti di camera* has flashes of virtuosic passagework, none of it suggests the flexibility and staying power demanded of the two tenor parts in, for example, Monteverdi's "Mentre vaga Angioletta." Guarini's poem was originally dedicated to Laura Peverara, one of the great singers in the Ferrarese *concerto delle dame*, but he later labeled it just "Gorga di cantatrice" (The female singer's throat).[77] It concerns how a male listener responds to such

---

revision to, say, "carco di spoglie, o gran Fernando Augusto" (so, Ferdinand II), which would fit the music. If it was not, then this has implications for dating the piece. Rinuccini's text was originally dedicated to Jacopo Corsi (who died in 1602) and probably comes from 1600, when Henri IV married Maria de' Medici. Most of the topical references to Henri could easily be adjusted, such as the encouragement for him to undertake a crusade to the Holy Land, which was a common thread in the 1600 wedding festivities; see Carter, "Epyllia and Epithalamia," 390. Fighting the Turks ("l'Oriente sonar belliche squille"—changed from "Galliche squille") may not have been at the top of Ferdinand III's list of priorities in 1638, but they were still a concern on his Eastern Front.

[74] Stevens, "*Madrigali guerrieri, et amorosi*," 174.
[75] Arrigoni's collection has seven settings of Marino, six of texts by Nicolò Crasso (a Venetian *letterato* who published under the pseudonym Publio Licinio; he was later associated with the Accademia degli Incogniti), three by Guarini, and single texts by Luigi Groto and Pietro Petracci, plus two unidentified poems.
[76] Seifert, "Rapporti musicali tra i Gonzaga e le corti asburgiche austriache," 225–26.
[77] Battista Guarini, *Rime* (Venice: G. B. Ciotti, 1598), fols. 130v–131r. The poem appears in anthologies from 1585 on (with some variants). In *Della nova scelta di rime di diversi eccellenti scrittori del'età nostra: parte prima*, ed. Benedetto Varoli (Casalmaggiore: Antonio Guerino & Co., 1590), 73–74, it is headed "Descrive il cantar della Signora Laura" and comes at the end of a series of poems about Laura Peverara.

vocal fireworks, his heart moving in sympathy to every twist and turn of the ornamentation. There had already been various five- and six-voice settings of the poem, plus one for solo voice (C1 clef) and continuo by Giovanni Girolamo (Johann Hieronymus) Kapsperger published in 1612.[78] But Monteverdi turns a single listener into two vying with each other to match the sounds coming from the singer's throat described in terms that seem technical from a vocal point of view but that are, in fact, drawn from Pliny's account of singing nightingales (see Chapter 6).

In his eulogy on Monteverdi's death, Matteo Caberloti adopted a similar vocabulary when he was describing the abilities of the composer's son Francesco, who

> consecrated to music, almost as a humanized bird—now breaking up the voice, sometimes taking it up again, now by stopping and twisting it, often by making it full or thin, now low, now delicate—forms a long chain of sweetest passages; with such artifice in sum does he sing, that with all other cares cast aside, men, drawn outside themselves, admire the harmonious arrangement of his song.[79]

Another tenor in St. Mark's (from 1622 to 1635), Giovanni Felice Sances, was similarly adept at this virtuosic manner of singing, and his own vocal writing bears comparison with Monteverdi's in their notation of ornamented passages; whether in "Mentre vaga Angioletta" or in the one place where ornamentation is allowed by the composer in the *Combattimento di Tancredi e Clorinda* (Ex. 4.3).[80]

In terms of any performance in Vienna of the Eighth Book settings, Monteverdi may have been relieved that Sances had moved there by December 1636, joining the other musicians there whom he knew from his Mantuan days. Even so, Monteverdi provided a number of pieces in the Eighth Book with unusually detailed verbal instructions on the manner of performing them.[81] They are often located in the logical place for them, the Basso Continuo partbook, which was intended for the director of the ensemble, although some of them (not always consistently) are in the vocal and string parts. Monteverdi must have been nervous forwarding musical materials to where he had no direct control over their use. On 28 July 1607, he sent

---

[78] Settings for six voices were published by Georg Flori (as Giorgio Florio; 1589) and Tiburtio Massaino (1604), and for five by Giovanni Battista Caletti (1604) and Francesco Turini (1629). For Turini's setting, see Ossi, "A Sample Problem in Seventeenth-Century Imitation."

[79] *Fiori poetici*, ed. Marinoni (1644), 8: "Lo lasciò costei arrichito di due figliuoli, l'uno de' quali chiamato Francesco, consacrato alla Musica quasi humanato Ussignolo hor troncando la voce, talvolta ripigliandola, hor col fermarla, e torcerla, ben spesso col farla piena, o scema, hor grave, hor sottile forma un'ampia catena de dolcissimi passaggi, con si fatto artificio in somma ei canta, che posta gl'huomeni [sic] in oblivione ogn'altra facenda, uscendo di se stessi ammirano l'armonioso articolar del di lui canto."

[80] The reading in Ex. 4.3(b) is taken from the score of the *Combattimento* in the Eighth Book's Tenore Primo partbook. The continuo score has a simplified version, which is yet another difference between the two (see Chapter 3).

[81] These include "Altri canti d'Amor, tenero arciero," the *Combattimento*, "Non avea Febo ancora," and the *balli* at the end of each section of the book. What is not clear is whether these instructions were included in manuscripts sent to Vienna, copies of which then provided the basis for what Monteverdi submitted to his printer, or whether Monteverdi wrote them specifically for the Eighth Book. The incorrect reference in the instructions to the *Combattimento* to its being done "twelve years before" (not fourteen) suggests that here, at least, the former may have been the case.

Ex. 4.3 (a) Monteverdi, "Mentre vaga Angioletta" (Eighth Book, 1638); (b) *Combattimento di Tancredi e Clorinda* (1624/Eighth Book, 1638), Testo, end of the "Notte, che nel profondo oscuro seno" stanza (ornamented version in the Tenore Primo partbook); (c) Giovanni Felice Sances, "Venite ad me omnes" (*Motetti a voce sola*, 1638).

to Genoa a sonnet setting commissioned by Duke Vincenzo Gonzaga, but he asked the court secretary, Annibale Chieppio, to make sure it was delivered to Bassano Casola (Monteverdi's vice-*maestro*) so that it could be rehearsed by the "gentlemen singers" because "it is very difficult for a singer to represent a melody [*rapresentare un'aria*] that he has not first practiced, and greatly damaging to that musical composition" which would not be "completely understood" on a first rendition. When Monteverdi auditioned for the position of *maestro di cappella* at St. Mark's, he was granted time for rehearsal with the *cappella*, and to good effect to judge by the outcome. Those instructions in the Eighth Book—sent far away without knowledge of who might take charge—reveal similar anxieties. It was the performance of his music, not its notation, that would secure Monteverdi's reputation among his peers and patrons.

5
Poetic Voices

Just as Monteverdi needed to engage with the musical voices within his ensembles, he also had to consider the poetic voice or voices present within the texts he set for them. The question is this: Who is actually "speaking" in these madrigals?[1] There are multiple possibilities: the poet, any character(s) established by or in the poem, the performers in the musical moment, and Monteverdi himself. It is an obvious problem in the five-voice polyphonic madrigal, in which five singers with different voice ranges present a text that is usually in a singular poetic voice (the "I") that might also, however, address a "you" by way of a vocative or similar rhetorical gesture. Moreover, that "I" is often gendered male by virtue of its use of pronouns and adjectival agreements: poems in the female voice are relatively rare in this period, although some female composers (e.g., Maddalena Casulana) tried to seek them out, or have them written specially. In terms of contemporary performing resources, male-gendered poems might still square with the voices delivering it if male castratos or falsettists took the upper parts. But the virtuoso female sopranos of the famous *concerto delle dame* of Ferrara appear to have had no problem with such poems, to judge by the contents of Luzzaschi's *Madrigali . . . per cantare et sonare a uno, e doi, e tre soprani* (1601), that reflect a late stage of their repertory.[2] Equally, however, it is clear that in cases in which a female voice came to the fore in a poem, it might or might not be reflected by some upper-voice grouping (regardless of the intended singers). Marenzio's well-known "Tirsi morir volea" (in his First Book *a5* of 1580), which represents Tirsi and an unnamed nymph speaking one to the other, is particularly ambivalent in this regard. There are some odd cases in Monteverdi as well, at least before the continuo madrigal enabled a more verisimilar approach to voicing.

Having five voices "speak" for one had long been typical of the repertory, and one might just have to accept it just as some form of group expression to itself, or to plural listeners (or on their behalf): the "I" becomes a "we" within a community that shared a common discourse on matters of love. But the emergence of individual voices within the group opens up a number of questions. An oft-cited early example is Jacques Arcadelt's "Il bianco e dolce cigno," first published in 1539 and a staple in the repertory.[3] Here the homophonic SAT opening describing how the swan sings at

---

[1] Calcagno (*From Madrigal to Opera*, 92–97) provides a pioneering overview, to which my present discussion of poetic voices owes a great deal.

[2] Five of its twelve settings are explicitly in a male poetic voice; the others are grammatically neutral.

[3] Monteverdi curated an edition of the collection containing "Il bianco e dolce cigno," Arcadelt's First Book *a4*, in 1627, printed in Rome by Paolo Masotti on the commission of the bookseller Giuseppe Cesareo

the moment of death postpones the entry of the bass voice to complete the analogy with the weeping lover ("et io piangendo ..").[4] This does not disrupt Arcadelt's orderly presentation of the text, phrase by phrase. However, superimposing phrases of the text in contrapuntal juxtaposition alters their sequence within the poem and potentially makes their delivery unclear. This might or might not serve a rhetorical point. In the case of simple "I" poems, for example, it can represent emotional disarray. But in the "I"/"you" poems more typical in the repertory, the lover's eager statements often collide musically, obscuring what the beloved is meant to hear. In Monteverdi's "Donna, s'io miro voi, ghiaccio divengo" (First Book), the three segments of that first line—"My lady," "if I gaze upon you," and "I turn to ice"—are superimposed almost to the extent that any freezing occurs at the vocative. The second line of the poem—"se di mirar m'astengo" (if I refrain from gazing)—gets completely hidden in a brief statement in S^2 and T, as if looking away were impossible for most of the ensemble. Another "Donna" text, "Donna, nel mio ritorno" (by Tasso) in the Second Book, begins with an orderly enough presentation of the text in SS, but A enters with the beginning of the second line ("il mio pensiero")—not the first—and by the time TB have entered, three separate segments of the first two lines are one on top of the other ("Donna, nel mio ritorno" / "il mio pensiero" / "a cui nulla pon freno"), suggesting that the lover's thought indeed cannot be restrained. Monteverdi then continues with overlapping lines and no clear cadences until the first strong syntactic break, which comes very late in the poem. These first seven lines take up a long sixty-five measures of music, at which point Monteverdi seems to breathe a sigh of relief on arriving at the much more focused last two lines of the text with its "whenceforth" point ("onde sol per virtù ..."), to which he devotes twenty-five measures in a far more straightforward way. However, he seems glad to get to the end, and he avoids the customary repeat of those final lines.[5]

Even granting the fact that the "old" rule that each voice within a madrigal should have a more or less complete version of the text was breaking down, Monteverdi's early settings adopt a fair degree of leeway in how the voices should enter, or where internal lines can be omitted in one voice so long as they are present in others. As a consequence, the complete text is presented only in performance by the full ensemble. Moreover, a surprising number of madrigals in the First Book have one or more voices begin with something other than the initial words of the text. This is not necessarily odd in cases in which, say, a three-voice (SSA) opening precedes the entry of the lower voices to fill out the texture for expressive or rhetorical

(attached to the Collegio Romano). The title page says that the volume is "di nuovo ristampato, e coretto in Venetia da Claudio Monteverde."

[4] Calcagno, *From Madrigal to Opera*, 109–15.

[5] Tomlinson (*Monteverdi and the End of the Renaissance*, 40) makes a similar point about Monteverdi's setting of "Baci soavi e cari" (First Book), with its "long-winded" text by Guarini leading the composer to make "nonsense" of it. However, Tomlinson is probably too optimistic in claiming that the more mature Monteverdi tended to avoid texts "like this one, texts whose rhetorical gestures did not inspire complementary musical structures."

reasons. In "Se nel partir da voi, vita mia, sento" (see Ex. 2.1), T enters at the second line of the poem ("così gran tormento") to allow fuller four-part harmony and dissonances for "such great torment," and B at line 3, typically to reinforce the exclamation "deh."

But Monteverdi becomes increasingly adept at these musical *contrapposti*; he makes great use of them at least through his Sixth Book, and more so than such contemporaries as Marenzio, Pallavicino, or Wert. In part, they serve a musical purpose. If in traditional Renaissance polyphony, each phrase of text is associated with a particular musical idea that gets developed contrapuntally (a so-called point of imitation), then the chief way to present contrasting musical ideas simultaneously is, precisely, by superimposing different elements of the text. Wert does this to some degree, particularly at his openings—his setting of "Ah, dolente partita!" in his Eleventh Book *a5* (1595) is an obvious case in point—although his approach is largely formalist in design.[6] Monteverdi, however, can also use the technique for rhetorical or expressive purposes.

Take, for example, those cases in which a voice enters preemptively with a later part of the text before its time. Sometimes this occurs because the opening line of a poem is impenetrable, prompting Monteverdi to move on as quickly as possible to something more interesting: "A che tormi il ben mio" in the First Book is a case in point, with the preemptive entry of A and T for "s'io dico di morire."[7] Elsewhere in this book, however, Monteverdi seems out to make a point. Alberto Parma's "Filli cara et amata" begins with a vocative (l. 1) and an imperative (l. 2) before reaching the question that matters:

> Filli cara et amata,
> dimmi per cortesia:
> Questa tua bella bocca non è mia?

[Filli dear and beloved, / tell me, pray: / Is this your fair mouth not mine?]

Instead, Monteverdi has T² enter preemptively—one might even say, rudely—with "non è mia" directly underneath the statement of what "mine" might be: the beloved's fair mouth (Ex. 5.1). Meanwhile, B waits patiently counting measures for his predictable entrance at the exclamation, "Ahi." But in "Ardo sì, ma non t'amo," the sounding bass (here in C4 clef) is given the chance to make a similarly abrupt entry, where he presents the angry vocatives of the second line of the poem directed to the treacherous beloved ("perfid'e dispietata") even before the first line has been fully stated. Monteverdi seems to have liked this trick: he does the same

---

[6] For Wert's *contrapposti*, see Coluzzi, *Guarini's "Il pastor fido" and the Madrigal*, 246–50.
[7] The verb "torere" is a relatively rare form of the verb "togliere": i.e., to take away. For the similar case of a preemptive initial entry in "Non m'è grave il morire" (Second Book), see Pirrotta, "Monteverdi's Poetic Choices," 279.

Ex. 5.1 "Filli cara et amata" (First Book, 1587; C1, C3, C4, C4; B is silent).

with the tenor in "Se pur non mi consenti." It might seem rhetorical, but it is also performative, as one singer within the ensemble is allowed to assert a presence in ways contrary to the traditional decorum expected of an ensemble in sociable conversation with itself.

Gendered voices

The text of "Filli cara et amata" is in the male voice: the speaker addresses Filli. The fact that it begins with the three upper voices (SAT[1]) is a consequence of Monteverdi's typical strategy of beginning with a canzonetta-like texture before bringing the lower voices into play. Likewise, it would probably be a mistake to view the preemptive entry in T[2], or of the bass in "Ardo sì, ma non t'amo," as any attempt to assert a male presence within the poem. One possible exception is the *seconda parte* of "Non si levava ancor l'alba novella" (Second Book), where the bass enters at the moment of direct speech ("Anima, a Dio"; with a striking harmonic shift up a third), perhaps to anchor a poem that is gender fluid. But more often, Monteverdi is just playing the voices against one another.

However, those madrigals in the Second Book that begin with lower-voice groupings start to suggest some gendering in terms of how the text is delivered. In "Dolcemente dormiva la mia Clori" (Tasso), the lover comes across his beloved asleep and eventually steals a kiss. Monteverdi arranges the high-clef voices (G2, G2, C2, C3, F3) in seemingly careful ways (Table 5.1). He uses ATB as the narrative voice for two key lines: the first ("Dolcemente dormiva . . .") and line 8 ("All'hor io mi chinai . . .")—those lines do not appear in the other voices. The first entry of the upper voices for lines 2–3 ("e intorn'a suo bel volto . . .") at the top of a four-voice grouping (SSAT) is probably what would conventionally be described as word-painting (higher voices for the little cupids fluttering around Clori's face). The bass voice returns to establish the first first-person verb in the text ("Miravo"). But by

Table 5.1 Predominant voice groupings in "Dolcemente dormiva la mia Clori" (Second Book, 1590).

Dolcemente dormiva la mia Clori,	ATB
e intorn'al suo bel volto	SSAT
givan scherzando i pargoletti amori.	
Miravo io, da me tolto,	B + SSAT
con gran diletto lei,	SSB/AT
quando dir mi sentei:	SSATB
«Stolto che fai?	SST
quando dir mi sentei:	*SSATB*
«Stolto che fai?	*SST*
Tempo perduto non s'acquista mai.»	SSAT, SSATB, SSAT
All hor io mi chinai, così pian piano,	ATB
e baciandole il viso,	SSATB (various groupings)
provai quanta dolcezz'ha il paradiso.	

[Sweetly did my Clori sleep, / and around her fair face / circled little cupids in play. / I gazed, drawn outside of myself, / on her with great delight, / when I heard myself say: "Fool, what are you doing? / Time lost can never be regained." / So I leaned over, softly, softly, / and in kissing her face / I felt all the sweetness of paradise.]

line 6 ("quando dir mi sentei"),[8] the full ensemble as a homophonic unit has become the narrator.

None of this is unusual for Monteverdi. But he does something surprising when he uses SS (supported by T) for the direct speech in the second half of line 6, at "Stolto, che fai?" (twice, given that the line is repeated). The grammar is clear: these are words that the lover says to himself (Clori remains asleep), so there is no reason to gender them female unless Monteverdi has decided to do something possible only in a musical setting: to have us hear the lover hearing Clori's voice in his head. For the subsequent aphorism that justifies the lover's behavior ("Tempo perduto . . .")—that time lost can never be regained—Monteverdi has three statements of the text in fuller textures, as if the lover were trying to convince himself of the argument, or as if the full SSATB statement were Monteverdi speaking as Monteverdi. But once ATB have resumed the narration after the direct speech ("All'hor io mi chinai"), Monteverdi must inevitably move to a full five-voice texture, which he turns to his advantage. The repeated "e baciandole il viso" across all the voices suggests that the lover has stolen more than just one kiss, and the richer contrapuntal texture allows for a gloriously expansive expression of the resulting sweetness of paradise.

Even if the voices are somehow partitioned within a setting for rhetorical or other reasons, a madrigal must end with all the voices save in the most exceptional circumstances. Any prior illusion of different voices "speaking" therefore cannot

---

[8] The literary sources have "sentì," here to be read as "sentii," which is the more normal first-person singular of "sentire" in the past tense. Monteverdi avoids the danger of reading "sentì" as past-tense third-person singular by way of a regionalism ("sentei"), but as Georis (*Claudio Monteverdi*, 392 n. 15) notes, it also creates an internal rhyme with the prior "lei."

be sustained, given that they end in harmonious agreement. Coupling that requirement with Monteverdi's increasing preference to separate different voice groupings raises some intriguing possibilities, however. The setting of Guarini's "Crudel, perché mi fuggi" in the Second Book is a case in point.[9] The poem consists of a question (ll. 1–2), a statement (3), a question (4–5), and a final aphorism (6–7):

> Crudel, perché mi fuggi,
> s'hai de la morte mia tanto desio?
> Tu sei pur il cor mio.
> Credi tu per fuggire,
> crudel, farmi morire?
> Ah, non si pò morir senza dolore,
> e doler non si pò chi non ha core.

[Cruel one, why do you flee from me, / if you have so great a desire for my death? / You are indeed my heart. / Do you believe that in fleeing, / cruel one, you will make me die? / Ah, one cannot die without grief, / and one who has no heart cannot grieve.]

The point of the poem is that if the beloved flees with the lover's heart, then the lover cannot die because he has no heart to feel the pain of death. However, for any composer the strong words ("Crudel," "fuggi," "morte," "dolore") are likely to have been more attractive than any such tortuous reasoning.

This is the setting in which Monteverdi sets himself up in competition with Pallavicino and also quotes Marenzio (see Ex. 2.4). But he does something quite different by way of what was fast becoming two characteristic features of his style: creating lower- and upper-voice groupings in juxtaposition; and having one or more voices enter preemptively to interrupt the poetic and musical flow. Either technique taken separately might or might not have interpretative consequences, but when they come together, matters become clearer. Monteverdi has the first two lines of "Crudel, perché mi fuggi" delivered by ATB, but even before they reach a cadence (on "desio"), S^2 jumps in with "Tu sei pur il cor mio," followed by S^1. This seems less like the lover's statement following his question than a preemptive counterpunch against its accusation, undermining the statement that follows in ATB. Monteverdi then switches the voices: SSA have the first two lines of the poem, and TB preempt the statement (with A following), leading to a full five-part cadence on "cor mio." SSATB present the start of the next question ("Credi tu per

---

[9] Guarini has "Lasso, perché mi fuggi," but ten of the thirty-two composers setting this text (including Marenzio and Pallavicino) preferred "Crudel ... ," probably because of the stronger vocative; see the list in Vassalli and Pompilio, "Indice delle rime di Battista Guarini poste in musica," 205. Guarini also has a semicolon at the end of line 3; composers vary on how to handle the transition to line 4, but Monteverdi makes a strong break. The FCM edition treats line 1 on its own as a question, but as Georis (*Claudio Monteverdi*, 394 n. 19) points out, this is obviously wrong.

fuggire") in homophony but then again break into SSA and ATB groups prior to a homophonic presentation (twice) of the beginning of the aphorism ("Ah, non si pò morire..."). Although the five-part texture continues to the end, the voices, while singing together, are clearly split into two groups: SS on the one hand, and ATB on the other.

For harmonic reasons, a five-voice madrigal usually requires at least three voices to be singing at any one time save at the opening. Thus, the alto voice will serve double function either as the lowest or the highest voice of any grouping (so, SSA or ATB).[10] But given the clear separation of the upper and lower groups in "Crudel, perché mi fuggi," plus the preemptive SS entry toward the beginning and then the repeat of the ATB opening by SSA, it is hard to resist the conclusion that Monteverdi has turned an accusatory monologue into a no-less accusatory dialogue between ATB and SS(A): that is, between the lover and the beloved. As the ATB group asks its initial question, the beloved (SS) interrupts with an affirmative statement ("You are indeed my heart"), but then turns the question back on the lover, who himself is forced into offering preemptive assurance. The one thing that they can agree upon, and perhaps Monteverdi as well, is the final aphorism introduced by the exclamatory "Ah": the connection between the heart, grief, and death.

This restructuring of a poetic monologue into a dialogue that begins with an argument but ends in agreement is possible because the text of "Crudel, perché mi fuggi" is gender-neutral. Both a lover and a beloved can be "crudel," a shortened form of "crudele" (which is bi-gendered in the singular), and there are no subsequent pronouns or adjectival agreements to indicate whether the speaker is male or female. The heading of the poem in the first editions of Guarini's *Rime*, "Fierezza vana," is also careful to sit on the fence, even if "Vain pride" (or ruthlessness) is typical of any beloved. It is a game that cannot be played—obviously—with "she" (or more rarely, "he") poems, but "I," "you," or "they" ones are open to it, depending on the verbal and grammatical choices within the text. It is also striking that Monteverdi starts to exhibit a clear preference for such gender-neutral poems: there are two in the First Book (where fourteen are in the male voice and three in the female one), six in each of the Second and Third Books, and no fewer than ten in the Fourth.[11] One suspects that Monteverdi started to like them more and more because of the interpretative potential seen in "Crudel, perché mi fuggi." Moreover, given that Monteverdi had moved into a performance world (in Mantua) where

---

[10] This is independent of whether Monteverdi's alto parts in C3 clef are meant to be taken by a natural alto (female or male) or a high tenor. Either way, the part can be cross-gendered, as it were, speaking both with the upper voices and with the lower ones.

[11] This is possible because terms of affection such as "anima mia" and "cor mio," etc., work either way. In some cases, a poem is gender-neutral by way of ambiguity: Tasso's "Dolcissimi legami" (Second Book) might be presumed to be in a male voice (so it was captioned in the 1619 edition of his *Rime*), but it is internally ambiguous (depending on who or what the "egli" is in line 4), not helped by conflicting readings in the literary sources. Guarini's "Stracciami pur il core" (Third Book) is in the male poetic voice according to its caption in one poetic source; see Georis, *Claudio Monteverdi*, 410. However, the poem has some odd ambiguities, and Monteverdi's setting plays it both ways. It is significant that for "Cor mio, mentre vi miro" (Fourth Book), Monteverdi is one of ten out of twenty composers who prefer "Cor mio..." to Guarini's "Donna, mentre vi miro"; for a list, see Vassalli and Pompilio, "Indice delle rime di Battista Guarini poste in musica," 198.

both male and female singers could work together (see Chapter 4), he was perhaps tempted by settings that could, in effect, play out a battle of the sexes.

The performance opportunities of Monteverdi's re-gendering, or cross-gendering, his poetic texts are clear enough. In "O come è gran martire" (Third Book), Monteverdi reveals his first encounter with a *concerto delle dame* on the Ferrarese model, and with the kind of music written for such an ensemble by Luca Marenzio, Luzzasco Luzzaschi, and others. He sets a gender-neutral poem to do so. However, the striking opening for high-clef SSA (with A somewhat unusually in the C1 clef), for twenty-one measures, reads it in the female voice, at which point the TB entry to create a full ensemble for the exclamation "O soave mio ardore" feels like the lover's attempt to reassure an anxious beloved.[12] Monteverdi then alternates and exchanges lines between different voice groupings so that all the voices can agree that their love will last until death. This imaginative treatment also has the advantage of distracting our attention from a text that, on its own, lapses into obscurity.

Two settings in the Fourth Book further reveal the dialogic possibilities, and one in a very surprising way. "Luci serene e chiare," by Ridolfo Arlotti, is a "you" poem consisting of three tercets parallel in terms of meter and rhyme. The first speaks to eyes that set fire to the heart, and the second, to words that strike the breast; the third draws a conclusion concerning this "miracle of love."

>   Luci serene e chiare,
> voi m'incendete, voi, ma prov'il core
> nell'incendio diletto, non dolore.
>   Dolci parole e care,
> voi mi ferite, voi, ma prova il petto
> non dolor ne la piaga, ma diletto.
>   O miracol d'amore:
> alma ch'è tutta foco e tutta sangue
> si strugg'e non si duol, muor'e non langue.

[Eyes serene and clear, / you set me alight, you do, but my heart feels / delight in the flames, not pain. // Sweet words and dear, / you strike me, you do, but my breast feels / no pain in the wound, but delight. // Oh miracle of love: / the soul that is all of fire and all of blood / consumes itself but does not suffer, dies but does not languish.]

Carlo Gesualdo had already set this text at the head of his Fourth Book *a5* (1596), taking a surprisingly (for him) formalist approach to it. He delivers the second tercet to a repeat of the music of the first with a varied ending. He provides new

---

[12] Guarini has "O mio soave ardore, / o mio dolce desio." The "giusto desio" may have come from Flaminio Tresti's setting in his Second Book *a5* (1597), although Tresti has "o mio giusto desio." Monteverdi shifted the "mio" in both lines: they are easier to set that way, and also, arguably, more effective in rhetorical terms.

music for the third tercet that is then repeated save for an extension to the final cadence. Monteverdi adopts this *AA'BB'* structure as well, but with two important differences. First, his *A* section starts with a major triad on D and cadences on C, while *A'* is transposed up a tone (a major triad on E; cadence on D): the music is otherwise the same, with a fairly homophonic presentation of the text. Second, while *B'* follows the music of *B* (with a more expansive ending), Monteverdi significantly reworks his contrapuntal treatment of the last three line of the poem by way of inversion, also to produce a greater emphasis on SSA and ATB voice groupings.[13]

Monteverdi's setting of "Luci serene e chiare" might seem conventional, even down to the "eye music" gesture of the opening, with "luci" given two whole notes (semibreves) that on the page look like eyes. This therefore must be changed for the repetition at *A'*, beginning with "Dolci," which Monteverdi does quite neatly. His handling of the poem's sectional divisions, however, makes it far more interesting by once again turning a monologue into a dialogue. Although the text is gender-neutral in terms of the speaking voice, one might imagine that it is a lover's job to praise the eyes of his beloved (*A*), while her response, in different register (a tone higher), is to acknowledge gratefully the power of such sweet words (*A'*). Then the lover (ATB) and the beloved (SSA) can each agree separately and together, at great length (*BB'*), on the "miracle of love" revealed by this amorous exchange.

The first madrigal in the Fourth Book, "Ah, dolente partita!", is more surprising still, given its context. This was Monteverdi's first setting of a text taken directly from Guarini's pastoral play *Il pastor fido*, which was all the rage in the 1590s (and it was staged in Mantua in November 1598).[14] The madrigal was certainly composed before 1597 (when it was included in Kauffmann's anthology), and as noted earlier, it may have been planned for the Third Book but dropped for reasons of space. If so, it would have been the first published setting of the text, which otherwise was Girolamo Belli's in his Third Book *a6* of 1593. However, by the mid-1590s, the versions to which Monteverdi's treatment would have been compared were Marenzio's and Wert's five-voice ones published in 1594 and 1595 respectively.[15]

The context of this text in the play is clear. Mirtillo loves Amarilli, and she him, although she cannot reveal it by force of prophesy: thus, Mirtillo spends much of the play lamenting his sorry state. At the end of Act III, scene 3, Amarilli orders him to leave her sight, prompting his emotional response (during which she is present).

---

[13] Bianconi discusses Gesualdo's and Monteverdi's settings in his "Struttura poetica e struttura musicale nei madrigali di Monteverdi." Tomlinson (*Monteverdi and the End of the Renaissance*, 102–4) views Monteverdi's upward transposition of the *A'* section as raising "the emotional intensity" of the setting. Chafe (*Monteverdi's Tonal Language*, 34) treats the transposition as a purely musical issue with no regard for the text: it establishes "two keys" ("C major" and "D minor") that "can perhaps be considered to represent the establishing of the natural hexachord and the primary mode, respectively." His mixing of terms (key, hexachord, mode) is anachronistic and not very helpful.

[14] "O primavera gioventù de l'anno" in the Third Book probably set a text that Guarini later expanded for the play. For this and other examples, see Chater, "Un pasticcio di madrigaletti?"

[15] The comparison is certainly the strategy adopted by modern scholars, following Petrobelli, "Ah, dolente partita."

Mirtillo laments the sad parting and the end of his life (Ah, dolente partita! / Ah, fin de la mia vita!"). He then asks a question: "Da te part'e non moro?" (Do I leave you and not die?), even though he feels the pain of death ("E pur i' provo / la pena della morte").[16] His living death gives life to grief, with the result that the heart dies immortally ("per far che moia immortalment'il core").

It has proven almost impossible not to read Marenzio's, Wert's, and Monteverdi's settings of this text as some kind of five-voice staging of the singular Mirtillo's speech.[17] Marenzio (SATTB; in the A-aeolian mode) and Wert (SSATB; G-dorian) use *chiavi naturali*, and the fact that Wert begins with an SSA group—and a nice contrapuntal superimposition of the first two lines of the text taking advantage of the "partita"/"vita" rhyme—is not thought to weaken the "Mirtillo" reading, given the conventions of the polyphonic madrigal. Monteverdi shares a mode with Marenzio after a fashion, but his use of high *chiavette* gives pause for thought, and still more does his opening gesture:[18] SS begin on their own, starting on a unison e'' and then moving a semitone apart to create a spectacular chain of intense dissonances.[19] The alto enters at "ah fin de la mia vita," and then TB with "Da te part'e non moro?" while SS are still stretching out the "end of my life." The alto joins TB with "Da te part'e non moro?" focusing on the pain of death, as SS return to their opening ("Ah, dolente partita!"). Further contrapuntal development leads to an ingenious superimposition of multiple phrases of the poem heard so far. Its first four lines (to "la pena della morte") take up a quite astonishing fifty-six measures of the piece; Marenzio delivered that same text in twenty-seven measures, and Wert in forty-four.

Wholly unprecedented in all the many settings of "Ah, dolente partita!", however, is Monteverdi's decision to have Mirtillo's question—"Da te part'e non moro?"—just in ATB repeatedly, and absent from the two sopranos (with one exception in S^1 that eventually got changed).[20] If all five voices are meant to be speaking as, or for, Mirtillo, S^2 completely, and S^1 in part, lose out on any chance to express a key phrase of the text. At that point, it is worth taking Monteverdi's SS opening as a cue

---

[16] The line in the play is "Da te parto, e non moro? pur i' provo," but both Monteverdi and Wert have "E pur" (And yet).

[17] Compare McClary, *Modal Subjectivities*, 3, which reads "Ah, dolente partita!" as a "sound-image of subjective interiority on the verge of psychological meltdown." Tomlinson (*Monteverdi and the End of the Renaissance*, 100–101) tends to divorce "Ah, dolente partita!" from *Il pastor fido*—it is "in a lyrical style without dramatic connotations"—and suggests that the "dolente partita" might be the death of Giaches de Wert on 6 May 1596.

[18] The 1603 edition uses G2, G2, C2, C3, F3 clefs. Kauffmann's 1597 edition has the lowest part in C4. It follows that my reference to SSATB scoring here is somewhat misleading, given that A and T are "high" voices.

[19] Monteverdi must have known how spectacular this was: he used it again in "A un giro sol de' belli occhi lucenti" later in the Fourth Book as the lover claims that his death began at the birth of his cruel and wicked beloved ("Certo quando nasceste / così crudel e ria").

[20] I am grateful to Seth Coluzzi for confirming this unique handling of the text. It may not be an accident that the version of "Ah, dolente partita!" published by Paul Kauffmann in 1597 had "Da te part'e non moro?" just in TB near the beginning (the alto uses its music to repeat "Ah, dolente partita!"). The exception is the presence of "Da te part'e non moro?" in S^1 in mm. 32–36 (in the 1597, 1603, 1605, and 1607 editions), although this gets changed to a repeat of "Ah fin de la mia vita" in Amadino's 1611 and 1615 editions (as followed by Malipiero). The earlier reading is obviously correct, but it is odd that it should have been altered.

for a different reading of this madrigal. He has done what we have now seen him do elsewhere. "Ah, dolente partita!" is a wholly gender-neutral text—if we forget that Mirtillo is speaking—and therefore Monteverdi constructs a dialogue between the beloved (SS) and the lover (ATB). It becomes a typically erotic case of sexual parting, but of course, only the lover can physically "leave" the beloved in that circumstance, even if the beloved can regret that parting. Yet both partners can also stretch out that "end of life" moment, and can equally enjoy, at great length, the "pain of death."

This teasing with voices can be very witty, often to the extent of belying the apparent seriousness of much of this madrigal poetry. Lovers suffer endless torments, summon death (metaphorical or real), and cry out for mercy. In "Mentr'io mirava fiso" (Second Book), the lover is moved by the beauty of the beloved's eyes to shout "Pity, pity!" albeit in sweet, amorous lays ("con dolci ed amorosi lai"), a typical musical reference to which Monteverdi devotes considerable attention. But his turning poetic monologues into musical dialogues is much less common as lovers argue ("Crudel, perché mi fuggi"), cuddle up together ("Luci serene e chiare"), or consider the post-coital consequences ("Ah, dolente partita!"). Elsewhere in the Fourth Book, the lover and the beloved can equally share sighs ("Oimè, se tanto amate"), look forward to sex ("Sì, ch'io vorei morire"), or once more engage with its bittersweet aftermath ("Voi pur da me partite, anima dura"), often in rather knowing, humorous, or even dangerous ways.[21] Add to that the fact that the Fourth Book also contains settings of at least two poems explicitly in the female voice—and only six explicitly in the male one—and it seems clear that Monteverdi is becoming interested not just in reinventing single-voice poetic texts for a five-voice context, but also in freeing up his singers variously to emerge from what the genre would require to be a singular ensemble.[22] Five voices need not speak as, for, or to one, but instead they engage in dynamic conversations that can sometimes split down gender lines and sometimes not. While concluding in harmonious agreement might remain the norm, how the voices reach it varies quite widely.

---

[21] There is no secure attribution of "Sì, ch'io vorei morire" to Mauritio Moro, although it fits into a sequence of poems with the same opening (and closing) by him; see Tomlinson, *Monteverdi and the End of the Renaissance*, 110 n. 20 (which nevertheless raises doubts about the poem itself, for no good reason). Moro's poetry, including the other "Sì, ch'io vorei morire" texts, was placed on the Index in December 1602; see Bertolini, "Censurare la musica," 246. Monteverdi was to some degree playing with fire by setting such explicit verse, at least so far as the ecclesiastical authorities were concerned. Significantly, the copies of the Tenore and Quinto partbooks of the Fourth Book surviving in the Archivio del Duomo, Florence, have paste-overs covering indecorous words throughout the book (as noted in the preface to the FCM edition).

[22] The two texts in the female voice are "Anima mia, perdona" (part of Amarilli's response to Mirtillo's "Ah, dolente partita!" in *Il pastor fido*, III.4), and "Anima del cor mio." "Cor mio, non mori? E mori!" also comes close to being explicitly female in voice, although matters become confused toward its end in terms of who is speaking to whom (or to what).

He said/she said

Any dialogic freeing of the voices falls under narrower constraints in the case of madrigals that have internal passages of direct speech, whether delivered by a single speaker or, in the case of proper dialogues, two. Such direct speech is usually cued by some version of the verb "dire" (to say): someone speaks in the present tense ("dice"), the imperfect ("diceva"/"dicea"), the past ("disse"), or sometimes—to create narrative ambiguity—in more than one of them. The poetic voice can certainly speak to itself, as in "Dolcemente dormiva la mia Clori" in the Second Book. But if it quotes the speech of a second and/or third party, it takes on the role of a narrator, setting up a scene, reporting anything said by one or more participants in it, and (usually) passing some remark on the consequences. The technique was relatively new to lyric poetry (which had tended to prefer a single poetic voice), but was familiar within epic, which frequently mixes the diegetic voice (the poet as narrator) and one or more mimetic ones (the narrator puts words in the mouth of another character). It is important to note that such mimesis within diegesis is not in any way "dramatic": the poetic voice remains the ventriloquist-in-charge who (re)enacts the action. But it can certainly create vividness (what in rhetoric would be called *enargeia*), bringing something to life in the mind's eye, or in music's case, ear.

In such cases, the moment of switching from narration to direct speech needs to be marked in some kind of way. In "Dolcemente dormiva la mia Clori," Monteverdi does it, at least initially, by setting the speaker's "Stolto, che fai?" for a reduced scoring (SST). Another means at his disposal is to change texture from homophony (diegesis) to imitative counterpoint (mimesis) or vice versa. The setting of Ottavio Rinuccini's "Sfogava con le stelle" in the Fourth Book is a straightforward example:

> Sfogava con le stelle
> un infermo d'amore
> sotto notturno ciel il suo dolore.
> E dicea fisso in loro:
> «O imagini belle
> de l'idol mio ch'adoro
> . . .

[To the stars poured forth / one sick with love / his grief under the night sky, / and he said, his gaze fixed upon them: / "O beautiful images / of the idol whom I adore . . ."]

Monteverdi begins with a homophonic presentation of the text in all five voices, at times leaving the declamation entirely up the performers in an attention-grabbing gesture: he provides just a single chord for the first five syllables of the text, a technique drawing on the *falsobordone* used for choral recitation of the psalms within the church. He does so elsewhere in the setting as well.[23] But even before the voices finish their opening narration (at "loro"), the bass enters preemptively with the vocative "O" of the direct speech, then followed by the other voices in a wonderful contrapuntal expansion of that single vowel (a good one for singers), extending to the top and almost to the bottom of the ensemble's vocal range.

By any conventional notion of verisimilitude, Monteverdi's choice of homophony for the diegesis and counterpoint for the mimesis might seem counterintuitive. If five voices have to represent a single speaker who suddenly appears within the poem, homophony might seem the more plausible choice for the speaking moment, leaving counterpoint to set the scene.[24] This is certainly Monteverdi's preference in his First and Second Books. In "Fumia la pastorella" (First Book), a three-stanza canzone by Antonio Allegretti, the first and third stanzas are narration, while second contains Filli's direct speech as she asks the sun in this season of spring to change the wearisomeness of winter into happiness and joy. Monteverdi's setting of the outer stanzas is largely contrapuntal, while the central one begins with a solid homophonic vocative ("Almo, divino raggio . . .") and ends with a no less homophonic triple time ("cangia in letizia e in gioia").[25] This is conventional enough, down to the triple time to mark the idea of "change." In "Sovra tenere erbette e bianchi fiori" (Third Book), however, Monteverdi explores the alternative approach, with near-homophony for the diegesis, and polyphony to intensify the mimesis as both Tirsi (the "I" of the poem) and Filli speak, in Tirsi's case by way of a preemptive entry in S^1 and then S^2 ("Cara Filli . . .") overlapping with the "dissi" (I said) that supposedly should preface the shift. This works particularly well for Filli's final instruction to Tirsi that he should kiss her—repeatedly, according to the musical setting—which Monteverdi handles very wittily indeed. The point of the same technique in "Sfogava con le stelle," however, is that counterpoint can also be a richer resource for emotional expression: the contrasts are quite compelling, as if the lover's grief cannot be contained within simple chordal walls. Monteverdi does represent the lover trying to rein himself in at times, returning to homophony when issuing his various instructions to the stars: just as they reflect his beloved's beauty, so should they show to her his burning passion, and so (*falsobordone*) might they make her pity him just as they make him love her. But in each case, counterpoint intervenes to give added weight to his requests.

In "Sfogava con le stelle," Monteverdi does not need to worry about the other end of the process—returning from mimesis to diegesis—given that the lover's speech continues to the end of the text: this is also why he can use so many different musical devices within the speech itself, given that any narrator has disappeared from view.

---

[23] There is also a brief such passage in "Che dar più vi poss'io" (Fifth Book). For the dubious question mark in the incipit of that madrigal, see Georis, *Claudio Monteverdi*, 478.

[24] Compare the discussion of Wert's Tasso settings in O'Rourke, "Representation, Emotion, and the Madrigal in Sixteenth-Century Italy," 171–224, where a contrapuntal proem disposes the listener to pay attention to the subsequent declamation.

[25] Allegretti's poem appears to have been written in honor of a Neapolitan singer, Madama Eufemia; Pirrotta, "Monteverdi's Poetic Choices," 274.

Texts with a three-part structure of diegesis–mimesis–diegesis, or a more complex sequence of such units, pose other challenges. In the setting of Guarini's "Io mi son giovinetta" (also in the Fourth Book), the lover is the narrator. The text begins with his sweet shepherdess singing a version of the first two lines of Boccaccio's old *ballata* (SSA).[26] Thus, the lover says (SSAT), did she sing, when suddenly (SSATB) his heart began to sing like a bird, with music similar to the opening: (ATB) "Son giovinetto anch'io . . ." (I, too, am young . . .). But this pleasant scene then takes a turn for the worse. The lover praises the spring flowering in his beloved's eyes, but she reacts in an unexpected way:

> Et ella:
> «Fuggi, se saggio sei», disse, «l'ardore;
> fuggi, ch'in questi rai
> primavera per te non sarà mai».

[And she: / "Flee, if you are wise," she said, "the fire; / flee, for in these eyes / spring will never be there for you."]

Monteverdi's use of an SSA grouping for the beloved, and ATB for the lover, is sensible enough. But those last lines of "Io mi son giovinetta" pose a problem in terms of how to voice the diegetic "Et ella" and "disse." The text immediately preceding "Et ella" is the end of the lover's direct speech (ATB), and Monteverdi does not seem to want to take the time to reintroduce the scoring previously used for the diegetic voice (SSATB), given that the beloved's unexpected statement needs to come in, well, unexpectedly. Likewise, a single "disse" is too short to warrant a change of texture. In the absence of any better option, Monteverdi gives "Et ella" and "disse" to SSA, meaning that their presentation gets folded into the beloved's direct speech ("Fuggi, se saggio sei . . ."). This is not the only time that he gets wrong-footed by an interjected "disse." But in order to end the setting with a full five-voice texture, Monteverdi is forced to have both the beloved and the lover repeat her dismissive final remark, although in terms of the texture, he maintains a fairly clear distinction between SS (now without the "disse") and ATB (with it), also giving SS the most active music with rising scales in close canon, and leaving ATB to restate it in stolid resignation (Ex. 5.2).[27]

The fact that "Io mi son giovinetta" is in the past tense ("disse") means that even the mimetic passages (the beloved and the lover's direct speeches) are in the narrative voice of the lover telling the story. This lessens the problem of any "disse" in the seemingly wrong voice(s). It is also what enables the lover to repeat the final warning

---

[26] Boccaccio's text (at the end of *Decameron*, 9) is "Io mi son giovinetta, e volentieri / m'allegro e canto en la stagion novella."

[27] These canonic scales appear elsewhere in Monteverdi's madrigals without any obvious textual association, as in the following madrigal in the Fourth Book, "Quell'augellin che canta." They have some echoes of improvised *contrappunto alla mente*.

Ex. 5.2 "Io mi son giovinetta" (Fourth Book, 1603).

of his sweet shepherdess: he quotes what she said and then says it again as if trying to absorb its content. Such narrative distance works in favor of the polyphonic madrigal precisely because it loosens the requirement for mimesis to be verisimilar. In "Io mi son giovinetta," Monteverdi can choose to distinguish the beloved's speech from the lover's by way of high- and low-voice groupings (SSA versus ATB), but he has other options, and either way, those groupings remain framed within a narration delivered by the full ensemble, with individual voices emerging and then retreating. That ensemble still speaks as a whole for the poetic "I," however much it might address a "you" or describe a "she," and regardless of whether others are allowed to speak. But Monteverdi seems to have taken some delight in these kinds of texts that can introduce an ambiguity of voice, and in turn, allow performers to play with it.

The same is true of what one might call "they" poems: that is, those with an unidentified third-party narrator observing a scene but not directly involved in it. In "Non si levava ancor l'alba novella" (Second Book), the *prima parte* is a long narrative introduction establishing the typical scene at dawn when lovers must part after a night of passion. The *seconda parte* describes how the lover and the beloved spoke (past tense) their farewells, quoting their speech prior to a comment in the final line: "Dolce languir, dolce partita e fella" (Sweet languishing, parting sweet and cruel).[28] This line lacks a verb and therefore stands outside of time: although it is ostensibly in the narrative voice, it could just as well be a separate, external one, whether Tasso as Tasso (rather than as narrator) or the reader/listener commenting on the scene. Monteverdi responds by setting it in rich, five-part homophony (with nice suspensions), a texture noticeably lacking elsewhere in the setting.

In "Non si levava ancor," Monteverdi does not make any clear and consistent distinction between the three separate voices in the poem—the narrator, the lover, and

---

[28] For the mistake in the FCM edition ("... e bella"), see Georis, *Claudio Monteverdi*, 378 n. 1.

the beloved—although by the end of the *seconda parte*, the full ensemble seems to be speaking for itself (or for the composer). It may not matter: Tasso treats the two lovers ("i duo vaghi e leggiadretti amanti," gendered masculine) as interchangeable, for each is a "soul in love" ("alma innamorata," gendered feminine) and therefore attached to feminine pronouns ("l'una ... l'altra"). Something similar occurs in the setting of Guarini's "Era l'anima mia" in the Fifth Book, where one "anima" seeks to join another "anima" in pleasurable death. Monteverdi's ATB opening here might suggest that he views the poetic voice (the soul initially close to its final hours) as male, but the situation soon becomes vocally confused as two souls are locked in passionate embrace.

However, two texts in the Third Book create different problems because two lovers are each given a name and therefore separate identities, whether Filli and Tirsi in "Sovra tenere erbette e bianchi fiori" (the poet has not been identified), or Fillida and Tirsi in Angelo Grillo's sonnet "«Rimanti in pace» a la dolente e bella."[29] This final setting in the Third Book is obviously meant to be a display of particular compositional ingenuity—and it is, harmonically speaking—but Monteverdi had to wrestle with the poem. The first quatrain might seem clear enough:

> «Rimanti in pace» a la dolente e bella
> Fillida, Tirsi sospirando disse.
> «Rimanti, io me ne vò, tal mi prescrisse
> legge, empio fato, aspra sorte e rubella.»

["Stay in peace," to sad, fair / Fillida said Tirsi, sighing. / "Stay, I am leaving, so has it been ordained by / law, wicked fate, harsh and inimical lot."]

But the past-tense "disse" gave Monteverdi two choices: to treat Tirsi's initial "Stay in peace" as direct (mimetic) or indirect (diegetic).[30] He hints at the former by beginning with the alto on its own, but it quickly becomes the latter, as the rest of the ensemble enters in low-voice homophony before splitting into upper (SS) and lower (ATB) groups to continue the narration ("a la dolente e bella / Fillida"), then with the typical rests to represent sighing ("sospiran-do"). As Tirsi restates his instruction for Fillida to "stay" (low-voice homophony again), the diegetic voice seems to continue. However, S² enters preemptively with an impulsive "I" ("io me ne vò") as if Tirsi suddenly wants to speak for himself in what becomes an SSA combination prior to the text being developed in all five voices.

The use of SSA as a mimetic voice becomes clear in the sonnet's sestet (Monteverdi's *seconda parte*):

---

[29] This is another of the texts that Monteverdi probably took from Licino's *Rime di diversi celebri poeti dell'età nostra* (1587), where it is attributed (133) to Livio Celiano, the name under which Grillo, a Benedictine monk, published most of his secular poetry.
[30] Giles, *Monteverdi and the Marvellous*, 255.

> Ond'ei, di morte la sua faccia impressa,
> disse: «Ahi, come n'andrò senza il mio sole,
> di martir in martir, di doglie in doglie?»
> Ed ella, da singhiozzi e pianti oppressa,
> fievolmente formò queste parole:
> «Deh, cara anima mia, chi mi ti toglie?»[31]
>
> [Whereupon he, his face marked by death, / said: "Ah, how will I go without my sun, / from torment to torment, from grief to grief?" // And she, oppressed by sighs and tears, / faintly formed these words: / "Ah, my dear soul, who takes you from me?"]

Monteverdi returns to the low five-voice scoring of his opening for the narration ("Ond'ei . . ."), although the more strongly positioned "disse" enables him to move more directly to Tirsi's "speaking" voice (SSA, again moving to the full ensemble). He can do the same as Fillida responds "faintly" ("Deh, cara anima mia . . ."), introduced preemptively by A, then followed by SS.

Both Tirsi and Fillida are voiced by similar upper-voice groupings: there is no attempt to distinguish them by tessitura.[32] But as usual, Monteverdi needs to find a way to end the setting with the full ensemble. The lower voices repeat the same music as at the initial presentation of the final tercet ("Ed ella . . . parole"), but now Fillida's speech ("Deh, cara anima mia . . .") gets taken up by all five singers one after the other (A, S^1, B, S^2, T, S^1, A), still "faint" but now not in a single mimetic voice. The motive to which the phrase is set—a falling minor sixth, then rising by step—is a typical Monteverdian gesture for an emotional exclamation, as at the beginning of "O come è gran martire" (Third Book), with numerous examples following. But words assigned to one character are now delivered by two as Fillida and Tirsi utter the same words of regret—one "anima" to another—prior to their each asking the same final question ("who takes me from you?") in voice groupings (SS and ATB) now properly gendered.

In principle, the emergence of the continuo madrigal (from the last six madrigals of the Fifth Book on) lessened some of the problems of setting poetic dialogues to music by virtue of the fact that the instrumental accompaniment (via the basso continuo) permitted a single voice to sing on its own. In the setting of Giambattista Marino's four-stanza canzone, "Presso un fiume tranquillo," at the end of the Sixth Book, Monteverdi strictly divides his seven-part ensemble so as to distinguish the narrative voice ($S^2S^3AT^2B$) from the characters, Filena (S^1) and Eurillo (T^1), who each have direct speech for the last four lines of the first three stanzas (Eurillo in stanzas 1 and 3, and Filena in stanza 2).

---

[31] For the variant "chi mi vi toglie," see Georis, *Claudio Monteverdi*, 426.
[32] Something similar is true for Filli and Tirsi in "Sovra tenere erbette e bianchi fiori."

POETIC VOICES 97

The last stanza created a double problem, however. In Marino's *Rime* (1602), the poem continues the prior pattern and ends with Filena speaking:

> «Sì, sì», con voglie accese
> la ninfa allor riprese:
> «Facciam, concordi amanti,
> pari le gioie ai pianti,
> a le guerre le paci:
> se fur mille i martir, sien mille i baci.»

["Yes, yes," with inflamed desire / the nymph then resumed: / "Let us, as lovers in agreement, / make our joys equal to our laments, / to our wars, our peace: / if our torments were a thousand, so let a thousand be our kisses."]

But Monteverdi adopted a different reading for the first two lines of the stanza:

> «Sì, sì», con voglie accese
> l'un'e l'altro riprese:

["Yes, yes," with inflamed desire / the one and the other resumed:]

It is not clear whether this was Monteverdi's invention: his friend and former colleague in Mantua, Francesco Dognazzi, had the same "l'un'e l'altro" reading in his setting of the text in his *Il primo libro de varii concenti* (1614), published in the same year as Monteverdi's Sixth Book.[33] Dognazzi writes a duet for soprano and tenor in modified strophic form and in a rather relaxed triple time, also with a three-part instrumental sinfonia that returns as a ritornello. Each voice is a character, and both together, the narrator: thus, his variant allows Filena and Eurillo to sing the initial "Sì, sì" in alternation. But Dognazzi then makes another change: "Faccian, concordi amanti." That "Faccian" (third-person plural) for "Facciam" (first-person plural) means that what Dognazzi had set up as an exchange between Filena and Eurillo ("l'un'e l'altro") switches to the third-party narrative voice ("Let them, as lovers in agreement..."). This is convenient because it allows the narrative voice to conclude the setting. Monteverdi could have done the same thing to bring back the full ensemble. Instead, he continues the dialogue with "Facciam..." as a shared exchange, with Filena and Eurillo both stating at some length that joy, peace, and kisses are better than weeping, war, and pain. He then has to fudge the entrance of the rest of the ensemble with a repeat of the last two lines of the text ("a le guerre..."). This is ungrammatical, although it allows Monteverdi to explore some vigorous

---

[33] The other seventeen settings of this text, beginning with Domenico Maria Melli's in 1602, strongly prefer Marino's "la ninfa...." I am grateful to Roseen Giles for this information. The reading "l'uno e l'altro" given by Georis (*Claudio Monteverdi*, 524) is clearly incorrect: both Dognazzi and Monteverdi intend "l'un[a] e l'altro."

near-*concitato* writing for the wars that S¹ and T¹ (whether or not as Filena and Eurillo) continue to present by vocal flourishes before they alone, as bi-gendered "concordi amanti," insist on the need to turn to peace. Inevitably, the full ensemble (with S¹ and T¹ no longer in character, it seems) ends up agreeing that a thousand kisses are indeed a good thing, especially when given sonic form. Monteverdi's handling of the texture encourages listeners to concur.

Another dialogue in the Sixth Book, "A Dio, Florida bella, il cor piagato" (Marino), takes an even more expedient approach to the problem of the ending. This is a sonnet: Floro (T) speaks to Florida in the first quatrain, and Florida (S¹) to Floro in the second (over the same bassline a fourth higher). The first tercet is narration (SSATB), explaining that this scene is taking place on the banks of the Tiber at dawn, and noting the single sound of Floro and Florida's exchange, mixing sighs, kisses, and words, which prompts Monteverdi to make a witty reference to the "confused" textures typical of improvised *contrappunto alla mente*.[34] The dialogue resumes in the final tercet:

> «Ben mio, rimanti in pace.» «E tu, ben mio,
> vattene in pace, e sia quel che 'l ciel vole.»
> «A Dio, Floro» (dicean) «Florida, a Dio.»[35]

["My love, stay in peace." "And you, my love, / go in peace, and let heaven's will be done." / "Farewell, Floro" (they said) "Florida, farewell."]

Monteverdi should probably have paid a bit more attention here. Both a lover and a beloved can address each other as "Ben mio," but traditionally in these contexts, the man asks the woman to stay while she grants him leave to go, willingly or not. However, Monteverdi gives the initial "Ben mio ..." to Florida (S¹) and "E tu ..." to Floro (T), which would seem to be a mistake.[36] He then remedies it by allocating both speeches to both characters simultaneously—so they each order the other to stay and to go, eventually agreeing in rhythmic unison to accept heaven's will.

At this point, the logical thing would be to reestablish the proper voicing in the final line, as Florida bids farewell to Floro, and then Floro to Florida. However, that would have left the problem of yet another pesky one-word diegetic intervention: "dicean" (they said). For the final line, Monteverdi therefore starts to bring in the full ensemble. Florida's "A Dio, Floro" is delivered simultaneously by S¹AB, with

---

[34] For a similar (and no less witty) reference in "Nisi Dominus" in the 1610 "Vespers," see Carter, "Improvised Counterpoint in Monteverdi's 1610 Vespers."

[35] Calcagno's account (*From Madrigal to Opera*, 215) of Monteverdi's "variants" in his text is odd, because the composer does indeed follow the 1602 edition of Marino's *Rime*. One confusion between "dicean" and "dicea" is a result of a typographical error in the 1614 print. The Alto and Basso partbooks have "dicean"; the Canto partbook has "dicea" with a typical superscript indication of an abbreviation; the Quinto partbook has "dicea" without the abbreviation sign. However, "dicea" (singular) would require three syllables, whereas "dicean" allows two, which is how it is set in all voices.

[36] Giles, *Monteverdi and the Marvellous*, 56–57, views it not as a "mistake" but, rather, as a deliberate ploy to undermine any notion that a soprano and tenor were any real Florida and Floro in the first place.

S² following. Perhaps these are the confused sounds still echoing around the Tiber. However, the tenor stays in character, repeating "Florida, a Dio" to the end—as if left on his own—amid repetitions of the now plural-voiced "A Dio, Floro." Indeed, Monteverdi still tries to keep S¹ (Florida) and T (Floro) apart: only S²AB have the narrative "dicean."[37] But he cannot sustain it: S¹ is finally forced to join the narrating ensemble with her own "dicean" and a final "Florida, a Dio." She cannot say farewell to herself—and she no longer speaks as Florida—but the full ensemble can say farewell to both Floro and Florida, as can Monteverdi and his listeners.

In "Io mi son giovinetta," "Rimanti in pace," "Presso un fiume tranquillo," and "A Dio, Florida bella," Monteverdi is forced to find a solution to the problem of a text that ends with a speaking voice, for if that voice has been treated in some sense mimetically, he must find a way to bring back the full ensemble. One poem does the job for him, however. Guarini's "«T'amo mia vita!», la mia cara vita," one of the continuo madrigals in the Fifth Book, begins with what the beloved says (present tense) to the lover whether directly or in his imagination: "I love you, my life!" This is not a remembrance of things past but something happening in the moment, which is probably why Monteverdi uses the soprano to voice the beloved in so direct a way.[38] One wonders, too, whether he conceived it for, or in, the voice of his wife, Claudia Cattaneo. The lover revels in the statement, one that transforms his heart and is full of such sweetness and delight that he wishes to have it stamped in his breast to give him life. The beloved's direct speech becomes words to be engraved in perpetuity. This solves the "ending" problem, and Monteverdi appears grateful for it because he can now play more easily with other parts of the text. He does so in particularly cunning ways. S¹ speaks for the beloved, and ATB for the lover. But Monteverdi inserts restatements of S¹'s "T'amo mia vita!" at logical grammatical and rhetorical points in the text (as marked in italic here):

>   «T'amo mia vita!», la mia cara vita
>   dolcemente mi dice, *(«T'amo mia vita!»)* e in questa sola
>   sì soave parola
>   par che trasformi lietamente il core
>   per farmene signore. *(«T'amo mia vita!»)*
>   O voce *(«T'amo mia vita!»)* di dolcezza e di diletto,
>   prendila tosto, Amore;
>   stampala nel mio petto.
>   Spiri solo per lei l'anima mia:
>   «T'amo mia vita!» la mia vita sia.

---

[37] Calcagno, *From Madrigal to Opera*, 220.
[38] My reading differs from Calcagno's (*From Madrigal to Opera*, 202), which, at least so far as the poem is concerned, treats the beloved's declaration as a reminiscence in the lover's memory. But there is nothing in the poem (or in its caption in Guarini's *Rime*: "Parola di Donna amante") to suggest the past.

"I love you my life!", my dear life / sweetly says to me *("I love you, my life!")*, and in this single / so sweet word / she seems happily to transform her heart / to make me its master.³⁹ *("I love you, my life!")*. / Oh declaration *("I love you, my life!")* of sweetness and of delight, / take it now, Love; / stamp it in my breast. May my soul breathe only for it: / let "I love you, my life!" be my life.]

Those inserted repetitions are important.⁴⁰ And whether or not the beloved's present-tense statement is a figment of the lover's imagination, Monteverdi's approach is clear. The soprano's "T'amo mia vita!" is set to a motive outlining a descending fifth, with its three insertions cadencing on three different pitches: d' (as also at the beginning), g', and a'. The lover (ATB) responds in fairly strict homophony. But once he has decided that the beloved's statement should be stamped in his breast, the setting shifts to rich polyphony, now in five parts by virtue of the late appearance of S^2. Those three descending-fifth motives are repeated by S^1 and S^2 (moving in parallel thirds) at the same three pitch levels, but within a full texture that has "T'amo mia vita!" in all the voices. Monteverdi has seen the opportunity presented by Guarini's "voce di dolcezza e di diletto": for the poet, "T'amo mia vita!" is a spoken declaration ("voce"), but Monteverdi envoices it by way of music that is itself sweet and delightful.⁴¹ The beloved's musical utterances become fully absorbed by the lover, who repeats them himself to ensure that his life will indeed never end.

He/she said

A special case of "he said" or "she said" settings are those which appear to be wholly or predominantly in the voice of a single character who is not the poet, and with little or no diegetic intervention to explain who is speaking, or why. While a poet can legitimately give voice to any invented person, and often does, pure mimesis creates obvious problems for any musical setting in five voices, as well as a no less obvious trap for any modern reading of it. The point is clear in the five-voice version of the *Lamento d'Arianna* at the head of the Sixth Book, reworking the recitative lament that had caused such stir in the performance of Monteverdi's opera *Arianna* (libretto by Ottavio Rinuccini) in Mantua in 1608 for the festivities celebrating the marriage of Prince Francesco Gonzaga and Margherita of Savoy. As was noted in

---

³⁹ The lines "par che trasformi lietamente il core / per farmene signore" are tricky in terms of what the subject of "par" might be, how to construe the conjugation of "trasformi," whose heart is being transformed, and what the "-ne" is in "farmene."

⁴⁰ This may also be another case in which Monteverdi sets himself up in competition with Benedetto Pallavicino, whose setting in his Fifth Book *a5* (1597) simply runs straight through the text.

⁴¹ The "T'amo mia vita!" motive comes back in "A Dio, Florida bella, il cor piagato" (Sixth Book) and in *Tirsi e Clori* (Seventh), in the latter notably (but not only) at the beginning of Clori's second stanza ("Sì, Tirsi, mia vita"), which is probably another case in Monteverdi in which a textual echo gains a musical resonance. Its occurrences at key moments in "Con che soavità labra odorate" in the same book (Ossi, *Divining the Oracle*, 171–72) may also be deliberate, given that setting's agenda (see Chapter 3).

Federico Follino's official description of the event, "not one lady failed to shed some little tear" as Ariadne found herself abandoned by her beloved Theseus.[42] Her lament gained a wide dissemination: even though the five-voice treatment was the first appearance of the work in print—the solo-voice setting was only published (twice) in 1623—there were a number of manuscript copies of some version of the original in circulation. Monteverdi seems to have been reluctant to commit it to any press in its original form, however, perhaps because he felt it was "owned" instead either by his patron (Duke Vincenzo Gonzaga) or by the performer for whom, and with whom, it was most likely written: Virginia Andreini. But he may also have wanted to create some distance between himself and the opera for more personal reasons. There is a clear sense in the Sixth Book of Monteverdi trying to put his difficult times in Mantua behind him, with their professional disappointments and personal tragedies, including the premature death of his wife in 1607. This is clear not just in the re-voiced lament of an opera for a set of wedding festivities that, he said, had almost been the death of him by overwork, but also in "Incenerite spoglie, avara tomba" on the passing of the singer who was originally to have sung the role of Arianna. The Sixth Book is a curiously dark, even painful collection of madrigals—not helped in that regard by the two Petrarch settings—as Monteverdi seems to struggle through depression into some kind of light. In "Presso un fiume tranquillo," Filena and Eurillo might agree to find peace and kisses, but they have gone through wars on the one hand, and a thousand torments on the other.

The story of Ariadne abandoned by Theseus on Naxos stems from Plutarch but was most familiar from its narration in epic mode by Catullus (*c.* 84–*c.* 54 BCE) as a long digression in his Poem 64 (on the wedding of Peleus and Thetis).[43] Rinuccini also borrowed heavily from Ovid's *Heroides*, 10. Turning the tale into an opera necessarily involved giving mimetic voice to each character, and those women in the audience for Monteverdi's opera wept for seeing some "real" Arianna on the stage. The SSATB version of the *Lamento d'Arianna* necessarily breaks that illusion, putting the protagonist back within some kind of diegetic frame with an implicit "she said" left hanging in the air.[44] Ovid had cast his Ariadne's complaint in the written form of a letter to be

---

[42] Cusick, "There was not one lady who failed to shed a tear." For the broader circumstances, and the possible addition of the lament when Virginia Andreini took over the role on the death of the singer intended for it, Caterina Martinelli, see Carter, "Lamenting Ariadne?" The five-voice version of the lament omits its final section, probably because Arianna has already reached one conclusion, and her next one ("Così va chi tropp'ama e troppo crede") is more like a moral that would in some sense reintroduce the voice of the composer. But in this final section, Arianna also contemplates suicide in a manner that works in the opera (she is soon rescued by divine intervention), but not so well in a freestanding context wherein any happy ending cannot be predicted.

[43] The story of Ariadne and Theseus is represented in embroidery on the coverlet for the wedding bed, so Catullus's inset narrative is a case of *ekphrasis*: i.e., the vivid description of a work of art.

[44] Fabbri (*Monteverdi*, trans. Carter, 92) quotes the report of the Estense ambassador present at the 1608 wedding festivities that Arianna's lament was accompanied by string instruments ("viole et violini"). But it is very hard to imagine that the SSATB version involves some kind of transcription or arrangement of that accompaniment. The text is not complete in the upper voice (a line and a half is omitted in the *seconda parte*), and the quite extensive repetitions make it implausible. It is possible, however, that the string instruments were used rather in the manner of Clorinda's speeches at the end of the *Combattimento*; compare Ossi, *Divining the Oracle*, 161–62. This may also have helped solve some of the tuning problems (see Chapter 8).

sent from Naxos ("quae legis, ex illo, Theseu, tibi litore mitto"), allowing her to narrate herself first in the past tense (as she describes how she rushed to the shore once she had discovered Theseus's flight) and then in the present (she considers her current condition). It becomes a carefully crafted rhetorical exercise rather than an instinctive outpouring of grief. Monteverdi's five-voice setting establishes a similar kind of distance as the voices speak for Arianna, but not as her.

Her audience changes as well. Rinuccini followed Ovid in having Arianna foresee her doom on dangerous lonely shores, prey to wild beasts. However, this does not square with his opening strategy in the operatic lament, given that she is surrounded by friendly fisherfolk: they are the "voi"—"you"—addressed at the outset by way of that initial imperative ("Lasciatemi . . .") and as Arianna despairs of their bringing any comfort ("E chi volete voi che mi conforte . . ."). On the stage, they also interject between the sections of Arianna's speech that Monteverdi treats as separate *parti* in the five-voice version.[45] But in the polyphonic version, the "voi" become the listeners who must consider their own views on Arianna's situation, perhaps bearing in mind that she is not entirely without blame for her actions. The Florentine music theorist Giovanni Battista Doni would have had none of this, however: he simply thought that the madrigal was a bad mistake foisted upon Monteverdi by some ill-informed Venetian patron.[46] And whichever way one reads it, Arianna remains a ghost in the machine, there but not-there, as what she said is now re-said by five voices each taking a brief lead in delivering successive portions of the text.

On 24 August 1609, Monteverdi wrote to Alessandro Striggio about a commission from Duke Vincenzo Gonzaga to set a particular text (unidentified). The composer was planning to write for solo voice, although if need be, he was willing to "rearrange the air for five voices" ("che riporti quel'aria a cinque"). However, the polyphonic *Lamento d'Arianna* is far more than just a rearrangement of the monodic version. Monteverdi distributes its melody across various voices, and he pauses at certain points in the text where there is room for rhetorical and musical expansion. For example, in the *seconda parte*, Arianna begs Teseo to turn back:

> Volgiti indietro a rimirare colei
> che lasciato ha per te la patria e 'l regno,
> e 'n quest'arene ancora,
> cibo di fere dispietate e crude,
> lascierà l'ossa ignude.

[Turn back to gaze upon her / who for you has left her homeland and kingdom, / and who yet on these shores, / food for harsh, cruel beasts, / will leave her bare bones.]

---

[45] These interventions are also removed in the solo-voice lament as Monteverdi published it in 1623, which makes sense if it was to be done in a chamber context.

[46] Fabbri, *Monteverdi*, trans. Carter, 140.

Ex. 5.3 "O Teseo, o Teseo mio," *seconda parte* of "Lasciatemi morire" (Sixth Book, 1614).

These five lines take up twelve measures of recitative, which Monteverdi now expands to twenty-one by repeating "Volgiti indietro . . . ," and then hitting the pause button, as it were, to create a six-measure insertion for a polyphonic expansion of lines 2–4, superimposing three separate textual moments: Arianna having left her homeland; her remaining on empty shores; and her being food for wild beasts (Ex. 5.3). By virtue of such fragmentation, repetition, and expansion, ideas that would be presented in succession in a single discourse become jumbled as if we were inside Arianna's head rather than hearing her speak.[47] It also means that the polyphonic lament is significantly longer than the monodic one, even though it omits the final eleven lines of the text. Monteverdi prolongs and plays with time, using his polyphony to force the listener to stay in the moment, however painful it might be.

As the *Lamento d'Arianna* reveals, these kinds of mimetic texts will usually be drawn either from drama or from epic. Marc'Antonio Ingegneri did not include epic poetry in his curated curriculum for his young student, and a fair number of prominent madrigalists avoided it because of its continuous eleven-syllable lines and its problems of narrative voice. However, Monteverdi's move to Mantua expanded his literary horizons. Thus, his Third Book has two extended settings from Tasso's *Gerusalemme liberata* (1581), which had gained some fame in the period. Both Wert and Marenzio were setting passages from it in the 1580s, including "Giunto alla tomba, ove al suo spirto vivo" (their madrigals were published in 1581 and 1587 respectively).[48] This is Tasso's account (Canto 12) of Tancredi standing before the tomb of the Saracen warrior, Clorinda, whom he loved but had unknowingly killed

---

[47] Chafe (*Monteverdi's Tonal Language*, 169–70) also notes how the polyphonic version allows for a more thorough working out of the tonal implications of the monodic one, and comments (173–75) on the harmonic consequences of the insertion shown in my Ex. 5.3.
[48] Owens, "Marenzio and Wert Read Tasso."

in hand-to-hand battle (as Monteverdi represented in his later *Combattimento di Tancredi e Clorinda*). But no one had hitherto set a slightly earlier scene for Tancredi following Clorinda's death, "Vivrò fra i miei tormenti e le mie cure" (Canto 12, stanzas 77–79). Likewise, the other *Gerusalemme liberata* text in the Third Book, "Vattene pur, crudel, con quella pace"—with a vengeful Armida cursing her lover Rinaldo, who has abandoned her—was also new to the madrigal.[49]

In the sixteenth century, epic poetry could be, and often was, performed by a solo voice to the lute, usually using standard recitation formulas that provided music for two lines of text that could be repeated for the pairs of lines within the *ottava rima* stanzas (eight eleven-syllable lines rhyming *ABABABCC*) that were standard for the genre. There were plenty of these *arie da cantar ottave* from which to choose. Polyphonic settings, however, faced a different set of challenges, given epic's typical mixture of diegesis and mimesis that therefore required some musical choices to be made in the manner of those lyric poems involving a narrator and direct speech attributed to one or more characters. "Giunto alla tomba" is typical from that rhetorical point of view. The first six lines of the first stanza set by Wert and Marenzio (Canto 12, stanza 96) are narration, and the last two, plus three more stanzas (97–99), are what Tancredi said, preceded by the typical "disse." "Vivrò fra i miei tormenti" is entirely mimetic, however: Tancredi speaks from beginning to end, with no narrative intervention. In neither case is he given his name; nor is Clorinda, if that matters. In other words, absent knowledge of *Gerusalemme liberata*, it is hard to tell precisely what these settings are about.

Starting in midstream creates problems, too. Prior to the passage set by Monteverdi, Clorinda and Tancredi have been found on their battlefield, one dead and the other nearly so. They are both carried back into the Christian camp and placed in separate tents. Doctors tend to Tancredi, and as he revives (stanzas 75–76), he curses the fact that he still breathes, and urges his own hand to end his life, although he realizes that he must, instead, live as a wretched example of ill-fated love, worthy only of suffering for his dreadful act. Monteverdi's setting begins as Tancredi continues to speak (stanza 77): he will live in torment, wandering out of his mind ("forsennato") through the shadows, scorning the sun, trying to flee from himself but never succeeding. In stanza 78 (Monteverdi's *seconda parte*), Tancredi's thoughts turn to Clorinda, wondering where the remains of her fair, chaste body now lie (ll. 1–2):

> Ma dove (o lasso me!) dove restaro
> le reliquie del corpo e bello e casto?

He fears that they are even now being devoured by the beasts of the forest (ll. 4–5):

---

[49] The following discussion draws heavily on the more comprehensive account of these two settings in Giles, *Monteverdi and the Marvellous*, chap. 6 ("Monteverdi's Earliest Laments"), although with some differences.

> Ahi troppo nobil preda! ahi dolce e caro
> troppo, e pur troppo prezioso pasto!

[Ah, too noble a prey! Ah, too sweet and dear, / too, too precious a meal!]

In stanza 79 (the *terza parte*), Tancredi resolves to go find those remains: if they have indeed been eaten, he will wait for the wild animals to devour him as well so that he can be with Clorinda in the same gastric tomb. Here Monteverdi's setting ends, although as Tasso's narration resumes (stanza 80), Tancredi is assured by his friends that Clorinda's body is indeed safe nearby, so he goes to see it for himself.

Unlike what he does with "Giunto alla tomba," Tasso situates all this in the historic present tense (Tancredi "dice" and "parla") rather than the past, presumably to make it more vivid: this may be why Monteverdi felt encouraged to divorce the speech from any narrative framework. Moreover, Tancredi's raving over his wretched future, Clorinda's body mauled by beasts, and his wish to join her in some bestial stomach would all seem to constitute some kind of mad scene. Monteverdi's choice of a high-clef scoring (G2, C1, C2, C3, F3) already seems to take the setting out of any normal range for a male character, and if this setting was indeed intended for the Pellizzari ensemble (see Chapter 4), it would have had female sopranos. But Tasso's text is complex grammatically, it involves very long sentences (e.g., the first six lines of the first stanza, and the last six of the third), and its emotive words are not best placed to allow Monteverdi to pause on them without losing track of the flow. His musical choices are therefore fairly limited. He opts for what one might call an epic Dorian mode that also appears in "Vattene pur, crudel" and the *Combattimento di Tancredi e Clorinda*, and he largely writes enlivened homophony where most of the voices move in rhythmic unison save where one is displaced by way of anticipation. One obvious exception is the opening of the *seconda parte*, where Monteverdi constructs a quasi-contrapuntal ATB opening to accentuate the start of Tancredi's question, "Ma dove..." (But where...), although with the slightly odd consequence that his exclamation that immediately follows ("o lasso me!") is not given much emphasis, because the question needs to continue.[50] Another exception is the opening of the *terza parte* ("Io pur verrò là dove sète; e voi") where the only first-person "io" in the piece (although it is all, of course, in the first person) gets allocated to an entrance in the bass voice, followed by the tenor. But for the rest, Monteverdi's expressive devices are largely limited to unusual harmonic juxtapositions, some of which are quite stunning, such as a minor triad on G to a major one on E.[51]

---

[50] The FCM edition gives the reading from the 1592 print (and in Amadino's 1594, 1600, and 1604 editions). Malipiero follows Amadino's 1607 edition, where S[1] has "Ma dove" in mm. 2–3 rather than mm. 6–7 (i.e., following S[2]). Giles (*Monteverdi and the Marvellous*, 246–48) notes the connection with the opening of Wert's "Ma che? squallido e scuro anco mi piaci" (from Erminia's lament over the wounded Tancredi) in his Eighth Book *a5* (1586).

[51] Monteverdi certainly seems to have liked the juxtaposition of a minor triad on G with a major one on E (or vice versa): it is found also in *Orfeo* (1607), during the Messenger's narration of Euridice's death.

Given these limitations of the text, Monteverdi moves through it fairly quickly: the three *parti* add up to 158 measures of music, a surprisingly low number for twenty-four dense eleven-syllable lines. But he does grasp at rhetorical straws. In the *seconda parte*, the text following that "Ma dove..." does not offer much opportunity, and even the next strong exclamation—"Ahi troppo nobil preda!" (Ah, too noble a prey!)—is unlikely to inspire. But Monteverdi catches sight of the next one, in line 7: "Ahi sfortunato!" Here, at last, is something straightforward that he can get his teeth into, and it takes up nineteen measures by way of a motive descending stepwise through a fifth as other text is presented above and below. Monteverdi is fond of these stepwise descents, also because of their modal clarity (see Chapter 8). Here they produce a gloriously rich musical moment, marred only by the fact that it is not entirely clear what is "ill-fortuned," whether the "meal" ("pasto") in line 6, Clorinda's body ("corpo") in line 2, or Tancredi himself. Perhaps Monteverdi does not care about such grammatical niceties. Rather, there is a strong sense here of him interjecting his own comment into the text, a diegetic musical intervention, as it were, that reveals his own role as narrator even within a text that denies the need for one.[52]

The other *Gerusalemme liberata* setting in Monteverdi's Third Book, "Vattene pur, crudel," is simpler in narrative terms, given that Tasso situates it in a past-tense framework. But it is also more complex insofar as it forces Monteverdi to deal with a closer juxtaposition of diegetic and mimetic voices. Here we have a female character, Armida (she names herself), and Monteverdi opts for a high-clef combination with two equal soprano voices. Like "Vivrò fra i miei tormenti," "Vattene pur, crudel" sets three *ottava rima* stanzas (Canto 16, stanzas 59, 60, 63), but not contiguous ones, meaning that it requires more careful explanation. The Saracen witch Armida has seduced the Christian knight Rinaldo, trapping him by way of the delights of her magic island, from which he is rescued by two other knights, Carlo and Ubaldo, who bring him back to the path of righteousness. Rinaldo has come to his senses by stanza 35, and stanzas 36–51 mostly concern Armida's attempts—wheedling, threatening, pleading, seducing—to persuade him to stay. The narration resumes in stanza 52: Rinaldo has been moved by Armida's pleas, so (stanzas 53–55) he tries to reason with her, given the military tasks that lie before him, and offers to return once honor has been gained on the battlefield. He then takes his leave (stanza 56):

> Rimanti in pace; i' vado: a te non lice
> meco venire; chi mi conduce il vieta.

[Remain in peace. I am going. To you it is not allowed / to come with me. Who leads me on forbids it.][53]

Tomlinson (*Monteverdi and the End of the Renaissance*, 67–72) also notes the influence on this progression of Wert's "Misera, non credea ch'a gli occhi miei" (in his Eighth Book *a5* of 1586), as on other aspects of Monteverdi's setting.

[52] Compare Giles, *Monteverdi and the Marvellous*, 248.
[53] Rinaldo's "Rimanti in pace" (not set here by Monteverdi) is taken over by Angelo Grillo (Livio Celiano) as the beginning of the sonnet set at the end of Monteverdi's Third Book, "«Rimanti in pace» a la dolente e bella,"

Armida knows full well that Rinaldo's promise to come back counts for naught, and in stanzas 57–58 she turns to scorn, speaking first to him, then to herself, and then (stanza 59) back to him, which is where Monteverdi begins:

> Vattene pur, crudel, con quella pace
> che lasci a me: vattene iniquo omai;

[Go then, cruel one, with that peace / which you leave to me; go now, unjust one.]

She then continues with threats: she will always be on his back, a relentless spirit and a new Fury tormenting him with snakes and torches as much as she loved him ("tanto t'agiterò quanto t'amai"). And if fate allows Rinaldo to enter battle... (stanza 60), there, lying among the bloodied and the dead, will he repay her suffering, calling for Armida in his last sighs, and she hopes to hear that often... (she breaks off).

Thus, Armida's "Vattene pur, crudel" comes at the end of a very long sequence, and the "quella pace" to which she refers is the "peace" in which Rinaldo urged her to remain in stanza 56. Tasso's enjambment between the end of stanza 59 and the beginning of stanza 60 works against dividing the two stanzas into a *prima* and *seconda parte*, although Monteverdi tries to smooth over it harmonically by ending the first on the co-final (a major triad on A) leading to a minor triad on D (the final) for the beginning of the second. The fact that Armida breaks off in the middle of stanza 60 also creates a problem in terms of marking the shift to narration (the last four lines of the stanza) describing how Armida's spirits failed—such that she could not even express her last thought completely—and she fell senseless on the ground. That narration continues in stanzas 61 and 62 (both dropped by Monteverdi), and in a rather curious way, not by describing what happens but, instead, by addressing Armida directly (shifting to the present tense). This is a rather neat trick sometimes adopted by Tasso as his narrative voice speaks to his characters, rather than about them or on their behalf. By having closed her eyes, Armida is missing out on what might provide comfort in her suffering; she should, instead, open them to see what impact her speech has had on Rinaldo: his tears, his sighs, and his pitying gaze toward her. Now (stanza 62), the narrative voice asks itself, or us, a question, which is another Tasso trick to engage the reader: "Hor che farà?" What will Rinaldo do?—leave Armida half dead on the shore? Courtesy restrains him; pity constrains him; but harsh necessity drives him on. Tasso then reverts to simple narrative: Rinaldo leaves, his sails taken by the wind, while gazing at the shore soon hidden in the distance.

This is complicated in narratological terms, and it is not surprising that Monteverdi jumps from stanza 60 to 63.[54] But he is not yet entirely out of the woods.

---

the love scene between Filli and Tirsi. For the notion that this might be viewed as some kind of attempt to reconcile Armida and Rinaldo, see Giles, *Monteverdi and the Marvellous*, 253.

[54] As Giles (*Monteverdi and the Marvellous*, 235–36) notes, dropping these stanzas also removes Rinaldo entirely from the scene conjured up in Monteverdi's "Vattene pur, crudel," where Armida is already on her own.

For the first two lines of stanza 63 (the *terza parte*), the narration returns to Armida, who revives and sees everything around her empty and silent. She is left with a question (ll. 3–4):

«Ito se nè pur», disse, «ed ha potuto
me qui lasciar de la mia vita in forse?

["Has he gone," she said, "and could he / leave me here in doubt over my life?]

She then has still more to ask: did he leave without a moment's thought; does she still love him; is she really just standing on the shore weeping and unavenged? She speaks to herself, but also to us. However, all these questions will be hard to handle: music is much better at delivering statements, given that cadences tend to force a descending motion in their upper lines.[55]

For the opening of "Vattene pur, crudel," Monteverdi probably had Wert once more in mind, who had set a slightly earlier passage in Armida's invective against Rinaldo, "Forsennata gridava: «O tu che porti" in his Eighth Book a5 of 1586. Here Wert uses a different combination of voices (C1, C2, C3, C4, F4), but he has a striking opening, his only "mistake" being that those first two words set to a rising tenth, as Armida shouted in fury, are delivered by the narrating voice, so when Wert moves to more straightforward homophony for her direct speech, it seems anticlimactic (Ex. 5.4). Monteverdi has the advantage—he must have realized—of beginning with Armida speaking, and he certainly gives the impression of a female voice echoing around the shore as S^1, then A and S^2 repeat her initial imperative. However, this places him in the slightly odd situation that when Armida switches from "you" (Rinaldo) to "me" ("Me tosto..."), this part of the text begins in T, and is the first allocated to B (in homophony with the upper voices).

Monteverdi then reverts to enlivened homophony while looking out for words that can allow for some more extended musical development: in the *prima parte*, the waves ("l'onde") over which Rinaldo will sail; and in the *seconda parte*, how he will call for her in his last sighs on the battlefield ("chiamerai"). By now, however, Armida is being voiced by all five parts, and having ended Armida's initial speech with full homophony, Monteverdi can mark the switch to diegesis ("Hor qui mancò...") only by way of reducing the texture to SS followed by B (and much later, T, and finally A). The music here is powerful and very artfully constructed: a long contrapuntal development (eventually in all five voices) over twenty measures

---

[55] Monteverdi sometimes tries to inflect questions musically. For the six of them in "Anima dolorosa, che vivendo" (Fourth Book), he sets each to a V–I progression with a rising motion in the top voice and the resolution delayed by a quarter note (crotchet). The same pattern can be found in madrigals by Wert (e.g., in the *quinta parte* of "Qual musico gentil prima che chiara") and by Gastoldi ("O misera Dorinda" in his Fourth Book a5 of 1602; see Coluzzi, *Guarini's "Il pastor fido" and the Madrigal*, 389). Monteverdi also uses it for the questions in the middle (but not the beginning) of "Ferir quel petto, Silvio?" (the *quinta parte* of "Ecco, Silvio, colei che in odio hai tanto") and elsewhere in the Fifth Book. In other places, he weakens cadences so as to give some sense of the interrogative. But this is not something that can be done easily within a polyphonic texture.

Ex. 5.4 (a) Giaches de Wert, "Forsennata gridava: «O tu che porti" (Eighth Book *a*5, 1586; C1, C2, C3, C4, F4); (b) Monteverdi, "Vattene pur, crudel, con quella pace" (Third Book, 1592; G2, G2, C2; T [C3] and B [F3] are silent).

of downward chromatic steps spanning a fourth.[56] It also serves to resolve the unstable harmony at the end of Armida's speech (the one she could not finish): she ended on a major triad on D, which the narrative voices eventually take to a cadence on G precisely when they note her inability to express her entire final thought ("né quest'ultimo suono espresse intero"), almost as if they are trying to do it for her. These last four narrative lines of the *seconda parte* take up forty-three measures (out of sixty-eight), and there is a similarly expansive treatment of the narration in the first two lines of the *terza parte*, albeit a more proportionate twenty measures out of eighty-two. This helps explain why "Vattene pur, crudel" in its entirety is significantly longer than "Vivrò fra i miei tormenti" (206 measures against 158): Armida's story is part-narrated, whereas Tancredi's is not, and its diegetic moments are more amenable to musical expansion than its mimetic ones.

---

[56] Monteverdi reversed it, but to similar effect, in his handling of another of Tasso's female figures in lamenting mode, Nicea (in *Gerusalemme conquistata*, substituting for Erminia in *Gerusalemme liberata*), in the narrative "Piagne sospira; e quand'i caldi raggi" at the end of the Fourth Book.

Ex. 5.5 "Poi ch'ella in sé tornò, deserto e muto," *terza parte* of "Vattene pur, crudel, con quella pace" (Third Book, 1592), Canto, Quinto, Alto.

This is a typical paradox in epic poetry: the context of what is said is often more richly described than what is said itself. But in the *terza parte*, the text puts Monteverdi in an impossible position. As Armida begins to speak again with her final questions ("Ito se nè pur"), Tasso inserts a parenthetical "disse" (she said), as he must to make the shift to mimesis clear. Monteverdi follows the logic of his musical opening to the *prima parte*: if Armida is represented by SSA there, so should she be here (Ex. 5.5). The case is similar to the interjected "disse" in "Io mi son giovinetta" noted earlier. If a female character's speech is already marked by a high-voice grouping, any "disse" is rhetorically redundant. But Monteverdi seems to think that he has nowhere else to put it, unless he is somehow reading the text differently ("disse" as "di sé").

Once again, diegesis contradicts the notion that Monteverdi is somehow trying to create within the polyphonic madrigal any kind of "dramatic" reading of a text. Armida is not speaking here, even if she is somehow represented as speaking. But any detachment caused by the polyphonic delivery of her words serves a purpose. Armida is often read as a wicked witch uttering curses willy-nilly once she has lost her evil sway over Rinaldo: her threat to torment him as much as she loved him ("tanto t'agiterò quanto t'amai") got taken over by another problematic female character, Dido, whom Monteverdi set to music (now lost) for one of the *intermedi* for Tasso's *Aminta*, staged in Parma in 1628.[57] What we lose in his setting of "Vattene pur, crudel," however, is an account of any response to Armida's complaint. In the omitted stanzas 61 and 62, the narrative voice seems sympathetic to her, and Rinaldo is certainly moved to tears, sighs, and pity (so we are told), even if "harsh necessity" drives him away. Having bypassed those two stanzas, Monteverdi instead leaves the listeners to stand in for Rinaldo, forcing us to reach our own conclusion over his dilemma: should he stay or go? In the context of *Gerusalemme liberata*, the answer is clear. But "Vattene pur, crudel" prompts some ambivalence on the part of both the performers and the listener.

[57] Carter, "Intriguing Laments," 53.

Monteverdi kept both Tancredi and Armida in mind: his *Combattimento di Tancredi e Clorinda* (included in the Eighth Book) was performed in Venice in 1624, and shortly thereafter, he composed a long Armida setting in a similar vein, starting nineteen stanzas before "Vattene pur, crudel" (at Canto 16, stanza 50: "Forsennata gridava: «O tu, che porte")—where Wert had also begun—although we do not know how long a piece it was. Monteverdi first mentioned what he called *Armida abbandonata* in his letter to Alessandro Striggio of 1 May 1627 (also noting where the setting began). Both the *Combattimento* and *Armida abbandonata* may also have been implicated in Monteverdi's evident competition with his chief rival in the 1620s, Sigismondo d'India, a composer largely associated with the courts of Savoy and then Modena, but who in 1621 was given the honorary title in Venice of Cavaliere di San Marco.[58] The *Combattimento* appears to make direct reference to d'India's setting of parts of the same text in his *Le musiche . . . libro quarto* (Venice: Alessandro Vincenti, 1621).[59] They were also in competition for the commission to write the music for the Farnese wedding celebrations, for which d'India composed a (now lost) *Lamento d'Armida* as proof of his abilities in theatrical music.[60] This may, in turn, relate to Monteverdi's own Armida setting (also lost), which seems to have been done in the vein of the *Combattimento* with a narrator and separate singers for the characters.[61] Given that Tasso's pastoral play, *Aminta*, was performed during the celebrations in Parma in December 1628, the poet's name was in the air. It is striking, however, that after the two epic settings in the Third Book, Monteverdi otherwise turned away entirely from the genre in his subsequent printed collections until he included the *Combattimento* in the *Madrigali guerrieri, et amorosi* in 1638. In the Fourth and especially the Fifth Books, epic texts are replaced by ones by another favorite poet with some presence in Mantua, Battista Guarini, whether his epigrammatic lyric verse or texts taken from his own pastoral play, *Il pastor fido*.[62]

---

[58] Morales, *Sigismondo d'India et ses mondes*, 192–95.
[59] Carter, *Monteverdi's Musical Theatre*, 181–85.
[60] D'India sent his *Lamento d'Armida* to Marchese Enzo Bentivoglio (who had charge of the Farnese festivities) on 2 September 1627 as proof of his skills in composing theatrical music; see Carter, "Intriguing Laments," 35–37. Monteverdi told Striggio on 10 September that Bentivoglio had approached him about writing music for Parma "as long as a month ago." D'India's Third Book of *Musiche* (1618) also contains solo-voice settings of Petrarch's "Voi ch'ascoltate in rime sparse il suono" (*RVF* 1) and "Or che 'l ciel e la terra e 'l vento tace" (*RVF* 164) that Monteverdi set for larger ensembles.
[61] Monteverdi promised Striggio to have a copy of the score of his *Armida* made for Mantua, which he did in mid-December 1627. That score was sent there by Monteverdi's friend and colleague, the bass singer Giacomo Rapallini, on 19 February 1628: see Sogliani, "La Serenissima e il Ducato," 594. In his letter accompanying the score, Rapallini requested that he be considered for the role of Ubaldo, given that he had already "digested" it on a previous occasion ("et se occorresse a caso . . . che nella Armida facesse bisogno la parte di Ubaldo, quale ho digesta benissimo in altro tempo, Vostra Signoria Illustrissima mi commandi ch'io lo riceverò per singolarissimo et segnalatissimo favore"). In the relevant portion of *Gerusalemme liberata* (Canto 16), Ubaldo has one stanza (51) of direct speech, and Rapallini's request would seem to mean that he had sung the role at some performance, presumably alongside an Armida, Rinaldo, and Testo.
[62] Tomlinson (*Monteverdi and the End of the Renaissance*, 84–89) discusses Guarini's "epigrammatic" style, defined by way of short texts usually in a two-part format establishing a situation and making a point of it. However, Monteverdi's setting of this poetry can be quite long, given his penchant for text repetition in varied scorings.

A pastoral conundrum

If the mixture of diegesis and mimesis within epic poetry creates one set of musical problems, the "pure" mimesis of drama adds still more. We have seen the five voices of a polyphonic madrigal speak as, or for, generically named characters—Tirsi, Clori, Eurillo, Filli, or Filena—who inhabit some feigned pastoral world. However, when such characters are taken from a newly invented play with stories that have a beginning, a middle, and an end, matters become more complicated. Battista Guarini's pastoral "tragicomedy," *Il pastor fido*, was the subject of great literary controversy, given its mixing of purportedly incompatible genres and other improprieties.[63] The play received a spectacular staging in Mantua on 22 November 1598 to honor the progress of Margaret of Austria on her way to Madrid to take her place as Queen of Spain. Just a week before, she was in Ferrara, at the same time as Monteverdi's nemesis, Giovanni Maria Artusi, encountered the composer's madrigals, prompting his stern criticisms of them in his treatises published in 1600 and 1603. All five settings by Monteverdi cited by Artusi were of texts by Guarini, with four of them drawn from the play. Monteverdi published one of those five in the Fourth Book ("Anima mia, perdona" and its *seconda parte*). The others appeared at the head of the Fifth: "Cruda Amarilli, che col nome ancora," "O Mirtillo, Mirtill'anima mia," "Era l'anima mia" (not from *Il pastor fido*), and "Ma se con la pietà non è in te spenta" (the *seconda parte* of "Ecco, Silvio, colei che in odio ha tanto"). Their prominent position seems deliberate; they are also in the order criticized by Artusi. Moreover, putting "Cruda Amarilli" first allowed Monteverdi to face head-on Artusi's most prominent attack—on its outrageously unprepared dissonant ninth falling to a seventh. But he may also have found another use for the piece: the amaryllis flower was commonly identified with Rome, and Artusi, representing the Church, had certainly been "cruel" to the composer over this particular madrigal.[64]

Guarini's tragicomedy deals with the vicissitudes of two pairs of star-crossed lovers: Mirtillo and Amarilli, and Silvio and Dorinda. In his earlier *Pastor fido* settings, Monteverdi had set either a version of a text probably written by the poet prior to its insertion into the play ("O primavera gioventù de l'anno" in the Third Book), or one that, by whatever means, was shorn of its connection to it. In the case of "Quell'augellin, che canta" (Fourth Book), the text set by Monteverdi is a new conflation of a portion of Linco's speech in Act I, scene 1 with the end of a related madrigal published separately by Guarini ("Dolce canoro e garulo augelletto").[65]

---

[63] Coluzzi, *Guarini's "Il pastor fido" and the Madrigal*, 296–97, notes the similarities between the common criticisms of Guarini's play, and Artusi's of Monteverdi's madrigals.

[64] Carter, "E in rileggendo poi le proprie note," 145. This is one reason that songs such as Giulio Caccini's "Amarilli, mia bella" (in his *Le nuove musiche* of 1602) become popular in recusant circles in northern Europe.

[65] Georis, *Claudio Monteverdi*, 68–69. Marenzio, on the other hand, sets the text from the play in his Seventh Book *a5* (1595), save for changing "Silvio" to "Tirsi." As Coluzzi (*Guarini's "Il pastor fido" and the Madrigal*, 315) notes, Monteverdi's version of "Quell'augellin, che canta" omits the reference to Silvio in Linco's speech.

For that matter, although "Anima mia, perdona" is indeed part of Amarilli's address to Mirtillo (Act III, scene 4), who has just left the stage, his name is dropped from the beginning of its first line—"E tu, Mirtillo (anima mia), perdona"—changing an eleven-syllable line into a seven-syllable one.[66] The play therefore becomes irrelevant by way of textual dissociation. The same is perhaps true of "Ah, dolente partita!" at the head of the Fourth Book, where Mirtillo's comment on being dismissed by Amarilli in Act III, scene 3, could well be read in Monteverdi's setting as a dialogue between two anonymous lovers.

"Cruda Amarilli, che col nome ancora" might seem to sit in the same hinterland. As with a number of Monteverdi's other settings from, or related to, *Il pastor fido*, it entered into a very large nexus of madrigals drawing on the play by composers close to him in professional terms (Pallavicino, Rossi, Wert), or who had already had some influence on him (Marenzio, Monte), as well as many others.[67] Indeed, the competition might help explain that outrageous ninth and seventh as Monteverdi tried to stand out from the pack. Mirtillo's speech in Act I, scene 2, is an apostrophe—"cruel" Amarilli is not present—delivered in the presence of his friend, Ergasto. Monteverdi sets just the first eight lines, ending at the point where the shepherd says that since his speaking causes such offense, he will die in silence ("i' mi morrò tacendo"). Marenzio (1595), Pallavicino (1600), and Wert (1595) had continued into a *seconda parte*, as did most other early settings of this text. Far from staying silent, Mirtillo resumes with a "but" as he claims that the slopes, mountains, woods, and springs will speak for him instead, lamenting in his place ("Ma grideran per me le piagge e i monti"). By ignoring that continuation, Monteverdi loses any sense of pastoral place within the text, and save for the reference to Amarilli, the "I" becomes a generic lover suffering in typically unrequited fashion.

As the Fifth Book progresses, however, the named characters of *Il pastor fido* interject themselves more forcefully within the texts set here. The second madrigal, "O Mirtillo, Mirtill'anima mia," cannot be so easily detached from the play. It comes from Act III, scene 4, and is Amarilli's immediate response to Mirtillo's "Ah, dolente partita!" at the end of scene 3 (the "Anima mia, perdona" that Monteverdi set in the Fourth Book comes from later in that same speech). Placing it immediately after "Cruda Amarilli" therefore seems to construct an exchange between two characters who are closely attached in *Il pastor fido*, but by way of texts that are not contiguous within it.[68] However, in the play Amarilli is speaking to herself—Mirtillo has

---

[66] There are similar variants in other settings of this text (including Marenzio's "Deh, Tirsi, Tirsi, anima mia, perdona" in his Sixth Book *a5* of 1594); see Coluzzi, *Guarini's "Il pastor fido" and the Madrigal*, 274–75.

[67] Ossi, "Monteverdi, Marenzio, and Battista Guarini's 'Cruda Amarilli.'" Marenzio's Seventh Book *a5* (1595) appears to have had some influence on Monteverdi in other ways as well; see the list of contents in Calcagno, *From Madrigal to Opera*, 162. Given that Marenzio may have been angling for a position in Mantua in the late 1590s (*From Madrigal to Opera*, 176–77), there could be some point to the competition. The perhaps surprising exception to this "Mantuan" competition is Giovanni Giacomo Gastoldi, who did indeed set many texts from *Il pastor fido*, but not, on the whole, those marked out as "classics" from the play; see Coluzzi, *Guarini's "Il pastor fido" and the Madrigal*, 368–69.

[68] La Via, "Monteverdi esegeta"; Ossi, *Divining the Oracle*, 85. Ossi then goes further (89–90) to propose reading the two independent madrigals inserted within the *Pastor fido* settings in the Fifth Book, "Era

left—although she is overheard by Corisca, who is also in love with Mirtillo. This means that the initial vocatives in both "Cruda Amarilli" and "O Mirtillo" are indirect, and each character dissolves the "you" within an expression of the "I."[69] Indeed, Monteverdi has made a rather cunning move, given the inherent implausibility of the medium he has chosen to present "dramatic" texts that turn out not to be very dramatic: he makes us hear what Ergasto (I.2) and Corisca (III.4) hear, but filtered through a polyphonic lens.

The fourth madrigal in the Fifth Book permits no such connivance. It presents a fairly continuous exchange between Dorinda and Silvio from Act IV, scene 9, beginning at "Ecco, Silvio, colei che in odio hai tanto."[70] This is the crunch scene for the other principal pair of lovers in Il pastor fido. Silvio has been sternly resisting Dorinda's advances, given his devotion to the hunt, but now he has struck her by accident with one of his arrows—she had disguised herself as a wolf to follow him—which forces him to view her in a different light. Monteverdi divides the setting into five *parti*, the first two presenting lines delivered by Dorinda (ll. 1237–59), the third and fourth by Silvio (ll. 1260–67, 1275–85), and the last, Dorinda's grateful response (ll. 1286–1305).[71] This amounts to over sixty lines of poetry, but the fact that Silvio and Dorinda's speeches are relatively short compared with Mirtillo's and Amarilli's means that Monteverdi can at least put the two characters directly alongside each other as in the play, albeit without any clear musical distinction between them: this sequence is all in high clefs (and in an unusually high range), and the fact that it is the Tenore (in C3 clef) that often takes the lead or otherwise stands out, whether in the "Dorinda" sections or the "Silvio" ones, makes matters just about as ambiguous as they can be.

The next extended madrigal in the book returns to Mirtillo in an earlier part of Act III, scene 3 ("Ch'io t'ami, e t'ami più de la mia vita"), creating a setting in three *parti* from passages from his speech (ll. 296–303, 332–46, 347–62; the last with a cut) delivered directly to Amarilli prior to a long exchange with her that ends with her final dismissal (and hence, Mirtillo's "Ah, dolente partita!" beginning at line 498).[72] The *Pastor fido* settings in the Fifth Book then end with "M'è più dolce il

---

l'anima mia" (by Guarini) and "Che dar più vi poss'io" (unidentified), either as a commentary on Mirtillo and Amarilli's condition, or as additional words put into their mouths. But save as a case of wish fulfillment, this seems hardly plausible for the openly erotic "Era l'anima mia," wherein love's pleasures are shared on both sides.

[69] Calcagno (*From Madrigal to Opera*, 128) notes the staging of Act I, scene 2, but misses the point of Amarilli's being overheard by Corisca in Act III, scene 4. The conversation between Mirtillo and Ergasto parallels the one between Silvio and Linco in Act I, scene 1: using dialogues to explain the plot is a typical introcuctory strategy in pastoral plays.

[70] Marenzio sets similar (but not always the same) portions of this part of IV.9 in his Eighth Book *a*5 (1598). The musical differences are quite striking, to the extent that any apparent references to Marenzio in Monteverdi's setting (e.g., in "Ferir quel petto, Silvio?") appear very casual, if they are present at all.

[71] In lines 1268–74, not set by Monteverdi, Silvio offers Dorinda her revenge, saying that he deserves no less cruelty than he had meted out to her because of his pride.

[72] The lines omitted between the *prima* and the *seconda parte* (ll. 304–31) have Mirtillo saying that his love is as constant as the forces of nature, ending with the question of whether Amarilli will at least take pity on his death. The smaller cut in the *terza parte* (ll. 356–58) is a rather convoluted parenthetical insertion.

penar per Amarilli," which is yet another declaration by Mirtillo, taken from Act III, scene 6, of how sweet it is to suffer over Amarilli. Here he is speaking directly to Corisca as she seeks to persuade him of the futility of his undying love. But although "Ch'io t'ami" and "M'è più dolce il penar" have an interlocutor on stage, they can easily enough be read as soliloquies when removed from the play as a polyphonic madrigal.

In these *Pastor fido* settings, the situation is different from the narrative structure of epic, wherein even the mimesis is still narrated and therefore enables a certain detachment of the music from the text. While one might argue over the proper voicing of a Tancredi or an Armida, having a five-voice narrator is not per se implausible: a polyphonic setting can legitimately speak for itself. When it comes to Mirtillo, Amarilli, Silvio, and Dorinda, however, the same seems not to apply save by way of some narratological sleight of hand such as placing an implied "he said" or "she said" prior to each madrigal.[73] Moreover, although mimetic passages within epic tend to be relatively short and focused, especially in the case of dialogic exchanges, equivalent passages in drama are not. And while Guarini's play is in *versi sciolti*, his extensive use of enjambment creates a form of lyric prose with fewer rhymes, meaning that phrases are less clearly delineated in ways that might help the composer. In the long Dorinda/Silvio exchange in the Fifth Book, Monteverdi plods along in the enlivened homophony that served him well enough in his settings of the mimetic voice in epic (as in "Vivrò fra i miei tormenti e le mie cure" in the Third Book), but now at much greater length. He cuts lines when he can (ll. 1268–74); he plays with different voice-groupings (but not to any gendered effect); he tries to find words or phrases—or just exclamations (often marked by an entry of the bass voice)—that will allow for at least some musical expansion; he sneaks in some rhetorical repetitions until the relentless text forces him on; he modifies Guarini's syntax to break up his very long sentences;[74] and at one point in the *seconda parte*, he even adds a line ("dolcissima parola") to try to bring in some further musical interest both harmonically and contrapuntally (it gets juxtaposed with Guarini's "voce cortese e pia").[75] He also creates some quite stunningly beautiful vocal sonorities and harmonic shifts: this is Monteverdi, after all. But if this is what he means for music's subservience to the delivery of a text within the *seconda pratica*, it runs the risk of becoming very wearing in the end, unless the point is to challenge performers somehow to pull it off (few can).

It is important to note that of all these settings, only the scene between Dorinda and Silvio ("Ecco, Silvio, colei" and its subsequent *parti*) forces an indelible connection with *Il pastor fido* in the senses that it makes scant sense outside of the play, and that it involves a direct dialogue between two characters from it. The others can

---

[73] Coluzzi, *Guarini's "Il pastor fido" and the Madrigal*, 335.
[74] In "Deh, bella e cara e sì soave un tempo" (the *seconda parte* of "Ch'io t'ami, e t'ami più de la mia vita"), Monteverdi's "chi mi scorse ad amare" for Guarini's "che mi..." forces the "chi" to mark the beginning of a new sentence rather than a relative clause. Georis (*Claudio Monteverdi*, 476) does not note this discrepancy.
[75] For the addition, see Georis, *Claudio Monteverdi*, 468 n. 9.

work as freestanding lyric madrigals, albeit long ones. This alone should prompt some caution over the common view of their role in Monteverdi's trajectory toward the creation of a new form of dramatic music.[76] They are often read as being proto-operatic, and indeed as proof that the sixteenth-century madrigal would find its consummation in some form of musical drama. This hinges in part on the notion that they were somehow intended for use in the production of *Il pastor fido* in Mantua in November 1598, with Monteverdi then performing the same exercise as he later did with the *Lamento d'Arianna*, rearranging as a polyphonic madrigal a setting originally for solo voice and instrumental accompaniment. There is no doubt that music was used in that Mantuan production both in the lavish *intermedi* that accompanied the play and within the play itself: notably in the *Giuoco della cieca* in Act III, scene 2, and, probably, for the end-of-act choruses.[77] But the idea that its principal characters somehow delivered lines in an early attempt at musical recitative scarcely seems credible. No one suggests that the entire play could have been delivered in that manner, so we are left with the odd notion that its lead characters occasionally interjected musical delivery into their long speeches. Songs were not uncommon in Renaissance spoken comedies, but they were most often introduced in plausibly realistic ways: that is, as "songs." That hardly applies here. Moreover, converting the polyphonic *Pastor fido* settings in the Fifth Book back to some kind of solo-voice version would seem harder even than in the case of the *Lamento d'Arianna*.[78]

There is no strong reason, however, to link them directly to the theater; indeed, some of the texts Monteverdi set here were cut from the performance of the play in Mantua on 22 November 1598.[79] Monteverdi makes scant effort to identify a single "speaking" voice, which is something that concerns him more in the continuo madrigals at the end of the Fifth Book setting Guarini's lyric, not dramatic, poetry. But he certainly cares about what is being said, and the polyphonic madrigal had long been adept at such expressive explorations. At least two of the settings that Artusi encountered in Ferrara in November 1598 had been performed twice during a musical evening at the residence of Antonio Goretti, suggesting that they were a matter of some curiosity and discussion.[80] In the dedication of the Fifth

---

[76] Compare Tomlinson, *Monteverdi and the End of the Renaissance*, 114–31; it leads him to say surprisingly little about the Fifth Book settings themselves save where their gestures become adopted (or transformed) in the solo-voice *Lamento d'Arianna*. Ossi (*Divining the Oracle*, 10) also views the Fifth Book as "a first point of arrival in Monteverdi's search for musical drama," an argument he pursues in his subsequent detailed account of the book itself.

[77] Act III, scene 2—in which Amarilli's companions play a game of blindman's buff to get her and Mirtillo in contact with each other—contains four choruses. Gastoldi published music for them in his Fourth Book a5 (1602), and it seems likely that it was used in 1598. His setting of a portion of the chorus ending Act II ("Ciechi mortali, voi che tanta sete") is in the same book. However, no music for the other choruses survives that could plausibly have been used in Mantua.

[78] Thus, they are quite different from the two *Pastor fido* settings in Salamone Rossi's First Book a5 (1600) among the six that have an accompaniment in chitarrone tablature, potentially allowing a performance for solo voice (the Canto) in addition to a polyphonic one.

[79] Coluzzi, *Guarini's "Il pastor fido" and the Madrigal*, 86–87.

[80] In *L'Artusi, overo Delle imperfettioni della moderna musica* (1600), fol. 39r, Artusi's "Luca" says that the madrigals were sung "una, et due volte" and that they made a good overall impression ("era la tessitura non ingrata").

Book to Vincenzo Gonzaga, Monteverdi noted that the duke had deigned to hear its contents in his royal chambers ("regie camere") when they were in manuscript; that they were particularly appreciated (the duke "diede segno di singolarmente gradirli"); and that as a result, the composer was placed in charge of his musical establishment. Gastoldi suggested something similar in his own collection of *Pastor fido* madrigals, his Fourth Book *a*5 of 1602, where he noted how various of his settings (he does not say which) had found favor in concerts done in Mantua.[81] There can be no doubt that all these madrigals reflect the current mania for *Il pastor fido*, and by extension, for Guarini (the poet responsible for all but three settings in the Fifth book). Equally, the controversial play was a matter of debate in many different circles. But these musical settings clearly had a place within the chamber rather than on the stage.

More striking, in fact, is Monteverdi's apparent fascination with Mirtillo's feelings about Amarilli and vice versa, which take up four settings in the Fifth Book. If "Cruda Amarilli," the first, was one cause of Monteverdi's downfall in his encounter with Artusi, by the last madrigal of the book before the six continuo settings—"M'è più dolce il penar per Amarilli"—he seems to have decided to agree with Mirtillo that it is indeed "sweet" to suffer over her, and that he would not renounce his "cruel Amarilli" for any other. It is a powerful biographical statement. But Monteverdi did not produce any further settings from *Il pastor fido*: having worked through the angst of Artusi's attack on him, he was ready to move in new directions.

Monteverdi says . . .

Treating "M'è più dolce il penar" as some kind of personal declaration from the composer might seem to be a dangerous strategy. Monteverdi can speak for, or as, anyone he chooses, but it is also worth paying attention to when he speaks as himself. Poets are able to do this easily enough by interjecting a comment that seems to come from outside the text: the final line of Tasso's "Non si levava ancor l'alba novella" in the Second Book is an obvious case in point. Monteverdi can respond accordingly. But he can also manipulate a poem to insert his voice more forcefully still.

The last six madrigals of the Fifth Book reveal the possibilities in various ways. They return to the familiar world of texts that might complain about the pains of love but manage to deal with them in short order, and certainly in less time than the multiple acts of a pastoral play. Monteverdi sets them apart by noting on the title page of the book that they in particular require an instrumental accompaniment (for harpsichord, chitarrone, or other such instrument) by way of a basso

---

[81] Gastoldi dedicated the book to Camillo Gonzaga, Conte di Novellara, on 10 April 1602, noting, first, how the count had distinguished himself in the tournaments held in Mantua during the previous Carnival, and second, that he had given clear signs of his musical taste by taking delight in "alcune mie composizioni" sung "ne' concerti del nostro Serenissimo Prencipe."

continuo, which is optional ("a beneplacito") for the others. This was not entirely new. Salamone Rossi's First Book *a5* (1600) had included in the Canto partbook a chitarrone tablature for six of its madrigals, implying the possibility of some kind of performance as solo songs, and his Second (1602), Third (1603), and Fourth (1610) provided a part for basso continuo in that same partbook. However, Monteverdi's "optional" continuo parts do not seem to allow for reduced vocal forces, and the last six madrigals in the Fifth Book are nothing like Rossi's.

In all but those last madrigals, the continuo functions mostly as a *basso seguente*: that is, duplicating the lowest sounding voice, which is not always the bass.[82] However, there are exceptions. At the end of "Ma se con la pietà non è in te spenta" (the *seconda parte* of "Ecco, Silvio, colei che in odio hai tanto"), the wounded Dorinda says that she would die happily if Silvio just uttered some tender word such as "Go in peace, my beloved" ("Va in pace, anima mia"). She does indeed seem to be failing by the minute: in the final measures, "Va in pace..." is delivered by AT and then just SS. However, the "optional" continuo provides a bassline on its own to support the final cadence and therefore seems essential unless it was just placed there haphazardly. Modern performers have to decide whether to include it or not.

In the case of the six madrigals which require a continuo, it still tends to act as a *basso seguente* when supporting the full ensemble—which is not, in fact, surprising—and so it is not harmonically necessary at those points. Elsewhere, however, it is. The difference is clear in the first of them, "Ahi come a un vago sol cortese giro." This presents a vocal scoring that is wholly unprecedented in Monteverdi's output: SSTTB. Almost all his previous madrigals have been for some version of SSATB (whether in low or high clefs), and indeed his only previous madrigals with two tenor parts were "Filli cara et amata" in the First Book, and "Cor mio, non mori? E mori!" and "Longe da te, cor mio" in the Fourth. Yet in "Ahi come a un vago sol," the strongest of leads is taken by those two tenors: Monteverdi now had some good ones in his ensemble in Mantua (see Chapter 4). They also sing in the modern style, with extensive vocal embellishments. Likewise, "Amor, se giusto sei" casts the spotlight on Monteverdi's best singers in turn: a soprano for lines 1–3 of the text, a bass for the "io" in lines 4–5, and a tenor for lines 6–7—only then does the full ensemble enter for the final four lines of the poem. That division of the text is sensible enough. The soprano is the lover (male) asking Love to make his beloved act justly; the bass says that he loves her but she torments him; and the tenor adds that she is fickle.[83] It is then up to the full ensemble to make the final plea to Love ("Non sostener, Amore..."): that in his kingdom, disdain should not be the reward for fidelity, and

---

[82] In his 1615 editions of the Third and Fourth Books, the Antwerp printer Pierre Phalèse provided instrumental *basso seguente* parts for them (also with some indication of intended harmonies), but purely on his own initiative, it seems.

[83] The tenor's accusation is set in a manner already heard for five voices in "Ma tu, più che mai dura" (the *terza parte* of "Ch'io t'ami, e t'ami più de la mia vita") as Mirtillo accuses Amarilli of refusing to speak even as he dies ("e l'armi d'una sola / sdegnosa e cruda voce").

Table 5.2 Text and scoring in "Troppo ben può questo tiranno Amore" (Fifth Book, 1605; "Ms" is S² in C2 clef, slightly lower than S¹ in C1).

SMsATB	Troppo ben può questo tiranno Amore, poi che non val fuggire a chi no 'l può soffrire.	This tyrant Love is too powerful! For useless is it to flee for one who cannot suffer him.
S	Quand'io penso tal'hor com'arde e punge,	When I think how he burns and strikes,
S (+ MsATB)	io dico:	I say:
S	«Ah, core stolto.	"Ah, foolish heart,
MsATB (+ S)	Non l'aspettar, che fai?	do not wait for him, what are you doing?
	Fuggilo sì che non ti prenda mai.»	Flee him so that he never catches you."
S	Ma non so com'il lusinghier mi giunge,	But I know not how the flatterer reaches me
S (+ MsATB)	ch'io dico:	such that I say:
S	«Ah, core sciolto.	"Ah, heart unchained,
MsATB (+ S)	Perché fuggito l'hai? Prendilo sì che non ti fugga mai.»	why have you fled him? Seize him so that he never flees you."

the recompense for love should be love returned. The conversations between the singers often lying hidden within the polyphonic madrigal now come out into the open. Here we have five singers (plus an instrumentalist) in apparent conversation: S, B, and T each make their point one after the other, and SSATB agree on the matter to be addressed by the god of love.

Monteverdi's polyphonic madrigals also use contrasted vocal groupings that can stand apart within the full ensemble but then merge into it. However, the presence of the continuo means that any single voice can be represented by a single singer rather than two or three of them, and therefore that even a text in a single poetic voice can be parsed in different ways. Another of the continuo madrigals in the Fifth Book, "Troppo ben può questo tiranno Amore," is a case in point (Table 5.2).[84] In fact, Monteverdi has been sneaky here. The gender-neutral poetic voice begins with a statement about the excessive power of Love; it reports on, and quotes, what it ("I") says when considering Love's ability to strike (flee him at all costs); it then returns to a statement on how Love still manages to insinuate himself; and it finally quotes a response (seize him). The eleven-line text breaks down into 3 + 4 + 4 lines. The two four-line groups match in terms of meter and rhyme, and Monteverdi does what one might expect: the last three lines of each group each have exactly the same music (with an extension for the end of the second), and the music for the first of

---

[84] Monteverdi's text conflates different versions of Guarini's poem, also causing a grammatical slip; see Georis, *Claudio Monteverdi*, 73–74. My parsing of it differs quite markedly from the chart in Ossi, *Divining the Oracle*, 78.

them is not so different.[85] But that musical repetition means that he can perform the same trick twice.

Monteverdi begins logically enough with the full ensemble for the opening statement. He also shifts to a solo soprano for the first "I" moment ("Quand'io..."). Each time we reach a "speaking" verb ("io dico" and "ch'io dico"), Monteverdi uses the full ensemble with the same music, although the soprano is kept distinct by way of an embellishment. The beginnings of each passage of direct speech are also allocated to the solo soprano, who therefore seems to speak on behalf of the ensemble. But Monteverdi crucially changes the position of the closing quotation marks. The poetic voice addresses its "foolish" heart and then its "unchained" one, each time posing a question about Love ("Non l'aspettar, che fai?" and "Perché fuggito l'hai?"). Monteverdi's setting handles it differently. The solo soprano has the vocatives ("Ah, core stolto" and "Ah, core sciolto"), but the questions are instead placed in the lower voices, who therefore appear to address the soprano, not the heart, as "you." The soprano then submits to asking the question and joins the full ensemble in the imperatives that follow, offering the advice first to flee Love ("Fuggilo...") and then to seize him ("Prendilo..."). The triple play is quite delicious: the soprano speaks with the ensemble, then on its behalf, but the ensemble speaks to the soprano before everyone agrees first on one thing and then on its opposite.

The notion that the ensemble can speak as a group in response to statements by one or more singers individualized within it poses an obvious question: On whose behalf is the ensemble speaking? Following the conversational model, the ensemble would seem to be the group of friends supporting one or more of their number in emotional turmoil. At times, however, the ensemble's comments seem to come from an outside observer. Two of the six continuo madrigals in the Fifth Book set texts that were the first and third of three in Guarini's *Rime* (in both the 1598 and 1599 editions) grouped under the heading "Recidiva d'amore" (a relapse of, or into, love), each of them in a gender-neutral voice. "Ahi come a un vago sol cortese giro" and "E così, a poco a poco" deal with that relapse in various ways, in the first case caused by the beloved's eyes, and in the second, the gaze. Each also ends with a one-line aphorism that stands alone, not assigned directly to the speaker's voice even if it plausibly comes from it.[86]

"Ahi come a un vago sol" has the poetic "I" voiced by two tenors in virtuosic vein. The final aphorism, that any wound from Love never heals ("Ah, che piaga d'Amor non sana mai"), is presented more straightforwardly by the full ensemble, as one would expect. However, Monteverdi also interjects that final line twice earlier in the

---

[85] Pirrotta ("Monteverdi's Poetic Choices," 296–97) views the text as a *ballata* missing its final *volta*. This is how Guarini cast it in his *Rime*, although the first version of the poem (in Licino's *Rime di diversi celebri poeti dell'età nostra* of 1587) was longer (fourteen lines rather than eleven) and less regular.

[86] The middle one in Guarini's three-poem sequence, "Oimè, l'antica fiamma," has the same final-line aphorism as in "E così, a poco a poco." The latter, in turn, repeats the "Ah, che piaga d'Amore" exclamation in "Ahi come a un vago sol cortese giro" with a different continuation. For Monteverdi's tendency in general to select texts that were contiguous or nearly so in his poetic sources, see Georis, *Claudio Monteverdi*, 53–55.

poem, in both cases delivered by SAB (without TT), making it a refrain; by the end, it is the only line that has been sung by the entire ensemble. He does the same thing in "E così, a poco a poco," set for six voices (SSATTB). An S^1T^1 duet represents the lover(s) returning like a moth to the flame, while AT^2B interject the final aphorism in mid-stream: that extinguishing an old flame just makes it immortal ("Chi spegne antico incendio il fa immortale"). This final line gets treated more expansively at the end by the full ensemble, including a late-entering S^2. Something similar occurs in "Qui rise, o Tirsi, e qui ver' me rivolse" in the Sixth Book (a comment on the happy memory of a joyful day). These constructed refrains are often read as Monteverdi's seeking to bring new types of formal organization into the madrigal.[87] But one might also plausibly ask whether they are intended as interjections by Monteverdi himself.

That possibility hinges on the ambiguity over the status of these one-line aphorisms—whether they are delivered by the poetic voice on the inside, or by the poet's voice from the outside. Monteverdi has to make a choice, and he tends to treat them as comments by the ensemble responding to things said by individual singers within it, and with which those singers eventually agree. But the highly unusual step of interjecting them in the middle of the setting also gives Monteverdi some agency in the matter. Add to that his use of "Ah, che piaga d'Amore non sana mai" to make an overt reference to Pallavicino (see Chapter 2), and something quite personal emerges. The ensemble speaks not just for itself, but also for Monteverdi, or even better, as him. Monteverdi, in turn, takes a double role, as the "I" of any poem, or the "we" who respond to it.

This forces further thought about those earlier polyphonic madrigals wherein the texture permitted reading them as some kind of dialogue or other form of exchange. It is certainly possible to read "Crudel, perché mi fuggi" (Second Book) and "Luci serene e chiare" (Fourth) as involving a discussion between a lover and a beloved ending in harmonious agreement, but that agreement is generally expressed by way of a statement referring to a third-person "one" or "it" somehow separate from any previous "I" or "you": that one needs a heart to feel love's anguish, or that the miracle of love is that the soul can die without pain. Indeed, any poem that ends with such a statement is going to raise the question of who is making it, whether any character(s) presented in the poem or someone standing outside it. That "someone" might just as well be Monteverdi, fashioning a narrative, and commenting upon it, in ways that best suited his purpose, whether in sympathy or with some detachment.

---

[87] Ossi, *Divining the Oracle*, 77–79. Ossi then relates this to a type of formalist musical thinking to be found in the canzonettas of the 1607 *Scherzi musicali*, and also in *Orfeo*.

6
Songbirds

The two-tenor opening of "Ahi come a un vago sol cortese giro" in the Fifth Book exploits the new types of ornamented singing that had become highly prized during Monteverdi's lifetime. He then provides textbook examples of them in his setting of Battista Guarini's "Mentre vaga Angioletta" in the Eighth Book.[1] This also offers a lesson in listening as Monteverdi musically instructs his audiences—performers and listeners alike—on how best to respond to his music:

> Mentre vaga Angioletta
> ogni anima gentil cantando alletta,
> corre il mio core, e pende
> tutto dal suon di quel soave canto;
> e non so come intanto
> musico spirto prende,
> fauci canore, e seco forma e finge
> per non usata via
> garrula e maestrevole armonia.

[While charming Angioletta / entices every well-born soul with her singing, / my heart races and hangs / completely on the sound of that sweet song; / and I know not how, in the meantime, / it takes on a musical spirit,[2] / songful jaws, and with them shapes and feigns, / in an unaccustomed manner, / a garrulous and masterful harmony.]

"Angioletta" can be a personal name or a "little angel," but either way, her ability to entice the "well-born soul" is not enough for the poet, who experiences something far more profound. His heart hangs completely on the sound ("suono") of the voice, taking on a musical spirit that then moves in sympathetic vibration to it:

---

[1] For "Mentre vaga Angioletta," see Carter, "Listening to Music in Early Modern Italy," 44–48. There is a more in-depth treatment in Wistreich, "Inclosed in this tabernacle of flesh" (from which I also borrow aspects of the translation of the poem). The text I give here generally follows the reading in Guarini's *Rime* (1598), fols. 130v–131r, from which Monteverdi has some minor variants; see Georis, *Claudio Monteverdi*, 654–56.

[2] The syntax is problematic: the subject of "prende" in line 6 is sometimes taken to be the "musico spirto" that takes on songful jaws.

> Tempra d'arguto suon pieghevol voce,
> e la volve e la spinge
> con rotti accenti e con ritorti giri
> qui tarda, e là veloce;
> . . .

[It tempers with sparkling sound the lissom voice, / and turns it and pushes it / with broken accents and twisting turns / here slowly, and there quickly . . .]

Again, the emphasis is on "suono": we are never told exactly what Angioletta is singing, and it does not matter so far as the heart is concerned. Guarini then continues at great length with yet more detail of such sonorous acrobatics, switching at the end to the consequences of their action:

> Così cantando e ricantando, il core,
> o miracol d'amore,
> è fatto un usignuolo,
> e spiega già per non star meco il volo.[3]

[Singing thus and singing again, the heart, / oh miracle of love, / becomes a nightingale, / and spreads its wings in flight so as not to stay within me.]

Monteverdi's setting was unusual enough to require some performance rubrics within the Eighth Book. It begins with a solo tenor on *a* much in the manner of Testo in the *Combattimento* (was it for the same singer?), although in "Mentre vaga Angioletta" he is unaccompanied. The opening therefore establishes a narrative mode, although Guarini's speaker, and Monteverdi's singer, then become more and more entranced by the musical experience: the musical *passaggio* on "corre il mio core" might just be word-painting, but it opens up a different world. The continuo enters only after sixteen measures, with a resonant minor triad on *G* struck as the tenor feels the onset of a "musical spirit" that is quite literally ensounded by the instrument.[4] Then comes a second surprise: the "garrulous and masterful harmony" created by the heart, or its musical spirit, needs two tenors, not just one—the second starts as an echo but increasingly asserts its own presence as the singers now try to outdo each other in virtuosic display. Then the double-voiced heart, singing and singing again, miraculously becomes a single nightingale, taking flight on wings of song. At "Così cantando e ricantando," Monteverdi shifts to a gloriously

---

[3] Monteverdi has "per non star mesto il volo" (and spreads its wings in flight so as not to remain sad), which also appears in earlier versions of Guarini's poem; see, for example, *Della nova scelta di rime . . . parte prima*, ed. Varoli (1590), 73–74.

[4] Monteverdi notes in the Tenore Primo partbook, "Qui entra l'istromento." The use of the singular is revealing, but the type of "instrument" is ambiguous unless we read it as a typical reference to a harpsichord.

lyrical triple time as we move from narration into a quite different kind of musical statement.

"Mentre vaga Angioletta" is the third of the "Canti amorosi" in the Eighth Book. The second is the setting of Petrarch's sonnet "Vago augelletto che cantando vai" (*RVF* 353; just the two quatrains), for seven voices (SSATTTB), two violins, a *violone* ("contrabasso"), and continuo.[5] Here it is the violins that provide an additional layer of "sound" as the speaker, represented by the late-entering T^3, hopes that the "vago augelletto" (charming bird) that sings as winter approaches might come to share its song with him in his grief. The intended resonance between the "vago augelletto" and "vaga Angioletta"—at least so far as the arrangement of the Eighth Book is concerned—is obvious, and it may also explain why Monteverdi adopts an early reading of the end of Guarini's poem, where the heart-as-nightingale spreads its wings in flight so as not to stay sad ("e spiega già per non star mesto il volo"): thus, the heart's doubled singing is meant to ease grief. Guarini's final version with the transcendent heart ("per non star meco il volo") is more concerned with the same out-of-body experience in response to virtuoso singing that Matteo Caberloti claimed was achieved by Monteverdi's son Francesco, a "humanized bird" whose vocal brilliance transported the listener onto a different plane (see Chapter 4). For the composer, however, that singing has a different purpose: to turn one emotion into another.

Nightingales

The music theorist Lodovico Zacconi made a similar connection between singers and songbirds in his treatise *Prattica di musica* (1596) when discussing how performers should add ornaments to their vocal lines:

> Embellishments and accents are made by splitting and breaking the notes every time that within a *tactus* or half of one a number of notes are added of a kind that are delivered quickly. They cause such pleasure and delight that we seem to hear a great many well-taught birds that with their singing seize our heart, and leave us very contented by their song.[6]

---

[5] The rubric in the Basso Continuo partbook is a little odd: "Vago augelletto" is headed "A 6 e 7 voci con doi violini e un contrabasso." The "seventh" voice is a third tenor, which enters at the second quatrain, where the text shifts to the poetic "I."

[6] Lodovico Zacconi, *Prattica di musica utile et necessaria si al compositore per comporre i canti suoi regolatamente, si anco al cantore per assicurarsi in tutte le cose cantabili* (Venice: Bartolomeo Carampello, 1596), fol. 58r (chap. 66: "Che stile si tenghi nel far di gorgia, et dell'uso de i moderni passaggi"): "Le vaghezze, et gli accenti si sono fatti col spezzar, et rompere delle figure, tutta volta che in un tatto, ò mezzo si aggiunge una quantità di figure che hanno natura di esser velocemente pronuntiate: le quali rendano tanto piacere, et diletto, che ci pare d'udir tanti bene amaestrati Augelli, che col cantar loro ci rapiscono il cuore, et ci fanno rimanere del cantar loro molto ben contenti."

But Guarini's command of musical terminology in "Mentre vaga Angioletta"—all those *accenti*, *giri*, and the like—is more apparent than real, given that his account of these vocal gymnastics is lifted almost word for word from Pliny the Elder's (23–79 CE) *Naturalis historia*, 10.43, which provides a lengthy account of how the nightingale sings nonstop for a fortnight to announce the arrival of spring, and engages in songful competition with its rivals even to the point of death, singing its heart out, as it were.[7] Guarini makes a version of this his final point: just as nightingales compete with one another, so does the listener's double-voiced heart vie to match the movements of the singer's throat, and with mortal consequences. This is another reason that Monteverdi sets the text as a duet.

Did birdsong count as music? St. Augustine answered strongly in the negative: some sounds of the animal world might appear "musical," but they lacked the rational foundation to grant them the status of "art." However pleasant these sounds might sometimes be, their wordlessness could also seduce the listener down dangerous paths that were often gendered feminine.[8] But the mythological origins of that most musical of birds, the nightingale, opened up both sides of the debate. According to Ovid's *Metamorphoses* (customarily dated to 8 CE), 6: 401–674, Procne was married to Tereus, King of Thrace, who raped her sister, Philomela, cut out her tongue, and left her abandoned in the woods. The sisters gained their revenge by having Tereus eat the flesh of his and Procne's son (Itys); he pursued them in fury; and they escaped by way of metamorphosis—Procne into a swallow and Philomela, a nightingale. Thus, the nightingale's song became strongly associated with the disembodied human voice expressing some manner of lament.

Several treatises document the interest in avian utterances in early-seventeenth-century Italy, including Antonio Valli da Todi's discussion of sixty types of songbirds in *Il canto de gl'augelli: opera nova . . . dove si dichiara la natura di sessanta sorte di ucelli, che cantano per esperienza* (Rome: Heirs of Nicolò Mutii, 1601), and another that borrows heavily from it: Giovanni Pietro Olina's *Uccelliera, overo Discorso della natura e proprietà di diversi uccelli e in particolare di que' che cantano* (Rome: Andrea Fei, 1622).[9] Olina says in the preface to his treatise that there are many things one might discuss concerning birds, but he has decided to focus on what interests him most about them: the admirable sweetness of a song that comes from such small

---

[7] *The Natural History of Pliny*, trans. John Bostock and H. T. Riley, vol. 2 (London, 1855), 510. Guarini himself acknowledged the connection. In a letter of 20 August 1581, he told Duke Alfonso II d'Este that in writing the poem he had attempted something not done before save for attempts by Pliny and Ariosto; see Durante and Martellotti, *Cronistoria del concerto delle dame principalissime di Margherita Gonzaga d'Este*, 145. Guarini does not further identify his two sources, but the second is Ariosto's *Carmen* 18 in praise of a singer called Giulia ("Qualem scientem carminis et lyra").

[8] I present here a vastly oversimplified summary of the far more complex, and nuanced, reading in Leach, *Sung Birds*.

[9] Antonio Valli was the fowler to Cardinal Girolamo Rusticucci (to whom the treatise is dedicated), and he cared enough about his text to secure a ten-year privilege from Pope Clement VIII protecting its copyright, probably because of its extensive series of engravings of individual birds by the noted artist Antonio Tempesta. Olina's treatise is dedicated to Cassiano dal Pozzo (1588–1657), a famed scholar, collector, and patron who also had some musical interests; see Dragosits, *Giovanni Girolamo Kapsperger*, 191–97.

bodies but that fills the air, woods, and fields with varied and strange melodies that exceed the abilities of what even the best-trained singers can produce from their more robust vocal apparatus.[10] The marvel of birdsong is that its "melodia" offers an out-of-body experience ("qual maraviglia s'io confessarò di sentirmi rapir fuori di me stesso, da qualunque melodia") with an impact no different from the way that the music of Orpheus and Amphyion moved the natural world. Moreover,

> if of all musical instruments, the ones most prized are those that most realistically resemble the variations of the human voice, we see every day that the efforts and study of excellent singers are no more focused on anything other than on resembling the movements, the rests, the fugues, the passages, the lingerings, the interruptions, the suspensions, the re-foldings, the turns, the jagged ornaments, the variation of sound production—clear, veiled, full, thin, high, low, bottom, middle, elevated, fast, slow, sparkling, and restrained in tone—and the changing of all the aforesaid movements together through which the *melodia* of birds causes us such unbelievable delight . . .[11]

Zacconi said the same thing. But in fact, Olina's terminology is slippery. His association of "melodia" with birdsong ignores Plato's careful definition of the constituent parts of *melos* as oration, harmony, and rhythm (as cited in Giulio Cesare Monteverdi's defense of the *seconda pratica*). Given that birdsong lacks words, it cannot produce *melodia* in the proper sense of the term. But another Roman amateur musician took the same liberty. Gratioso Uberti was a jurist in Rome who moved in the circles of the Papal curia, and in 1630 he published his *Contrasto musico* (Rome: Lodovico Grignani), a "musical debate" intended for the "delight" of its readers and constructed as a dialogue between two characters called Severo (Stern) and Giocondo (Cheerful).[12] Severo attacks music both on personal grounds (he hates the caterwauling coming from the music school near his house) and by way of a barrage of citations from Classical sources, the Bible, and the Church Fathers. Giocondo defends it in similar legalistic ways, also taking Severo on a tour of places in Rome where music is performed, and justifying its efficacy in each one.

---

[10] According to Olina's preface, "mi son sentito rapire da occulta violenza, ad ammirare con desiderio di godere l'amabile soavità del canto, che da un così picciolo corpicciuolo uscendo, et altamente risonando di tanto varia, e strana melodia riempie l'Aria, e le Selve, e le Campagne, che in vano con lei gareggiano le più canore fauci, et i più robusti petti degl'esercitatissimi cantori." Athanasius Kircher was similarly fascinated by different birdsongs in Book 1 of his *Musurgia universalis* (1650) to the extent of transcribing them in musical notation, paying special attention to the nightingale.

[11] "Perché se tutti gli stromenti musici tanto più son prezzati, quanto più al vivo rassomigliano il variar dell'humana voce, tutto il dì veggiamo, che lo sforzo, e lo studio degl'eccellenti Cantori non è altrove impiegato, che nel rassomigliare i movimenti, i riposi, le fughe, i passaggi, le dimore, i rompimenti, le sospensioni, i ripiegamenti, i giri, le tirate, i precipitii, il variare del mormorante, chiaro, fosco, pieno, sottile, acuto, grave, basso, mezano, elevato, frettoloso, lento, frizzante, e dimesso tuono, e l'alterar di tutti i detti movimenti insieme, onde incredibilmente ci diletta la melodia degl'Uccelli, e di quelli massimamente, che nel seguente discorso sono espressi."

[12] Gratioso Uberti, *Contrasto musico: opera dilettevole* (Rome: Lodovico Grignani, 1630), facs. ed. Giancarlo Rostirolla, "Musurgiana" 5 (Lucca: Libreria Musicale Italiana, 1991); all following references are to the original pagination. Uberti's treatise is discussed further in Carter, "Listening to Music in Early Modern Italy."

One of cranky Severo's many complaints about music—made during his and Giocondo's visit to a princely apartment—is that he can never understand the text as it is delivered by singers. Giocondo's cheerful response is to invoke the origins of music in burbling streams, garrulous birds, and whistling breezes (citing Lucretius, *De rerum natura*, 5: 1379–91), none of which, he says, needs words:

> it is therefore not cause for reproof even if when many sing together that one does not understand precisely the words, which properly belong to poetry, for it suffices to hear the *melodia*, which is proper to music.[13]

Severo persists: those who sing solo to the instrument make so many *passaggi*, *gorgie*, and *trilli* that the words are lost to all understanding. Giocondo responds by reverting to definitions: "canto" properly refers to a solo voice, and "melodia" to voices singing together, just as "suono" refers to a single instrument and "sinfonia" to many. But the "canto" of a solo voice with embellishments causes great delight, and it seems to be the song of the nightingale described so elegantly by Pliny, whom Giocondo quotes at length.[14] Thus,

> from this description one can gather that the sweetness of song [*canto*] does not consist of delivering and making understood the words, but in the sweetness of the voice, in the variety of the sound, now low, now high, now slow, now diminished.[15]

This would seem to be an extraordinary admission, given the emphasis on the clear and effective rhetorical and expressive delivery of the text presumed to lie at the heart of the *seconda pratica* and of other similar aesthetic positions held around 1600. No less striking, however, is the ongoing slippage in use of the word "melodia." We might forgive Olina for it, but Uberti knew exactly what he was doing: he cited the standard Platonic reading elsewhere in his treatise, yet almost as a historical curiosity, to be quoted when useful but otherwise ignored. However, the meaning of *melodia* was shifting from the whole musical package (oration, harmony, and rhythm) to some lyrical quality within it. This has a strong bearing on the emergence of new types of expressive triple-time writing in the 1620s and 1630s.

---

[13] Uberti, *Contrasto musico*, 83: "non è dunque cosa di riprensione, ancorché quando molti cantano insieme, non s'intendano precisamente le parole, che proprie sono della Poesia; perche basta di sentire la melodìa, propria della musica."

[14] Ibid., 84: "*Sev.* Hora sento, che canta una voce sola con l'instromento; ma fà tanti passaggi, tante gorgie, e trilli, che si perde qualche parola, che non s'intende. *Gioc.* Il canto si dice propriamente di una voce sola, e melodìa di più voci concertate. Come anco suono si dice di un solo stromento, e sinfonia di molti accordati insieme. Il canto d'una voce sola con passaggi, gorgie, e trilli diletta assai, sembra il canto del Rosignuolo, descritto elegantemente da Plinio…"

[15] Ibid., 85: "da questa descrittione si può raccogliere, che la dolcezza del canto, non consiste nel proferire, e fare intendere le parole; ma nella soavità della voce, nella varietà del suono, hor grave, hor acuto, hor tardo, hor diminuto."

Table 6.1 Monteverdi madrigal books (Second to Eighth) with texts mentioning birds (*augello, us[c]ignolo, rossignuolo*, etc.).

Second	"Non si levava ancor l'alba novella" (Tasso); "Intorno a due vermiglie e vaghe labra"; "Ecco mormorar l'onde" (Tasso)
Third	"O rossignuol ch'in queste verdi fronde" (Bembo)
Fourth	"Io mi son giovinetta" (Boccaccio); "Quell'augellin, che canta" (Guarini)
Fifth	"Questi vaghi concenti"
Sixth	"Zefiro torna e 'l bel tempo rimena" (Petrarch); "A Dio, Florida bella, il cor piagato" (Marino); "Presso un fiume tranquillo" (Marino)
Seventh	"O come sei gentile" (Guarini); "Augellin che la voce al canto spieghi"
Eighth	"Or che 'l ciel e la terra e 'l vento tace" (Petrarch); "Ogni amante è guerrier: nel suo gran regno" (Rinuccini); "Vago augelletto che cantando vai" (Petrarch); "Mentre vaga Angioletta" (Guarini); "Dolcissimo uscignolo" (Guarini); "Su, su, su, pastorelli"

Not for nothing is early modern lyric poetry full of warbling songbirds—usually the nightingale. Monteverdi's first eight books of madrigals include plenty of settings that mention birds in one or other capacity with texts by the likes of Petrarch, Pietro Bembo, Torquato Tasso, Battista Guarini, and Giambattista Marino (Table 6.1). These birds echo the happy state of the lover or console the sadness of the unrequited; both the bird and the lover are imprisoned within a cage (real or metaphorical) created by the beloved; the bird might serve as messenger between a couple unable to communicate in any other way; or the lover-singer engages in a competition with the bird to the mortal peril of now one, and now the other.[16]

Any reference to birds is almost certain to prompt some musical representation. It cannot be a coincidence that the first quatrain of Monteverdi's "O rossignuol ch'in queste verdi fronde" (Third Book) excludes the two lower voices to focus on a high-voice trio that may have been intended for the Pellizzari ensemble. In the *concertato* madrigals, birdsong almost always prompts vocal acrobatics. They might just be contained within a short flourish, as for a bird flying to its favorite food in "A Dio, Florida bella, il cor piagato" in the Sixth Book, or they can be more extended within a context somehow formalized as song by way of repetitive basslines or of other structural devices. In one of the Seventh Book "bird" madrigals, "O come sei gentile," the lover compares the bird's song ("tu canti") with his own ("io canto"), and the two sopranos play themselves off against each other over a repeating four-measure bass pattern, continuing to sing at great length even as they are "dying." In the same book's "Augellin che la voce al canto spieghi" (TTB), the first tenor begins solo for eight measures; the second tenor interjects himself at the cadence with a repeat of the opening; T^1 tries to regain his authority (another repeat of the opening)

---

[16] The classic early-seventeenth-century example of the contest between the singer and the nightingale is in Giambattista Marino's *L'Adone* (1623), Canto 7, stanzas 32–62. This, too, borrows from Pliny in describing the bird's vocal abilities.

but then admits defeat, singing in thirds below T^2 until he can find a way to get on top again. This is not so much a bird letting loose its voice in song as one tenor competing with another, and it falls upon the late-entering bass singer to remind them of the point being made here: the purpose of the opening vocative, "Augellin," is to ask the bird to take pity on the lover's grief ("per pietà del mio duolo") and fly to the beloved with a message. But Monteverdi's staged fight between the two tenors, and the delayed appearance of the exasperated bass, produces something very funny indeed.

Olina goes one step further in his birdsong treatise, however, arguing that nightingales have a striking sympathy for *sinfonie* and for *musica*, such that if in the room they are kept one makes a sweet *conserto* of instruments or voices, they are wondrously roused to sing themselves.[17] This prompts a different reading of another of Monteverdi's "bird" pieces, "Questi vaghi concenti," written, I have argued, for the nine male singers and string players under his control as *maestro della musica* in Mantua (see Chapter 4). The text by an as yet unidentified poet is a two-stanza canzone, with the first establishing the premise:

> Questi vaghi concenti
> che gli augelletti intorno
> vanno temprando a l'aparir del giorno,
> sono, cred'io, d'amor desiri ardenti.
> Sono pene e tormenti,
> e pur fanno le selve e 'l ciel gioire
> al lor dolce languire.

[These charming sounds / that the birds all around / temper at the break of day / are, I believe, ardent desires for love. / They are pains and torments, / and yet they make the woods and heaven rejoice / at their sweet languishing.]

In the second stanza, the lover—represented by a newly appearing S^2—wishes that he could sing as sweetly so that his beloved would welcome his laments.

Monteverdi's setting is unusual in that it is the first in his madrigal books to include a purely instrumental sinfonia, once at the beginning and then repeated in a shorter form prior to the second stanza. It is not at all surprising that he should have used "Questi vaghi concenti" to display his skills as both a composer and an ensemble director, drawing attention to the "sweet sounds" he was able to produce with his fellow musicians, whether in the setting itself or in the book of madrigals that it concludes. But the sinfonia provides what Olina called a "sweet *conserto*," in his case to provoke birds to sing, but in Monteverdi's, as the "vaghi concenti" produced by

---

[17] Olina, *Uccelliera*, fol. 3r ("Per stimolar' il rusignolo al canto"): "Opera anco infinitamente la Sympathia, che quest'Uccelletto hà con la Sinfonia, e musica. Onde quando nella Camera dove si tiene, si farà Conserto suave di suoni, ò di voci, s'accenderà maravigliosamente al canto." Olina's other advice to achieve this goal is like Antonio Valli's and largely concerns appropriate types of bird food.

the birds themselves singing so sweetly at dawn, to which the voices then respond. Unlike a number of his contemporaries, Monteverdi wrote almost no independent instrumental music other than the sinfonias, ritornellos, dance movements, and the like to be found in his theatrical works and in some of his settings for church and chamber. However, the instrumental ritornellos that represent La Musica in the prologue to *Orfeo*, the echoes in "Possente spirto e formidabil nume" at the heart of that opera as the eponymous hero stands on the bank of the River Styx, or the sinfonia in "Tempro la cetra, e per cantar gli honori" as the poet "tunes" the lyre at the beginning of the Seventh Book, all make it clear that Monteverdi was intrigued by the question of what instrumental sound might bring to the musical experience. Indeed, the entrance of the continuo in "Mentre vaga Angioletta" suggests that it represents some form of musical spirit. Monteverdi's handling of sound, whether instrumental or vocal, is as much a part of his compositional technique as his treatment of text.

Music about music

In another of Monteverdi's "bird" settings, of Guarini's "Dolcissimo uscignolo" in the Eighth Book, the lover envies the bird the power of its song to attract its mate, whereas his own singing avails him naught ("A me canto non vale"). When Gastoldi set this text in his *Concenti musicali, çon le sue sinfonie, a otto voci* (1604), he prefaced it with an instrumental sinfonia representing the songful bird in a manner that may have influenced "Questi vaghi concenti." Monteverdi, on the other hand, has the "sweetest bird" addressed just by the five-voice ensemble (plus continuo). But despite the lover's despair over his vocal limitations, the group sings prettily enough in what is identified as the "French style" ("alla Francese"). As a more extreme example, even when the lover is torn between the merits of speaking or staying silent, in "Parlo, misero, o taccio?" (Seventh Book), the two sopranos and the bass sing at length about the problem, using the ornamental passagework typical of Monteverdi's modern style of vocal writing. Music must always be music even when it claims not to be musical.

But if the music is about music, then so much the better, not least because it justifies the apparent absurdity of its use as a medium of expression. The singers delivering the text of a madrigal need to have some reason for doing so. By having them comment on how sweetly it is being done, or how great the delight that follows, the benefit is doubled. The musical play in "Questi vaghi concenti" had already been anticipated in the Fifth Book's "«T'amo mia vita!», la mia cara vita," where the solo soprano's declaration of love contains "sweetness and delight" ("O voce di dolcezza e di diletto"), then taken up by the full ensemble. But Monteverdi learned the trick early on. Tasso's "Non sono in queste rive" (Second Book) has the lover respond to the beloved's singing. Her lips are redder than any flowers in the field, and the summer breezes rustling across springs, roses, and lilies cannot create any sweeter

Ex. 6.1 "Non sono in queste rive" (Second Book, 1590).

harmony than her song that pleases and enflames the lover, who wishes it only to be interrupted by an exchange of kisses. The beloved's "song" ("canto") is represented by typical melismas, while at "sweeter harmony" ("più dolce armonia"), the young Monteverdi tries something daring: a progression of major triads built on G, C, E, A, and G (Ex. 6.1). Both C–E and A–G are not standard progressions according to any textbook that Ingegneri might have given his young student, although Monteverdi could easily have picked them up from Marenzio or other such composers.[18] But even here the young Monteverdi makes a joke of a kind that would become typical for him: the point of the poem is that kissing is preferable to singing, but he keeps the music going for longer than it should, delaying those kisses ("i baci") until the very last two measures.

---

[18] Compare Tomlinson, *Monteverdi and the End of the Renaissance*, 48, which further notes another movement by thirds (C–A) in "Tutte le bocche belle" (Second Book). There is a neat performance problem in Ex. 6.1. Monteverdi's notation makes clear the intended synaloepha between the last syllable of "dolce" and the first of "armonia," as is required by the poetic meter, although there will be a strong tendency for singers to separate the two words in some way.

He must have enjoyed demonstrating his grasp of sweet harmony. The issue is central to the argument of "Con che soavità, labra odorate" in the Seventh Book, for solo soprano and "nine" instruments.[19] The poem presents a typical wish to resolve an amorous paradox by a speaker who is gender-neutral in Guarini's poem, but female in Monteverdi's setting. She takes delight both in kissing the lips of her beloved and in listening to the words that emerge from them, but she cannot do both at the same time. How exquisite would be the harmony if kisses and words could at once do sweet double duty, kisses speaking, and words kissing. It is a witty enough conceit compressed into eleven lines of poetry. Monteverdi extends his setting to a luxurious 121 measures, repeating single lines or groups of them to stretch out what no longer seems to be an argument pursued to any logical conclusion.[20] The solo voice and the instruments intertwine, the singer's words and the instruments' sounds superimposed in ways that fulfill the lover's desire, words and not-words united in a languid moment of intense erotic pleasure that can last some five or more minutes in performance.

Monteverdi devotes three-fifths of those measures to the last four lines of the poem, prompted by that notion of exquisite harmony. He pushes the harmonic boundaries almost to the edge of what was possible within the tuning systems in use at the time (see Chapter 8): his setting of "Che soave armonia" begins with a major triad on D leading to a cadence on G, and he then repeats the music up a tone (a typical gambit), with a major triad on E and a cadence on A. By the end of the setting, Monteverdi has covered a wide harmonic range, from the sharp side to the flat one (B♭ toward the end). There is a logic to these progressions. But his frozen moment has a striking harmonic breadth and depth.

Not all poetry set by Monteverdi is musically inclined, but when it is, some response is to be expected. Trigger words included not just "armonia" but also the likes of "accenti," "cantare," "suono," and "voce." His First Book is full of them. In "Fumia la pastorella," the eponymous shepherdess was gathering flowers in the field, singing the while ("sen già cantando in un prato di fiori"); she spoke to the sun, asking it to spread springtime happiness and joy over the land; then all the shepherds and nymphs united to sing in Fumia's praise. In "Usciam, Ninfe, omai fuor di questi boschi," the speaker calls upon the nymphs to come together and make the valleys resound with song, and to dance to sweet sounds. In "La vaga pastorella," the present-tense lover pursues a fair shepherdess who moves through the meadow, sweetly singing the while ("cantando dolcemente"). Then comes the twist. In these three madrigals, the characters exploiting their musical talents are all female. But in "La vaga pastorella," the lover pursuing the charming shepherdess is

---

[19] This is another text also set in Gastoldi's *Concenti musicali* (1604). He has two groups each of four singers (SATB) in a kind of dialogue with each other, although each group has the same text, and for the standard repetition of the final lines of the poem, Gastoldi just switches their music from one to the other.

[20] Gastoldi's setting is more compressed at seventy-one measures (plus an initial sinfonia of thirty-four).

a bearer of suffering ("carco di martiro"), and he begs her not to flee because he is at death's door ("ch'io mi sento a morire"). Of course, he is nothing of the sort. But in the pastoral tradition, nymphs sing while shepherds die (eight of them, in fact, in the First Book), and only the most precocious of nymphs can join their male companion in death so sweet that they come back to life to die again.

Any poetic reference to singing is going to draw attention to itself precisely because singers are singing, regardless of the human or avian source of any such musical utterance within the poem. In the polyphonic madrigals, the standard musical device prompted by it is some running and/or turning motion in eighth notes (quavers), as seen in "Non sono in queste rive" (in Ex. 6.1), although this has the potential to get confused with whatever word(s) are being set in the moment. In this same madrigal, four or more eighth notes are used to represent "l'aure" (breezes), for metrical emphasis ("queste" and "vermigli"), and even, somewhat oddly, on the final syllable of "paci" in a misjudged attempt to maintain a contrapuntal flow (in thirds with "canto" in the bass voice)—this is a typical student mistake. Similar motives could also represent—and do in various madrigals—"giro" (turn), "vago" (charming), or any other such word. The text of Guarini's "Io mi son giovinetta" (Fourth Book) is an extreme case. Its first eight lines have no fewer than four uses of the verb "cantare" in present and past tenses, and one "canto" as a noun. Monteverdi's use and reuse of similar musical patterns becomes very confusing in terms of who is singing what, where, and when, especially when the opening "io" is not, in fact, the principal poetic voice.

Any slippage between these musical signs and their verbal associations can sometimes be helpful, however. In the setting of Tasso's "Ecco mormorar l'onde" in the Second Book, water murmurs, leaves rustle in the early morning breeze, and birds sing sweetly in the trees (a nice "cantar" moment in the top two voices). The east smiles as the sun rises and is reflected in the sea, making serene the heavens, and causing the snow on the high mountains to glisten. The poem then ends with a proclamation to the dawn (or to its goddess, Aurora):

> O bella e vag'aurora,
> l'aura è tua messaggiera, e tu de l'aura
> ch'ogni arso cor ristaura.

[O beautiful and charming dawn, / the breeze is your herald, and you [the herald] of the breeze / that restores every scorched heart.]

The text does not make much sense without understanding Tasso's play on "l'aura," the breeze, and Laura Peverara, the virtuoso soprano in the Ferrarese *concerto delle dame* who was also the subject of Guarini's "Mentre vaga Angioletta" when he first wrote that poem. Monteverdi's melismatic setting of "l'aura" could just as well be a setting of some version of "cantare" (Ex. 6.2). But that is the point: the breeze and Laura are made of the same musical breath.

Ex. 6.2 "Ecco mormorar l'onde" (Second Book, 1592).

However, such pastoral-musical evocations can often take a turn for the worse. In Monteverdi's setting of Petrarch's iconic sonnet, "Zefiro torna e 'l bel tempo rimena" (*RVF* 310), in the Sixth Book, spring returns in all its visual and sonic glory, the latter created by warbling Procne (transformed into a swallow) and lamenting Philomena (a nightingale). Jove rejoices in seeing his daughter (Proserpina, on her seasonal return from the Underworld), and the air, sea, and land are full of love as every animal recommits to amorous entanglements. But the sestet shifts to the long-suffering lover by way of a typical "but" ("Ma per me, lasso"): he cannot draw any pleasure from such delightful sights and sounds, given the sighs pouring forth from his heart. Monteverdi sets each of the first two quatrains to the same music in a jolly triple time. This is his first extensive use of that meter in his madrigals, and the unusual (for Monteverdi) repetition of the music suggests that he is worried about sustaining it over eight eleven-syllable lines.[21] At "Ma per me, lasso," however, he shifts into a dissonant duple-time world that once more moves into dangerous harmonic domains in terms of tuning (a major triad on B). Triple time returns briefly, but for the lover's wretched state, that duple time—now even more intensely dissonant—is the only possible response as Monteverdi also makes what seems to be a bow to Giaches de Wert's setting (1581) of another of Petrarch's sonnets of despair, "Solo e pensoso, i più deserti campi" (*RVF* 35).

"Zefiro torna e 'l bel tempo rimena" is generally viewed as one of Petrarch's sonnets on the death of his beloved Laura—which explains its sestet—although by the late sixteenth and early seventeenth centuries, it could be read as reflecting the situation of any lover kept distant from the delights of the pastoral world by the intransigence of the beloved: Arcadia was full of such ill-fortuned figures. The

---

[21] It was more common for solo-voice settings of sonnets to adopt some manner of strophic repetition, and particularly those in the vein of the "arie da cantar sonetti": i.e., with music for any first quatrain that can be repeated for the second and adapted for the two tercets. Polyphonic settings, however, traditionally tended to be through-composed.

same shift occurs in Ottavio Rinuccini's play on Petrarch, "Zefiro torna e di soavi odori," set for two tenors and continuo as "Zefiro torna e di soavi accenti" in the 1632 *Scherzi musicali*. Here the celebration of pastoral delights lasts to the end of the first tercet. Zephyr murmurs through the trees and the flowers dance to his sound; Filli and Clori make the mountains and valleys resound with their cheerful notes; dawn spreads from the east and the sun makes everything sparkle. Then comes the inevitable switch:

> Sol io, per selve abbandonate e sole,
> l'ardor de' due begli occhi e 'l mio tormento,
> come vuol mia ventura, hor piango, hor canto.

[Only I, through abandoned and solitary woods, / of the fire of two fair eyes and my suffering, / as my fortune would have it, do now weep, now sing.]

Monteverdi again starts in triple time, now adopting a relatively new technique to extend it over longer stretches of musical time (113 measures): an ostinato pattern in the continuo—an offbeat *ciaccona*—over which the voices can weave variations that also respond quite specifically to individual images in the text. It is a highly virtuosic compositional technique. But at "Sol io" things must change: Monteverdi moves into a more declamatory duple time, intensified by its use of two voices and by the same radical harmonic shifts (to a major triad on B) as in his Petrarch setting. Rinuccini's text creates an additional problem, however. For Petrarch, the pastoral soundscape is external to the tormented lover in a desert wilderness. Rinuccini, however, keeps him sonically engaged, now weeping, now singing. When Monteverdi reaches the first statement of the final line of the sonnet, "hor canto" prompts him to make a brief return to the triple-time *ciaccona*. When he restates it, he does the same but then realizes that it is hard to produce a strong final cadence in triple time, so he shifts to a different representation of "singing": ornamental passagework in duple time. The despairing "I" moments at the end of these two different "Zefiro torna" settings, and the shifts of style that represent them, intrude quite drastically upon the musical world established thus far, forcing the listener—as they do the lover—back into a quite different, more wretched place. And even though Rinuccini's sonnet, unlike Petrarch's, ends with singing, Monteverdi's final embellishments with their notated *trillo* (fast repeated notes) seem to lapse into inconsolable sobs.

In "Or che 'l ciel e la terra e 'l vento tace" in the Eighth Book, Petrarch's sonnet (*RVF* 164) offers no opportunity for a vocal celebration of the delights of nature, however violent their contrasts might be with the state of the lover. It is set at night, when beasts and birds are all asleep. All is calm save the troubled mind of an insomniac lover in a perpetual state of a war replete with anger and grief ("guerr'è il mio stato, d'ira et di duol piena"), and while thoughts of the beloved offer some brief respite, she both heals and wounds him: therefore, he dies and is reborn a thousand times each day. This is one of the "Canti guerrieri" in the Eighth Book, and its text provides the violent contrasts that Monteverdi claimed in its preface were what animated his musical exploration of the passions by way of the three *generi* that, he said, were used in Classical Antiquity: the *molle* (soft), *temperato* (temperate), and *concitato* (aroused). Their differences were construed in terms of sound, chiefly rhythmic but also with melodic and harmonic consequences. Monteverdi was particularly proud of having revived the *concitato genere* that he had developed within the *Combattimento di Tancredi e Clorinda* and then continued to explore in various sacred and chamber works, leading other composers to admire and imitate him (so he says in the Eighth Book preface to establish his claim for precedence). In "Or che 'l ciel," "guerr'è mio stato" prompts plenty of vocal and instrumental fanfares in "battle" mode. But Monteverdi also has to deal with the sonnet's initial account of a world in silent sleep. He begins in low-scored homophony with little harmonic movement in the manner to which Artusi took such exception in "Era l'anima mia" in the Fifth Book. Now a full eleven measures are on the same chord before the voices suddenly break cover at the first-person "veglio, penso, ardo" (I wake, I think, I burn). This opening is presumably in what Monteverdi considered to be the *molle genere* in terms of rhythm and pitch, the polar opposite of the *concitato genere*. What sits between them, however, can change in terms of expressive style and function.

Singing and "singing"

The ending of "Zefiro torna e di soavi accenti" suggests that Monteverdi now has two modes for representing singing, his "birdsong" one in duple time with ornamental flourishes, and a more lyrical one in triple time. Those modes are both present in sequence in "Mentre vaga Angioletta." The first part of the setting concerns all those sympathetic vibrations responding to the singer's vocal acrobatics. Thus, the heart sings, re-sings, becomes a nightingale, and takes flight. Monteverdi marks the shift in the argument articulated by that "thus" ("Così") by moving to triple time (Ex. 6.3). This is not at all birdlike, even though it is rich in song.

Ex. 6.3 "Mentre vaga Angioletta" (Eighth Book, 1638).

In his Seventh and Eighth Book madrigals, Monteverdi uses this device with some frequency. The short passages of triple time in "Dice la mia bellissima Licori" and "Perché fuggi tra' salci" in the Seventh are probably for rhetorical effect, while Tirsi's triple-time stanzas in *Tirsi e Clori* suggest a rather bumptious shepherd who needs taming by Clori's more sensuous duple time. Things seem different, however, in the same book's "Non vedrò mai le stelle" (the poet has not been identified). Here the lover states that he will never look at the stars without seeing in them the eyes of his faithless beloved, and this is what he will say:

«O luci belle,
deh, siate sì rubelle
di lume a chi ribella è sì di fede,
ch'anzi a tanti occhi e tanti lumi ha core
tradir amante sotto fé d'amore.»

["Oh beautiful lights, / ah, deny / your light to her who so denies faith, / who before so many eyes and so many lights has the heart / to betray a lover even while pledging love."]

This is doggerel, but Monteverdi can make enough sense of it to realize that in structural terms, he is in a situation similar to "Sfogava con le stelle" in the Fourth Book, with an opening statement (in that case, narration) moving to direct speech cued by a vocative "O." In "Sfogava con le stelle," Monteverdi had five voices and so could use that vocative to shift from homophony to polyphony. In "Non vedrò mai le stelle," he has two tenors. He first broaches the vocative "O" with an expansive rising scale in T^1: "O luci belle, deh siate sì rubelle di lume." He then gets stuck at the point where the poem starts to make no sense, so T^1 returns to "luci, luci belle," soon joined by T^2: "luci, luci belle, o luci belle." Desperate (I imagine) to put off trying to figure out the meaning of what follows, Monteverdi then shifts to triple time: "O luci, o luci, o luci belle . . ." He bites the bullet to tackle the continuation (to "fede") but then decides to return to the portion of the phrase that at least makes some sense: "siate sì rubelle, siate sì rubelle, siate sì rubelle, sì rubelle, sì rubelle di lume" (to quote T^1; adding T^2 would multiply the repetitions). This eventually reaches a cadence on "a chi ribella è sì di fede," at which point, Monteverdi returns to duple time for "ch'anzi a tanti occhi" to the end. But he has evidently enjoyed giving his singers thirty-eight measures of pure lyricism, the text be damned. They wallow happily in it, losing all track of the meaning of the poem. It probably does not matter.

There is no harm in wallowing: Gratioso Uberti's cheerful Giocondo made precisely that point by way of his sneaky redefinition of the term "melodia." In one of the two tenor duets in the Eighth Book, "Ardo, e scoprir—ahi lasso!—io non ardisco" (two stanzas of *ottava rima*), the lover fervently desires to express his feelings to his beloved, but the necessary words cannot pass his lips ("si troncan su le labbra le parole"): the music shifts to a stuttering triple time that fails to shape itself into a properly lyrical love song. In the other duet, however, song takes full flight. "O sia tranquillo il mare o pien d'orgoglio" (a sonnet) presents a male lover playing the role of an Armida or Arianna: his beloved has sailed away but he sits on a rocky cliff as he waits for her return, treating the winds as messenger to tell her of his suffering and torment. The final tercet deals with the inevitable outcome and the moral to be drawn from it:

> Ma tu non torni, o Filli, e 'l mio lamento
> l'aura disperge. E tal mercè ne speri
> chi fida a donna il cor e i prieghi al vento.

[But you do not return, o Filli, and my lament / is scattered by the breeze. And such a reward may one expect, / who entrusts the heart to a woman and prayers to the wind.]

The ambiguity within that final moral is neat: "speri" is both second- and third-person present subjunctive (and second-person present indicative), but either way, it is some kind of address to the listener. Prior to that point, however, the abandoned lover is most concerned with the fact that Filli does not return ("Ma tu non torni, o Filli"), and Monteverdi's response is now predictable enough, with forty-eight measures of triple time for half a line of verse. There are various possible triggers for Monteverdi's shift here, whether the "But" ("ma" is always a good word to mark a change), or some notion of turning with "return." More important, however, is how the lover defines it: as "mio lamento." Of course, the entire sonnet is some kind of lament, but the quatrains and the first tercet present narrative statements. While "Ma tu non torni, o Filli" is also a statement, Monteverdi in effect puts it in the quotation marks of direct speech. But if lyrical triple time can be some form of lament, we enter a quite different musical world.

The increasing emotional weight granted to triple-time songs is clear in a repertory to which Monteverdi made a relatively small contribution in proportion to his total output, but nonetheless a significant one. The three-voice canzonettas in his 1607 *Scherzi musicali*, collected by his brother, Giulio Cesare, are mostly settings of texts by, or in the vein, of Gabriello Chiabrera, in multiple stanzas each generally six to eight lines long. The verse tends to be in meters other than the mixed seven- and eleven-syllable lines of madrigal poetry—five- and eight-syllable lines are common—and structured by way of regular groupings: "I bei legami" (five-syllable lines: *ababccdd*), "Damigella" ($a^4a^4b^8c^4c^4b^8$), or "La violetta" ($a^5a^5b^7c^5c^5b^7$) are typical examples, although there is a fair amount of variety. The texts tend to be "light" in tone, praising the beloved or, if chiding her, steering clear of the more painful consequences of unrequited love. These settings are scored for two sopranos and a bass, but a rubric allows other possibilities (the internal stanzas by a single soprano or that line taken down an octave). Each *scherzo* has a ritornello to be played twice at the beginning and then after each stanza: this is for two violins and a continuo line to be played by a chitarrone, harpsichord, "or other similar instrument."

Chiabrera admitted that he had taken this type of poetry from the French anacreontic verse of Pierre de Ronsard, and Giulio Cesare Monteverdi also associated his brother's settings of it with what he called the "canto alla francese" (song, or manner of singing, in the French manner), which he said his brother had first brought back from Spa (in the Ardennes) in 1599, where Monteverdi had gone as part of the entourage of Duke Vincenzo Gonzaga.[22] The meaning of the term remains unclear—whether referring to a genre or a manner of performance—as is how it might relate to the contents of the *Scherzi musicali*. However, there is clearly some connection to the strophic chansons in *vers mesurés* of Claude Le Jeune with their strongly homophonic, syllabic settings and clear-cut phrases determined by the length of the poetic line: eight-syllable ones are particularly characteristic, given their tendency toward hemiola patterns. But whatever that case, the *scherzi* are definitely "songs," and their poetic and musical idioms are treated as such in Monteverdi's opera *Orfeo*, when Orfeo sings what are explicitly or implicitly identified as songs (in Acts II and IV) that are kept poetically and musically distinct from the prevailing recitative.

The kinds of strophic verse found in the *Scherzi musicali* remained popular, although it started to change in style and function. Remigio Romano's five collections of *canzonette musicali* issued between 1618 and 1626 reveal the shifts.[23] They contain just poetic texts, and Romano does not note their authors, although many can be identified from other sources. Some of these songs, however, have their harmonies indicated by way of letter-tablature for the Spanish guitar, an instrument gaining in popularity among amateur musicians because it was relatively easy to play. Moreover, given that chords created by particular fingering patterns were indicated by letters (A, B, C, etc.), it did not require musical notation, or any music-theoretical knowledge, to provide an accompaniment. But there is no indication of their melodies, which must therefore have been well known.

Some of Romano's texts go back a fair way (indeed, to Giulio Caccini's *Le nuove musiche* of 1602). Others, however, are more up-to-date, including canzonettas with longer stanzas and more complex structures, sometimes mixing a wider range of poetic meters, and making greater use of end-accented *versi tronchi* rather than

---

[22] In the "Dichiaratione" appended to the 1607 *Scherzi musicali*, Giulio Cesare Monteverdi justified his brother's laying claim to the term "seconda pratica" (so that it would not be appropriated by others) by saying that the "canto alla francese" was now being widely used in motets, madrigals, canzonettas, and arias without regard for the fact that Claudio deserved the credit from bringing it back from Spa. The exact meaning of the term is still a matter of debate: Monteverdi was certainly not the first to set Chiabrera's poetry to music. Whenever "alla francese" appears in his later secular and sacred music, it seems to mean the setting of syllables to paired eighth notes (quavers), often slurred. Such slurred patterns can also be found in numerous settings in the 1607 *Scherzi musicali*, and briefly in the Fifth Book, in "Troppo ben può questo tiranno Amore" (at "Ah, core stolto," etc.). It is not clear, however, what the performance consequences might be.

[23] Miller, "New Information on the Chronology of Venetian Monody." Not all of the texts are canzonettas, strictly speaking: some are poetic madrigals or are in other forms.

the more customary *versi piani*.[24] There is also an increasing attempt to link the stanzas within a stronger narrative arc rather than treating them as distinct, separate units. Longer texts meant longer musical settings; *versi tronchi* were better suited to musical cadences than *versi piani* by virtue of their weak–strong endings; and narrative arcs sometimes prompted composers to provide new music for all or part of the final stanza of any given setting.[25]

A number of Monteverdi's contemporaries in Venice in the 1620s contributed to the repertory: Carlo Milanuzzi's *Primo scherzo delle ariose vaghezze* of 1622 was followed by eight similar books by him to 1643, and Giovanni Pietro Berti's two books of *Cantade et arie* (1625, 1627) contain similar pieces, if also others in a more expansive vein. Both composers appear in Alessandro Vincenti's collection of *Arie de diversi* of 1634, in which Monteverdi probably had a hand. Moreover, Milanuzzi included three settings by Monteverdi in his *Quarto scherzo delle ariose vaghezze* of 1624, plus two each by Monteverdi's son Francesco and by Berti and Guglielmo Miniscalchi.[26] The first by Monteverdi, "Ohimè, ch'io cado, ohimè," is what would usually have been labeled a "cantata" (not to be confused with later uses of the term): it is a set of strophic variations wherein the six stanzas of the text are set in duple time to the same "walking" bass moving in quarter notes (crotchets), but the melody is varied in each one.[27] The other two are straightforward canzonettas with music provided for the first stanza with the others printed as text, save in the case of "La mia turca che d'amor," which has additional music for the final stanza prompted by its rhetorical shift at the end.

The third canzonetta merits further consideration:

> Sì dolce è 'l tormento
> ch'in seno mi sta,
> ch'io vivo contento
> per cruda beltà.
> Nel ciel di bellezza
> s'accreschi fierezza
> et manchi pietà:
> che sempre qual scoglio
> all'onda d'orgoglio
> mia fede sarà.

---

[24] For these kinds of poetic structures, see also Badolato, "Soluzioni metriche e motivi poetici nei testi intonati da Benedetto Ferrari e Nicolò Fontei."

[25] Monteverdi's "Più lieto il guardo" in the 1634 *Arie de diversi* is a case in point: stanzas 2–4 are repeated to the same triple-time music as provided for stanza 1, but stanza 5, marked "recitato," shifts to recitative.

[26] The single surviving copy of the 1624 edition is identified as "novamente ristampata, e corretta," also with two "new" arias (by Milanuzzi) at the beginning of the book. However, its first edition must have appeared soon before, given that Milanuzzi's *Terzo scherzo delle ariose vaghezze* came out in early 1623 (with a dedication dated 1 December 1622).

[27] Other examples are Monteverdi's "Quel sguardo sdegnosetto" (in triple time) and the long "Et è pur dunque vero" (with instrumental ritornellos), both in the 1632 *Scherzi musicali*.

Ex. 6.4 (a) Carlo Milanuzzi, "Sì dolce è 'l tormento" (*Primo scherzo delle ariose vaghezze*, 1622), 12; (b) Monteverdi, "Sì dolce e 'l tormento" (in Milanuzzi, *Quarto scherzo delle ariose vaghezze*, repr. 1624), 44.

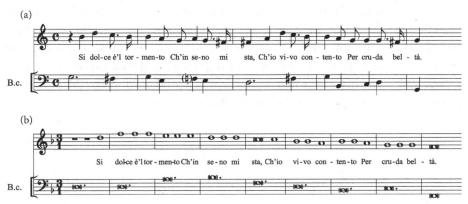

[So sweet is the torment / that rests in my breast, / that I live content / for such cruel beauty. / In the realm of beauty / let harshness increase / and pity be lacking: / for always as a rock / against the waves of pride / will my faith stand.]

In terms of its content, this first stanza of the text comes close to any poetic madrigal. Its meter does not, however: the poem has four ten-line stanzas in six-syllable lines with periodic end-accented *versi tronchi* that rhyme (in the first: "mi sta," "beltà," "pietà," "sarà").[28]

Monteverdi may have caught sight of this text in the setting included in Francesco Petratti's *Il primo libro d'arie a una et due voci* (Venice: Alessandro Vincenti, 1620), which he helped shepherd through the press as a favor to Paolo Giordano II Orsini, Duke of Bracciano. But his focus lay on the setting in Carlo Milanuzzi's *Primo scherzo delle ariose vaghezze* of 1622 (Ex. 6.4). The typical approach for such texts in a single poetic meter was to identify a rhythmic pattern suitable for each line that could be repeated as often as necessary. Milanuzzi does precisely that, in a rather stolid duple time (so does Petratti). Monteverdi, however, opts for a suave triple time, also making a virtue of a supremely simple melodic line moving down by step measure-by-measure. By the second half of the stanza, he gives that descending line still more force by way of painful dissonances and an obsessive repetition of notes that do not fit the harmony. The lover's faith might stand firm as a rock, but it is at some cost.

In 1624, Monteverdi was fifty-seven years old, and Milanuzzi some twenty years his junior. We do not know how the younger composer might have felt at being bested by the *maestro di cappella* of St. Mark's: it may be significant that none of Milanuzzi's subsequent surviving volumes of *ariose vaghezze* (the Fifth is lost)

---

[28] The other three stanzas each contain the other possible *tronco* endings: -è, -ò, and -ì.

contains music by other composers. But by now, Monteverdi probably had carte blanche to publish whatever he wanted. His choice of triple time for "Sì dolce è 'l tormento" remains significant, however. It is not just a nod to what was, or would become, a Venetian fashion. If in "O sia tranquillo il mare," two tenors can sing what they call a "lament" in triple time, then the same meter here is no less suggestive of some new kind of emotional intensity in music generated purely by vocal lyricism—by singing. This celebration of the qualities of the human voice is a dangerous tool, as we discover when it fills the moral void of Monteverdi's last opera, *L'incoronazione di Poppea*. But it is also ineffably beautiful.

7
Monteverdi's "Mistakes"

Not all of Monteverdi's birds are quite so well behaved: indeed, they sometimes lead him astray. Petrarch's sonnet "Vago augelletto che cantando vai" (*RVF* 353), set in the Eighth Book, twists the "charming bird" trope because the bird is not just singing about times past but also weeping over them ("che cantando vai, / over piangendo, il tuo tempo passato"), given the onset of the dark nights of winter, the gay months left behind. The text begins with a vocative ("Vago augelletto") plus a relative clause ("che cantando . . .") that continues through the first quatrain, leading to an "if"-clause at the beginning of the second:

> se, come i tuoi gravosi affanni sai,
> così sapessi il mio simile stato,
> verresti in grembo a questo sconsolato
> a partir seco i dolorosi guai.

> [if, just as you know your own heavy sorrows, / so were you to know my like state, / then you would fly to the breast of this disconsolate lover / to share with him your grievous pains.]

Monteverdi instead turns Petrarch's rather elliptical "if . . . then" construction into an "as . . . so" one ("sì come i tuoi gravosi affanni sai"). This also confuses Petrarch's careful use of tenses, from present ("sai") through imperfect subjunctive ("sapessi") to conditional ("verresti").[1]

Editors vary on whether to treat Monteverdi's "sì" for Petrarch's "se" as a slip of the pen, or a typographical error, and therefore to correct it. Another option is to imagine that by way of early-seventeenth-century Italian usage, Monteverdi could well have understood "sì come" ("siccome") as introducing an "if" clause in the first place. He does not help matters, however, by having already set the second quatrain off from the first, therefore breaking the enjambment and leaving the first quatrain hanging unresolved grammatically. Moreover, he does so by turning Petrarch's first line ("Vago augelletto che cantando vai") into a songful refrain interjected repeatedly throughout the setting—therefore separating the first quatrain from the

---

[1] Compare Georis, *Claudio Monteverdi*, 652 n. 12, which, however, is a bit more generous to Monteverdi's reading.

second—and having it return at the very end. These repetitions have as much to do with building some kind of formal structure as with expressing the text, or even just delivering it: we find the same thing in some of his sacred settings where a portion of a psalm text (a statement or an imperative) returns in seemingly odd places. But Monteverdi's bird is indeed just singing, even though Petrarch's is doing something else as well, or instead.[2]

There is a great deal invested in the notion that Monteverdi was acutely sensitive to the rhetorical and affective nuances of the poetry he set, not least in light of his own claims for the *seconda pratica*. There may therefore be a certain iconoclastic pleasure to be gained from pointing out where he slips up. Resistance to any such critical move will vary in direct proportion to one's belief in the value of Monteverdi's claim in the first place. But accepting that he could have made a mistake tends to be a counsel of last resort: most would prefer to argue that a musical approach to a poetic text in *seconda pratica* vein can legitimately distort its grammar or even its meaning—indeed, that it is incumbent on the composer to find, or invent, new things in a text precisely because of the opportunities presented by setting it to music.[3] Monteverdi offers many examples to prove the point. But once one has identified and acknowledged such "errors," one can begin to ask how and why they might have occurred, and what they might tell us about a particular musical mind at work.

"Vago augelletto" is a good example of a typical challenge for editors accustomed to identifying, documenting, and taking action on perceived errors in their sources in order to produce a "correct" version of a given musical text that best represents what the composer wanted, or should have wanted, to produce. That process tends to assume that composers sometimes need saving from themselves—anyone can make mistakes—and/or that some interference has occurred in the transmission of a text, for example, by way of copying errors or typographical ones. Such errors are convenient, given that they absolve the composer of some responsibility for them. In "Misero Alceo, del caro albergo fore" (Sixth Book), the typesetter clearly made a slip in giving "more" (dies) for "mentre" (while).[4] It must be corrected, but we do not know whether it was his fault in the act of typesetting, or a problem in his source where the word was wrong or somehow illegible.

It is harder to dismiss the problem in the first line of the *seconda parte* of "Or che 'l ciel e la terra e 'l vento tace" (Eighth Book), given as "Così suol d'una chiara fonte viva" in all the relevant partbooks, including the Basso Continuo, which just has a

---

[2] Rosand ("Monteverdi's Mimetic Art," 114–15) notes how Petrarch's sonnet "succumbs under the weight of Monteverdi's interpretation," and that the composer "may have been the most extreme textual deconstructor" in the history of the madrigal.

[3] Compare Ossi's account of "Vago augelletto" in his "Monteverdi as Reader of Petrarch," which also notes the canzonetta elements within Monteverdi's representation of the singing bird. However, he does not discuss the "se, come"/"sì come" problem.

[4] Georis, *Claudio Monteverdi*, 518 n. 32. The incorrect "more" is clear in Amadino's 1615 edition of the Sixth Book. Something is odd in the first (1614), which may originally have had "me[n]tre" (with an abbreviation sign above the "e").

short-form incipit so as to identify the piece ("Così suol d'una fonte").[5] Monteverdi, or his copyist, must have written "suol" in the manuscripts delivered to the printer, even though the verb (from "solere": i.e., "as is wont") makes no sense absent any subsequent infinitive. Most editors will happily correct the text to Petrarch's "Così sol d'una chiara fonte viva." It is true, however, that Petrarch's wording is fairly obscure: his point is that the sweet and the bitter on which the poet feeds come from a single clear, living spring ("d'una sola fonte chiara e viva," as it were). The "sol" is awkwardly positioned, and one can see why Monteverdi might have thought it meant something else, even if, as with "Vago augelletto," he should probably have read his Petrarch more carefully in the first place.

In the case of the *Combattimento di Tancredi e Clorinda*, again in the Eighth Book, someone had already done this kind of editing for the composer. There are two scores for the piece, one in the Tenore Primo partbook and the other in the Basso Continuo one (see Chapter 3). Broadly speaking, the one in the vocal partbook has better readings for the music, but worse for the text. Thus, the tenor partbook probably reflects the piece as it was copied by Monteverdi and used in rehearsal and performance—hence the musical improvements—while the continuo score was prepared by someone else (I have suggested his printer, Alessandro Vincenti).[6] Those textual improvements in the continuo score included correcting at least some of Monteverdi's errors in reading Canto 12 of Tasso's *Gerusalemme liberata*. For example, in the case of the tenor partbook's "Non danno i colpi hor finti, hor pieni, hor tardi" (stanza 55, line 3), the continuo score gives the correct conclusion to the line as "hor scarsi," restoring the proper rhyme word fixed by the *ottava rima* pattern ("ritrarsi," "scarsi," "urtarsi"). This poses an editorial conundrum. Monteverdi's musical setting would work for blows either "tardi" (slow) or "scarsi" (glancing), so a more general conclusion must be reached on whether consistently to prefer one source over another, whether or not in relation to what Tasso wrote.[7]

The Eighth Book has a number of these kinds of problems, some of which can be fixed easily enough, although others cannot. In "Altri canti d'Amor, tenero arciero," at least part of the first tercet as presented in the text underlay in the (solo) bass voice is untenable as it stands:

> Tu cui tessuta han di Cesare alloro
> la corona immortal mentre Bellona
> gradite il verde ancor novo lavoro
> . . .

---

[5] Ibid., 600 n. 8. "Or che 'l ciel" has other problems as well, including the incorrect Quinto part (S²) toward the end of its *prima parte*.

[6] However, one place where the continuo score fixes a musical error in the partbooks concerns the second violin part in the battle music; see Holman, "Col nobilissimo esercitio della vivuola," 586–87.

[7] For another, far more intractable issue in the *Combattimento*—what to do with Monteverdi's assignment of Testo's "e ferma attende" (in the second stanza) to Clorinda—see Carter, "Another Monteverdi Problem." There are only two viable solutions to it: either letting the error stand, or transposing Clorinda's music down an octave for Testo.

This seems to involve a combination of copying errors and misreadings. Monteverdi's setting makes it clear that he means "di cesareo alloro" (with the musical accent on the second syllable of "cesareo," whereas "Cesare" would have it on the first). The "mentre Bellona" left hanging at the end of the second line is almost certainly an error for "Marte e Bellona" (the subject of "han"): thus, Mars and Bellona have woven an immortal crown from imperial laurel.[8] In general, however, this sonnet by an as yet unidentified poet is made of poor cloth: Monteverdi appears to have commissioned it for the specific purpose of opening the Eighth Book, and he was left making the best of it he could.[9]

Even with a "better" poet, however, Monteverdi feels justified in having a text changed to suit his purpose. Some such changes may have been done by a poet: one cannot quite imagine Monteverdi coming up with the revision to the end of the first section of Rinuccini's "Ogni amante è guerrier: nel suo gran regno" (Eighth Book) to close with a rhyming couplet.[10] The same may be true of the revision to the first two lines of the *Combattimento* so as to set the scene (Tasso's text is in midstream). But Monteverdi could have made other changes on his own, whether by design or accident. In "Tempro la cetra, e per cantar gli honori" (Seventh Book), Monteverdi switches a rhyme word in Marino's first tercet—"vanto" to "canto"—even though "canto" is used in the last line of second tercet (rhyming, precisely, with "vanto"). Monteverdi's "canto . . . canto" seems linked to other changes made here better to link this initial setting in the book to the references to Apollo and the Muses in the dedication to Caterina de' Medici. Another problem in this same tercet—perhaps stemming from the same need—is whether Monteverdi is invoking Marino's sublime "tromba" (trumpet) of heaven, as he does in the score in the Continuo partbook, or its sublime "lira" (lyre), in the tenor part. But that repeated "canto" cannot be correct in poetic terms. Nor can Monteverdi's alteration of the first line of Rinuccini's sonnet "Zefiro torna e di soavi odori" to ". . . e di soavi accenti" (in the 1632 *Scherzi musicali*), changing "sweet perfumes" to "sweet accents," even though "odori" rhymes with "fiori," "Clori," and "canori."[11] But here, at least, one can see the point of Monteverdi's change, preferring musical "accents" over "perfumes," especially given that those "accenti" are presented by two tenors over a jaunty *ciaccona* ground bass. In this case, at least, it would be foolish to change the text in pursuit of literary correctness, even though some have proposed doing so.[12]

---

[8] Denis Stevens suggests the "Marte e Bellona" reading in his "*Madrigali guerrieri, et amorosi*," 173–74, although Pirrotta ("Monteverdi's Poetic Choices," 309 n. 124 [on p. 448]), proposes "mentr'è Bellona" (while Bellona is present), which does not solve the "han" problem.

[9] One gets a similar impression from the entire setting of the sestet. It is first presented complete by the solo bass (with instruments); the full ensemble then repeats the last tercet, although it is not a separate syntactical unit.

[10] Georis, *Claudio Monteverdi*, 608 n. 22.

[11] Carter, "Two Monteverdi Problems." Salamone Rossi uses the correct reading in the setting (SSB, bc) in his *Madrigaletti a due voci* . . . , op. 13 (Venice: Alessandro Vincenti, 1628). Monteverdi seems to have had an aversion to "odori": he changed the last line of Marino's sonnet "A quest'olmo, a quest'ombre et a quest'onde" (Seventh Book) to end with "honori" instead.

[12] Pirrotta, "Monteverdi's Poetic Choices," 313 n. 144 (on pp. 451–52).

In that "Zefiro torna" duet, however, there is an insoluble problem in Monteverdi's handling of the second quatrain. Fillide and Clori sing sweet love songs,

> e da monti e da valli ime e profonde
> raddoppian l'armonia gli antri canori.

[and from the mountains and the valleys deep and low / the echoing caves redouble their harmony.]

Monteverdi engages in some typical word-painting here, with a rising line for the mountains and a descending one for the valleys (Ex. 7.1). He then matches that with high notes for "ime" and low ones for "profonde": thus, he appears to assume that the mountains are "ime" and the valleys "profonde." That cannot be the case: mountains (a masculine noun in Italian) would be "imi," not "ime," but one would never apply the adjective to them anyway, given that "imo" is an archaic, literary word for "deep" (drawing on "imus," the poetic contraction of the Latin "infimus" as often used by Virgil). Tasso also makes it clear that valleys can be "ime e profonde" (*Gerusalemme liberata*, Canto 12, stanza 11, line 2): that is, deep in two directions, both horizontal and vertical. There is nothing one can do about Monteverdi's misreading of the word—if this is what his setting of "ime" is—although one might fix those translations of this text that regularly adopt some version of "the high mountains and deep valleys," influenced by Monteverdi's setting rather than consulting a standard dictionary.

Monteverdi seems to have had other difficulties, however, with what parts of the natural world can produce what kinds of sounds. Zephyr's "sweet accents" make the flowers dance to his murmuring ("e mormorando tra le verdi fronde . . ."), but Monteverdi gets confused by another case of murmuring breezes. In his setting of the sonnet "Movete al mio bel suon le piante snelle" (the *ballo* introduced by "Volgendo in ciel per immortal sentiero") in the Eighth Book, the Canto partbook has the correct "d'aure odorate al mormorar giocondo": clouds and storms should give way to "the cheerful murmuring of perfumed breezes," with "giocondo" rhyming with "biondo," "fondo," and "mondo." The other voices, however, have

Ex. 7.1 "Zefiro torna e di soavi accenti" (*Scherzi musicali*, 1632).

an aquatic "d'aure odorate al mormorar dell'onde," where the murmuring streams break the rhyme and make no grammatical sense. Monteverdi uses a similar "murmuring" musical motif for "mormorar" here as he does for "mormorando" in "Zefiro torna e di soavi accenti." But in "Movete al mio bel suon," he seems instinctively to have gone for a faint echo of "Ecco mormorar l'onde" in the Second Book. In the later setting, some editorial fix is needed, and the arguments seem strongly weighted in favor of "giocondo."[13]

Cases in which Monteverdi has misread the syntax of a poem are no less revealing. In the case of "Vattene pur, crudel, con quella pace" in the Third Book, there was little he could do about the enjambment from the first to the second stanza, given the division of the setting into separate *parti*. But he had no excuse for ignoring a similar situation in "O rossignuol ch'in queste verdi fronde" in the same collection. This is the first stanza of a canzone by Pietro Bembo, and it falls into three four-line segments (it started life as a sonnet).[14] The first is a vocative addressing the nightingale, extended by two relative clauses, so it leads directly to the second segment, which, in turn, has an enjambment to the third (shown in italic here):

> alterna teco in note alte e profonde
> la tua compagna, e par che ti consoli.
> A me, perch'io mi strugga, e pianto e duoli
> versi ad ogn'hor, nissun *giamai risponde,*
> *né di mio danno* si sospira e geme.
> E te, s'un dolor preme
> ...

[there alternates with you in notes high and low / your companion, and she seems to console you. / To me, for all that I suffer, and tears and sobs / do I scatter everywhere, *no one ever responds, / nor for my injury* sighs and weeps. / And for you, if pressed by grief...]

Monteverdi has no business creating a strong cadence (on G) for "giamai risponde" and a new start (on C) for "né di mio danno" (the continuing "nor for my injury sighs and weeps"). However, he does realize that there is a full stop at the end of that line, meaning that "E te..." prompts another new start.

---

[13] This is not the only problem here. The double sonnet "Volgendo in ciel"/"Movete al mio bel suon" was written by Rinuccini to celebrate a birthday of King Henri IV of France, so as in other cases in the Eighth Book, the poetry needed to be modified to suit Viennese circumstances. The text in the Canto partbook (S¹) is in general closer to Rinuccini's original: for example, it gives "in sì bel dì"—a reference to the "fine day" of the birthday—rather than the more neutral "in questo dì" in ATB (S² also has "in sì bel dì," but not the other variants in S¹). However, S¹ also reflects an intermediate version: it has "e lasciato del mar il ricco fondo" for Rinuccini's "e lasciato di Senna il ricco fondo" (the Seine), whereas S²AB have "e lasciato dell'Istro il ricco fondo" (the Danube), and T, "e lasciato dell'Istro il negro fondo." Other differences (and better readings) suggest that in this case, the manuscript for the Canto partbook may have been copied by someone different from Monteverdi, and one more attentive to literary issues. In other words, the situation here is similar to the different sources for the *Combattimento* typeset in the Eighth Book (see Chapter 3).

[14] Georis, *Claudio Monteverdi*, 412 n. 12.

There are numerous other examples in the Third Book where Monteverdi misplaces a hiatus within his text setting. In "Ch'io non t'ami, cor mio?" the poem ends with a four-line question:

> Ma se tu sei quel core onde la vita
> m'è sì dolce e gradita,
> fonte d'ogni mio ben, d'ogni desire,
> come poss'io lasciarti e non morire?

[But if you are that heart wherefrom life / is so sweet and welcome to me, / fount of all my happiness, of all desire, / how can I leave you and not die?]

Here "fonte d'ogni mio ben, d'ogni desire" is a parenthetical adjectival phrase within an "if . . . how" construction. But Monteverdi treats it as a vocative: he makes a new start at "fonte d'ogni mio ben," and only the last two lines of the poem are repeated at the end of the setting.[15] This seems to be a typical behavior of his: when texts are too long, when the principal clause is too far away from the start of a sentence, and/or when there are too many questions (which I have noted are hard to deal with in musical terms), he breaks them down into shorter, more manageable units, even if that means losing sight of the broader syntactical or even rhetorical structure.[16]

"Volgea l'anima mia soavemente" (Fourth Book) suffers on all these grounds and more. Guarini's poem begins with a long four-line sentence where the principal verb comes only at the end—the "parea dire" that introduces the direct speech of what the beloved "seemed" to say:

> Volgea l'anima mia soavemente
> quel suo caro e lucente
> sguardo, tutto beltà, tutto desire,
> verso me scintillando, e parea dire:
> «Dami il tuo cor, ché non altrond'i' vivo.»

[My beloved sweetly turned / her dear, shining / gaze, full of beauty, full of desire, / toward me, sparkling, and seemed to say: / "Give me your heart, for nowhere else do I live."]

---

[15] In terms of last-line repetitions, Monteverdi makes a similar mistake in "Occhi, un tempo mia vita" (Third Book). The penultimate line of Guarini's poem is a question ("forse per non mirar come v'adoro?") and the last, an imperative ("Mirate almen ch'io moro"). However, Monteverdi treats these two lines as a single syntactic unit and repeats them as such. In "La piaga c'ho nel core" (Fourth Book), Monteverdi does the reverse, repeating the last line at great length (for exactly half of the setting) divorced from the preceding line that makes it part of a question.

[16] Compare also "Non sono in queste rive" (Second Book), where Monteverdi loses track of the syntax created by a "né" clause.

150   MONTEVERDI'S VOICES

A simpler version of the opening, in two seven-syllable lines, would be "Volgea l'anima mia / suo sguardo, e parea dire" (My beloved turned / her gaze, and seemed to say), although of course Guarini would never be so crass. But Monteverdi has to break down this complex syntax (my full stop indicates a strong cadence, and semicolons, weak ones):

> Volgea l'anima mia soavemente.
> Quel suo caro e lucente sguardo;
> quel suo caro e lucente sguardo;
> tutto beltà, tutto desire, verso me scintillando;
> e parea dire: «Dami il tuo cor . . .

He loses the enjambment between Guarini's lines 1–2 but makes it reasonably clear between lines 2–3 (after a repetition of l. 2). He then builds up a nice progression in all five voices through "tutto beltà . . . scintillando." His handling of "e parea dire: / «Dami il tuo cor," however, poses one of those typical voicing problems for the introduction of direct speech. He moves to the three upper voices (SSA), but overlaps the "dire" with the beginning of what the beloved "appears" to say (Ex. 7.2). Monteverdi must have realized the advantage of the three voices arriving on the same consonant ("Dami" and "dire"), and also the offbeat entry in S^2 of "Dami il tuo cor": simple homophony would have given too strong an impression of something actually said. Moreover, had he put "e parea dire" in a different voice grouping (ATB?), it might have contradicted the idea that all this is happening in the mind of a lover tending to hear whatever is wanted to be heard. But when it comes to the lover's direct speech at "sospirando gridai" ("sighing, I cried out: 'Wretched and deprived / of my heart, who gives me life?'"), Monteverdi hedges his bets on where it starts (at "Wretched . . ." or "Who . . ."). He manages to recover only when the beloved replies ("Io, che son il tuo core"), making the typical double play of a "female" voice (SSA) followed by the lover repeating and reveling in what she says, with a glorious descending line spanning an eleventh first in T and then, within the full texture, in B. Here things come into musical focus precisely because the poetry becomes clear.

Ex. 7.2 "Volgea l'anima mia soavemente" (Fourth Book, 1603; TB are silent).

Parenthetical clauses that separate a subject from its main verb leave Monteverdi in a quandary. In the TT setting of "Tornate, o cari baci" in the Seventh Book, Marino's text has a typically roundabout way of getting to the point of what kisses should do:[17]

> Voi di quel dolce amaro
> per cui languir m'è caro,
> di quel vostro non meno
> nettare che veleno,
> pascete i miei famelici desiri:

[You, with that sweet bitterness / which makes languishing dear to me, / of your no less / nectar than poison, / feed my famished desires:]

Monteverdi clarifies the "Voi . . . pascete" construction by having T[2] twice deliver the line containing the verb early, leaving the rest of the words to T[1]:

> T[1]:   Voi di quel dolce amaro . . .
> T[2]:   *pascete i miei famelici desiri*
> T[1]:   di quel dolce amaro / per cui languir m'è caro,
> T[2]:   *pascete i miei famelici desiri*
> T[1]:   di quel dolce [sic] non meno / nettare che veleno,
> T[2]T[1]: pascete i miei famelici desiri, pascete i miei . . .

This seems like an act of despair and is very hard to bring off in performance. Once more, things come back into focus only with the last line: "baci, in cui dolci provo anco i sospiri" (kisses, in which I also feel sweet sighs). This is a somewhat irregular vocative with a dependent clause, but Monteverdi appears not to care about the grammar: perhaps he is glad just to have reached the end.

In "Tornate, o cari baci," Monteverdi seems to have been carried away by Marino's "dolce" (which he sets by way of a glorious chromatic slide), given that he adds an extra one in lieu of Marino's "vostro" ("di quel dolce non meno" for "di quel vostro non meno"). We might argue over whether this is a "mistake," but it is not untypical of the composer's willingness to make direct changes to the poetry if needed. Some of them are logical enough. In the Fourth Book, the poet's "La piaga del mio core / onde si lieta, o bella Silvia, hor sei"—the text is by Alessandro Striggio the younger—becomes "La piaga c'ho nel core, / Donna, onde lieta sei," turning the reference to Silvia into a generic "lady."[18] Similar changes can serve a music-rhetorical

---

[17] Giles, *Monteverdi and the Marvellous*, 154–55.

[18] For the prior (mis)attributions of the poem to Aurelio or Alessandro Gatti, see Georis, *Claudio Monteverdi*, 442 n. 18. Its author can now be properly identified, given that in the collection *Ghilranda* [sic] *dell'aurora*, edited by Pietro Petracci (Venice: Bernardo Giunti & Giovanni Battista Ciotti, 1609), 383, it is attributed "del Ritenuto Academico Invaghito," and "Il ritenuto" was Alessandro Striggio's academic name within the Mantuan Accademia degli Invaghiti.

purpose. In "Vorrei baciarti, o Filli" (Seventh Book), Marino's lover cannot decide where first to kiss Filli ("ma non so prima"): whether on the eyes or the mouth. Monteverdi's does not know "how" to kiss her ("ma non so come"), which allows for a witty repetition ("Ma non so, non so come, non so come").[19]

Other changes, however, seem to reflect a moment of confusion on his part. In "Anima mia, perdona" (Fourth Book), Monteverdi makes two significant alterations to Amarilli's speech in Act III, scene 4 of Guarini's *Il pastor fido*, one more plausible than the other. Amarilli has just sent Mirtillo away: she cannot admit her love for him, although it is powerful enough.

> E tu, Mirtillo (anima mia), perdona
> a chi t'è cruda sol, dove pietosa
> esser non può: perdona a questa solo
> nei detti, e nel sembiante
> rigida tua nemica, ma nel core
> pietosissima amante.

[And you, Mirtillo (my soul), forgive / her who is wont to be cruel to you, when pitying / she cannot be. Forgive her who only / in words and in look / [is] your inflexible enemy, but in her heart / [is] a most pitying lover.]

Changing the first line to "Anima mia, perdona" makes sense so as not to mention Mirtillo, and it remains metrically correct, now as a seven-syllable line. But Monteverdi also removes the "solo" at the end of line 3 (producing "perdona a questa nei detti . . ."). This misses Amarilli's point (she is cruel only in words and look but not in her heart) and produces an irregular line. However, he may have worried about whether "solo" should be "sola" (an adjective agreeing with the female Amarilli), even though its role as an adverb is clear. There is no such justification, however, for the change to the first stanza of the Sestina in the Sixth Book, where Monteverdi ends line 5 with "in pianto, in foco" rather than the correct "in foco, in pianto"; he may have thought that "foco" rhymes with Glauco (producing a rhyming couplet to form the end of the stanza), but the line must end in "pianto," which is the word repeated in subsequent stanzas according to the sestina format. Elsewhere in the Sestina, too, Monteverdi sometimes seems just to give up in despair: the end of its *seconda parte* ("Ditelo, o fiumi, e voi ch'udiste Glauco") comes close to nonsense.[20]

Poetry can often be confusing in this manner—and Guarini's more than most—both on a local level and more broadly. Thus, Monteverdi's apparent resistance to complex or confusing syntax occasionally leads, whether consciously or not, to

---

[19] Georis, *Claudio Monteverdi*, 72–73.
[20] For the *seconda parte*, Monteverdi appears to be worried about line 5 ("letto, o sasso felice, il tuo bel seno"), which makes scant sense. He therefore sets the last three lines of the stanza as lines 4, 6, 4, 6, 5 + 6 (superimposed), 6.

significant intervention in the poetry he sets, however unwarranted it might be in purely literary terms.[21] There is a rather drastic example in "Deh, bella e cara e sì soave un tempo" in the Fifth Book (the *seconda parte* of "Ch'io t'ami, e t'ami più de la mia vita"). In Act III, scene 3 of *Il pastor fido*, Mirtillo asks Amarilli to turn her eyes to him:

> E dritto è ben, che se mi furo un tempo
> dolci segni di vita, hor sien di morte
> que' begli occhi amorosi,
> e quel soave sguardo,
> che mi scorse ad amare
> mi scorga anco à morire,
> e chi fù l'alba mia,
> del mio cadente dì l'Espero hor sia.

[And indeed it is well, that if once to me were / sweet signs of life, now are of death / those fair, loving eyes; / and that sweet gaze / which saw me fall in love / should also see me die; / and she who was my dawn / should now be the evening star of my dying day.]

Guarini wrote three successive "and" clauses here: "E dritto ... ," "e quel ... ," and "e chi ... ." This is too complex, and Monteverdi turns it into two four-line sentences: "e quel soave sguardo" gets linked to the "occhi amorosi," and "che mi scorse" is turned into the start of a new sentence as "Chi mi scorse." His reading therefore changes the argument:

And indeed it is well, that if once to me were / sweet signs of life, now are of death / those fair, loving eyes, / and that sweet gaze. / She who saw me fall in love / should also see me die; / and she who was my dawn / should now be the evening star of my dying day.

Still greater interventions appear elsewhere. When Monteverdi cuts a line from a poem, as in Rinuccini's "Sfogava con le stelle" (Fourth Book), it is not clear whether it is by accident or intentional; there does not seem to be any justification for it in any of the poem's poetic sources or in other musical settings.[22] But intentional cutting

---

[21] But sometimes all it takes is a change of preposition. In "Altri canti di Marte e di sua schiera" (Eighth Book), Monteverdi's setting changes line 5 of Marino's sonnet from "Io canto, Amor, da questa tua guerriera" to "... di questa tua guerriera." Marino's syntax is complex, spanning two lines: "I" am singing of the mortal offenses delivered by the beloved, whereas Monteverdi's "I" is singing about the beloved, [and] how many mortal offenses he has received (so two lines are kept separate). However, Monteverdi's setting then makes a "mistake" with the following "quant'hebbe" in all voices save T^1, which has the correct "quant'hebbi." This is another case within the Eighth Book where different scribal mannerisms are apparent in different parts.

[22] The same appears true of Monteverdi's turning an *endecasillabo* into a *settenario* in "Ecco mormorar l'onde" (Second Book), noted in Tomlinson, *Monteverdi and the End of the Renaissance*, 49 n. 21.

is certainly the case in the *lettera amorosa*, "Se i languidi miei sguardi" (Seventh Book), which loses a large amount of Claudio Achillini's excessively verbose text, with just under two hundred lines reduced to seventy-eight. Monteverdi had more respect for Ottavio Rinuccini to the extent of keeping his *partenza amorosa*, "Se pur destina e vòle," intact (108 lines). However, Rinuccini's paraphrase and expansion of Ovid in "Ogni amante è guerrier: nel suo gran regno" (Eighth Book) is cut by about a half (to eighty-four lines), probably to make it more plausible as an encomium to Emperor Ferdinand III. On the other hand, the "missing" lines in the SSA setting of "Su, su, su, pastorelli" in the Eighth Book—which leave the poem making no sense whatsoever—are almost certainly accidental: Monteverdi seems to have taken the text from the bass part of the TTB setting eventually included in the Ninth Book, forgetting that some phrases of the poem were presented only by the tenors.[23]

Adding lines to a poem poses different questions. Creating a return to the opening of "Non è di gentil core" (Seventh Book) at its end, with an added "Dunque" (Therefore) certainly makes sense for a poem that otherwise falls completely flat, and it allows for the same music to round off the setting.[24] The added lines in the setting of Tasso's "Al lume delle stelle" (Seventh Book) have greater impact, however. This is for four voices and continuo, and an opening narration (SSTB) sets the nighttime scene as Tirsi sits under laurel, pouring forth his grief "in these accents" ("in questi accenti"). The text then moves to direct speech for his address to the stars, to which Monteverdi adds two lines (in italic here):

«O celesti facelle,
di lei ch'amo ed adoro
rassomigliate voi gli occhi lucenti.
Luci care e serene,
sento gli affanni, ohimè, sento le pene.
Luci serene e liete,
sento le fiamme lor mentre splendete.»

["O heavenly torches, / of her whom I love and adore / do you resemble the shining eyes. / *Lights dear and serene, / I feel the torments, alas, I feel the pains.* / Lights serene and happy, / I feel their flames while you shine."]

Monteverdi makes one change within Tasso's text, where the final line has just a singular flame ("sento la fiamma lor mentre splendete"). More drastic, however, are those two new lines. They seem prompted in part by the circumstances of a

---

[23] Carter, "Two Monteverdi Problems," 427–32.

[24] For the addition, which is unique to Monteverdi's setting, see Georis, *Claudio Monteverdi*, 536 n. 12. As Georis notes, the common attribution of this poem to Francesco degli Atti is incorrect (although Degli Atti did produce a musical setting of it in 1613). Pirrotta ("Monteverdi's Poetic Choices," 305–6) reads the text as a ballata because of the return of lines 1–2, but if it is, that is Monteverdi's doing.

four-voice setting. For the direct speech ("O celesti . . ."), Monteverdi moves logically enough from his SSTB narration to a TB duet as Tirsi speaks "in these accents," with embellishments to match. Yet he cannot leave his two sopranos out of the reckoning: therefore, they enter with the added "Luci care e serene . . ." The tenor and bass respond with "Luci serene e liete" but are soon joined by the two sopranos to produce a four-voice ending, which is what the setting requires.

Those two lines are not the best poetry, but they do more than just allow the two sopranos to sing. The "luci" addressed by Tirsi in the last two lines of the poem are the stars that make him feel the flames of his beloved's eyes. The added lines seem to suggest that those same stars first make him feel torments and pains. But allocating them to the sopranos confuses the issue of who is addressing what, or whom, and what the source of any lights might be (stars or eyes) that now contain plural "flames." The result hints at some kind of dialogue in the manner of "Luci serene e chiare" in the Fourth Book, although in that case Monteverdi did not need to have words added to the text. But his treatment of "Al lume delle stelle" fits in with the whole program of the Seventh Book directed to Caterina de' Medici, Duchess of Mantua, as she negotiates a tricky marriage with her "Tirsi," the duke.

There is one strange case, however, where Monteverdi seems to have felt the need for an added line, even though he did not act upon it. The setting of Guarini's "O come sei gentile" (Seventh Book) takes full advantage of the comparison between the lover and a songbird imprisoned in its cage. There is one problem in the text, however. It first appeared as follows in the poet's 1598 collection of *Rime*:

> O come se' gentile,
> caro augellino: o quanto
> è 'l mio stato amoroso al tuo simile.
> Tu prigion, io prigion; tu canti, io canto,
> tu canti per colei,
> che t'ha legato, ed io canto per lei.
> Ma in questo è differente
> la mia [sorte] dolente,[25]
> che giova pur a te l'esser canoro.
> Vivi cantando, ed io cantando moro.

[Oh how kind you are, / dear bird, oh how / is my amorous state like yours. / You are a prisoner, I a prisoner; you sing, I sing. / You sing for her / who has bound you, and I sing for her. / But in this is different / my sad fate: / that it benefits you to be songful. / You live singing, and I, singing, die.]

---

[25] Guarini typically has ellipses for "sorte" (fate) for fear of backlash from the Inquisition.

Monteverdi's setting changes line 4 of the poem to "Io prigion, tu prigion" (reversing the "io" and "tu") so as to create a neat chiasmus ("I ... you ... you ... I"). But he does something odder later on.

The English lute-song composer John Danyel (1564–c. 1626) published a setting of this text in translation in his *Songs for the Lute, Viol and Voice* (London: T[homas] E[ast] for Thomas Adams, 1606). The book contains other settings of texts modeled on Italian poets: in one case Guarini (again) and in another, Petrarch.[26] The influence seems to have come from Danyel's elder brother, Samuel (1562–1619), who was a poet and later playwright of some distinction: his published poetry includes translations of Tasso and Marino, and he was also closely associated with the newfound craze for Guarini in Elizabethan and Jacobean England, having made a trip to Italy sometime around 1590 when he met the poet himself.[27] In the case of "O come se' gentile," the version set by John Danyel follows the Italian closely, with one significant exception (in italic, below).

> Thou pretty bird, how do I see
> Thy silly state and mine agree;
> For thou a prisoner art,
> So is my heart.
> Thou sing'st to her, and so do I address
> *My music to her ear that's merciless.*
> But herein doth the difference lie:
> That thou art grac'd, so am not I;
> Thou singing liv'st, and I must singing die.

There is no known Italian source for that added line: either it is pure invention, or it comes from a version of Guarini's poem that existed prior to its first publication in 1598 (to which, one might suggest, Samuel Danyel gained access in 1590). Whatever that case, it does solve a problem, for Guarini's "Tu canti per colei, / che t'ha legato, ed io canto per lei" (You sing for her / who has bound you, and I sing for her) is singularly inelegant both for the "colei"/"lei" rhyme in two consecutive lines, and for the fact that "I sing for her" seems to require some continuation ("I sing for her who ..."). Danyel's added line is much more satisfactory.

---

[26] Danyel's "I die when as I do not see" (no. 14) treats as two parallel stanzas Guarini's "Io mi sento morir quando non miro" and "Parlo, misero, o taccio?" (Madrigals nos. 55 and 54 in the *Rime*; the English version is attributed to "Jo: Richards" in a manuscript source of the poem). Likewise, Danyel's "Now the earth, the skies, the ayre" adapts two Petrarch sonnets (*RVF* 164, 310). His volume was dedicated to the young Anne Grene; he was currently a household musician and tutor to the Grene family of Great Milton, near Oxford.

[27] Samuel Danyel (Daniel) is well known for his poem beginning "O happy age of gold" (headed "A Pastorall") that is a line-by-line translation of the Act I chorus from Tasso's *Aminta*. His poetic output also includes "A Description of Beauty, Translated out of Marino." His dedicatory poem to Sir Edward Dymoke in *Il Pastor Fido, or The Faithfull Shepheard. Translated out of Italian into English* (London: for Simon Waterson, 1602) refers to them both having met Guarini, who had little good to say about "the vertues of the North" (i.e., England), including its graceless coasts and its "barbarous tongues" incapable of poetry.

Ex. 7.3 "O come sei gentile" (Seventh Book, 1619).

Monteverdi had just the version of the poem published by Guarini in 1598. However, if we can trust the use of uppercase letters in the text underlay in the Canto partbook of the Seventh Book, he seems to have parsed lines 4–5 thus:

> Tu canti per colei che t'ha legato,
> Et io canto per lei.[28]

This is also how Monteverdi sets the text in terms of what now becomes a mid-line "colei," which is treated as two syllables ("co-lei") rather than the three that would be required at the end of a poetic line ("co-le-i"). This is neutral in poetic terms, with Guarini's two lines of seven then eleven syllables split differently into an eleven-syllable line and then a seven-syllable one. But whether one takes Guarini's reading or Monteverdi's, the "lei" at the end of "et io canto per lei" should definitely be a two-syllable "le-i" (Ex. 7.3). It is not.[29] This is unprecedented in Monteverdi's madrigals: whenever he encounters an end-of-line "lei" (or "sei," etc.), he always sets the diphthong to the correct two syllables.[30] Two suggestions follow. One is that he simply wanted to match what he had done for "co-lei." The other is that when he set "et io canto per lei" to music, he somehow sensed that the text should continue to complete an eleven-syllable line, even if he was going to separate that continuation by way of a cadence. But John Danyel was probably right: something is indeed missing.[31]

---

[28] So it is styled in the Canto partbook, which continues "ma in questo è differente la mia sorte dolente..." The Quinto partbook (S²) has "tu canti per colei che t'ha legato Et io canto per lei ma in questo E differente La mia sorte dolente..."

[29] And to forestall an obvious objection, the text underlay in the Canto partbook is absolutely clear (but it is less so in the Quinto): "-to" is under the b♭', "per" under the a', and "lei" under the g'. It would also be wholly implausible in light of the standard rules for text underlay to push everything back one note ("-to" under the quarter-note a' at the end of the dotted run) therefore allowing a two-syllable "le-i."

[30] Likewise, he quite properly treats such diphthongs as one syllable in mid-line: the opening of "Volgea l'anima mia soavemente" (Fourth Book) is a typical example ("mia" rather than "mi-a"). The same is true of his entirely correct treatment of the eleven-syllable line "de le speranze mie. Tu ben sei quella" in "O primavera gioventù de l'anno," confounding the insistence of some editors on treating it as two separate lines of verse; compare Georis, *Claudio Monteverdi*, 418.

[31] There is another English setting of a version of this poem, by Orlando Gibbons (1583–1625) in his *The First Set of Madrigals and Mottets of 5. Parts Apt for Viols and Voyces* (London: Thomas Snodham, 1612). His "Dainty fine bird that art encaged there" solves the problem by way of an adaption that is closer to Guarini, if still with a significant difference: "Both prisoners be; and both singing, thus / Strive to please her that hath imprisoned us."

Some of these kinds of issues in Monteverdi's presentation and parsing of his texts may be due to his specific poetic sources: surprisingly few of them have yet been pinned down in any precise manner, whether from literary collections or from musical settings by other composers. One wonders, too, about the extent to which they may have arisen by some manner of oral transmission, or just by faulty memory. Some of his "mistakes" in fact give hints of the latter: when he was writing out the score in that tenor partbook for the *Combattimento di Tancredi e Clorinda*, he did not conscientiously consult some printed copy of Tasso's *Gerusalemme liberata* on a line-by-line basis, even if the editor of the continuo score did something of that kind. There is also no doubt that Monteverdi could be careless at times. But other interventions must have been deliberate on his part. They reveal a great deal about what Monteverdi expected of his texts, and what he was willing to do if they failed to deliver it.

8
Musical (Im)pertinence

When Artusi launched his critique of Monteverdi's madrigals in his *L'Artusi, overo Delle imperfettioni della moderna musica* in 1600, he paid no attention to their poetic texts. Indeed, he printed his notated music examples without any words. Giulio Cesare Monteverdi, in turn, viewed that lapse as opening the door to his own defense of his brother's music by way of the *seconda pratica*. If this "second" practice, unlike the "first," was predicated upon the *oratione* taking precedence over other musical elements, then the music needed to be judged according to its expression and delivery of the text, and its licenses could be explained and excused accordingly. Looking just at the musical notes completely missed the point.

No music theorist was going to accept that argument, given that the rules governing musical harmony and rhythm were well established by tradition on the one hand, and by reason on the other. Artusi, now in his late fifties, felt that younger would-be modern composers were too ready to cast them aside just to tickle the fancy of ignorant ears. He constructed his treatise as dialogue in which he, as "Vario," gently but sternly instructs his friend, "Luca," on various musical matters. "Luca," in turn, just happens to have brought with him scored-up passages of two madrigals that he heard "yesterday" (Monday, 16 November 1598) at a performance at the house of Antonio Goretti in Ferrara: Monteverdi's "Cruda Amarilli, che col nome ancora" (Fifth Book) and the *prima* and *seconda parte* of "Anima mia, perdona" (Fourth).[1] Luca then brings to Vario's attention another piece he had encountered "not too many days ago": Monteverdi's "O Mirtillo, Mirtill'anima mia," also published later in the Fifth Book. If Luca is to be believed, he was present on two separate occasions on which Monteverdi's madrigals were performed, presumably both in Ferrara when the future Queen of Spain was present in the city.[2] The composer is not named, but until Monteverdi's defender with the academic name "L'Ottuso" came into the frame (as noted by Artusi in the *Seconda parte dell'Artusi*

---

[1] Stras (*Women and Music in Sixteenth-Century Ferrara*, 316–17) suggests that the performers on that evening might have been Livia d'Arco and Laura Peverara (two singers from the former *concerto delle dame*) plus Ippolito Fiorini, and Luzzasco Luzzaschi.

[2] This is curious. Artusi represents the dialogue between Luca and Vario as taking place on two days, the first part on 16 November, and the second (concerning Monteverdi's madrigals) on the 17th. Luca says that he was invited to visit Goretti's house later on the 16th; hence his bringing the actual music of Monteverdi's two madrigals the next day. Of course, Artusi himself was writing after the fact—so this could all be fiction—but it is still not clear why he should have separated out the performance of "O Mirtillo" as not, in fact, taking place on the 16th.

in 1603), his madrigals are the only ones submitted as examples of modern improprieties.

Artusi's criticisms hinged on the patent irregularities within Monteverdi's handling of dissonances on the one hand, and mode on the other. In his second treatise of 1603, he also complained about "Era l'anima mia" and "Ma se con la pietà non è in te spenta" (the *seconda parte* of "Ecco, Silvio, colei che in odio hai tanto"), both in the Fifth Book, because of their homophonic openings reiterating a single chord and therefore creating just "concento" (a combination of high, middle, and low sounds) but not the "modulatione" (movement from one sound to another) that was essential for music.[3] As the controversy heated up, Artusi (under the pseudonym Antonio Braccino da Todi) later added a third proof of Monteverdi's musical ignorance: his patent misunderstanding of the correct mensuration signs that governed the *tactus* and its potential subdivision in duple and triple proportion (we would now call them time signatures, although their meaning is different). So far as those signs are concerned, Artusi had a point: the use or misuse of them by early-seventeenth-century composers remain a matter of controversy even today in terms of proportional shifts from duple to triple time or back, which is a matter of some importance for performances of this music.[4] As for his criticisms of Monteverdi's treatments of dissonances and mode, Artusi was on the wrong side of history. But the fact that he was the only figure of the time to engage in Monteverdi's music in any analytical depth means that he still serves a useful purpose in pointing out what might deserve attention within it.

An impertinent beginning

After a lengthy critique of the dissonances in "Cruda Amarilli," Luca goes on to complain to Vario about its modal irregularities by beginning in Mode 7 (G-mixolydian), then shifting to Mode 12 (C-hypoionian) or 8 (G-hypomixolydian) before ending back in Mode 7. This manner of composing is an "impertinence," he says ("essendo questo modo di comporre una impertinentia"). He continues by bringing another of Monteverdi's madrigals into play, for which he did not have the music to hand, it seems, although he was able to describe it well enough:

> Not too many days ago, I heard a madrigal that began on a note of the twelfth mode in the flat system. Then, if I remember it well, it ended up in the natural system and furnished the first [mode]. And it seems to me that the words of the madrigal were

---

[3] For "Ma se con la pietà," Artusi added a twist to his criticism: its repeated sonorities at the opening were more redolent of a popular *giustiniana* or a "spifarata alla Mantovana" than a madrigal proper. In the *Seconda parte dell'Artusi*, the theorist also extended his criticisms of modern composers in terms of their use of awkward intervals (presumably in terms of tuning) and extreme vocal ranges: Monteverdi was guilty of both.

[4] For the issues, and a summary of prior controversies, see Kurtzman, *The Monteverdi Vespers of 1610*, 433–57. The broader problems are discussed in DeFord, *Tactus, Mensuration, and Rhythm in Renaissance Music*, 169–79, 200–206.

Ex. 8.1 "O Mirtillo, Mirtill'anima mia" (Fifth Book, 1605).

"O Mirtillo" by Guarini, taken from *Il pastor fido*. This gave me much to think about, nor do I know how someone who professes to be capable should let himself be led astray into such imperfections, known even by boys who first begin to put their lips to the fount of Helicon.[5]

Thus, Luca complains about the opening of Monteverdi's "O Mirtillo, Mirtill'anima mia" (Ex. 8.1). His point is that its initial sonority, a major triad on B♭, belongs to transposed Mode 12 (Hypoionian in the flat system: C–C with a final on F), whereas the rest of the madrigal is in Mode 1 in the natural system (Dorian; D–D), eventually cadencing on D. This mixture of systems and modes in a single work is not to be condoned, especially when it creates an inconsistency between its beginning and its end. A marginal annotation at this point in Artusi's treatise directs the reader's attention to the "impertinence of a beginning of the madrigal 'O Mirtillo'" ("Impertinentia d'un principio del Madrigale ò Mirtillo").[6]

Luca is correct. But he seems unaware of what Monteverdi has done here. The opening of "O Mirtillo" is a direct quotation of a passage in "Cor mio, mentre vi miro" (Fourth Book).[7] The latter text, also by Guarini, notes how the lover is transformed on seeing the beloved:

---

[5] *L'Artusi, overo Delle imperfettioni della moderna musica* (1600), fol. 48v: "Ascoltai un Madrigale non molti giorni sono, che incominciava in una Corda del Modo duodecimo per b molle; dipoi se bene mi raccordo, si ridusse per b quadro, e fornì del primo; e parmi che le parole del Madrigale dicessero, ò Mirtillo, dal Guerino tolte nel Pastor Fido; il che molto mi dette che pensare, nè sò come uno che facci professione di valent'huomo, si lasci scorrere in simili imperfettioni, note sino a' putti che all'hora incominciano, à mettere il labro sul fonte d'Helicona."

[6] Artusi's comment, and "O Mirtillo" itself, have become something of a cause célèbre for those seeking to redeem Monteverdi, while also trying to justify the composer's "impertinence," or even just to figure out what mode the madrigal is in; for an overview, see Coluzzi, "Se vedesti qui dentro."

[7] I am not the first to notice the connection (see Chafe, *Monteverdi's Tonal Language*, 72), although it has not hitherto been used to engage with issues of mode. McClary (*Modal Subjectivities*, 188) builds on Chafe's observation to argue that the out-of-order opening of "O Mirtillo" reflects Amarilli's ambivalent emotional state, and is a "stammered response" to Mirtillo's harsh accusation in "Cruda Amarilli, che col nome ancora."

Ex. 8.2 "Cor mio, mentre vi miro" (Fourth Book, 1603; C1, C2, C3, F4; T [C4] is silent).

O bellezza mortale,
o bellezza vitale,
poi che sì tosto un core
per te rinasce, e per te nato more.

[Oh death-giving beauty / o life-giving beauty, / for as soon as a heart / is reborn for you, then born for you, it dies.]

Monteverdi switched those first two lines: Guarini has "O bellezza vitale, / o bellezza mortale," matching the "nato"/"more" opposition in his final line. But Monteverdi's "mortale," then "vitale," allow him to have an expressive exclamation in five-part homophony that he then repeats up an invigorating tone (Ex. 8.2).

In this part of "Cor mio, mentre vi miro," Monteverdi makes four statements of a harmonic pattern (in effect, a IV–[I^6]–V–I cadence) with the last note of one becoming the first of the next:[8]

	O bel-	lez-	za,
1	B♭[–F^6]	C	F
	bellezza mor-	ta-	le,
2	F[–C^6]	G	C
	o bel-	lez-	za,
3	C[–G^6]	D	G
	bellezza vi-	ta-	le,
4	G[–D^6]	A	D

Tomlinson's earlier "Madrigal, Monody, and Monteverdi's 'Via naturale alla immitatione,'" 68–69 n. 11, reversed the chronology, suggesting that "Cor mio, mentre vi miro" was composed after "O Mirtillo" on the basis of the repetition of "bellezza" extending Guarini's *settenario* to get closer to an *endecasillabo*. But that repetition is conventional enough.

[8] Compare Chafe, *Monteverdi's Tonal Language*, 63–64.

For "O Mirtillo" Monteverdi uses the same first statement of the pattern and elides it with the third:

	O Mir-	til-	lo,
1	B♭[–F⁶]	C	F
	Mirtill'anima	mi-	a,
3	C[–G⁶]	D	G

"Cor mio" has a sequence of V–I cadences each ending a fifth above (or a fourth below—it is the same) the previous one: F–C–G–D. Monteverdi then has the tenor restate "O bellezza mortale, o bellezza vitale"—underneath "poi che rinasce..." in the upper voices—backtracking to step 2 but continuing to what would be step 5 (D[–A⁶]–E–A). In the case of "O Mirtillo," Monteverdi's omission of step 2 does not alter the basic progression, given that the first note of step 3 (C) is a fifth above the final note of step 1 (F). These rising fifth progressions are quite typical of Monteverdi, and they have broader consequences for his gamut: that is, the overall harmonic range within which he can operate.[9] But to connect these two madrigals, he may also have been triggered by a grammatical resemblance (the vocative."O"), and still more, by an intertextual memory: in the penultimate line of "O Mirtillo," Amarilli rhetorically asks Mirtillo, "cor mio," what good it does him to be loved ("Che giova a te, cor mio, l'esser amato?").

"Cor mio, mentre vi miro" might well be read as being in the Dorian mode in the natural system: there is no flat in the key signature, and any B♭ required by standard voice-leading rules (such as *fa supra la*) is introduced by way of single accidentals. Its medial shift into what Luca identifies in "O Mirtillo" as a sonority specific to the transposed Hypoionian mode would not have caused a music theorist much anxiety: most admitted that so long as the beginning and end of a piece were clear, what happened in the middle was more open to compositional invention. However, even if Artusi had known the "Cor mio" connection, he would not have approved of Monteverdi's taking something permitted in the middle of a Dorian piece and putting it at the beginning.

---

[9] For rising or descending fifths, see Chafe, *Monteverdi's Tonal Language*, 35. Chafe views them as derived from the pitch content of hexachords, treating each pitch as the potential root of a triad and rearranging them: thus, the C-hexachord (pitches C, D, E, F, G, A) contains the roots of six triads (major or minor does not matter) related by fifths (E–A–D–G–C–F). He argues that this circle of fifths can be extend sharpward by way of the G-hexachord (B–E . . .) or flatward by the F-hexachord (. . . F–B♭) and the double-flat hexachord (. . . B♭–E♭); see the chart in *Monteverdi's Tonal Language*, 47. The notion of hexachords presenting a collection of triadic roots comes from Dahlhaus, *Studies on the Origins of Harmonic Tonality*, where they offer the potential for "component keys" (*Teiltonarten*) that exist independently of any functional or hierarchical significance in relation to the primary key or mode. However, this involves a leap of faith, given the very specific purpose of hexachords as a tool for determining the position of any *mi-fa* semitone. They do not present pitch classes for harmonic rearrangement.

Giulio Cesare Monteverdi responded to Artusi's criticism of "O Mirtillo" by claiming that it was unfair to judge parts of a madrigal without considering the whole. He also cited other examples of mixed-mode pieces, including Cipriano de Rore's "Quando, signor, lasciaste a entro le rive" (in his Fourth Book a5 of 1557). This sets a sonnet concerning the departure of Prince Alfonso d'Este from Ferrara and his return, so the text prompts some modal wandering.[10] But Giulio Cesare simply suggests that if Rore can begin his *prima parte* in Mode 11 and pass through Modes 2 and 10 before ending in Mode 1 (and Mode 8 in the *seconda parte*), then Monteverdi's beginning in Mode 12 and ending in Mode 1 in "O Mirtillo" has a clear precedent.

In this regard, even Artusi seems to have felt that he was on shaky ground. When Luca points out the impertinence of the opening of "O Mirtillo," Vario sidesteps the issue—it would take decades to discuss these modern compositions, he says— and he shifts into a conventional account of the modes that takes up the rest of his treatise. One can see why. Understanding the modes was an essential step in any musical training, but as Luca's subsequent questions to Vario reveal, students usually got confused, as any discussion quickly got bogged down in the links between modern modes and those of Classical Antiquity (Plato's Dorian, Phrygian, etc. "modes"), the difference between modes and psalm tones, whether there were eight or twelve modes, and so on. Monteverdi would have known full well that modes were octave species each made up of a rising stepwise fifth (a *diapente*) conjoined with a stepwise fourth (*diatessaron*); that what distinguished these octave species and their component segments were different patterns of tones and semitones; that the "final" of a mode (the note on which its scale began) required due prominence in structural cadences; that the fifth above the final (the co-final) had some importance save in the Phrygian mode on E, which was always a special case; and that each mode had particular characteristics in terms of the other notes of the scale on which cadences could be constructed.[11] He knew that "authentic" modes had the *diapente* below the *diatessaron* (so the final is the first degree of the scale), whereas the "plagal" ones (Hypodorian, etc.) had the *diatessaron* below the *diapente* (the final is the fourth degree of the scale), and that in writing polyphony, one was forced to mix both authentic and plagal versions of a mode if the piece was to be modally consistent (see Chapter 4). No less standard was the practice of transposing modes down a fifth/up a fourth by placing them in the flat system (the B♭ enables the preservation of the same sequence of tones and semitones), or more rarely, up a fifth/down a fourth by way of incorporating an F♯.

This was basic music theory covered, as Luca says, even by boys taking their first musical steps. Ingegneri would have drummed it into his young student, and if Monteverdi forgot any of it, he could refresh his memory by turning to his own

---

[10] Luoma, "Relationships between Music and Poetry."
[11] The semitone between the first two steps of the Phrygian mode (E–F) created a problem for final cadences in the mode, and also for the formation of any triad on its fifth degree (B; given the B–F tritone).

copy of the standard music treatise of the period, Gioseffo Zarlino's *Istitutioni harmoniche*.[12] But mode, on its own, is not a particularly useful analytical tool for dealing with Monteverdi unless one engages with its structural elements and their consequences. Even at the most basic level of descriptive labeling, it does not serve much purpose to know that such and such piece is in, say, the transposed Dorian mode (in the flat system with a G final). An exception might usefully be made in situations that could lead to interpretative misunderstanding. One case in point is the Phrygian-mode "Ch'io non t'ami, cor mio?" (Third Book), which ends with a perfectly standard cadence for that mode that will nevertheless sound unresolved to modern ears (because of the final chord sounding like a "dominant"), therefore prompting some (mis)reading that Monteverdi wanted its final line left hanging as the lover asks how he can leave his beloved and not die ("come poss'io lasciarti e non morire?").[13] But more recent arguments over the mode(s) of "O Mirtillo, Mirtill'anima mia" have not borne much fruit, and indeed the fact that all the settings in Monteverdi's Fifth Book have either a D or a G final (in the latter case, in the natural or flat system) suggests that categorizing them as Dorian, transposed Dorian, or Mixolydian is not going to help account for their musical conduct or their rich harmonic variety.

This is true for much of Monteverdi's music. However, it is not to deny that modal elements are built into the fabric of his madrigals. The *diapente* fifth and *diatessaron* fourth that comprise the modal octave set tangible, while flexible, limits within which melodic and harmonic activity can take place.[14] The "rules" allow extending that octave by one note on either side, producing an effective range of a tenth. But Monteverdi tends to use that upper extension quite carefully. He also treats the *diapente* as the primary field of activity. The Canto part at the beginning of "Cor mio, mentre vi miro" first operates within the *diapente* of its authentic Dorian mode, articulating a descent from the fifth degree to the second ($a'-e'$). The next phrase ("visibilmente mi trasform'in voi") moves into the upper *diatessaron* (plus one note, an e'' that will become important), cadencing on the co-final, a'. That initial descent ($a'-e'$), left incomplete on the second degree of the *diapente*, requires completion to the final (d'), which comes at the end of the first complete

---

[12] Zarlino's treatise was first published in 1558. The copy of the 1573 edition signed by Monteverdi (now in the Beinecke Rare Books and Manuscript Library, Yale University) is shown in Reese, *Music in the Renaissance*, Plate IV (between pp. 366 and 367).

[13] The A–E final cadence, with a major triad on the E, is absolutely standard in the Phrygian mode, given the impossibility of a more normal authentic/perfect (V–I) cadence because of the difficulties of building a triad on B. The problem is that it will "sound" to modern ears as a half (imperfect) cadence (i–V) in A minor. Susan McClary (*Modal Subjectivities*, passim) tends consistently to treat such settings as being in some version of the Aeolian mode and ending on the "dominant," but see the counterarguments in Coluzzi, "Black Sheep." One might, of course, argue that Monteverdi chose the Phrygian mode (which is extremely rare for him) for this text precisely because of this problem with its cadences, but that still raises the question of whether one can or should listen to this music with "tonal" ears.

[14] My discussion of *diapente* descents owes some obvious debts to McClary, *Modal Subjectivities*, plus the Schenkerian twist added by Seth Coluzzi in his "Structure and Interpretation in Luca Marenzio's Settings of *Il pastor fido*." McClary's resistance to Schenkerian analysis is not unusual, although her *diapente* descents (and their subsidiary extensions) are very amenable to such analysis, and her notation of them would benefit from it.

Ex. 8.3 "Cor mio, mentre vi miro" (Fourth Book, 1603; C1, C2, C3, C4; B [F4] is silent).

sentence of the text as the lover expires in a single sigh (Ex. 8.3). Having taken the Canto up to *e″* also allows Monteverdi to have two stepwise descents of a fifth covering two statements of "l'anima spiro," one to the co-final (*e″–a′*) and then from the co-final to the final.[15] The second descent enables the cadence on D, although Monteverdi reduces it to just two voices as the lover "expires" off the beat: this serves the text but also signals that matters textual and musical are not yet finished. With a Dorian mode so clearly established, however, what comes next—the B♭ chord on "O bellezza" (see Ex. 8.2)—cannot really disrupt it, however disruptive that same chord might seem at the beginning of "O Mirtillo, Mirtill'anima mia."

That cadence on D at "l'anima spiro" has been anticipated (by the initial incomplete *diapente* descent), delayed (by a secondary descent), and finally achieved, although only in two out of the five voices. Having a *diapente* descent to a note other than the final (as the *e″–a′*) also has the potential to open up different spheres of melodic and harmonic activity that might still operate within the primary mode but can also suggest a different one, generating what Artusi would have called modal mixture. This is clear in a madrigal that turns the *diapente* descent into a motto: in "«T'amo mia vita!», la mia cara vita" (Fifth Book) the lover rejoices in hearing the beloved's separate statements of "I love you, my life" descending to different degrees of the Dorian scale until they merge in an outpouring of contrapuntal ecstasy.

These short-, medium-, and even long-term *diapente* descents bear significant weight in Monteverdi's musical thought, both for expressive purposes and, when they are on a larger scale, to maintain control of the broader structure. The question, however, is how to offer harmonic support for the five notes of the descent. The easiest option is to treat each one save the last as the fifth of a triad: thus, the descent of the *diapente* defining the A-aeolian mode, E–D–C–B(–A) would be supported

---

[15] These 5–2(–1) descents outlining primary (to the final) and secondary diapentes (e.g., to the co-final) are particularly clear in "Darà la notte il sol lume alla terra" (the *terza parte* of "Incenerite spoglie, avara tomba") in the Sixth Book. Tomlinson (*Monteverdi and the End of the Renaissance*, 144–45) reads them as descending 8–5 tetrachords, which misses the point.

in the bass by A–G–F–E(–A), producing the chord sequence i–VII–VI–V(–i). This is exactly what Monteverdi does at the beginning of "A un giro sol de' belli occhi lucenti" (Fourth Book), and he tries, but largely fails, to avoid the obvious problem with this model: the consecutive fifths between the outer parts. They were a common feature of the more "popular" villanella and canzonetta, and Monteverdi also takes the formula into his madrigals in multiple modal contexts.[16]

Although Monteverdi's earlier madrigals tended to be derived from the structures and idioms of the three-voice canzonetta, consecutive fifths were not on the whole to be condoned in more sophisticated polyphony. They might be useful in "Io mi son giovinetta" (Fourth Book), in G-hypodorian (although the parts extend far beyond the modal octave), where they represent a shepherdess singing an old text by Boccaccio. But while the following madrigal in the Fourth Book, "Quell'augellin che canta," seems to form a pair with it, its treatment of the initial *diapente* descent (in a similar G-hypodorian) avoids the infelicities by way of a different harmonic support: i(–III)–VII–i–V(–i).[17] The key to understanding Monteverdi's broader treatment of these descents, however, is that the initial and final degrees of any complete or incomplete *diapente* descent, and often the steps in between, can each be harmonized in various ways without necessarily losing the directional force of the descent itself, even though it might dilute or divert it for lesser or greater periods of musical time. This also offers one explanation for Monteverdi's penchant for transposing specific musical units to different degrees of the scale—with correspondingly different harmonic support—as a means of prolonging single elements within, or connected to, a single *diapente*.

The technique seems quite instrumentally conceived, which is how Monteverdi may have been thinking of it. It also allows him to move quite far afield in harmonic terms. The second of the two "O bellezza" statements in "Cor mio, mentre vi miro" is a direct transposition of the first up a tone. Monteverdi moves up by fifths with cadences on F, C, G, and D (and beyond in its subsequent repetition). But the Canto (S^1) remains within the Dorian octave, plus that one note above, e'', which Monteverdi has previously established as the possible, then actual, initiation of a *diapente* descent to a'. Indeed, at the second "O bellezza" that e'' remains an upper neighbor note to the d'' in S^1 that was used for the initial "O," and on which the voice cadences at "vitale." In "Anima del cor mio" (Fourth Book), however, Monteverdi stretches out the neighbor-note prolongation and adds a harmonic twist (Ex. 8.4). The Dorian mode is clear at the outset, as is the Dorian *diatessaron* in the vocatives presented in S^1 (d''–a'), echoed by S^2 an octave lower. At "cor mio," Monteverdi makes another intertextual play with the opening of "Cor mio, mentre vi miro,"

---

[16] Compare Chew, "The Perfections of Modern Music," which establishes the model of a *diapente* descent supported by a bassline moving in consecutive fifths. Chew then identifies different ways of deviating from it, in part by way of "rhetorical substitutions."

[17] This starts getting close to the typical Romanesca chord sequence (or its *passamezzo antico* sibling), which itself supports a G-dorian *diapente* descent and therefore becomes a typical fingerprint of G-dorian settings: compare Monteverdi's "Ohimè, dov'è 'l mio ben, dov'è 'l mio core?" (Seventh Book), his only explicit Romanesca setting, and one in what was now the typical modern style for *ottava rima* stanzas.

Ex. 8.4 "Anima del cor mio" (Fourth Book, 1603; C1, C2, C3, C4, F4).

but in ATB rather than SSB, and ending on a different sonority. The harmonic progression consists of a series of descending fifths, D–G–C, and the C provides initial support for the upper-neighbor-note e'' in S^1, exactly as occurred at the second "O bellezza" in "Cor mio, mentre vi miro." But Monteverdi then switches that C harmony to a stunning major triad on E, with the alto sliding up a chromatic step from G♮ to G♯ (compare the same move in Ex. 6.1). S^1, echoed by S^2, then outline an e''–b' diatessaron. Thus, mm. 7–12 is a repetition of mm. 1–6 up a tone, still prolonging e'' as an upper neighbor note to the initial d''.[18] Whereas the first "cor mio" (mm. 4–6)

---

[18] Chafe, *Monteverdi's Tonal Language*, 33–34, treats mm. 7–12 as moving from flat to sharp by way of upward transposition by two fifths (G–[D]–A) spanning what he calls a "three-hexachord range." The neighbor-note reading is certainly more elegant, but Chafe would probably not approve of the term, nor of my use of "prolongation" with its obvious Schenkerian overtones. His resistance to Schenkerian analysis (like McClary's) is typical, but also odd, given that it is no less anachronistic than his own combination of modes, hexachords, and systems, and that it offers a much simpler way to engage with matters over which he labors at great length. Nor is there any reason that Monteverdi could not have been thinking here of stretching out a *sol–la–sol* motion (and its *re–mi–re* counterpart a fourth below) in the G-hexachord.

Ex. 8.5 "Oimè il bel viso, oimè 'l soave sguardo" (Sixth Book, 1614).

was supported by D–G–C in the bass, the second has an E–A–D progression that then continues down another fifth to G for the return to d'' in S^1 (at "Poi che"). But just as Monteverdi made that striking move from a triad on C up a third to one on E, he now takes the one on G to a major triad on B (with a tricky $c\sharp'$–$d\sharp'$ in the alto), taking us back into E territory. The textual prompt is a woeful "da me, misera," but this is very far sharpward for Monteverdi. He will need to pull back from it by way of cadencing a few measures later on A, the co-final of the Dorian mode.

Artusi would probably have regarded that repetition up a tone in mm. 7–12 as an improper case of modal mixture by virtue of the insertion of a new modal *diatessaron* (e''–b' rather than d''–a') and its harmonic support. The other reading is that Monteverdi has just found a different way of elaborating a neighbor-note progression (d''–e''–d'') with a chromatic chord under the e'' rather than a diatonic one within the mode. Either way, this is a progression that Monteverdi remembered. I have already suggested that Monteverdi took a longer musical passage from the beginning of "Luci serene e chiare" (Fourth Book) and repeated it up a tone in order to bring a new poetic voice into the equation: this also supports a neighbor-note prolongation on a much larger scale. Doing the same at closer quarters, however, becomes a strikingly expressive move, and we find Monteverdi compressing the procedure even more at various "alas" or similar moments in his subsequent madrigals. Two examples are the *sesta parte* of the Sestina in the Sixth Book, lamenting the death of Caterina Martinelli (at "Ahi, Corinna"), and in the madrigal that follows it, the setting of Petrarch's "Oimè il bel viso, oimè 'l soave sguardo" (*RVF* 267), as an "alas" gets painfully repeated (Ex. 8.5).[19]

---

[19] Tomlinson, *Monteverdi and the End of the Renaissance*, 146–47, notes the connection. The same technique appears in Venere's exclamations in the *Ballo delle ingrate*, and at a repeated "alas" in "Se pur destina e vòle" (Seventh Book); see the music examples in *Monteverdi and the End of the Renaissance*, 207.

The fact that all these neighbor-note progressions are in some kind of Dorian mode might indicate that this particular mode prompts Monteverdi to do certain kinds of things, just as he does in mode-specific ways in other contexts (G-dorian, F-ionian, etc.). A mode puts him in a particular musical frame of mind and creates a field of operation. What he does within that field, however, is not always modally determined, at least in ways that music theorists would have understood the term. Most striking, however, is the fact that when Monteverdi quotes or echoes himself, he often does so in pitch-specific ways. The direct connection between "Cor mio, mentre vi miro" and "O Mirtillo, Mirtill'anima mia" is an obvious case in point, but so are those $d''-e''-d''$ neighbor-note progressions, however varied they might be in their harmonic support or in the ways they are stretched out. Monteverdi's musical memory seems to have stored things by way of particular sonorities often triggered, in turn, by textual associations.

"Ahi lasso"

Artusi may not have wanted to spend too much time on treatments of mode, but he certainly sank his teeth into his chief complaint about those Monteverdi madrigals he encountered: their irregular dissonance treatment. The rules on handling seconds (or ninths), fourths, and sevenths as suspensions or passing tones were absolutely clear, and Monteverdi broke them. He was not alone. But the first of Artusi's nine examples was an egregious case: the famous dissonant ninth and then seventh in "Cruda Amarilli, che col nome ancora" (Ex. 8.6). "Vario" makes short shrift of the various defenses that "Luca" reports being made of the a'' and f'' in S[1] above the g in the bass: that they are consonant with the $f'-d'$ in the Quinto part; that the quarter-note (crotchet) rest before the a'' contains an implicit g'' (which S[1] has

Ex. 8.6 "Cruda Amarilli, che col nome ancora" (Fifth Book, 1605; G2, C1, C3, C3, F3).

Ex. 8.7 "Oimè, se tanto amate" (Fourth Book, 1603), Canto, Quinto, Basso.

C: e do - lo - ro - so ohi - mè sen - ti - re;

Q: e do - lo - ro - so ohi - mè sen - ti - re;

B: [dolo-]ro - so ohi - mè sen - ti - re;

just been singing); that modern singers tended anyway to create such dissonances in performance by way of the embellishments ("accenti") they conventionally added to their notated parts; and that such passages do not necessarily offend the ear.[20] And since Artusi gives only these two measures, he allows no sense of what Monteverdi is doing here. For example, the Canto part (S¹) in "Cruda Amarilli" begins with a mode-defining *diapente* descent from d' to g' in the natural system (so, G-mixolydian), followed by one to its fourth degree (g''–c'').[21] It then rises back up to g'' to initiate a repeat of that second descent, of which the f''–e'' forms a part (and it will eventually carry on). But even that does not excuse the a'', although Monteverdi probably had fun poking a stick at Benedetto Pallavicino's more conventional handling of exactly this cadential situation, unless Pallavicino was instead showing Monteverdi how to do things properly.[22]

That escape-note ninth falling to a seventh appears in madrigals in the Fourth Book as well, including "Oimè, se tanto amate," this time doubled at the lower third to create another illicit seventh (Ex. 8.7). Here, Monteverdi has already established a falling third as an appropriate means of conveying a languid "alas," as distinct from a mournful one; it becomes almost as strong a fingerprint as his falling minor sixth

---

[20] The dissonances so upset Artusi that he even ignores the consecutive fifths by contrary motion between Alto and Basso (over the last bar line in Ex. 8.6). The point about the implied g'' within the quarter-note rest is that the a'' is an "escape" note and the f'', a passing one.

[21] McClary would regard this as a subsidiary descent to a degree within the primary descent. The other option is to treat it as substituting an "authentic division" of the G-G octave (G-D-G; Mixolydian) with a plagal one (G-C-G; Hypoionian), which is precisely how Artusi's Luca viewed "Cruda Amarilli" when he said that it moved from Mode 7 to Mode 12. Chafe's discussion of "Cruda Amarilli" (*Monteverdi's Tonal Language*, 11–17) focuses on Monteverdi's somehow establishing the subdominant (C) as a cadential goal no less valid than the dominant (D) in the context of the key of G, which he then uses to suggest a tonal allegory based (inevitably) on conflict and musical resolution. Chafe is correct that C had "no place" in Artusi's notion of cadences appropriate to the G-mixolydian mode (*Monteverdi's Tonal Language*, 11). However, that is because Artusi was relying on Gioseffo Zarlino's neat, but illogical, insistence on the first, third, and fifth note of any mode being its cadence points (which does not work for any mode beginning *ut–re–mi*: i.e., with a major third). Other theorists treated cadences on C as perfectly acceptable within the G-mixolydian mode (and likewise the fourth degree of any *ut* mode), and even Zarlino grudgingly accepted the fact; compare Meier, *The Modes of Classical Vocal Polyphony*, chap. 4. So Monteverdi was not deviating from any norms at least in this regard, and any notion of a "subdominant" was way beyond his ken.

[22] Tomlinson (*Monteverdi and the End of the Renaissance*, 107) provides the comparison between "Cruda Amarilli" and Pallavicino's "Se ben al vincer nacqui" from his posthumous Sixth Book of 1604, but does not note the obvious problem in terms of which madrigal came first.

Ex. 8.8 "Sfogava con le stelle" (Fourth Book, 1603).

for expressive exclamations. But had Artusi seen "Oimè, se tanto amate," he would have thought its dissonances no less wrong than those of "Cruda Amarilli."

This is typical of Monteverdi's Fourth Book, which becomes a virtuoso exercise in new (at least for him) manners of dissonance treatment and other melodic or harmonic irregularities that, in turn, might suggest a degree of tongue-in-cheek humor. He seems to develop a fondness for those ninths and sevenths. Toward the end of "Sfogava con le stelle" we get first a ninth and then a seventh at the two statements of "pietosa sì," which inserts a fair degree of pain into the lover's request that the beloved have pity for him (Ex. 8.8).[23] This is yet another of Monteverdi's mistakes in reading his texts: the "sì" is not a reinforcement of "pietosa" but, rather, part of a comparison ("sì come" as "siccome"): the stars should make the beloved feel pity just as they make the lover fall in love.[24] But that misreading is also prompted by the fact that Monteverdi needs the "sì" to complete a progression that has struck harmonic gold.[25] There are three components to it: a consonant preparation, a dissonance, and a resolution. Monteverdi handles the first two regularly enough: in the first "pietosa sì," Monteverdi prepares the d'' in S^1 over a consonant minor triad on g, then holds it over the c in the bass. But the resolution goes awry in any standard theoretical terms, leaving the performer perplexed and the listener, hanging. That c should then be sustained while the d'' resolves to c'' (hence a 9–8 suspension), but neither occurs: the c moves down to $B\natural$ as the d'' falls to g'. The resolution of the

---

[23] Salamone Rossi used the same dissonances in his own setting of Rinuccini's text published in his Second Book a5 of 1602; see Carter, "'Sfogava con le stelle' Reconsidered," 150–55.

[24] Aquilino Coppini's contrafact as "O stellae coruscantes" (1609) had to deal with this problem. He recognizes Monteverdi's error but cannot change the music, which forces him into some very awkward text underlay (the four-syllable "pietosa sì" as a repetitive "vos eum, vos"). Coppini is usually better than this, but Monteverdi had painted him into a corner.

[25] The same dissonant ninth appears twice at the end of "Era l'anima mia" (Fifth Book) for "se mori, ohimè" (if you die, alas), which ends with a number of other echoes of "Sfogava con le stelle" (both settings are in some form of D-aeolian).

Ex. 8.9 (a) "Ch'io t'ami, e t'ami più de la mia vita" (Fifth Book, 1605); (b) "Cruda Amarilli, che col nome ancora" (Fifth Book; C3, C3, F3; C [G2] and A [C1] are silent).

suspension is certainly consonant, as resolutions are meant to be, but it is the wrong consonance. The second "pietosa sì" does a similar trick with a 7–6 suspension, with the additional sin of simultaneously sounding the dissonant a' against its note of resolution g' (in S^2).

Monteverdi doubled down. The last madrigal in the Fourth Book, "Piagn'e sospira; e quand'i caldi raggi," is filled with almost every harmonic and melodic "error" one can imagine, and even stretches out at gorgeous contrapuntal length the harmonic progression at the beginning of "O Mirtillo, Mirtill'anima mia" that had caused such modal complaint.[26] Monteverdi pushes the boundaries even further in the Fifth Book, especially in terms of suspensions that have proper preparations and dissonances, but highly improper resolutions. "Ch'io t'ami, e t'ami più de la mia vita" provides an extreme example (Ex. 8.9). As Mirtillo tells Amarilli that if she doubts his love, she would gain confirmation of it from the woods and its beasts, hard branches, and rocks. Those branches and rocks begin well enough, but on the "-ri" of "duri," the f'' in S^1 over the c in the bass sets up a 4–3 suspension, and the d''

---

[26] See the list of "errors" in Carter, "E in rileggendo poi le proprie note," 153 n. 44.

Ex. 8.10 "Ma te raccoglie, o Ninfa, in grembo 'l cielo," *quarta parte* of "Incenerite spoglie, avara tomba" (Sixth Book, 1614).

in S^2 a 9–8 one, albeit in the "wrong" metrical position. Those two suspensions resolve correctly in linear terms (to e'' and c''), but the lower voices have moved to a minor triad on D, so the SS resolution creates another double suspension (9–8 and 7–6) that again resolves to a dissonance as the lower voices ascend. Monteverdi had used a similar progression in "Cruda Amarilli, che col nome ancora," where at least he made some pretense at resolving the suspensions properly. In "Ch'io t'ami," however, S^1 and S^2 each move a half note (minim) too late against ATB.

All these examples suggest that Monteverdi was curious about the power of dissonance. He produces a quite extraordinary one in "Ma te raccoglie, o Ninfa, in grembo 'l cielo" (the *quarta parte* of the Sestina) in the Sixth Book (Ex. 8.10). Here the sonority on the first syllable of "lamenti" is perfectly consonant, but while S^1S^2T each repeat their same notes for the second syllable, B and A have moved, creating a chordal combination that makes no sense whatsoever save as an excruciating cry of anguish. Monteverdi has just had the same progression a fifth higher for SAT, so this cannot be a mistake in the parts that needs editorial intervention.[27] Here, at least, he seems to be thinking in linear rather than vertical ways, and may even have been surprised by a sonority that sounds painfully right, even though it is patently wrong in any music-theoretical terms.

Temperamental moments

Monteverdi can certainly set words such as "lamenti" to an intense dissonance, but for any ongoing act of lament, he has other options. The opening of "Piagn'e sospira;

---

[27] Chafe (*Monteverdi's Tonal Language*, 175, 177–78) makes the same point about a seemingly implausible $c♯/c♮''$ clash in the second and third parts of the five-voice version of the *Lamento d'Arianna*, which also has roots in the monodic version.

e quand'i caldi raggi" is built on the contrapuntal development of a motif rising chromatically through a major third: B♭–B♮–C–C♯–D, imitated at the fifth above as F–F♯–G–G♯–A. This linear, rather than vertical, treatment of lamentation gets developed in numerous ways by way of ascending or descending chromatic tetrachords. In the *seconda parte* of "Vattene pur, crudel, con quella pace" (Third Book), the narration of Armida's collapse into silence places a chromatic descent through a fourth from D to A underneath one from A to E displaced in such a way as to create parallel sixths.[28] Something similar occurs in reverse in Monteverdi's canzonetta "Non partir, ritrosetta" (Eighth Book), at "tu non senti i lamenti" (you do not hear my laments).[29] Here, a chromatic ascent E–F–F♯–G–G♯–A is imitated at the fifth below again in such a way to create parallel sixths and then (with the entry of the third voice) to overlap the cadence:

A: e' f'–f♯' g' g♯' a'

T: a   b♭   b   c'–c♯' d'

B: A   B♭–B

This can also work in different contrapuntal ways: there are stretched-out versions (with entries further apart) in "Tu dormi? Ah crudo core" in the Seventh Book (at "Io piango, e le mie voci lagrimose") and in the trio of Seneca's Famigliari in Act II of *L'incoronazione di Poppea* ("Non morir, Seneca, no").[30] But in "Così sol d'una chiara fonte viva" (the *seconda parte* of "Or che 'l ciel e la terra e 'l vento tace"), Monteverdi shifts the contrapuntal coordination of the chromatic steps:

T¹: e   –   –   f

T²: e' f'   f♯' g' – g♯' a' –

B: A–B♭ –   B   c   –   c♯   d

In this case, the parallel sixths and then thirds in "Non partir, ritrosetta" get distorted by way of chromatic passing tones to represent "the sweet and the bitter" ("il dolce e l'amaro") that nourishes the lover.

---

[28] There is a similar passage in "«Rimanti in pace» a la dolente e bella" (Third Book) at "stillando amaro humore," although it is not fully chromatic.

[29] This passage in "Non partir, ritrosetta" replays a progression that Monteverdi had used in his motet "Christe, adoramus te" (1620) at the mention of the Crucifixion; see Carter, *Monteverdi's Musical Theatre*, 283–86. Obviously, it is meant to be serious in the motet, but it seems parodic—and therefore funny—in the madrigal.

[30] Tomlinson (*Monteverdi and the End of the Renaissance*, 179 n. 24) traces it back to the opening of Marenzio's "Solo e pensoso, i più deserti campi" in his Ninth Book *a5* of 1599, which certainly has a striking chromatic ascent in the Canto from g' to a", though it is not imitated contrapuntally.

176　MONTEVERDI'S VOICES

Ex. 8.11 "Così sol d'una chiara fonte viva," *seconda parte* of "Or che 'l ciel e la terra e 'l vento tace" (Eighth Book, 1638). All accidentals here are as given in the print.

In both these cases, the A–A octave breaks down into two rising fourths, A–D, and E–A. But a few measures further on in "Così sol," Monteverdi adds what appears to be another chromatic rising fourth, B–E, first in S², then followed by the bass (Ex. 8.11). This creates significant problems in the original parts. The first *B* in the continuo is figured sharp, indicating a raised third (D♯), whereas it should be a minor triad, not major. Moreover, S² obviously should move from a *d♮"* through *d♯"* to *e"*, although there are two possible positions for the *d♯"* depending on whether one follows T¹ two measures earlier, or S¹ a measure later. But whichever one chooses, the sharp figured for the first *B* in the continuo needs shifting somewhere within the second.

This third chromatic tetrachord (B ascending to E) supplies the D♯ missing in the first two tetrachords (A–D, E–A) and therefore creates a fully chromatic A–A octave. This is not the case in "Non partir, ritrosetta," which keeps its two tetrachords distinct, not filling out the chromatic step between D and E. However, "Non partir" does have a quite prominent E♭ later in the setting (in the Alto part). Within any tuning system used in the early seventeenth century other than equal temperament, D♯ and E♭ are not the same note, so both pitches can be used only with difficulty with any instrumental accompaniment. Indeed, D♯ both as a pitch and as part of any chord is always going to be a problem, which may be why the parts for "Così sol d'una chiara fonte viva" get so confused.[31]

Artusi's 1600 treatise on "the imperfections of modern music" is itself divided into two "ragionamenti" (argumentations). The second concerns dissonance

---

[31] What follows is a vastly oversimplified account of a complex set of issues. For a broader discussion, see Duffin, *How Equal Temperament Ruined Harmony*; Levenberg, "*Seconda pratica* Temperaments, *Prima pratica* Tempers."

treatment and mode with Monteverdi as the target. The *Ragionamento primo*, on the other hand, engages in a different dispute that had been playing out with the Bolognese music theorist Ercole Bottrigari on the subject, precisely, of tuning and temperament. They had been tussling at some length over a particular set of problems and how or how not to solve them. Voices on their own will tend to sing in what we now call just intonation, with pure thirds and fifths across the range (this is why a cappella choirs can sound so wonderful). Keyboard instruments would be tuned to some form of mean-tone tuning, allowing for pure thirds and fifths in the center of the gamut (roughly speaking, from B flat major to D major in tonal terms), but getting into difficulties at G♯/A♭ and D♯/E♭ because of so-called wolf intervals: in such cases, G♯ tended to be tuned as G♯ and not A♭, and D♯ as E♭.[32] Fretted instruments of the plucked variety (lutes, etc.) or bowed (viols) were generally considered to play in some version of equal temperament as it was understood at the time: when all semitones are equal, sharps and flats sound the same note, but neither is "pure." Unfretted string instruments (of the violin family) could play "in tune" across the gamut by bending G♯ or A♭, and so on, as required. All this was certainly acknowledged by contemporary theorists, who also agreed that plucked and keyboard instruments could not, by definition, sound well together, even though it was common enough to combine them (so Monteverdi shows).[33] It is important to note, however, that when using multiple continuo instruments of different types, they do not each have to play full triads, and it is often better if they do not in extreme harmonic circumstances.

These were facts of musical life with which Monteverdi was well accustomed. In his polyphonic madrigals without continuo, he can range quite widely because the tuning will remain pure. For example, "«Rimanti in pace» a la dolente e bella" (Third Book) has striking major triads on E♭ at the return to diegesis ("ed ella") following Tirsi's first speech to Fillida, and it goes even further flatward at the beginning of the *seconda parte*, to a major triad on A♭ as Tirsi's face is imprinted by death ("di morte"), and then later as well. This is as far flat as Monteverdi goes. Likewise, the Aeolian-mode madrigals in the Fourth Book can move far sharpward (to cadences on E preceded by a major triad on B, with a D♯): this is the case in "Voi pur da me partite, anima dura" and "A un giro sol de' belli occhi lucenti," which seem to act as a pair,[34] though not in "Sì, ch'io vorei morire," perhaps because this setting is more obviously

---

[32] This therefore provides G♯ as a raised leading tone to A, and E♭ as a perfect fourth above B♭.

[33] Nuti, *The Performance of Italian Basso Continuo*, 40–42, notes the problems for modern performers but declines to offer a solution. For other options, see Dolata, *Meantone Temperaments on Lutes and Viols*. Modern chitarrone players tend to be flexible, moving the frets (or adding half frets) and/or choosing one version of a chord over another so as to match a given keyboard temperament (when playing with one), or simply preferring mean-tone tunings because they do indeed sound better in the middle of the harmonic spectrum, The same was almost certainly true in the early seventeenth century. The point remains, however, that equal temperament facilitates a different kind of harmonic thinking.

[34] The two texts come one after the other in Giovanni Battista Licino's collection of *Rime di diversi celebri poeti dell'età nostra* (1587), 204.

in the plagal version of the mode.[35] However, none of the continuo madrigals goes so far to the flat side (E♭ is Monteverdi's limit), in part, one assumes, because of the tuning issues. And when the madrigals go beyond any feasible sharpward limit, Monteverdi seems out to make a point of it. In "Augellin che la voce al canto spieghi" (Seventh Book), the lover commissions a bird to ask the beloved whether she will always force him to be distempered by weeping ("ch'in pianto chi v'adora si distempre"). Monteverdi often responds to these potential musical references: in "Voi pur da me partite, anima dura" (Fourth Book), "dura" leads him to a major triad on A, which by one reading is certainly *durus*.[36] The "distempre" in "Augellin che la voce al canto spieghi" becomes a yet more forceful musical pun by going one step further to a distempered musical cadence on E (forcing a major triad on B) that is only partially redeemed by its repetition to cadence on A (therefore requiring a G♯). But with only a few other such exceptions that need special consideration, his settings with instrumental accompaniment tend to remain in relatively safe tonal areas, which is also why they are not as modally varied as one might expect.

Monteverdi's gamut gets defined early on by way of those circle-of-fifth progressions that he often uses in direct sequential succession. In "Anima dolorosa, che vivendo" (Fourth Book), the lover questions his soul in terms of what it hears, says, thinks, sees, and feels amid its pains and torments. The music moves into a strong circle of fifths, A–D–G–C–F (Ex. 8.12).[37] In "È questa vita un lampo" in the *Selva morale e spirituale*, Monteverdi adds one degree extra to either side of that sequence, starting on E and ending on B♭, covering almost his entire harmonic range.[38] These fifth progressions have a strong directional force. But their other advantage is that one can stop them at any point, either to return to where one started (in "Anima dolorosa" Monteverdi begins on A and breaks the sequence to end on A) or to head in a different direction. The further sharp or flat one goes, however, the more one gets into potential difficulties of tuning. This does not matter in an unaccompanied madrigal, but it does raise questions in one with a continuo accompaniment, given the issues of tuning and temperament that ensue.

---

[35] Still more striking is the shift in "Ma tu, più che mai dura" (the *terza parte* of "Ch'io t'ami, e t'ami più de la mia vita" in the Fifth Book), where a change of system from *cantus mollis* (G-dorian) to *cantus durus* enables a setting that starts on the flat side to move far sharpward at the peak of Mirtillo's grief, with an internal B–E cadence that then prompts a circle of fifths to cadence on a major triad on G; compare Chafe, *Monteverdi's Tonal Language*, 116. Chafe misses Monteverdi's textual point, however. That shift of system is at a key point in the text where Mirtillo pauses, awaiting some response from Amarilli (to whom he is speaking in *Il pastor fido*, III.3), which never comes. A similar shift is worked out in more leisurely harmonic ways in "Zefiro torna e 'l bel tempo rimena" in the Sixth Book (*Monteverdi's Tonal Language*, 188–91).

[36] Chafe, *Monteverdi's Tonal Language*, 99.

[37] The same progression appears in the middle section of "Perché fuggi tra' salci" (Seventh Book), which Dalhaus (*Studies on the Origins of Harmonic Tonality*, 322) views as being initiated by a prior B–E motion that, however, is kept separate from it. Monteverdi goes through a similar sequence in "Or che 'l ciel e la terra e 'l vento tace" (Eighth Book) at "veglio, veglio, penso, ardo"—and thus to similar rhetorical effect—with two cycles: first D–G–C–F(–B♭), then A–D–G–C. There are plenty of examples in the Sixth and Seventh Books as well.

[38] Rising fifth progressions, as in Ex. 8.2, have a similar potential; see Chafe, *Monteverdi's Tonal Language*, 216, 232. Compare also another typical Monteverdian fingerprint involving paired V–I progressions, this time up a fourth then down a second (so each pair moves up by thirds) supporting an ascending scale, as toward the end of "Sì, ch'io vorei morire" (the rising "Ahi bocca, ahi baci...").

Ex. 8.12 "Anima dolorosa, che vivendo" (Fourth Book, 1603).

The title page of Monteverdi's Fifth Book states that the continuo is "for harpsichord, chitarrone, or other similar instrument" and that it is necessary for the last six madrigals but "optional" for the others ("Col Basso continuo per il Clavicembano, Chittarone od altro simile istromento, fatto particolarmente per li sei ultimi, e per li altri a beneplacito"). The Sixth Book simply notes that it has a basso continuo to enable performance "with the harpsichord and other instruments ("Con il suo Basso continuo per poterli concertare nel Clavacembano, et altri Stromenti"). Here, it seems, the continuo is not optional at all.[39] However, the partbooks identify in the table of contents those settings which are to be "concertato," and all but the last two of them are headed with some version of "Concertato nel Clavacembano" in the Basso Continuo one.[40] In the Seventh and Eighth Books, everything is accompanied by the continuo in some manner. In all these cases, however, Monteverdi's continuo lines have very basic figuring, comprising sharps for raised thirds and flats for lowered ones. No continuo player can just play from that part without some more concrete evidence, or at least awareness, of what the voices are doing, and even then, ambiguities remain.[41] The problem in "Così sol d'una chiara fonte viva" (see Ex. 8.11), is by no means the most extreme case.

The two "concertato" settings in the Sixth Book not marked "with the harpsichord" come at the end: "Batto, qui pianse Ergasto. Ecco la riva" and "Presso un fiume

---

[39] In the Fifth Book, the "optional" continuo parts functioning as a *basso seguente* lack figuring, but (*pace* the suggestion in the FCM edition), they still seem to require a harmonic instrument. The *basso seguente* parts in the Sixth Book do have figuring.

[40] "Una donna fra l'altre onesta e bella" and "A Dio, Florida bella, il cor piagato" are "Concertato nel clavacembano," and "Qui rise, o Tirsi, e qui ver' me rivolse" and "Misero Alceo, del caro albergo fore" are "Concertato nel Clavacimbano." "Batto, qui pianse Ergasto. Ecco la riva" and "Presso un fiume tranquillo" have no such heading. In the table of contents in the vocal partbooks, "Una donna fra l'altre" is labeled "Concertato nel Clavicimbano," and others are just marked "concertato." The different stylings of "Clavacembano," "Clavacimbano," and "Clavicimbano" could just be a typical inconsistency, although they might also have a bearing on the manuscript sources given to the typesetter.

[41] Monteverdi's tendency not to use figures to indicate 6/3 chords, etc., save in special circumstances, creates problems. For example, Chafe (*Monteverdi's Tonal Language*, 227) treats as significant a minor triad

180 MONTEVERDI'S VOICES

Fig. 8.1 "Batto qui pianse Ergasto. Ecco la riva" (Sixth Book), Basso Continuo partbook, p. 29, first two staves (Museo Internazionale e Biblioteca della Musica, Bologna).

tranquillo." They each certainly require a continuo instrument, but the absence of a header indicating the harpsichord raises questions. One notational oddity in "Batto, qui pianse" is also curious (Fig. 8.1): what seems to be a straightforward neighbor-note progression in the bassline (A–G♯–A) in fact takes the middle note up an octave (A–g♯–A). The only logical reason for this to occur is that the continuo instrument is intended to be a theorbo/chitarrone with the lowest stopped string tuned to A and the first diapason, a G♮, meaning that a low G♯ is not available on the instrument.

If Monteverdi did indeed intend a theorbo/chitarrone as the continuo instrument here, its impact makes itself felt in other ways. The harmonies in Fig. 8.1 are quite striking: a very long stretch of a major triad on E resolving to a cadence on A that then moves via a circle of fifths to a minor triad on G (at "Hor qui tremante").[42] Thus, Monteverdi moves from the very sharp end of his gamut to the very flat one, while still avoiding the D♯/E♭ problem (E♭ appears earlier and later in the setting). But again, the continuo figuring does not provide sufficient information on its own properly to support the voices. For example, the first two tied e half notes (minims), each figured sharp, in fact support a 6/4 sonority in the voices (compare Ex. 9.2), so the player cannot (or should not) do what the figures instruct. The broader point, however, is that any sharp/flat juxtaposition that goes to extremes will work better on an instrument tuned in a near equal temperament rather than a mean-tone one.[43]

This is not to say that a harpsichord could not sound major triads on E, or minor triads on G. Both occur in the previous madrigal in the Sixth Book, "Misero Alceo,

on B toward the end of "Tornate, o cari baci" in the Seventh Book, but the continuo has a B and T^1T^2, b and d', meaning that it could just as well be (and probably is) a 6/3 sonority (with an implied G).

[42] The typesetting in Fig. 8.1 reveals a typical misreading of what may have been an unclear original: the second sharp positioned next to the tied e half note (minim) should be placed above it. For a similar example, see Carter, "Some Notes on the First Edition of Monteverdi's *Orfeo*," 505.

[43] There is a much broader discussion to be had about Monteverdi's continuo instruments, their range in the bass register, and their tuning. Nor is it clear why Monteverdi prefers the spinet (or what he sometimes called a "spinetta arpata") in parts of the Seventh and Eighth Books. Not everything he notates seems possible on, say, a keyboard instrument with a "short octave" below c, or a theorbo/chitarrone in most tunings.

Ex. 8.13 *Combattimento di Tancredi e Clorinda* (1624/Eighth Book, 1638), Testo and continuo (string parts omitted).

del caro albergo fore," where that instrument is specified. This setting even goes one step further sharpward to a major triad on B for a cadence to E. The *Combattimento di Tancredi e Clorinda*, which Monteverdi says had a harpsichord as the continuo instrument (plus a "contrabasso da gamba" doubling the bassline), similarly goes very far flat—with major triads on E♭ and minor ones on C—and very far sharp, with major triads on B as the "fatal hour" of the end of the battle draws near at "Ma ecco homai l'hora fatal è giunta" (Ex. 8.13). This must have sounded quite "out of tune" unless Monteverdi intended it for a split-key instrument (i.e., with E♭ and D♯ tuned separately, and likewise G♯ and A♭), or unless the figured sharp is, instead, a warning not to play any third at all (as we shall see).

But when Monteverdi wanted purer sonorities, he may have found it better to drop the harpsichord. At two points near the end of the *Combattimento*, the dying Clorinda is instructed to sing "solo with four *viole*" ("sola in 4. Viole"): that is, to the accompaniment of the four *viole da braccio* (soprano, alto, tenor, and bass) that have provided the instrumental material thus far.[44] Any *viola da gamba* is fretted, but any *viola da braccio* is not and so can "tune in" quite precisely to pure thirds and fifths. By this means, Monteverdi was also able to dictate the precise position of each note within a given harmonic unit (which is not the norm in any figured bass). The sequence of single chords (heard twice) at Clorinda's first passage, "Amico, hai vinto, io ti perdon, perdona" again spans the gamut: g–G^6–c–A^6–D (using upper case for major triads and lower case for minor ones). The one in her second passage at the end of the piece, to be played with "smooth bow strokes" ("soave arcate"), ranges even more widely: E–a–G–C–B♭–g–A–D (Fig. 8.2). This ends with a quite extraordinary cadence, with Clorinda holding the fourth above the *a* in the bass as what starts out like a 4–3 suspension (her *d″* should move to a *c♯″*), but it does not resolve. Monteverdi remembered this (in the same harmonic context) from the fifth stanza of "Possente spirto e formidabil nume" in *Orfeo*, on the word "vita" (life). In

His seemingly precise specifications in sections of his score for *Orfeo* need close examination in this light, as does the issue of when a bowed string instrument doubles the bassline (as Monteverdi specifies for the *Combattimento*). But this moves far beyond what can be covered here.

[44] The instruction is in two of the partbooks each containing one of the string parts (Alto Secondo and Tenore Secondo). It is also ambiguous (the "sola" applies to Clorinda). The continuo line is still figured, which seems to suggest that the harpsichord continues to play. However, it is possible that some decision was made in rehearsal to drop the harpsichord that therefore prompted an annotation that entered some of the parts but was not made consistent across all of them when Monteverdi's manuscripts were prepared for printing.

Fig. 8.2 *Combattimento di Tancredi e Clorinda* (Eighth Book), Basso Continuo partbook, p. 43 (Bibliothèque nationale de France, Paris).

Orfeo, the cadential A is not figured sharp, and the one marked for Clorinda is presumably a mistake, even if there was a continuo instrument to play it. Certainly it makes better sense just to have the bare octave-plus-a-fifth sonority in the strings.

Those single chords on bowed string instruments at Clorinda's "Amico hai vinto" invoke a performance practice, and a typical kind of sound, that have been an implicit presence throughout the *Combattimento*: the bard or ballad singer (*cantastorie*) reciting epic poetry to the accompaniment of the modern equivalent of the ancient plucked lyre, the bowed *lira da braccio*.[45] Monteverdi made the same reference in "Altri canti d'Amor, tenero arciero" (Eighth Book) when the solo bass takes up his extravagant eulogy of Emperor Ferdinand III ("Tu cui tessuta han di cesareo alloro").[46] Separate chords are played by "viole sole" with bow strokes that are to be "simple and sweet" ("ad arcate semplici, e dolci") in the first violin part, and "long and smooth" ("con arcate lunghe, e soavi") in the others. The first chord, a major triad on E, takes us into a world quite different from that of the previous fanfares based on a major triad on G in the *concitato genere*. A similar resonance probably lies behind the use of string instruments (*da braccio* and *da gamba*) in "Con che soavità, labra odorate," given its association with the Muses, and especially

---

[45] Carter, *Monteverdi's Musical Theatre*, 192–93. There is a similar echo of the improvising poet-singer in the first piece of the Seventh Book, "Tempro la cetra, e per cantar gli honori," with its opening sinfonia and ritornellos between the vocal sections, although the final instrumental saltarello (if that is what it is) takes things in a different direction.

[46] Ossi, "Between *Madrigale* and *Altro genere di canto*," 19–20. The Continuo part is headed "Voce sola con viole sole e spinetta."

Ex. 8.14 "Or che 'l ciel e la terra e 'l vento tace" (Eighth Book, 1638).

in the lower-scored third group of instruments brought in at "Che soave armonia," first on a major triad on D and then up a tone, on E (prior to a typical circle-of-fifths progression to land on F).

This also prompts reading "Or che 'l ciel e la terra e 'l vento tace" in a slightly different light. The two violin parts serve to reinforce the image of the lover in a state of war ("guerr'è mio stato") with *concitato* gestures. Elsewhere, however, they tend to double the voices, as with the low homophony at the beginning. But again they also serve a harmonic purpose. Monteverdi takes the setting very far sharp to major triads on B and even to a cadence on B (therefore preceded by a major triad on F♯). Such moments are handled with particular care (Ex. 8.14). For the continuo at the cadence on B for "ho qualche pace," Monteverdi does not figure a raised third above the *f♯*—it could not be played "in tune" on a harpsichord—although the necessary A♯ is present in S¹ (by way of a 4–3 suspension).[47] He marks a raised third over the *b*, but it is supplied by the *d♯*″ in Vln 2. And when in the *seconda parte* ("Così sol d'una chiara fonte viva") Monteverdi again moves into sharp realms—at "tanto da la salute mia"—and uses a solo tenor for the poetic "I," the harmony is filled out by the two violins. Indeed, every single D♯ figured in the continuo part of "Or che 'l ciel" is actually provided by one of the other parts (vocal or instrumental), at which point one wonders whether the continuo player is meant to treat the figuring less as an instruction than as a warning not to play a major third when matters get tricky in terms of tuning.[48]

---

[47] Compare the cadence to B in the 1623 version of the monodic *Lamento d'Arianna*, noted in Chafe, *Monteverdi's Tonal Language*, 180. Here the prior *a♯* is supported instead by a *c♯* in the continuo (hence an implied 6/3 chord). Even this seems to have caused some confusion for the manuscript versions of the piece, and perhaps significantly, the passage was treated quite differently in the five-voice setting.

[48] The same is true for that "distempered" moment in "Augellin che la voce al canto spieghi" (Seventh Book) cadencing on E (therefore with a major triad on B) noted earlier, although there are cases elsewhere in the Seventh Book ("Ecco vicine, o bella tigre, l'hore," "Perché fuggi tra' salci," and "Tu dormi? Ah crudo core") where any D♯ seems left to the continuo. In general, however, ambiguities often occur such that the continuo

Most modern music theorists would treat Monteverdi's shifts from the temperamental center of the circle of fifths to its sharp or flat extremes as a move from so-called *cantus naturalis* to *cantus durus* (sharp) or *cantus mollis* (flat). The terminology derives from the "natural," "hard," and "soft" hexachords (on C, G, and F respectively) by way of which singers solmized their path through successive pitches. It then gets transferred to the notion of "system," with *cantus mollis* in the flat system (with a one-flat signature), *cantus naturalis* in the natural system with no signature, and *cantus durus* heading sharpward, although still without a signature (given that one-sharp key signatures were a thing of the future). But hexachords are one thing, systems another, and harmonic movement still another. And while Monteverdi can certainly move to the sharp side, the *durus* (hard, harsh, whatever) affect seen in his polyphonic madrigals tends to be dissipated in his later harmonic language. The shift from a major triad on G to one on B marking the end of the battle in the *Combattimento* certainly forces an immediate change in narrative tone, as the text requires (see Ex. 8.13). But even if the shift goes into a system four-times *durus* by one theoretical reckoning, that is not at all its rhetorical or emotional effect. Similarly, while Clorinda's "Amico, hai vinto," starting with a minor triad on G, is in *cantus mollis*, her final appeal to heaven ("S'apre il ciel"), starting on a major triad on E, is not, and its move to B♭ seems prompted more by local than systemic circumstances.

Matters become still more complicated when one tries to overlay these tripartite divisions onto Monteverdi's own scheme outlined—vaguely, it must be said—in the long preface to the Eighth Book of madrigals.[49] Here he notes the distinction made in Classical Antiquity between three *generi*: the soft (*molle*), temperate (*temperato*), and aroused (*concitato*). He also says that he is particularly interested in the *concitato genere* because he has not hitherto found it in modern musical compositions. Many have noted its impact in the Eighth Book, not least in the *Combattimento*, where Monteverdi uses the string band, and different playing techniques (including pizzicato), to imitate the various sounds of battle. They do so usually in triads built on G, whether because that is *durus* or because it is a good key for string instruments (or both). Monteverdi certainly associates the *generi* with rhythm and pacing by reference to Classical poetic meters (at their extremes, the "fast" pyrrhic foot of two short syllables and the "slow" spondee with two long ones) and to some degree with pitch (high, middle, and low to indicate, respectively, anger, temperance, and humility or supplication). But hexachords, systems, or modes do not figure in his theoretical account here, even though Monteverdi

---

player might be best advised to leave a chord without any third at all. The same is true of final chords in cadences that might or might not have a raised third. That cadence to E in "Augellin" is left ambiguous in that the voices have no third in the chord above it, so the continuo player must choose either to supply one (G♯ or G♮), bearing in mind the following major triad on C (with G♮ in T[1]), or to omit it. The final chord of the setting (on A) also has no third in the voices (and no figuring in the continuo), and one might argue over whether and how it should be added.

[49] Ossi, *Divining the Oracle*, 189–210, tries to untangle its complex threads.

could in principle have extended his argument in that direction by way of Plato's own association of different modes (in the ancient Greek sense) with different affective results.

That discussion of the *generi* in the preface to the Eighth Book does not always stand up to close scrutiny.[50] Monteverdi was no music theorist. He admitted to Giovanni Battista Doni that he was discouraged from pursuing ancient Greek music theory by his attempt to grapple with part of one treatise that tried to untangle its complexities: Vincenzo Galilei's *Dialogo della musica antica, et della moderna* (1581).[51] He also never finished—or even, perhaps, started—the treatise on *seconda pratica* composition that he had promised in response to Artusi's attack on his madrigals. But he was certainly attuned to music's practicalities, with an intense curiosity about their potential for performers and listeners. In a *sonetto caudato* that Monteverdi's friend and admirer, Bellerofonte Castaldi, wrote probably in the late 1630s, Castaldi complained about the labored, constipated music written by those who relied on the "paralytic" harpsichord to compose in ways that always sounded the same ("Il compor musical stentato e stitico / . . . / tolto dal Clavicembal paralitico / par che sia sempre una medesma cosa"). Monteverdi, Castaldi says, is different and without equal: in terms of musical invention, he is daring, practical, noble, varied, beautiful, and forever green ("Però nel inventioni ardito e prattico, / nobile, vario e bello e sempre verde").[52] He then explains why:

> La cagion chi la vuole
> saper, e perch'ei dia tanto diletto,
> la Tiorba il dirà c'ha sempre al petto.

[The reason, for who wishes / to know, and why he gives such delight, / will be told by the theorbo which he has always at his chest.]

If Monteverdi did indeed compose with a theorbo (chitarrone) to hand, that could explain a great deal of the harmonic language and range of his madrigals, even if he then had to accommodate their performance to instruments of other tempers.

There are broader consequences. The continuo tended to encourage "bottom-up" thinking in terms of chordal progressions that were now conceived vertically, however much linear voice-leading might still play its part. Any attempt to work top-down, as it were, would miss the point. For example, an early manuscript version of

---

[50] It also contains a spectacular mistake when it refers to Plato's treatise on "rhetoric," meaning Aristotle's.

[51] See Monteverdi's second letter (of two) to Doni of 2 February 1634, where he mentions looking at Galilei's treatise twenty years before. Monteverdi was not particularly comfortable writing to Doni, who in turn was less than impressed with the outcome. The composer's reaction to erudite music-theoretical texts may also be clear from the fact that Doni complained about the lack of acknowledgement of the receipt of the copy of his *Compendio del trattato de' generi e de' modi della musica* (1635), which the theorist had sent to Monteverdi sometime before August 1638; see Ossi, *Divining the Oracle*, 191.

[52] For the sonnet, see Fabbri, "Inediti Monteverdiani," 81 (I have edited it slightly). Subsequently, Fabbri (*Monteverdi*, trans. Carter, 308 n. 172) expressed some skepticism about Castaldi's claim, given that the theorbo was the latter's own instrument. Nevertheless, it remains provocative in the present context.

"Misero Alceo, del caro albergo fore" has a quite different continuo line for Alceo's central episode.[53] This seems to have been created by someone working just from the voice part, which is quite like the published one. It works harmonically but bears no relation to Monteverdi's more chromatic treatment, and it fails to realize his use of strophic variation, with the same bassline repeated for different segments of the text. Bottom-up thinking also forces individual sonorities being considered in terms of their connection one to the other, and of any larger-scale structure by way of a coherent field of harmonic relationships. Clearly, Monteverdi conceived his music in multiple ways: vertically, linearly, top down, bottom up, or even inside out. This is one reason that it is such a delight to perform. Another is the fact that what Artusi's decried as impertinence seems, rather, to be a preference for a kind of musical brinkmanship in all these dimensions, often setting itself up for a fall that is usually avoided only at the last minute.

---

[53] Watty, "Zwei Stücke aus Claudio Monteverdis 6. Madrigalbuch in handschriftlichen Frühfassungen," 130–31 (transcribing Kassel, Landesbibliothek und Murhardsche Bibliothek, 2° Ms. Mus. 57f).

9
The "Representative" Style

Monteverdi's means of energizing his text setting changed significantly with the emergence of the continuo madrigal in the last six pieces of the Fifth Book. The presence of an instrumental accompaniment built upon a figured bass meant that the voices were not required to provide or maintain a full harmonic texture. That bass also permitted a more flexible approach to harmonic rhythm: single chords could be sustained for longer, their rate of change could alter according to rhetorical or expressive need, and their drive toward cadential goals could be manipulated to stronger or weaker effect. All this made it easier to control the musical pace and vary the degrees of forward melodic, harmonic, and rhythmic motion. The voices, in turn, were freer in terms of how many needed to sing at once—with solo sections now becoming a distinct, at times preferred, possibility—and there was more room for ornamental passages to show off the singers, to act as a particular form of word-painting, or to provide rhetorical emphasis. "Troppo ben può questo tiranno Amore" has already provided a case in point (see Table 5.2): here Monteverdi takes a text in a single poetic voice speaking as or for itself, but sets it in such a way that allows singer(s) X variously to speak to singer(s) Y, or more directly to us. One trade-off was the loss of the nuanced play of textual superimpositions and repetitions that we saw in the polyphonic madrigals and even in the five-voice *Lamento d'Arianna*. But to have singers as functional personas delivering a text in direct, comprehensible ways with immediate emotional impact became identified in the early seventeenth century with the so-called *stile rappresentativo*, first in association with theatrical music (in particular, early opera), but then more broadly as a new form of musical rhetoric to arouse the listener.

For example, the *Combattimento di Tancredi e Clorinda* is one of the pieces promised on the title page of Monteverdi's Eighth Book of madrigals as "some little works in [the] representative genre, which will serve as short episodes between the songs without action" ("alcuni opuscoli in genere rappresentativo, che saranno per brevi Episodii frà i canti senza gesto").[1] Two other pieces in the book to which some version of the "rappresentativo" label is applied are placed within the "Canti amorosi": the central section of "Non avea Febo ancora"—the *Lamento della ninfa* ("Rapresentativo")—and the final *Ballo delle ingrate* ("in genere rappresentativo").

---

[1] The internal preface to the *Combattimento* provides instructions for the work "volendosi esser fatto in genere rappresentativo." The *Combattimento* is labeled just "rapresentativo" in the table of contents.

All of these might well be identified as "canti con gesti," as it were—certainly in the case of the action in the *Combattimento* and the *Ballo delle ingrate*, and possibly for the *Lamento delle ninfa*, depending on how the nymph is meant to act out her grief on being abandoned at dawn. As for their being in any "representative genre," Monteverdi had already used the term for the *lettera amorosa* and the *partenza amorosa* in the Seventh Book, both "in genere rapresentativo," and that label was repeated on the title page of Bartolomeo Magni's 1623 edition of those two works (plural "lettere amorose in genere rapresentativo") preceded by the solo-voice version of the *Lamento d'Arianna*. Monteverdi himself noted in his letter to Alessandro Striggio of 4 April 1620 that as a result of sending a newly copied score of *Arianna* to Mantua for potential performance of the opera there, he felt inspired to compose daily more works "in tal genere di canto rapresentativo."[2]

Here we enter a terminological minefield. Giulio Caccini had identified his opera *Euridice* as being composed "in stile rappresentativo," so it is styled on the title page of its first edition of 1600. By this he seems to have meant in the "theatrical style," although in the preface to his *Le nuove musiche* (1602), he suggested that this style had derived from the earlier solo songs included in that vocal collection. In turn, Pietro de' Bardi said (1634) that "il canto in istile rappresentativo" had been developed by Vincenzo Galilei in Giovanni de' Bardi's Camerata, with which Caccini was also associated.[3] Other composers linking the term with the theater include the Bolognese Girolamo Giacobbi, who set the text of Ridolfo Campeggi's *L'Aurora ingannata* (1608) "in Musica di stile rappresentativo."[4] Giacobbi then published this music that same year as "canti rappresentativi." However, the *lettera amorosa* and *partenza amorosa* in Monteverdi's Seventh Book are not "theatrical" in any literal sense of the term; nor are the *Dialoghi rappresentativi* that Francesco Rasi published in 1620. Moreover, when Bernardino Borlasca published his contrapuntal *Scherzi ecclesiastici sopra la cantica a tre voci* in 1609, he said on the title page that they were "appropriate for singing amid solemn concertos in *stile rappresentativo* ("appropriati per cantar fra Concerti gravi in stile rappresentativo"), which seems to mean that they could provide a contrast with more serious sacred motets that took a different approach to the delivery of their texts. Even just by Monteverdi's terms, not all "representative" works are meant to be staged. Nor, at least in the Seventh and Eighth Books, are all the "staged" works labeled "representative": the two *balli—Tirsi e Clori* in the Seventh and "Volgendo in ciel per l'immortal sentiero"/"Movete al mio bel suon le piante snelle" in the Eighth—are cases in point.

---

[2] The single consonant in "rapresentativo" (not "rappresentativo") is typical of Monteverdi's preference for so-called *consonanti scempie* rather than *doppie*. If one finds them in his printed editions, it is a strong clue that the printer is following the composer's orthography.

[3] In his letter to Giovanni Battista Doni given in Solerti, *Le origini del melodramma*, 144.

[4] The term is noted in the libretto (Bologna: Heirs of Gio. Rossi, 1608). *L'Aurora ingannata* served as *intermedi* for Campeggi's spoken play *Il Filarmindo*.

The "stile recitativo"

Monteverdi's rubrics for the *lettera amorosa* and *partenza amorosa* in the Seventh Book added further qualifications; they are for solo voice and are to be "sung without a beat," in other words, in unmeasured time.[5] We would now identify them as being in free "recitative" in the early-seventeenth-century sense of the term. But this creates another problem of terminology that the music theorist Giovanni Battista Doni, working in Rome in the 1630s and 1640s, tried without much success to resolve.[6] For him, anything in the *stile rappresentativo* was by definition intended for dramatic action on the stage. But

> by *stile recitativo* is today understood that sort of composition [*melodia*] which can be recited elegantly and with grace, that is, sung by solo voice in the manner that the words are understood, whether done on the theatrical stage, or in churches or oratorios in the manner of dialogues, or, indeed, in private chambers or elsewhere. And finally, with this term one understands every kind of music that is sung solo to the sound of some instrument, with few drawn-out notes and in such a manner as to come close to common speech, but yet in an emotional way.[7]

Doni realized, however, that even just this broad use of the term *stile recitativo* was not very helpful, so he tried to narrow it down:

> And although all might use the term "recitative" for every composition that is sung by a solo voice, it is, however, very different when one sings formally in the manner of madrigals, and when predominates that simple, flowing style that one sees in two *lettere amorose* published by Monteverdi with his *Lamento d'Arianna*.[8]

For Doni, then, the *lettera amorosa* and *partenza amorosa* were examples of the *stile recitativo* rather than the *stile rappresentativo*. However, he does not appear to have been convinced by either piece. According to a later comment about recitative (in this case, within the *stile rappresentativo*), he felt that any style midway between speech and artful song ("un canto mezzano tra il recitare, e il modulare artifiziosamente") was neither fish nor fowl and therefore would not cause much

---

[5] Canto partbook: "Lettera amorosa a voce Sola in genere rapresentativo et si canta senza batuta." Tenore partbook: "Partenza Amorosa in genere represntivo / voce sola et si canta senza battuda."
[6] The following draws on the discussion in Privitera, "Leggete queste note."
[7] Doni, "Trattato della musica scenica," ed. Gori, 29: "Per stile dunque Recitativo s'intende oggi quella sorte di melodia, che può acconciamente, e con garbo recitarsi, cioè cantarsi da uno solo in guisa tale, che le parole s'intendano, o facciasi ciò sul palco delle scene, o nelle Chiese, e Oratori a foggia di Dialoghi, o pure nelle Camere private, o altrove; e finalmente con questo nome s'intende ogni sorte di Musica, che si canti da un solo al suono di qualche instrumento, con poco allungamento delle note, e in modo tale, che si avvicini al parlare comune, ma però affettuoso." Doni's treatise was written sometime before 1647.
[8] Ibid., 27: "E sebbene tutto chiamano Recitativo, intendendo ogni melodia, che si canti ad una voce sola; è però molto differente, dove si canta formatamente quasi alla guisa de' Madrigali, e dove regna quello stile semplice, e corrente, che si vede in due lettere amorose, pubblicate dal Monteverdi col suo lamento di Arianna..." Doni is clearly referring to the 1623 edition.

delight.[9] The very long *lettera* and *partenza amorosa* might seem to prove his point. Although Monteverdi made some massive cuts to Claudio Achillini's "Se i languidi miei sguardi" (in *versi sciolti*), it still had seventy-eight lines of poetry, and Ottavio Rinuccini's "Se pur destina e vòle," its rhyming couplets left uncut, had 108. In setting both texts, Monteverdi had scant choice but to set them in a declamatory manner save for some lyrical expansion at heightened rhetorical moments.

Creating long poems as an epistolary declaration to a distant beloved ("Se i languidi miei sguardi"), or as direct speech to one whom the lover is about to leave on a long journey ("Se pur destina e vòle"), was a convenient conceit that had an obvious precedent in Ovid's *Heroides* and elsewhere. They also enabled poets to write to commission, giving voice to patrons who might wish to impress their inamoratas. Achillini's "Se i languidi miei sguardi" offers paeans of extravagant praise to the beloved's hair, eyes, and mouth; Monteverdi sticks just with the hair, taking much longer to say something that was far more neatly compressed in one of the two canzonettas toward the end of the Seventh Book, "Chioma d'oro." The oddity that he sets it for a soprano voice (C1 clef) did not escape Doni, who thought it more capricious than rational that while the letter was ostensibly addressed to a lady who knew how to sing and play, it did not seem to be right and proper to have her sing words that should be delivered by her lover.[10] The scoring certainly plays into one agenda behind the Seventh Book: to present what Caterina de' Medici hoped to hear from her husband. But Doni, like modern scholars, also misses the point that what "speaks" here could well be the *lettera* itself (the noun is gendered feminine in Italian).

"Se i languidi miei sguardi" is presented as something written: its recipient is told to read what the lover has penned in ink.[11] "Se pur destina e vòle," however, is meant to be heard by the beloved, who is repeatedly urged to "listen to" and "hear" what is being said (or sung) as the lover laments his imminent departure at dawn.[12] Therefore, Monteverdi sets it more properly in the C4 clef. Rinuccini adopted the same tropes in another such text, "Fornito ha 'l corso aprile," that was seemingly set by Monteverdi but is now lost. Here the moment of parting (in this case, by the beloved) casts a pall over the delights of May. Remigio Romano included the poem, typically without attribution, in his *Prima raccolta di bellissime canzonette musicali e moderne* (1618) with the heading "On the departure of the beloved, there was one who left written the following notes, which were then set to music with

---

[9] Ibid., 27. Doni's analogy is that if one preferred things betwixt and between, then one would rather eat otter (half fish and half meat) than a capon or a sturgeon ("che altrimenti più gusterebbe la Lontra, che è mezza pesce, e mezza carne, che la carne di Cappone, e il pesce Storione").

[10] Ibid., 26: "Ma l'invenzione delle Lettere ha più del capriccioso, che del ragionevole: perciocché benché siano state raccontate, come s'ha da credere, a qualche Dama, che sapesse cantare, e sonare; tuttavia non pare che abbia del buono, che quello, che dovrebbe dire, o cantare l'amante, la Dama stessa lo cantasse." Doni was evidently not open to the idea of "Se i languidi miei sguardi" being sung by a castrato lover.

[11] Lines 7–10: "leggete queste note, / credete a questa carta, / a questa carta in cui, / sotto forma d'inchiostro, il cor stillai." By the Italian "note," Achillini meant written notes, although the potential musical pun is obvious.

[12] Lines 4, 10: "ascolta, alma mia diva / . . . / odi le voci estreme." Giles notes the difference in *Lettera amorosa*.

a most excellent recitative style."[13] Unlike many of the texts here noted already to have been set to music, there is no obvious source for this one. But Romano seems to have had some access to Rinuccini's poetry in manuscript: the *Seconda raccolta* (also 1618) included a chorus from his *Narciso*, a libretto that was never printed or set to music, although Monteverdi considered it for a while.[14]

Rinuccini refers to "Fornito ha 'l corso aprile" in a long ode in rhyming couplets, "Sparito è luglio ardente," that turns out to be in praise of Grand Duke Cosimo II de' Medici and his wife, Archduchess Maria Magdalena of Austria.[15] In search of inspiration, the poet asks a favor of Clori, his personal muse (the italics are mine):

> Indi la bella mano
> porgi alla cetra d'oro,
> e deh, di quel canoro
> cigno che l'Adria ammira,
> alla cui dotta lira
> cede ogni Musa il vanto,
> non l'ammirabil pianto
> *Lasciatemi morire*,
> ma deh, fammi sentire
> in men flebile stile
> *Fornito ha 'l corso aprile*,
> canto che sì sovente
> rapì la nobil gente
> delle gran cure al pondo
> . . .

[So turn your fair hand / to the golden lyre, / and, ah, of that songful / swan admired by Adria [Venice], / to whose learned lyre / each Muse yields the prize, / [sing] not the admirable lament / *Lasciatemi morire*, / but, ah, let me hear / in less mournful style / *Fornito ha 'l corso aprile*, / a song that so often / snatched noble folk / from the weight of great cares . . .]

Despite the indirect reference, "Fornito ha 'l corso aprile" is clearly attributed to Monteverdi (the "swan" admired by Venice). It also seems to have become a favorite

---

[13] *Prima raccolta di bellissime canzonette musicali e moderne* (Vicenza/Venice: Angelo Salvadori, 1618), 61–64: "Nella partita della cosa amata fù chi lasciò scritto le seguenti note, che furono poscia ridotte alla Musica con eccellentissimo stile recitativo." This collection also includes the texts of the *Lamento d'Arianna* and "Non avea Febo ancora" (containing the *Lamento della ninfa*), although its source for the latter is unclear. "Fornito ha 'l corso aprile" and its connection to Monteverdi counts as a joint discovery by me and Roseen Giles, since it emerged from one of our many fruitful exchanges about the composer. The poem (with some minor variants) is attributed to Rinuccini in a manuscript probably from the early 1640s: Florence, Biblioteca Nazionale Centrale, Magl. VII.902, fol. 97r–v. In it, Rinuccini addresses Filli, who seems to be a singer (as mentioned at the end).
[14] See Carter, "Ottavio Rinuccini's *Narciso*."
[15] Ottavio Rinuccini, *Poesie*, ed. Pierfrancesco Rinuccini (Florence: Giunti, 1622), 173–76. The dedication of this book is dated 4 January 1622 *stile fiorentino*; it appeared in early 1623.

piece of female singers: Francesco Rasi reported in 1621 that the Roman virtuosa Ippolita Recupito sang it particularly well.[16] But while the text was certainly less mournful than the *Lamento d'Arianna* ("Lasciatemi morire"), its recitative style would indeed have had to be "most excellent," as Remigio Romano says, to make so powerful an effect.

Monteverdi viewed recitative as a manner of "speaking" the text: an instruction prior to Clori's first stanza in *Tirsi e Clori* (Seventh Book) notes that she responds to Tirsi "saying as follows" ("dicendo come segue"). But her music is not declamatory in the "simple and flowing" style that Doni identified in Monteverdi's *lettere amorose*. This more lyrical form of delivery is used to great effect in the *Ballo delle ingrate*, and in pieces styled in the manner of operatic prologues, including "Tempro la cetra, e per cantar gli honori" (Seventh Book) and "Volgendo il ciel per l'immortal sentiero" (Eighth). It can also be given some structural cohesion by way of strophic variation: each quatrain and tercet of "Tempro la cetra" varies the vocal line over the same harmonic sequence in the bass, as do the two quatrains of the sonnet "Volgendo il ciel," and, for that matter, Clori's own stanzas in *Tirsi e Clori*.

"Volgendo il ciel" serves as a preface to the *ballo* "Movete al mio bel suon le piante snelle" and is delivered by a "Poeta" who refers to himself in the first person. The score is also provided with stage directions as the poet makes an entrance and is handed a chitarrone by a nymph, who then places a garland on his head. Strophic variation appears in the *Combattimento di Tancredi e Clorinda* as well, where the "speaking" Testo moves into a more lyrical mode as he calls upon Night to allow him to bring Tancredi and Clorinda's actions to the light of the world: the two quatrains of the "Notte, che nel profondo oscuro seno" stanza are each delivered over the same bassline. This is one of the passages in the *Combattimento* where Monteverdi modified the text of Tasso's *Gerusalemme liberata* (Canto 12) by way of the poet's reworking of the episode in *Gerusalemme conquistata* (Canto 15), with additional editorial intervention.[17] It is probably no coincidence that it is the only place in these *Gerusalemme liberata* stanzas where Testo refers to himself with a first-person pronoun ("io"), which he does not in the equivalent place in the *Conquistata*.[18] Monteverdi allows the singer an expressive moment—with ornamental flourishes to boot—but still within the frame of what Testo quite literally represents: the "text."

Typically for epic, the narrative structure of the *Combattimento* is quite complex in terms of shifting between diegesis and mimesis. The diegetic Testo sets the scene, describes the action, and makes clear any shift to mimesis with a "disse"—"(s)he said"—or the like. Given that Monteverdi is writing for a solo voice, he can vary the melodic, harmonic, and rhythmic intensity of his declamatory recitative to match

---

[16] Carter, "Monteverdi, Early Opera and a Question of Genre," 34 n. 58.
[17] The texts are laid out for comparison in Georis, *Claudio Monteverdi*, 635–43.
[18] *Gerusalemme liberata*, Canto 12, stanza, 54, line 5: "Piacciati, ch'io ne 'l tragga, e 'n bel sereno." *Gerusalemme conquistata*, Canto 15, stanza 68, line 5: "Piacciati, ch'indi il tragga, e 'n bel sereno." Monteverdi mostly follows the *Conquistata* reading in this stanza, although with some input from the *Liberata* one. Elsewhere he tends to stick more closely (but not exactly) to Tasso's original.

the narrative pace. Yet matters are not quite so straightforward when Tasso himself intervenes to move the "text" beyond a straightforward narrative role. A case in point is when Tancredi and Clorinda take pause in the middle of their bloody battle, resting on their swords (from the end of Tasso's stanza 58—beginning at "Vede Tancredi in maggior copia il sangue"—through stanza 59). Edward Fairfax's translation (1600) makes things clear:[19]

> Tancred beheld his foe's out-streaming blood,
> And gaping wounds, and waxed proud with the sight,
> Oh vanity of man's unstable mind,
> Puffed up with every blast of friendly wind!
>
> Why joy'st thou, wretch? Oh, what shall be thy gain?
> What trophy for this conquest is't thou rears?
> Thine eyes shall shed, in case thou be not slain,
> For every drop of blood a sea of tears:
> The bleeding warriors leaning thus remain,
> Each one to speak one word long time forbears,
> Tancred the silence broke at last, and said,
>
> . . .

Here Testo continues to tell the story ("Tancred beheld . . ."); makes a pronouncement on Tancredi's pride ("Oh vanity of man's unstable mind . . ."); speaks directly "to" Tancredi ("Why joy'st thou, wretch? . . ."); and then returns to his narrative task, introducing the mimesis in the stanza that follows ("Tancred . . . said"). Tasso does this quite often in his epic poetry.[20] The question is how Monteverdi might best respond.

In Armida's "Vattene pur, crudel, con quella pace" in the Third Book, Monteverdi omitted two stanzas where Tasso did the same thing, "speaking" directly to Armida and also to the reader/listener (see Chapter 5). He has less room for maneuver at this point in the *Combattimento*, given that those rhetorical shifts occur in very close succession. But while he can handle one change of register easily enough, two in succession create greater problems even within a declamatory style that should allow for it. Testo's account of Tancredi's moment of pride ("ne gode e insuperbisce") ends on a straightforward major triad on G, and the exclamation on the vanity of man's mind ("Oh nostra folle mente") jumps in and takes the music far sharpward (Ex. 9.1). However, Monteverdi is less able to mark the subsequent shift from Testo's general comment to his vocative addressing Tancredi ("Misero, di che godi?"). It is

---

[19] Given in http://www.italianverse.reading.ac.uk/liberata. Fairfax typically turns Tasso's historic presents ("guarda," "appoggia," and so on) to the past tense ("beheld," "stood," etc.).

[20] Calcagno, *From Madrigal to Opera*, 197. It can happen in lyric poetry, too: in the setting of Guarini's "Quell'augellin, che canta" (Fourth Book), the poetic voice shifts from describing the bird to addressing it directly in the last two lines ("Che sii tu benedetto . . .").

Ex. 9.1 *Combattimento di Tancredi e Clorinda* (1624/Eighth Book, 1638), Testo and continuo (from Tenore Primo partbook).

left to the singer to make the change of direction clear, who must take over where Monteverdi leaves off.

But while this *stile recitativo*, as Doni would have called it, necessarily deflected compositional control to the performer, Monteverdi found a way to regain it. As Clorinda is baptized and takes her last breath, she sees heaven open and leaves in peace ("S'apre il ciel, io vado in pace"). According to Tasso, this is what Clorinda "appeared" to say ("dir parea").[21] In his polyphonic madrigals, Monteverdi was able to fudge this kind of construction, given that the plural voices left room for ambiguity over whether something is actually "said" or just appears to be so. In principle, Clorinda's final words should be delivered by Testo. However, Monteverdi seizes the moment to give her the last word, and himself, too, as the string instruments stretch and fade out their final chord on a single bow stroke (as the parts instruct, "Questa ultima nota va in arcata morendo").

"Musica rappresentativa"

A different notion of what is "representative" was adopted by Aquilino Coppini, a Milanese professor of rhetoric who in 1607–9 provided three volumes of spiritual contrafacts of *Musica tolta dai madrigali di Claudio Monteverdi e d'altri autori*, to cite the title of the first. Here Coppini replaces the Italian texts of madrigals by Monteverdi and others (only Monteverdi in the third volume) with Latin texts of a religious kind. This posed something of a challenge: Coppini first had to transcribe the parts into score and then come up with Latin prose that would match Italian poetic meters, Monteverdi's own fragmentation of a given text, and, where possible, the music's rhetorical and expressive content. Some rather strange clashes occur, as when the highly erotic "Sì, ch'io vorei morire" (Fourth Book) becomes a plea for beloved Jesus, "my life" ("light," "hope," etc.), to embrace the speaker in eternity ("O Jesu mea vita" in Coppini's third volume). It was no doubt Coppini's intention to turn Italian poetry bordering on the illicit into something more palatable for those feeling uncomfortable with blatant musical orgasms. However, this does raise

---

[21] Calcagno, *From Madrigal to Opera*, 229.

a question of how Monteverdi's seemingly legible musical gestures and rhetorical gambits for one set of words can feasibly apply to another.

Coppini's enthusiasm for Monteverdi is clear in the preface to his second volume (1608):

> The representative music of Signor Claudio Monteverdi's Fifth Book of madrigals, governed by the natural expression of the human voice in moving the affections, stealing into the ear in the sweetest manner and thereby making itself the most pleasant tyrant of souls, is indeed worthy of being sung and heard not (as others said out of spite) in pastures and among the herds, but in the houses of the most noble spirits, and in royal courts. And it can also serve many as an infallible norm and idea of how to compose madrigals and canzones harmonically in conformance with the best rule.[22]

The reference to the Artusi-Monteverdi controversy is clear, as is Coppini's siding with the composer. But his praise of Monteverdi's "musica rappresentativa" had little if anything to do with it being theatrical in any way: rather, it was a question of how he used the "natural expression of the human voice" to move the emotions by way of a form of *enargeia*.[23]

What Coppini felt was "representative" about these madrigals concerned the effective oratorical delivery of the text treated as the prime directive of the *seconda pratica*. Unlike Doni, he would not have complained about Arianna speaking to the absent Teseo in five voices, or of Glauco addressing the dead Corinna in the same manner in "Incenerite spoglie, avara tomba." The five voices represent them in the same way as they do Tancredi in "Vivrò fra i miei tormenti e le mie cure" in the Third Book, or Mirtillo, Amarilli, Dorinda, and Silvio in the *Pastor fido* settings in the Fifth, at several steps removed from any notion of verisimilitude. The same is true of the poetic "I" in the other *basso seguente* madrigals in the Sixth Book: "Zefiro torna e 'l bel tempo rimena" and "Oimè il bel viso, oimè 'l soave sguardo." Both of those texts are Petrarch sonnets (*RVF* 310, 267), and they each come immediately after a first-person lament (the *Lamento d'Arianna* and the Sestina respectively).[24] However, the Sixth Book madrigals that are "concertato" with the basso continuo all

---

[22] Given in Fabbri, *Monteverdi* (1985), 152: "La musica rappresentativa del quinto libro de' madrigali del signor Claudio Monteverde regolata dalla naturale espressione della voce umana nel movere gli affetti, influendo con soavissima maniera negli orecchi, e per quelli facendosi degli animi piacevolissima tiranna, è ben degna d'esser cantata et udita non già (com'altri per livore disse) nei pascoli e tra le mandre, ma ne' ricetti de' più nobili spiriti e nelle regie corte; e può anco servire a molti per infallibile norma et idea di comporre armonicamente conforme alla legge migliore madrigali e canzoni . . ." I have not been able to trace who said that Monteverdi's madrigals were fit only for herds (was it from Antonio Braccino da Todi's now lost treatise of 1606?).

[23] Compare Giles, *Monteverdi and the Marvellous*, 168, on Quintilian's notion of *enargeia* (also called "representation") as a rhetorical imperative of vividness.

[24] The Sixth Book is often read as being divided into two, with the *Lamento d'Arianna* at the head of the first half, and the Sestina, the second; compare Ossi, *Divining the Oracle*, 15–16. However, this may be to misconstrue its initial table of contents, which certainly has in the middle of the list a centered heading, "Sestina" (in upper case), but for what reason remains unclear. Had there been a lament for Hero and Leander (e.g., prior to the last two *concertato* settings), the book might have divided into three.

play with more complex narrative structures, whether by describing a single "she" with no direct connection to the narrative voice—as in "Una donna fra l'altre onesta e bella"—or by introducing third-party characters that speak to one another, or to themselves. Coppini had already published (1609) a contrafact of "Una donna fra l'altre" as "Una es, o Maria," addressing the Virgin Mary and therefore turning a "she" into "you." But he would have had a harder time with the other *concertato* settings here.

In the continuo madrigals in the Fifth Book, any specific persona adopted by one or more individual singers tends to be a generic male or female lover, or both. In the Sixth, they shift to being named characters, whether Tirsi, Alceo, Batto, and Ergasto, or, in the case of the two dialogues, Floro/Florida and Eurillo/Filena.[25] In each case, some additional narrative voice intervenes, and while those named characters might be voiced in a verisimilar fashion by a single singer (as with a tenor Floro and a soprano Florida), Monteverdi can also confound any such expectation, almost as if he wished to show that writing for solo voice and continuo was not the only, nor the best, use of the new *concertato* idioms. This is especially the case with texts in mixed narrative modes in which he could, in turn, wrest control of the musical and rhetorical argument.[26] Thus, these Sixth Book madrigals confound any sense of being narrowly representative even when narrow representation had become feasible, expected, or even required.

Monteverdi's setting of "Misero Alceo, del caro albergo fore" (Sixth Book) makes a striking change to Marino's sonnet. In the first (1602) edition of Marino's *Rime*, the text is headed (in the table of contents) "A shepherd who leaves his nymph" ("Un Pastore, che si diparte dalla sua ninfa"), and the beginning is clear enough:

> Misero Alceo, del caro albergo fore
> gir pur conviemmi, e ch'al partir m'appresti.
> Ecco, Lidia, ti lascio, e lascio questi
> poggi beati, e lascio teco il core.

> [Wretched Alceo, out from the dear home / am I required to go, and I must prepare myself to leave. / So, Lidia, I leave you, and I leave these / blessed hills, and I leave my heart with you.]

Thus, Alceo begins by speaking to himself (I–me), and then to Lidia (I–you). Monteverdi's setting, however, changes the pronouns, also forcing a shift to direct speech:

---

[25] For these issues particularly in Monteverdi's Sixth Book, see Carter, "Beyond Drama," which also unpicks the literary threads and their resonances.
[26] Calcagno (*From Madrigal to Opera*, 208–9) links this directly to the aesthetics of Marino's poetry with its plurality of perspectives.

> Misero Alceo, del caro albergo fore
> gir pur convienti, e ch'al partir t'apresti.
> «Ecco, Lidia . . .

[Wretched Alceo, out from the dear home / are you required to go, and you must prepare yourself to leave. "So, Lidia . . ."]

This revision to the opening makes Monteverdi's purpose clear. Lines 1–2 are delivered by the full SSATB ensemble addressing Alceo (as "you"). Line 3 shifts the focus as he (a solo tenor) speaks to Lidia in recitative-style declamation set as strophic variation over three statements of the same harmonic sequence.[27] That direct speech lasts for nine lines, until the end of the first tercet, at which point the full ensemble returns to conclude with a final narration—"Thus spoke the shepherd . . ." ("Così disse il pastor . . .")—leading to a comment: how the parting of Alceo and Lidia divided one heart into two. The full ensemble therefore serves two purposes: as a group speaking in the present tense to Alceo, and as the narrative voice speaking in the past tense to us.[28]

Monteverdi also has fun at the point when Alceo's speech ends. He has two tasks here. First, the speech is in a harmonic area (starting on a minor triad on E) somewhat removed from that of the initial narration (a minor triad on D), so the music needs to return to it. Second, the tenor representing Alceo needs to re-enter the full ensemble. He first has just the word "Così" (Thus) on his own on his cadential *e*, as if he were continuing his speech, but that *e* pivots to being the fifth of a minor triad on A as the other voices jump in with "Così disse" to cut "Alceo" off, forcing a narrative shift as well as a gradual move back to the initial modal region.[29] Monteverdi then spends just under a third of the setting on the final line and a half of the sonnet, reveling in the image of a single heart divided by way of different vocal combinations within the full ensemble.

The mimetic center of "Misero Alceo"—his speech—is placed within a narrative context in a manner typical of epic poetry. Thus, to read it as some kind of dramatic *scena* is to confuse poetic genres, just as it is in the case of the *Combattimento*.[30] Indeed, Monteverdi's other *concertato* settings in the Sixth Book provide a rather stern warning against any such reading. It may be clear that the two dialogues "A Dio, Florida bella, il cor piagato" and "Presso un fiume tranquillo" are set in a more realistic

---

[27] One might expect those three statements of the bassline each to cover the same amount of poetry, but Monteverdi rather craftily matches them to the syntax of the poem (ll. 3–4, 5–8, 9–11).

[28] Calcagno, *From Madrigal to Opera*, 216.

[29] Calcagno (*From Madrigal to Opera*, 218–20) takes a different tack: Alceo's preemptive "Così" keeps him as a separate voice in a final narration that also brings a separate musical Lidia into the equation.

[30] Compare Tomlinson, *Monteverdi and the End of the Renaissance*, 162 ("Misero Alceo" is "a dramatic *scena* framed by polyphonic narrative passages"). Similarly, "«T'amo mia vita!», la mia cara vita" (Fifth Book) is "a semidramatic *scena* for soprano with lyric comment by the lower voices" (*Monteverdi and the End of the Renaissance*, 156). The broad thrust of Tomlinson's argument—that Monteverdi is heading toward musical drama—still has its influence in the field; compare Calcagno (*From Madrigal to Opera*, 213) on "Batto, qui pianse Ergasto. Ecco la riva" as "a miniature opera."

Ex. 9.2 "Batto, qui pianse Ergasto. Ecco la riva" (Sixth Book, 1614; ATB are silent).

C: Deh___ mi - ra, (e - gli di - cea) se fug-gi-ti-va fe-ra pur sa-et-tar tan - to ti pia - ce,

Q: Deh___ mi - ra, (e - gli di - cea) se fug-gi-ti-va fe-ra pur sa-et-tar tan - to ti pia - ce,

B.c.

manner than, say, the dialogue in the five-voice "«Rimanti in pace» a la dolente e bella" in the Third Book. Floro and Florida, and Eurillo and Filena, are each (re)presented by a solo voice distinguished by gender (tenor and soprano), although as we have seen here and elsewhere, Monteverdi is forced to come up with a creative means to allow the setting to conclude with the full ensemble. "Batto, qui pianse Ergasto. Ecco la riva," however, is more complex.[31] This sonnet, again by Marino, follows the tripartite form of diegesis–mimesis–diegesis. An unnamed speaker tells Batto that "here" is the riverbank where Ergasto paused in his pursuit of his recalcitrant Clori who, in turn, was chasing a deer. "Ah, look!" Ergasto said, asking her to send her arrows into his heart. She briefly turned back, which made Ergasto burn with love all the more. Who, then, will say that the wet tears that fall from two eyes are not fire?

Marino's final oxymoron is typical, switching from narrative mode into commenting one. But there are two crucial differences between "Batto, qui pianse Ergasto" and "Misero Alceo." First is the use of tenses. "Misero Alceo" is all in the present tense until the final narrative "disse" (he said) and the following epigrammatic point (a single heart was divided). "Batto, qui pianse Ergasto," on the other hand, reverses the switch: Ergasto and Clori's actions are in the past ("qui pianse Ergasto," not "piange"), although the final point is framed as a question ("Hor chi dirà, che non sia . . .") that brings us into the present and forces us to consider our answer. Second, the story about Ergasto is being told by a second person to a third one. Thus, there is no constraint forcing Ergasto's direct speech to be represented by a solo voice. Monteverdi in fact allocates it to two sopranos who, moreover, remain in diegetic mode by also presenting the "he said" of "egli dicea" (Ex. 9.2). In the case

---

[31] So Tomlinson (*Monteverdi and the End of the Renaissance*, 159–60) notes. Here I draw on, and add to, his discussion.

of "Vattene pur, crudel, con quella pace" (Third Book), placing a narrative "disse" within the voices ostensibly representing Armida may have been a force of circumstance (compare Ex. 5.5). Monteverdi could have avoided the problem in "Batto, qui pianse Ergasto," save that it was not at all a "problem" in the context of reported, rather than direct, speech. The unnamed person(s) telling the story to Batto can use any means available to relate what Ergasto said.

A number of the sonnets by Marino set in the Sixth Book come from what appears to be a single sequence within the poet's *Rime boscherecce*, which therefore prompt a number of intertextual relations between them. A less recalcitrant Clori is described in "Qui rise, o Tirsi, e qui ver' me rivolse." According to the description of the poem in Marino's table of contents, the sonnet's unnamed speaker "shows to a shepherd the place where he kissed his nymph" ("Mostra ad un Pastore il luogo, dove baciò la sua ninfa"). That "place" is not specified (but its location will become clear). However, it is referenced constantly through the poem by a repeated "qui" (here) beginning lines 1, 3, 5, 7, 9, and 12 (each couplet in the two quatrains and at the beginning of each tercet), with additional internal repetitions. Tirsi is told that "here" Clori laughed and gazed upon her lover, made a garland for his hair while he played his pipes, spoke in exalting terms, sat next to him, placed her arm around his waist, and kissed him with a modest blush.[32] The sonnet ends as the speaker extols the happy memory of a joyful day ("O memoria felice, o lieto giorno"). Given that in "Batto, qui pianse Ergasto," someone tells Batto of Ergasto's less happy times with Clori, it seems reasonable to assume that the speaker in "Qui rise, o Tirsi" is Ergasto himself—recounting an event before Clori had turned her affections elsewhere—and even that the person telling Batto about the end of Ergasto's affair is Tirsi. In fact, Tirsi, Ergasto, Batto, and Clori are interconnected by way of a long literary history conflating references in Homer and Ovid with accretions by way of Sannazaro, Tasso, and Guarini. They are "real" people insofar as anyone in the pastoral world of Arcadia is real, and Marino plays with their separate and combined stories in highly creative ways.

So, too, does Monteverdi. "Qui rise, o Tirsi" is another of his settings that adopts an unusual SSTTB (plus bc) scoring. This would encourage SS and TT pairings, and he begins accordingly with SS (for Clori's laughter and gaze), and then TT (the garland). However, Monteverdi then chooses other combinations for Clori's angelic voice (S) and the graces and cupids that danced around her head (SST) as she braided her hair (SS), sat next to her lover (ST), and kissed him (TTB). Monteverdi segments the text by way of that repeated "qui," but he did not feel any obligation to represent the single speaker by a single voice, or by any consistent combination

---

[32] For Clori's speaking in exalting terms ("Qui l'angelica voce e le parole . . ."), Monteverdi's setting alters Marino's "Qui l'angelica voce in note sciolse," changing the rhyme word and omitting a necessary verb. It is a strange revision, especially given Marino's musical reference (as Clori unloosed her angelic voice in [musical] notes). Georis (*Claudio Monteverdi*, 516–17 n. 28) explains it as a reference to Petrarch's "Erano i capei d'oro a l'aura sparsi" (*RVF* 90).

within the ensemble; nor, again, did he need to do so, given that the text is all in the past tense. More striking, however, is the fact that he reserves the full SSTTB ensemble for just one line of the sonnet, the final "O memoria felice, o lieto giorno."[33] Monteverdi treats it as a refrain, placing a statement at the end of the first and second quatrains. He had done this before in the Fifth Book's "Ahi come a un vago sol cortese giro" and "E così, a poco a poco," and the effect in "Qui rise, o Tirsi" is the same. At this point, the ensemble is not a narrator but, instead, a commentator speaking for itself, for/as Monteverdi, or for the listener.

The question posed at the end of "Batto, qui pianse Ergasto" crosses those lines even more forcefully. The ensemble starts out as the narrator of a rather sad tale in the past, but shifts tenses as it seeks agreement ("Hor chi dirà ... ?") over the oxymoronic mixture of tears and fire. Again, it is worth glancing back at Armida's "Vattene pur, crudel." Here Tasso had used a similar not-quite-rhetorical question in his account of Rinaldo's departure: What will he do? Monteverdi avoided the problem of that "Hor che farà?" simply by omitting the stanza that contained it (plus one other). In the context of the polyphonic madrigal, the five-voice ensemble could act as narrator, could speak as one or more voices, and could, at a push, present other voices speaking. It was harder, however, for the ensemble to pose a question to itself, to the subject of its narration, or to the listener. That required a further degree of functional detachment from the narrative that was rendered possible, not entirely paradoxically, by a representative style that purported to remove it.

The bass "I"

In "Qui rise, o Tirsi," the speaker tells Tirsi how he played his pipes ("al suon de le mie canne") as Clori made a garland for his hair. The sonnet comes at the end of four of Marino's *rime boscherecce* (nos. 47–50) each concerning a happy dalliance with Clori (she is named directly in three of them). The first is "A quest'olmo, a quest'ombre et a quest'onde," which therefore explains the location left vague by the "here" in "Qui rise, o Tirsi": Clori and her lover sit in the shade of an elm tree on the bank of a river ("a quest'onde"), which might or might not be the same riverbank where Ergasto later tried to persuade his Clori not to flee, so we are told in "Batto, qui pianse Ergasto."

Monteverdi's six-voice setting of "A quest'olmo" toward the beginning of the Seventh Book has echoes of those Sixth Book sonnets in terms of the shared poetic source and theme, although the six-voice scoring (SSATTB in *chiavette*) and the presence of instruments make it quite different. I have already suggested (in Chapter 3) that Monteverdi may have been turning to personal ends the nostalgia

---

[33] Marino has "O memoria soave, o lieto giorno." Georis (*Claudio Monteverdi*, 518 n. 29) links Monteverdi's change to a line in Petrarch's "Due rose fresche e colte in paradiso" (*RVF* 245).

inherent in the poem, even if the setting fulfilled an additional purpose in the program of the Seventh Book.[34] The text once more invokes the memory of a happy day "when Clori gave her entire self and her heart to me" ("all'hor che la mia Clori / tutta in dono se stessa e 'l cor mi diede"). At that moment, Monteverdi shifts his instruments from two violins to two labeled "flautino o fifara" standing in for a shepherd's pipe. He also allocates the text to the bass voice, carefully noting in the partbook that it is singing "solo" on its own.[35]

Having the lowest sounding voice somehow represent a poetic "I" was not at all uncommon in the polyphonic madrigal. In the *concertato* settings in the Fifth Book, Monteverdi also used the bass for key "I" moments within "Amor, se giusto sei" and "Questi vaghi concenti" (see Chapter 5). The settings in the Sixth and Seventh Books further suggest that he had access to a singer with an unusually wide range ($D-e'$ in the case of "Parlo, misero, o taccio?" in the Seventh), which may have prompted a focus on the voice-type. In the context of any "representative" style, however, the bass potentially becomes an explicit poetic persona standing apart, however briefly, from the collective "I" or "we" of the ensemble. The point is clear in the first of the "Canti guerrieri" in the Eighth Book, "Altri canti d'Amor, tenero arciero." Following a brief but exquisite opening sinfonia, SST are given a luxuriously languid triple time to state that "others" may sing of the sweet pleasures of Love. The second quatrain of the sonnet, however, makes the point of the text clear by shifting to a first-person verb initially delivered by the bass:

> Di Marte io canto, furibondo e fiero,
> i duri incontri e le battaglie audaci;
> strider le spade e bombeggiar le faci
> fo nel mio canto bellicoso e fiero.

[Of Mars do I sing, furious and proud, / his harsh encounters and daring battles; / the clash of swords and flaming torches / do I make [appear] in my warlike, proud song.]

This anonymous sonnet has all appearances of an ad hoc creation for the purposes of the Eighth Book: no serious poet would have adopted that "fiero ... fiero" repetition in a key rhyming position (unless Monteverdi has made another mistake). But the bass compels that SST group to shift from amorous musings: "Di Marte," he sings sternly—SST repeat it, and then the full ensemble—"Di Marte io canto ..."

---

[34] Carter, "Beyond Drama," 10; compare Calcagno, *From Madrigal to Opera*, 210. Others have noted that "A quest'olmo" seems somehow misplaced in the Seventh Book; see Chafe, *Monteverdi's Tonal Language*, 211, and Ossi, *Divining the Oracle*, 18. However, I am now more inclined to think that "A quest'olmo" belongs where it is, harking back to Monteverdi's Marino settings in the Sixth Book rather than having been composed alongside them.

[35] Earlier in the setting, Monteverdi uses a tenor for a solo "I" moment, at the beginning of the second quatrain. This is a bit odd: T^2 begins the quatrain ("In voi"), imitated by T^1, but T^2 then drops out, and T^1 acts as the sounding bass of a three-part texture (with two violins above).

Here it is the bass as warrior who forcibly turns the attention to singing about the proper matter at hand: war, not love.[36] This then invokes the typical vocal and instrumental gestures of the *concitato genere*. Monteverdi also has the bass interject "fo nel mio canto," the beginning of the last line of the quatrain, prior to the third (B: "Fo nel mio canto" preceding TT: "strider le spade"). This makes the syntax clearer, but also puts the bass firmly in charge of the "canto," whether to spur the other singers on to bellicose enthusiasm or, for the last six lines of the sonnet, to issue the invocation to "gran Fernando," Emperor Ferdinand II/III, prior to its repeat by the full ensemble. Given that this invocation also includes a plea to welcome the Eighth Book—"il verde ancor novo lavoro"—one starts to suspect that the bass singer who makes war resound in "my song" speaks for Monteverdi himself.

The Eighth Book cannot sustain its warlike content for long without completing the metaphor: that war and love are two sides of the same coin in terms of how a lover lays siege to the beloved and might or might not win any battle that ensues. The argument is explicit in the sixth of the "Canti guerrieri," "Ogni amante è guerrier: nel suo gran regno." Ottavio Rinuccini's text starts out as a translation-cum-paraphrase of Ovid's "Militat omnis amans" (*Amores*, 1.9), but the poet moves far beyond the notion of the warrior-lover to praise the military virtues of Henri IV, King of France (changed in Monteverdi's setting to Emperor Ferdinand III). Rinuccini had dedicated the poem to his friend Jacopo Corsi (who died in 1602), and he addresses him in directly in the second line ("Corsi gentil, se meco mirar prendi").[37] This line is omitted by Monteverdi, logically enough, although it creates a problem for later that he has to solve in a quite creative way. His setting divides the text into four sections, also with some extensive cuts. The first section begins with T^1 ("Ogni amante è guerrier"), then joined by T^2. The second is a long section for bass solo ("Io, che nell'ozio nacqui e d'ozio vissi") with a very wide range (D–d'): its first four lines mark the end of Rinuccini's translation of Ovid prior to his shift into an account of how the "I" who was born and raised into leisure became a lover, and hence, an amorous warrior, prompting an extended digression on the battlefield abilities of the King of France (for Monteverdi, the emperor). As with "Altri canti d'Amor," the bass marks the entrance of the poetic "I" (the first section consists entirely of third-person statements), and again, the bass serves as both a warrior and a eulogist.

Monteverdi's third section comes at the point where Rinuccini decides to rein things in. His original text is the following:[38]

>Ma per qual ampio Egeo spieghi le vele
>sì dal porto lontano, ardita Musa?

---

[36] Compare Wistreich, "Of Mars I Sing"; Calcagno, *From Madrigal to Opera*, 199–200.

[37] "Every lover is a warrior: in his great kingdom / (noble Corsi, if you join me in considering the matter) / Love does indeed himself have his own army."

[38] Rinuccini, *Poesie* (1622), 115–19.

> Riedi, ché meco il mio cortese amico
> veggio ch'a sì gran corso, a sì gran volo,
> di pallido timor dipinge il viso.

> [But across what wide Aegean do you spread your sails / so far from harbor, ardent Muse? / Return, for with me my courteous friend / do I see, who, at so great a course, at such great flight, / colors his face with pale fear.]

The poet's appeal to his Muse, and the punning reference to his "friend" intimidated by "sì gran corso" (Jacopo Corsi) were not going to work in the present context. Monteverdi's setting therefore changes the "ardent Muse" to an "ardent lover" ("sì dal porto lontano, ardito amante"). But this remains puzzling, at least until one realizes what Monteverdi has done.

It is significant that this third section is delivered by just a solo tenor (T^1). The "ardent lover" whom he now accuses of having strayed too far is the bass delivering the second section ("Io, che nell'ozio"). And the "friend" standing by with timorous demeanor is T^2, who then joins T^1 in the fourth section:

> Riedi, ch'al nostro ardir, ch'al nostro canto,
> ch'ora d'armi e d'amor confuso suona,
> scorger ben pòte omai ch'Amor e Marte
> è quasi in cor gentil l'istesso affetto.

> [Return, for at our passion, at our song, / which now sounds of arms and love mixed together, / one can indeed now realize that Love and War / are almost the same emotion in a well-born heart.]

The bass adds his voice to the two tenors at "ch'Amor e Marte...," acceding to the final moral.

"Militat omnis amans" is in a single poetic voice (Ovid speaking to Atticus), as is Rinuccini's "Ogni amante è guerrier" (addressing Corsi). Monteverdi's setting presents three: a principal poetic voice (T^1) and his "friend" (T^2), plus a bass "I" who once luxuriated in idle pleasure but becomes an "ardent lover" and then a profuse eulogist for Emperor Ferdinand III before being brought back under control. One can then extend this reading back into the first section: T^1 begins the discourse, then his friend (T^2) joins in, reaffirming the initial premise that every lover is a warrior before the two then vie to come up with increasingly extravagant musical images as the text itself moves more and more into hyperbole. Thus, Monteverdi has found a rather neat way to justify the use of three singers to deliver a text that, in principle, requires just one. But then in the fourth section of the setting, yet someone else is brought into the mix: the "one" (the subject of the third-person singular "pòte": i.e., "puote") who can realize from "our song" that Love and War are indeed almost the same thing. That "one" is, of course, the listener, who should have been paying careful attention to the argument thus far.

"I"/"we"

The different possible meanings of any "representative" manner of composing—a direct relationship between a singer and a poetic voice, or a more general notion of affective *oratione*—come to a head in the duets that start to play a key role in Monteverdi's later madrigals. The conventional view is that he preferred this medium over the solo songs that were otherwise starting to dominate the repertory precisely because it allowed the development of a stronger musical argument in contrapuntal and/or harmonic terms. There is also no doubting the musical and even erotic thrills to be gained from hearing two voices in the same range (SS or TT, say) singing in close canon, in parallel thirds, with virtuoso flourishes, or by way of dissonant suspensions rubbing together to generate a friction that demands release. Monteverdi already exploited such dissonant duet textures within the polyphonic madrigal, as in the SS opening of "Ah, dolente partita!" (Fourth Book), and he may have enjoyed now being able to use them on their own. But when he chose to begin the first *concertato* madrigal in the Fifth Book, "Ahi come a un vago sol cortese giro," with two tenors, one is left asking whom they are meant to represent. The fact that the text delights in the beauty of the beloved's two eyes does not seem sufficient to justify the paired voicing, so one can only assume that here the two tenors are "speaking" as one, an impression that becomes all the stronger when they sing in rhythmic unison.

The mode of presenting a text within a duet is quite different from what was typical of the solo song, which tended to be linear, with little or no internal repetition. Monteverdi sometimes turns this to his advantage. The first five lines of Guarini's "Ahi come a un vago sol" as set by Monteverdi are once more grammatically obscure, with the main verb typically delayed until the fifth line, at "torna," followed by its subject, "mio core":

> Ahi come a un vago sol cortese giro
> de' duo belli occhi, ond'io
> soffersi il primo dolce stral d'Amore,
> pien d'un novo desio,
> sì pront'a sospirar torna 'l mio core.[39]

[Ah, how to a charming, single, kindly turning / of two fair eyes, from which I / suffered the first, sweet arrow of Love, / full of new desire, / so ready to sigh does my heart return.]

---

[39] Guarini has "di duo begli occhi" and "primo e dolce stral," neither of which makes things any clearer. The "sol" is often read as a contraction of "sole" (e.g., "a graceful, lovely sun"), but that does not work grammatically.

Aquilino Coppini's contrafact (in his 1607 volume) tried to produce something in better syntactic order by way of three separate sentences that match the music surprisingly well:

> Vives in corde meo, Deus meus,
> nec te dimittam. Tu tui
> me vulnerabis pharetra amoris.
> Deus meus,
> te quaeso: contine in meo corde,
> . . .

[You live in my heart, my Lord, / nor shall I forsake you. You yourself / wounded me with the arrow of your love. / My Lord, / I beg you: remain in my heart . . .]

But this is an after-the-fact rationalization of a situation wherein Monteverdi took the benefit of the text fragmentation inherent within the duet medium to avoid having to make any sense of the poem in the first place. Coppini in effect reconstructs a poetic rhetoric from Monteverdi's musical deconstruction of the text. But it comes as something of a relief when Monteverdi brings in the last line of the poem early, which at least provides a clearly understandable statement: that the wound made by Love never heals ("Ah che piaga d'Amor non sana mai").

If the two voices of any duet begin together homophonically, the notion that they sing "as one" is certainly more plausible, and it permits their subsequent separation to serve as rhetorical intensification: this is clear in "Ardo, e scoprir—ahi lasso!—io non ardisco" and "O sia tranquillo il mar o pien d'orgoglio" that sit side-by-side—and share some musical commonalities—in the "Canti amorosi" in the Eighth Book. Something similar is true if the voices each present a line of text one after the other. "O viva fiamma, o miei sospiri ardenti" (Seventh Book), a sonnet, has twelve lines each beginning with a vocative (with internal vocatives as well) prior to an "if" clause in line 13: that sequence is made grammatically complete only in the final line (14). Monteverdi therefore has to get to that line as efficiently as possible for the setting to make any sense. He allocates the first two quatrains line by line to S^1 and S^2, with overlapping entries and S^2 in canon, initially at the fourth. As a result, eight lines of text are delivered in just thirteen measures. The entries come closer together—with the canon now at the unison—at the beginning of the first tercet at the mention of flowers, a key word for the Seventh Book. But S^1 alone then marks the shift in the final two lines as the speaker asks that if any amorous spirits live on this earth, they should take pity at her bitter lament. The point is then intensified in its repetition by S^1 and S^2 together.

Here the two voices seem to be in competition with each other to pile vocatives upon vocatives. In other duets, however, one of the voices can appear to serve as an alter ego of the other, adding out-of-order interjections to bring a text to greater rhetorical life.[40] In "Ah, che non si conviene" (Seventh Book), the last lines of the poem have the speaker ("I") affirm the intention to stand firm like a rock in the waves, wanting to live and die in the beloved's name ("e viver vostro e morir vostro i' voglio"). Monteverdi brings the verb at the end of the line closer to the front and imposes a rhetorical repetition:

T^2:   e viver vostro
T^1:   i' voglio,
T^2:   e morir vostro
T^1:   i' voglio,
T^2:   e viver vostro
T^1:   i' voglio,
T^2:   e morir vostro
T^1:   i' voglio,
T^1T^2: e viver vostro e morir vostro i' voglio, i' voglio, i' voglio...

Monteverdi had already done this kind of preemptive trick in some of his polyphonic madrigals, although here it is much more noticeable as an affective and effective rhetorical device.[41]

Two male singers competing in canon start to raise other suspicions, however. In "Perché fuggi tra' salci" (Seventh Book), one of Marino's many "kisses" madrigals, the setting starts straightforwardly enough with a solo tenor as the lover asks his shepherdess why she flees among the willows. But as he heads into the cadence at the end of the third line, a second tenor abruptly enters with the text from the beginning, forcing T^1 back there as well, and extending those first three lines from twelve measures to twenty-five. The two tenors constantly compete in terms of who will take the lead and who will follow, although they end up agreeing that they were wholly innocent of stealing the kiss that prompted the shepherdess to flee in the first place, given that it was her fault for vindictively offering it ("fu più vendetta tua che mia rapina"). The first tenor on his own delivers the complete text in about thirty-three measures, but the competition with T^2 extends the entire setting to ninety. It is hard to avoid the conclusion that here there are two tenors each pursuing the same shepherdess even if they have arrived from different locations. Presumably, this is somehow meant to be comic.[42]

---

[40] Whenham, *Duet and Dialogue in the Age of Monteverdi*, 1: 165, notes how Monteverdi may have gained some of these and other techniques from the duets by his younger colleague in Venice, Alessandro Grandi, in the latter's *Madrigali concertati a due, tre, e quattro voci* (Venice: Giacomo Vincenti, 1615). Tomlinson, *Monteverdi and the End of the Renaissance*, 188–92, follows.

[41] Compare the similar interjection of "negli occhi, negli occhi" on the same falling-third pattern in "Vorrei baciarti, o Filli" (Seventh Book), where it seems to be humorous. It becomes a mannerism: Monteverdi uses it at "soccorso" in "Ardo, e scoprir—ahi lasso!—io non ardisco" (Eighth Book), as the lover cries for "help."

[42] For a reading of the Eighth Book's "Gira il nemico insidioso Amore" on different comic lines, see Ossi, *Divining the Oracle*, 245–47.

Bringing a third voice into the mix makes things seem funnier still. One of Monteverdi's contributions to the anthology *Madrigali del signor cavaliero Anselmi nobile di Treviso* (Venice: Bartolomeo Magni, 1624) was a trio (ATB), "Taci, Armelin, deh taci," where the speaker(s) try to keep the beloved's dog (Armelino) from barking so that he/they can secure a kiss. Three strophic canzonettas in the Eighth Book give a similar impression of multiple lovers in pursuit of the same woman. In "Non partir, ritrosetta," two altos and a bass accuse her of not hearing the laments of her singular faithful lover (". . . del tuo fedel amante / tu non senti i lamenti?") in ways that make us question whether this is serious or parodic. In "Ninfa, che scalza il piede e sciolta il crine" a tenor, then two tenors, and then two tenors and a bass seek to persuade a nymph running barefoot through the meadow—her hair loose to the wind, singing and dancing the while—that she should stop to stay with him/them and take rest under the shade of an ash tree to the sound of his/their instrument ("De l'usate mie corde"—where the bass enters, again almost as if he were Monteverdi). However, she continues her course, pursuing her beloved Lillo (so he/they fear), at which point he/they wish that her fleeing foot would be changed . . . into hard stone. Monteverdi rather wittily saves that abrupt final phrase to the end of a long passage in triple time. However, it gives the impression that our three singers are just grumpy old men leering at a nymph who has a different prospect in view.

"Ninfa, che scalza il piede" has four stanzas, the first three of which are clearly defined as such in Monteverdi's setting by way of the increasing number of voices singing: the music is not quite strophic but there are enough similarities in the first three stanzas to make it appear nearly so. In "Perché ten fuggi, o Fillide," an alto, a tenor, and a bass are together from the start (although with an imitative beginning), and its three stanzas run on as if the setting were through-composed. The joke here is that two tenors and bass are together trying to persuade Filli(de) with a none-too-tempting argument:[43]

> Già belva non son io, né serpe squallido:
> Aminta io son, se ben son magro e pallido.

[No wild beast am I, nor foul snake: / I am Aminta, even if I am scrawny and pale.]

No one "magro e pallido" is going to turn Filli's eye, and this "Aminta" (or Monteverdi's three of them) is not just wasting away from love but also past his prime. As in "Ninfa, che scalza il piede," the text setting is extravagant, to say the least.

Indeed, all three settings would seem to invoke a more sophisticated version of the Venetian *giustiniana* (or *canzona alla veneziana*), in which three old men (usually some combination of alto, tenor, and bass voices) mutter into their beards about

---

[43] She is named both Fillide and Filli in the text, the former to allow for the *versi sdruccioli* endings.

the impediments of age so far as love is concerned. The trope was a popular one in the madrigal comedies and similar "lighter" collections of the likes of Orazio Vecchi and Adriano Banchieri. Gabriello Puliti also provided a sanitized version of the genre in his *Ghirlanda odorifera di varij fior tessuta, cioè mascherate a tre voci, libro primo* (Venice: Giacomo Vincenti, 1612). Some of Puliti's *mascherate* adopt the typical dialectal mannerisms as three old lovers introduce themselves to young girls ("Vecchietti inamorai / nu semo care fie") to tell of the burning in their hearts ("per narrarve el brusor / ch'avemo dentro al cuor").[44] Another makes a more literate joke of three "ill-fortuned singers" (TTB) of love songs:[45]

> Noi siamo tre cantori
> ch'andiam sempre cantando,
> sfogando i nostri amori,
> ci andiamo consumando
> per queste donne ingrate e dispietate.

[We are three singers / who go always singing, / giving vent to our loves, / [and] we come here suffering / for these ungrateful, pitiless ladies.]

Those three trios in the Eighth Book fit the mold precisely.

The same is true of the low-voice canzonettas included in Monteverdi's posthumous Ninth Book (1651). It begins with a dialogue between a shepherdess (S) and her shepherd (T), "Bel pastor dal cui bel guardo," to a text by Ottavio Rinuccini organized as a loose canzonetta.[46] Here a rather stolid shepherd refuses to give the desired answer to the shepherdess's repeated questions about whether he loves her, and Monteverdi enjoys drawing out the argument without any conventional harmonious agreement at the end. The next five madrigals in the book are TT duets already included in previous publications by Monteverdi. Then follow ten canzonettas, all but one of which are for three male voices (ATB, TTB, TTT).[47] Their texts are in the newer style, with longer stanzas and with refrains. Monteverdi sets them all strophically (although sometimes as strophic variations), and his options are either to have all three voices sing throughout, or to allocate each stanza to a separate voice in sequence, with the ensemble coming together for any refrain. In the simplest cases in which all the voices sing in homophony, the canzonetta could equally be performed just by a solo voice: this is certainly the case with "Perché se m'odiavi" (TTB), a version of which was published

---

[44] Puliti, *Ghirlanda odorifera*, ed. Cavallini, 19–20. A significant number of Puliti's texts were drawn from prior publications (both poetic and musical).

[45] Ibid., 5–6. The song is headed "Cantori sventurati."

[46] A setting of this text by Marco da Gagliano had been included in Piero Benedetti's *Musiche* (Florence: Heirs of Cristofano Marescotti, 1611). Monteverdi seems to recall it, given the occasional musical similarities, although his text has some variants that might have come from the poet.

[47] The exception is "Come dolce oggi l'auretta" (SSS), a canzonetta from Monteverdi's *Proserpina rapita* (1630), to a libretto by Giulio Strozzi; see Carter, *Monteverdi's Musical Theatre*, 226–33.

by Monteverdi as a solo song (in C1 clef) in Alessandro Vincenti's collection of *Arie de diversi* of 1634.

These texts are all explicitly or implicitly in the male poetic voice. There is one striking case in the Seventh Book, however, where a text in the female poetic voice is set for a TTB trio. "Eccomi pronta ai baci" is one of sequence of six madrigals (nos. 20–25) in the *seconda parte* of Marino's *Rime* (1602). Here, "Cinzia" invites Ergasto to kiss her, but not in such way as to leave teeth marks on her face lest the act be noticed by others, to her shame.[48] Of course, Ergasto ignores the imperative (Monteverdi has an unusual pause mark where the action occurs), at which point Cinzia says that she will die before she kisses him again. The transvestite scoring is odd, however, and rendered even more so by the fact that for one line of the text ("nota non resti . . ."), T^2 voices Cinzia on his own, perhaps to draw out the musical pun ("nota" as a "mark" and a "note"). Setting this text as a four- or five-voice madrigal, as was done by Gabriello Puliti (1609), Antonio Taroni (1612), Pomponio Nenna (1613), and Vincenzo Ugolini (1615), is hardly problematic, given the genre. In any "representative" style, however, at least the gender of speaker should somehow be matched by the voices: Marc'Antonio Negri published a perfectly decent solo-voice setting (G2 clef) in his *Affetti amorosi . . . libro secondo* (Venice: Riccardo Amadino, 1611), as did Giacomo Fornaci (C1 clef) in his *Amorosi respiri . . . libro primo* (Venice: Giacomo Vincenti, 1617).[49] But in the case of Monteverdi's TTB treatment, one has to ask why three men should be exposing Cinzia in an orgy of barroom ribaldry, regardless of whether Ergasto is part of the group or he and Cinzia have somehow been spied upon by three others. Again, it is hard not to read this as anything but comic in intent.

"A delightful musical aria, and beautiful"

If three male observers intruding upon a scene might legitimately raise questions about their lewd intentions, this poses a dilemma for one of the key pieces marked "rappresentativo" in the Eighth Book, the central *Lamento della ninfa* within Ottavio Rinuccini's "Non avea Febo ancora." In his First Book of madrigals, Monteverdi had provided an innocuous setting of Antonio Allegretti's canzone "Fumia la pastorella." He allocated its three stanzas to three *parti*: in the first, the speaker describes a

---

[48] Cinzia is not named in the text, but the lover excuses himself to her in the next madrigal in Marino's sequence, "Al desir troppo ingordo" (headed "Scusa di bacio mordace"). For a broader discussion, see Ossi, "Pardon me, but your teeth are in my neck." The two madrigals immediately prior to "Eccomi pronta" in Marino's *Rime* are "Tornate, o cari baci" and "Vorrei baciarti, o Filli": Monteverdi's settings are placed earlier in the Seventh Book ("Vorrei baciarti" first), spaced out in what seems to be a quite deliberate fashion (five settings separate each of them).

[49] Marc'Antonio Negri set all six of these "baci" madrigals in his 1611 collection, plus the dialogue-canzone, "Poich'a baciar ne 'nvita" (between Aminta and Clori), that follows in Marino's *Rime*. They are not in sequence save for "Eccomi pronta ai baci" (G2 clef) and "Al desir troppo ingordo" (C3—presumably, given the high clefs, a "tenor" voice).

shepherdess singing through the fields; in the second, she herself celebrates the arrival of May; and in the third, the speaker tells how all the nymphs and shepherds of the Tiber rallied to Fumia's call, singing her praises. Monteverdi's options within the polyphonic madrigal were fairly limited in terms of how to reflect these different rhetorical registers. The "representative" style or genre made life easier from that point of view, although its consequences are not always straightforward.

The text of "Non avea Febo ancora" is a canzonetta in ten stanzas.[50] Monteverdi, however, grouped them into three sections by way of their diegesis (stanzas 1–3), mimesis (4–9; Monteverdi gave this part the title "Lamento dela ninfa"), and diegesis (10), creating a tripartite structure similar to "Misero Alceo" and "Batto, qui pianse Ergasto" in the Sixth Book. When Remigio Romano included the text anonymously in his *Prima raccolta di bellissime canzonette musicali e moderne* (1618; pp. 86–87), he labeled it a "Dilettevole aria di musica, e bello," and identified its subject as a woman abandoned by her faithless lover ("Donna abbandonata da infedele Amante"). Romano called the speaker a "donna"; for Rinuccini, she was "donzella" (within the text), and for Monteverdi, a "ninfa"—her changed status raises questions about how to read her complaint. Romano's term "aria" is also striking. It appears less frequently in the *Prima raccolta* than "canzonetta" or "canzona," although there is no discernible difference in the use of the terms. There is also some ambiguity over whether Romano's "aria di musica" is one that has been, or could be, set to music. Certainly, settings of some version of "Non avea Febo ancora" had already been published by Antonio Brunelli in 1614 (in C4 clef but labeled "Canto o Tenore") and Giovanni Girolamo (Johann Hieronymus) Kapsperger in 1619 (SS, bc).[51] But the text published by Romano differs from them in its sequence, and sometimes content, of the stanzas, and while both Brunelli and Kapsperger come closer to the version of the poem included in Rinuccini's posthumous *Poesie* (1622; pp. 223–24), as does Monteverdi, they also have some differences from it, and between themselves. The poem is therefore surprisingly unstable in its various poetic and musical sources, which may, in turn, reflect Rinuccini's tendency constantly to revise his poetry in his working manuscripts.[52]

The nymph's circumstances here are far less happy than was the case in "Fumia la pastorella." Rinuccini sets the scene at dawn—"Febo" (i.e., Phoebus) is the sun—in the first stanza, with a final two lines that become a refrain:

---

[50] We might argue over how to label it. Georis (*Claudio Monteverdi "letterato,"* 668) calls it an "ode-canzonetta," which is plausible, based on the model of Gabriello Chiabrera.

[51] Part of their music is presented for comparison in Ossi, *Divining the Oracle*, 179. There are other settings as well. The anonymous solo-voice one in Florence, Biblioteca Nazionale Centrale, Magl. XIX.144, has just the first stanza (and the music survives elsewhere with a different text). Giovanni Battista Piazza's setting (C1 clef), published in his *Canzonette ... Libro primo: a voce sola* (Venice: Bartolomeo Magni, 1633), takes a quite different approach. He sets only a version of the first stanza, adding a line that turns the final two (the refrain) into direct speech (with a shift to triple time): "dicea dolente e mesta: / «Misera che farò / tanto duol non soffrirò.»"

[52] See the examples in Carter, "Ottavio Rinuccini's *Narciso*."

> Non havea Febo ancora
> recato al mondo il dì,
> ch'una donzella fuora
> del proprio albergo uscì.
> (Miserella, ahi più no, no,
> tanto giel soffrir non può.)

[Phoebus had not yet / brought day to the world, / as a young girl out / from her own house came. / (Poor thing, ah, no more, no, / can she suffer such ice.)]

The unfortunate nymph has presumably woken to discover that her lover is no longer in her bed. The narrative voice explains how grief was spread across her face and sighs issued forth from her heart (stanza 2), as she wandered here and there (stanza 3), trampling on the flowers. Thus does she go forth weeping ("così piangendo va"). That shift from past to present tense cues the move from diegesis to mimesis, although the temporal ambiguity is already there in the refrain ("non può" is third-person present tense).

The nymph starts to speak in stanza 4:

> «Amor», diceva, e 'l piè,
> mirando il ciel, fermò,
> «dove, dov'è la fé
> che 'l traditor giurò?»[53]
> (Miserella, ahi più no, no,
> tanto giel soffrir non può.)

["Love," she said, and her foot, / looking at the sky, did she stop, / "where, where is the faith / that the traitor swore?" / (Poor thing, ah, no more, no, / can she suffer such ice.)]

In stanzas 5–7, she issues a series of complaints mixed with some threats until she reaches her main point (stanzas 8–9): that her lover's new beloved may be more beautiful but never so much in love, and her kisses will never be so sweet. At that point the nymph falls silent ("ah, taci"), prompting a return to narration (stanza 10):

> Sì tra sdegnosi pianti
> spargea le voci al ciel.
> Così ne' cori amanti,
> mesce Amor fiamme e giel.

---

[53] Rinuccini breaks the meter here, given that the previous and subsequent stanzas all have alternate *settenari piani* and *tronchi* (save for the refrain). He may have been using that to mark the shift to mimesis. Kapsperger, however, fixed the irregularity by having "piede...fede."

> (Miserella, ahi più no, no,
> tanto giel soffrir non può.)

[So amid scornful plaints / did she pour out the words to heaven. / Thus into amorous hearts, / does Love pour flames and ice. / (Poor thing, ah, no more, no, / can she suffer such ice.)]

By the time the nymph reaches her comparisons with her rival, her plaints have indeed become "sdegnosi"—a word that ranges from anger through scorn and indignation to resentfulness. This suggests that the nymph has more gumption than one might credit, with none of the subsequent ladylike retractions found toward the end of the *Lamento d'Arianna* in its operatic version. The "voci" in that final stanza also offers a typical pun between "words"—or what lies behind them—and (musical) "voices." However, Rinuccini's repetition of the refrain even at the end of this final stanza is strange, given that he has already drawn the final oxymoronic moral of the scene narrated here. Indeed, the refrain is odd in general. Inevitably, the initial narration is in the past tense, and the nymph's direct speech is in the present. The last stanza mixes past tense (closing off the narration) and present (for the moral). The present-tense refrain puts the three onlookers directly at the scene—as if speaking on the listener's behalf—rather than having them tell us about it. But at that point, its repetitions after each and every stanza, including the first three narrative ones, seem misplaced. Monteverdi prefers to omit a good number of them—and to shorten others—including the one at the end of the central lament's final stanza, where the nymph urges silence.

Brunelli and Kapsperger do what one would expect for a strophic canzonetta: they print the music for the first stanza (and the refrain), but only the text for the subsequent ones. Monteverdi instead creates a through-composed setting. The first three narrative stanzas are set in duple-time homophony for TTB, save for contrapuntal elaboration as the "donzella" tramples the flowers, wandering here and there. That texture returns for the final stanza. Monteverdi treats the lament itself as a separate section, labeled "Rappresentativo" precisely because his "nymph" is voiced by a solo soprano. He also reorders its first lines in a way that could just be one of his "mistakes" (we lose the "piè"/"fé" rhyme)—although it does make clearer the word order—and he repeats things for emphasis, in each case creating a line exactly double in length:

> «Amor», dicea, il ciel
> mirando il piè fermò,
> «Amor, Amor, dove, dov'è la fé
> che 'l traditor, che 'l traditor giurò?»

["Love," she said, at the sky / looking she stopped her foot, / "Love, Love, where, where is the faith / that the traitor, that the traitor swore?"]

This central *Lamento della ninfa* has come to play a key role in modern views of Monteverdi's late output. His other settings in the *genere rappresentativo* had tended to be "representative" not just by identifying a singer with a character but also by a predominant use of recitative. Here, in contrast, Monteverdi writes in triple time, and moreover, using a four-measure ground-bass pattern (thirty-four statements) descending stepwise through the modal *diatessaron*, from the final to the co-final (*a–g–f–e*). This descending tetrachord has been labeled an "emblem of lament," and it is certainly true that it appears in subsequent operatic and similar laments, whether in its diatonic form or with the steps filled in chromatically (as in Dido's lament near the end of Henry Purcell's *Dido and Aeneas*).[54] However, it appears in other contexts in the Eighth Book, as when it underpins the "sweet charms" of love in "Altri canti d'Amor, tenero arciero." The effect is quite different from the previous *locus classicus* of the "representative" lament, Arianna's in Monteverdi's opera of 1608. As many have noted, Monteverdi now appears to have moved away from recitative to triple-time aria as the most powerful medium for emotional expression or, perhaps better, experience. However, matters are not quite so simple.

While the *Lamento d'Arianna* could be translated into the medium of the polyphonic madrigal only with some difficulty, "Non avea Febo ancora" and its central lament were more straightforward precisely because of the explicit narrative frame. However, Rinuccini's decision to cast his tale in strophic form might seem odd in the context of what would seem to be intended as a "serious" piece. This is not entirely unique in the poet's output. Two more of his poems (never set to music, it seems) adopt a similar strategy, perhaps drawing on Chiabrera's Pindaric odes. His "Scorsemi un giorno Amore" develops a narrative over twelve seven-line stanzas in which the speaker recounts coming across a shepherd and quotes his lengthy lament at having left his beloved Orsilla until (back to narration) he is reassured by his companions that she will hear his words and come to him.[55] And in the very long "Al suon di questa cetera" (in four-line stanzas) the speaker (construed as Rinuccini himself) invites his listeners to draw near—a typical epic strategy—to hear the story of how he encountered a young woman by the Arno (the river running through Florence). He fell in love, but in vain, for she was in mourning for the death of her husband (so she recounts at length), at which point he promised to honor her in verse.[56] In their own settings of "Non avea Febo ancora," both Brunelli and Kapsperger allow for this manner of poetic delivery by way of a strophic setting for a single singer in the manner of a balladeer. It has pros and cons: the repetitive music focuses attention on the text and the story it tells, but save by performative intervention within narrow constraints, it cannot respond to shifts in content and

---

[54] Rosand, "The Descending Tetrachord."
[55] Rinuccini, *Poesie* (1622), 192–95. The structure of each stanza is unusual: $a^7b^7a^7b^7c^8c^8c^8$.
[56] Ibid., 134–52. There are 128 four-line stanzas, almost entirely in *settenari sdruccioli*. At one point, the speaker describes himself as a poet who had told the tales of Narcissus and of Daphne, making reference to two of Rinuccini's opera librettos.

tone in successive stanzas. Monteverdi tries for the best of both worlds: a through-composed setting over a repetitive bassline.

He also gives the nymph a separate voice, just as he did for Tancredi and Clorinda in the context of Testo's narration in the *Combattimento*, but now on a much larger scale, given her stronger presence in the text. Doing so created some dilemmas, however. Given that the narration continues after the nymph has begun ("«Amor», dicea . . ."), Monteverdi had no choice but to include in the central lament TTB as past-tense narrators ("dicea")—as they had been in the introductory stanzas—and as present-tense commentators (in the refrain). When Tasso performed the same mixed-tense rhetorical trick in the *Combattimento di Tancredi e Clorinda*, Monteverdi could leave it up to the singer in terms of how best to handle his recitative at such moments. He is more constrained by the triple-time ostinato of the central *Lamento della ninfa*, however, and he presents TTB's music in two different formats. For the outer sections of "Non avea Febo ancora" (the first three stanzas and the last), the voices are given separately in the appropriate partbooks, while for the central lament, they are contained within an abbreviated score (minus a fully written-out basso continuo) in the Alto partbook, and in full score in the Basso Continuo one. This also raises questions about how the different partbooks would have been used in performance.

Monteverdi explains this layout in his prefatory instructions for the piece in the Eighth Book ("Modo di rappresentare il presente canto"):

> The three [voice] parts, which sing outside the lament [*pianto*] of the nymph, are thus placed separately, because they are sung to the time of the hand. The other three parts, which proceed commiserating in weak voice with the nymph, are placed in score, so that they may follow her lament, which is sung to the time of the emotion of the soul, and not to that of the hand.[57]

His "to the time of the hand" means to a regular beat. But when it comes to the central lament, as TTB commiserate with the nymph "in weak voice" (their music is also marked "cantino piano"), they needed the score because the nymph's delivery was intended to be irregular, according to "the time of the emotion . . . and not to that of the hand." It is presumably for similar reasons that in the *Combattimento di Tancredi e Clorinda*, the two sections where Clorinda's speech is accompanied by the string instruments have her words printed in each string part.

Singing "without a beat" ("senza battuta") was explicitly associated with the recitative style of the *lettera amorosa* and *partenza amorosa* in the Seventh Book. The paradox of the *Lamento della ninfa*, however, is that it is not in any typical recitative style, and that its triple time forces at least some kind of regular beat that is further

---

[57] In the Basso Continuo partbook: "Le tre parti, che cantano fuori del pianto dela Ninfa; si sono così separatamente posto, perché si cantano al tempo dela mano; le altre tre parti, che vanno commiserando in debole voce la Ninfa, si sono poste in partitura, acciò seguitano il pianto di essa, qual va cantato a tempo de 'affetto del animo, e non a quello dela mano." Monteverdi's reference to "the other three parts" does not imply three new singers.

constrained by the four-measure ostinato bass. Monteverdi also has to deal with the repetitive metrical structures of Rinuccini's stanzas, which are quite different from the freer *versi sciolti* associated with recitative. And the poet's mixing of *versi piani* and end-accented *versi tronchi* tends to prevent the kind of free-flowing movement that one might associate with singing to "the time of the emotion."

Of course, Monteverdi finds a very clever solution to the problem, principally by way of the nymph singing against, rather than to, the ostinato. He does this harmonically by having her jump to dissonances that do not fit the prevailing harmony. But he also counters the regularity of the ostinato pattern in other ways. It descends by step from final to co-final (one note per measure), meaning that the end of one cycle and the beginning of the next form an authentic/perfect cadence (V–I). Monteverdi therefore needs to resist that cadential motion save at the end of each four-line grouping.

For example, the second stanza of the lament (the fifth of the entire sequence) alternates *versi piani* and *versi tronchi* (as do almost all the others) as the nymph continues her instruction to Love:

> fa che ritorni il mio
> amor com'ei pur fu,
> o tu m'ancidi, ch'io
> non mi tormenti più.

[make return my / love as indeed he was, / or kill me, so that I / may torment myself no longer.]

Those *versi tronchi* are useful in musical terms, given that they end with a strong accent rather than a weak one. But Monteverdi needs to make a distinction between the one ending line 2 ("com'ei pur fu") and the final one ("tormenti più") to avoid too strong a break in the middle. Therefore, he spaces the text out over the repetitions of the bass, and destroys the poetic meter (in the first line, "ritorni" and "il" should be elided, and "mio" set as two syllables):

fa che ri-	torni	il mio a-	mor co-
a	*g*	*f*	*E*
-m'e pur	fu,	o,	o tu m'an-
a	*g*	*f*	*E*
-cidi,	ch'io	non mi tor-	menti	più.
a	*g*	*f*	*E*	*a*

Monteverdi then repeats that final line, also to create the effect of an enjambment with the next stanza: "Non mi tormenti, non mi tormenti, non mi tormenti più. No, non vò più ch'ei sospiri . . ." But each four-line stanza ends with a cadence (and the same motion in the vocal line), while within each stanza, the placement of the text over the ostinato seeks to avoid any cadential motion, whether still moving synchronously with the bass or, at times, at odds with it, as in the painful suspensions on "Perché di lui mi struggo" when the nymph asks why she is "consumed" by her feelings for her lover.

In other words, Monteverdi's remark that the nymph's lament is sung to the time of the emotion is less a performance instruction than a statement of compositional fact; that "emotional time" is embedded within the musical fabric precisely because of the nymph's metrical and harmonic dissonances against the regularly moving bass. But there remains the question of those three onlookers. Monteverdi says that they "proceed commiserating" with the nymph, but they are also voyeurs, speaking on behalf of an audience that is no less voyeuristic. They have a prurient interest in watching an abandoned "donna," "donzella," or "ninfa" trampling the flowers at dawn: they seem to take some pleasure in their gaze, and their own musical dissonances contain a distinctly erotic charge.

Arianna also has observers as she laments her abandonment by Teseo, at least in the operatic version of the scene: the fisherfolk who have welcomed them to Naxos stand by, both speaking directly to her and commenting on her sad but noble state. But she, at least, can come to her own conclusion on her situation (again, in the opera): that this is what happens to one who loves and believes too much ("Così va chi tropp'ama e troppo crede"). As someone reduced to lesser, ambiguous status, the nymph, speaking only to herself, is left just with silence ("ah, taci," she says). Whatever sympathies the onlookers may have had for her during her lament seem to disappear in their final narrative stanza: her actions simply become an object lesson in how Love pours flames and ice into the hearts of lovers. Monteverdi's *ninfa* may be being offered up as further proof of the madrigal immediately preceding hers in the Eighth Book, "Chi vòl aver felice e lieto il core," which claims that anyone wishing to have a happy heart should steer clear of love altogether. In the following "Perché ten fuggi, o Fillide," however, another nymph gets firmly put back into the traditional position of callously refusing the amorous attentions of a "scrawny and pale" Aminta, while the next, "Non partir, ritrosetta," makes a similar complaint of a woman who refuses to listen to a lover's lament ("tu non senti i lamenti"). "Su, su, su, pastorelli" then has a female poetic voice summon shepherds to the fields at dawn to enjoy another day of the heart's "true joy." But the trajectory is clear. If women are not willing to provide such joy, then the final *Ballo delle ingrate* reveals their fate, condemned to eternal suffering in the afterlife for being ungrateful in love. These *Madrigali guerrieri, et amorosi* take a very one-sided view of the matters in hand. And while Monteverdi's settings here, as elsewhere, invoke a specific set of relationships between the composer, performer, and listener wherein playing with text and music is designed not just to arouse the passions but also to prompt a form of interactive engagement, an uncomfortable question remains: What, precisely, is any reaction to a lamenting nymph meant to be?

10
Playing with Time

The conclusion of any account of Monteverdi's madrigals as embodying and inspiring performative acts of various kinds by the composer, a musical ensemble, or the listener must be to force engaging with them in performance. While these works each have a "real"-time duration, they also invoke a subjective experience contrary to any external clock. Brunelli's and Kapsperger's settings of "Non avea Febo ancora" took the wholly predictable step of providing music just for the first stanza of Rinuccini's text, with the rest to follow. Each did so in an economical twelve duple-time measures, including the refrain (with Brunelli adding a two-measure instrumental ritornello at the end). Monteverdi is still more efficient for the first three stanzas (dropping the refrain), which take up a total of twenty-seven measures. However, the nymph's lament—six stanzas—extends to 137 measures, in part because of the more leisurely pace of the triple time, but also given Monteverdi's repetitions within the text. Moreover, his distinction between "the time of the hand" for the opening and closing sections, and "the time of the emotion" for the central lament, tells his musicians how they must alter the perceptions of their listeners. Performances of Monteverdi's "Non avea Febo ancora" tend to last somewhere between five and seven minutes. What we experience, however, goes beyond any such limit.

Rinuccini might not have approved, to judge by his account of an event in 1610. In June of that year, the virtuoso soprano Adriana Basile journeyed from Naples to Mantua to enter service at the Gonzaga court. She passed through Florence, where she stayed in the house of Giulio Caccini, the well-known singer. Caccini, in turn, invited a group of patricians to an impromptu concert for which Basile was joined by other Florentine musicians to perform five-voice madrigals by Alfonso Fontanelli. She impressed her audience by her abilities to hold her place in the music, whereas the other singers kept getting lost, which has an air of truth, given that Fontanelli's settings are extremely difficult to sing. However, Rinuccini had more fundamental criticisms to make of the madrigals themselves, given that after four of them, he and his fellow listeners were bored to an extreme: one musical beat seemed to last a whole year, and each word, two.[1] By now he was more accustomed to the new

---

[1] Carter and Goldthwaite, *Orpheus in the Marketplace*, 218–19, 292–93. The other singers were Giovanni Gualberto Magli (castrato), Antonio Brandi (alto), Jacopo Peri (tenor), and Lelio Ghirlinzoni (bass).

styles of solo song that tended to deliver poetry in a much more straightforward way word by word and line by line.

Not everyone would have agreed with him. Vincenzo Giustiniani ended his survey (c. 1628) of music in his lifetime on a rather ambivalent note. He appreciated the delights of contemporary singing, but he lamented the decline of the polyphonic madrigal and the increasing emphasis on music as a listener's art rather than one in which learned connoisseurs could actively participate. Like many Romans, he also doubted the merits of the new recitative, which often, he claimed, would lead to tedium. His comment on madrigals was followed by Giovanni Battista Doni in 1635 ("the madrigalian art is understood only by the experts") and by the composer Domenico Mazzocchi in 1638 ("today few are composed, and fewer are sung, given that to their misfortune they seem more or less banned from the academies").[2] Perhaps the most extreme example is the Florentine monk Severo Bonini, who in his *Discorsi e regole sovra la musica* (c. 1650) wrote with heavy heart:

> Do you not see that today one is only concerned with composing little arias for one and two voices concerted with harpsichords or similar instruments? Madrigals to be sung at the table without instruments have been sent to oblivion, as is church music, all of which are too composed, and so little by little one will carry on losing this art, because today hard work seems somewhat unhealthy...[3]

Monteverdi may have valued the demonstration of "hard work" in musical terms: even his "arias for one and two voices" are not so little. But he perhaps also felt that the "classic" five-voice madrigal was past its time. He conspicuously avoids the scoring in his Seventh Book (save in the final *ballo*, *Tirsi e Clori*), and the only five-voice settings in his Eighth (save again for the *ballo* at the end of the "Canti guerrieri") are the rather odd "alla francese" settings in the "Canti amorosi," of Guarini's "Dolcissimo uscignolo" and "Chi vòl aver felice e lieto il core." When he wants to write on a grand scale, he opts for six or more voices with instruments, just as he had done in "A quest'olmo, a quest'ombre et a quest'onde."

Monteverdi's return to five-voice writing, if sometimes now with instruments, in three of the five Italian settings at the head of his *Selva morale e spirituale* of 1640–41 might therefore seem a retrograde step.[4] The volume was dedicated to Eleonora Gonzaga, the dowager empress whose husband, Ferdinand II, was to have been the recipient of the *Madrigali guerrieri, et amorosi*. Its opening madrigals are the "moral" component—Monteverdi labels the first two of them as such—of what is

---

[2] Carter, *Music in Late Renaissance and Early Baroque Italy*, 241–42. Mazzocchi's comment comes from the preface to his *Madrigali a cinque voci, et altri varii concerti* (Rome: Francesco Zannetti, 1638). For a broader discussion, see Holzer, "Sono d'altro garbo," 269.

[3] Carter, *Music in Late Renaissance and Early Baroque Italy*, 242.

[4] Some of the partbooks of the *Selva morale e spirituale* are dated 1640 and others, 1641; the dedication is dated 1 May 1641. As for the separate contents of the volume, one can plausibly assume that they were composed over a lengthy period of time. In the case of the Italian settings, however, there is no strong evidence to support the statement made by Moore ("*Venezia favorita da Maria*," 328, 353) that they were "almost certainly" performed in June 1630 as part of Venice's ceremonies responding to the plague.

otherwise a large collection of sacred music in Latin for liturgical purposes (the majority) or devotional ones (the final contrafact of the *Lamento d'Arianna* as a lament of the Madonna, "Iam moriar, mi fili"). None of the Italian settings is a "spiritual madrigal" in the narrow sense of the term, but they each comment on the futility of earthly pleasures in the face of divine judgment. Indeed, the two canzonettas here use the ostensibly light-hearted genre itself to make the point. "Spuntava il dì" (to a text by Francesco Balducci) and "Chi vòl che m'innamori" are set to Monteverdi's now typical low-voice combination (ATB; in the latter case, with two violins). But their invocation of worldly delights is undermined by their refrains, which turn the typical "seize the day" argument on its head: everything will pass.

Monteverdi was now in his seventies, and there is a clear sense here of an old composer looking back on a long career. He was not yet done. He had already revived *Arianna* in Venice in the 1639–40 Carnival season, which was also when his new opera, *Il ritorno d'Ulisse in patria*, received its premiere there. While publishing the *Selva morale* he was finishing off his next work for the stage, *Le nozze d'Enea con Lavinia* (1641), which may be why the volume was delayed in the press. *L'incoronazione di Poppea* (1643) was still to come. But in the second of his "moral" madrigals, Monteverdi takes the opening sonnet of Petrarch's *Canzoniere*, "Voi ch'ascoltate in rime sparse il suono" (set for an unusual combination of STTTB, with two violins), to make an apologia similar to the poet's: he hopes to find both pity and forgiveness for his youthful transgressions and for the varied style in which he weeps and speaks, while acknowledging that worldly delight is but a brief dream.[5]

The first madrigal, however, looks outward rather than inward, and in a quite astonishing way. "O ciechi, il tanto affaticar che giova?" is for a more typical SSATB combination plus violins. The text is taken from the first *capitolo* of Petrarch's *Trionfo della Morte*, in *terza rima*, although not precisely in sequence.[6] Here mankind is blind to the eternal truth that earthly labor is in vain: Monteverdi has the initial vocative—"O ciechi, ciechi" in his reading—recur throughout. But that generic warning is given a specific twist as the composer now seems to address the Habsburgs directly (his replacement for one word in the text is noted in italic):

> Che vale a soggiogar gli altrui [*M: tanti*] paesi
>   e tributarie far le genti strane
>   cogli animi al suo danno sempre accesi?
> Dopo l'imprese perigliose e vane,
>   e col sangue acquistar terre e tesoro,
>   vie più dolce si trova l'acqua e 'l pane,
> e 'l legno e 'l vetro che le gemme e l'oro.

---

[5] Calcagno (*From Madrigal to Opera*, 87–88) finds a similar apologetic thrust in the final setting in the *Selva morale e spirituale*, the contrafact of the *Lamento d'Arianna* as the *Pianto della Madonna*.

[6] Monteverdi sets lines 87–100 followed by 82–85, He changes line 100 (the first line of a new *terza rima* stanza) to "e 'l vetro e 'l legno che le gemm'e gl'ori," switching the last word from "l'oro" in order to provide a rhyme for his backtracking to lines 82–85, with which the setting ends. Therefore the *terza rima* structure breaks down for the last five lines of the setting.

[What worth lies in subjugating others' (*M: so many*) countries / and to make foreign peoples tributaries, / their spirits set aflame to your harm? // After campaigns perilous and vain, / and gaining land and treasure with blood, / sweeter it is to find water and bread, // and wood and glass, than gems and gold.]

If the *Madrigali guerrieri, et amorosi* had been conceived during a lull in the Thirty Years' War, the ferocious renewal of combat in the successful campaigns of the Franco-Swedish alliance took the Habsburg cause from bad to worse. Monteverdi's appropriation of Petrarch's antiwar statement takes on a powerful edge, as do his brief references to the *concitato genere* that are now far less strident. He may have hoped that Empress Eleonora, at least, might take the message to heart. But at least one of the eulogists writing on the composer's death rued the fact that his music could no longer create peace for a world in crisis.[7]

The third piece in the *Selva morale* returns to the broader theme. "È questa vita un lampo" is to a text by Angelo Grillo (Livio Celiano), with whom Monteverdi had been associated earlier in his career.[8] However, he once more modifies the poem, switching Grillo's grammatical constructions addressing the reader ("you" and "us") to a first-person-singular verb and pronoun. This turns the setting into a very personal statement on Monteverdi's part.

> È questa vita un lampo,
> ch'a l'apparir dispare
> in questo mortal campo.
> Ché se miri [*M: miro*], il passato
> è già morto, il futuro ancor non nato,
> il presente, partito[9]
> non bene anco apparito.
> Ahi lampo fuggitivo, et sì n'alletta [*M: m'alletta*];
> e dopo il lampo pur vien la saetta.

[This life is a flash of lightning, / which disappears as soon as it appears / in this mortal domain. / For if you (*M: I*) consider it, the past / is already dead, the future not yet born, / (and) the present, gone / scarcely as it has appeared. / Ah, fleeting

---

[7] One of the contributors to the *Fiori poetici raccolti nel funerale del Molto Illustre e Molto Reverendo Signor Claudio Monteverdi*, ed. Marinoni (1644), Paulo Piazza, provided a sonnet deploring Monteverdi's death in a time of military crisis ("Al fiero suon di furibondo Marte / scomposta è ogni armonia, roca ogni tromba"; p. 14). In another madrigal ("Gloria à Dio, pace all'huom, musici egreggi"; p. 26), he noted how Monteverdi's presence in paradise now prevented him from bringing peace to the world ("... Ma da barbara guerra / vietato ei d'annuntiar la pace in terra / ... / gito e a cantar la gloria in paradiso").

[8] For Monteverdi's earlier connections with Grillo (1557–1629), see Fabbri, *Monteverdi*, trans. Carter, 118–19. The poem "È questa vita un lampo" was published in Grillo's *Pietosi affetti, et lagrime del penitente* (Venice: G. B. Ciotti, 1601), 330. It is possible that some version of Monteverdi's setting was one of the two spiritual madrigals (otherwise lost) that the composer sent to Grillo in August 1614 (along with his Sixth Book); Fabbri, *Monteverdi*, trans. Carter, 141–44.

[9] Monteverdi has "sparito" in some parts.

flash of lightning, and yet it so delights us (*M: me*), / but after the lightning comes the thunderbolt.]

Grillo's text deals with the temporal fragility of life, which passes in a flash between a dead past and a future still to come. Monteverdi's setting is the most ostensibly conservative of the "moral" madrigals: the basso continuo is a *basso seguente* throughout, and the madrigal could be done as well, if not better, without it. He also exploits extreme contrasts of pace: the first line, "È questa vita un lampo" is delivered in two measures, whereas the same number of syllables in "Ché se miro, il passato" takes up six. Monteverdi draws out his three temporal moments—past, present, and future—but is still more fascinated by "il presente": even though it is lost as soon as it appears, he devotes no fewer than fifteen musical measures (out of sixty-seven) to it, dragging out its birth and death across all five voices. Rinuccini may have complained about madrigalian beats seeming to last a whole year, and each word, two, but Monteverdi milks them for all their worth. The present must become the past, and Judgment Day awaits us all, but he is going to use music to delay that moment for as long as possible.

When Monteverdi discussed with Alessandro Striggio a new libretto by Giulio Strozzi, *La finta pazza Licori*, for possible performance in Mantua in 1627, he thought it had some good moments because its lead character, Licori, needed to feign madness, which therefore "must take into consideration only the present, not the past or the future" (so he wrote on 7 May). He proposed achieving this by using the music to emphasize single words and "not the sense of the phrase." That was a logical choice for any solo song, but polyphonic music offered different options. Most lyric poetry operates within a present-tense limbo, a painful or pleasurable moment frozen forever in time that traps the lover between a past that might be remembered (someone or something was) and a future that can only be imagined or hoped for (someone or something might be).[10] It also often arrests an instant in time so that it can be seen, heard, or felt from all angles: a sigh, a kiss, the act of parting, the moment of death (whether metaphorical or real). Music plays with time as well.[11] In "Dolcemente dormiva la mia Clori" (Second Book), the aphorism that justifies the lover stealing a kiss from the sleeping Clori—"Tempo perduto non s'acquista mai" (Time lost can never be regained)—is stated three times as the lover not only plucks up courage but also freezes a temporal moment that will soon pass; the repetition seems tinged with a note of regret. "Piagn'e sospira; e quand'i

---

[10] Of the eighty-six settings included in Monteverdi's first five books of five-voice madrigals, only ten have texts in part in the past tense, and nine of those do so according to the convention of mixing past-tense narration and present-tense direct speech. The exception is "Piagn'e sospira; e quand'i caldi raggi" (Fourth Book), in which Nicea weeps and sighs, and carved her lover's name on the trees. This is epic (from Tasso's *Gerusalemme conquistata*), where mixed tenses are not unusual, in part because of the use of the historic present. Those eighty-six madrigals of course include dramatic texts (from Battista Guarini's *Il pastor fido*) that by definition must largely be in the present tense.

[11] See Giles, *Monteverdi and the Marvellous*, 9–11. Giles goes on to link this directly with contemporary concepts of *meraviglia* (the marvelous) as stretching or compressing time, and as making simultaneous that which cannot be so in any objective world.

caldi raggi" (Fourth Book) has Tasso's Nicea (or Monteverdi's Monteverdi) inscribe a complaint over an extraordinary eighty-seven slow-moving measures of dense counterpoint.[12] "Era l'anima mia" (Fifth Book) draws out the lovers' anticipation of mutual orgasm over a languid seventy-four measures. In "Con che soavità, labra odorate" (Seventh), the solo soprano stretches time to the limit in the hope of achieving the impossible: that words and kisses can simultaneously, rather than separately, produce "sweet harmony"—a simultaneity that can occur only in music. The refrains inserted by Monteverdi within the continuo madrigals in his Fifth and Sixth Books both stop time and render it cyclical. In "Ahi come a un vago sol cortese giro" (Fifth), Love's wound never heals. In "Qui rise, o Tirsi, e qui ver' me rivolse" (Sixth Book), a "happy memory" keeps coming back to mind. As for the *Combattimento*, the action moves more quickly or more slowly, or even stops entirely as Testo pauses the narrative to extol the need to bring Tancredi and Clorinda's memorable actions from night into the bright light of day in a "full theater" ("pieno Theatro")—clearly meaning something more than just Girolamo Mocenigo's residence. Monteverdi sets the "Notte, che nel profondo oscuro seno" stanza apart by way of a solemn sinfonia, a shift to strophic variation (for the two quatrains in the *ottava rima* stanza), and an instruction that here—and only here—is the singer playing Testo permitted to add ornamentation, some of which gets notated.[13] Any sense of narrative motion is dropped in a freeze-frame moment before Tancredi and Clorinda take to battle: Testo has just told how they are approaching each other with halting, slow steps like two angry bulls protective of their terrain ("e vansi incontro a passi tardi e lenti, / quai duo tori gelosi e d'ira ardenti"). They might still move during the instrumental "passeggio" at the end of the sinfonia, and closer still during its repeat between the two halves of Testo's stanza, but their actions are limited as our attention is turned elsewhere.[14]

This playing with time reflects broader contemporary issues. Measuring, and therefore controlling, its passing was a matter of concern in early-seventeenth-century Italy, both for scientific purposes (not least, astronomy) and as means of regulating urban social and economic life. The typical day became regulated less by the visible motion of the sun, or by the bells marking ritual sacred or civic schedules, and more by clocks that were becoming more precise and accurate.[15] Time had always been a musical concern, too, not least by way of the *tactus* and its possible proportional subdivisions. But the ability to measure time's inexorable forward motion in ever smaller increments raises the question of how music might now be used

---

[12] Giles, *Monteverdi and the Marvellous*, 213–14.

[13] See Ex. 4.3(b). According to the internal preface to the *Combattimento*, Testo "non doverà far gorghe né trilli in altro loco, che solamente nel canto dela stanza, che incomincia 'Notte'; il rimanente porterà le pronuntie à similitudine dele passioni del'oratione."

[14] This section of the *Combattimento* always creates problems for the piece; see Ossi, *Divining the Oracle*, 225 (the "Notte" stanza acting as if in a "stop-action sequence"); Calcagno, *From Madrigal to Opera*, 233 (discussing the production by Pierre Audi). But Ossi's "tension between dramatic and narrative time" would be lessened by just accepting the fact that the *Combattimento*, as epic, has little to do with "dramatic time" in the first place.

[15] Long, *Hearing Homophony*, 96–97.

to alter temporal perception, speeding things up, slowing them down, or stopping them altogether.

A poem spoken or read remains bound by its linear sequence: the second line must follow the first, and the third the second. Musical settings change the nature of the poetic game. Lines can be repeated in varied ways; they can come out of order; and their delivery can be paced over a far wider range of speeds. Indeed, Monteverdi often manipulated his texts precisely for these temporal consequences. Time folds in on itself in greater or lesser circular motions, escaping the mundane to place the listener in quite different aesthetic and emotional worlds. The more time became measured, the more the arts—and in particular, the musical arts—sought to resist its constraints.[16]

When Aquilino Coppini sent his three volumes of contrafacts to his fellow rhetorician, Henrik van den Putte, in July 1609, he noted that Monteverdi's madrigals in particular required in performance a very flexible approach to tempo in terms both of its initial choice and of slowing down and speeding up as needed: only then, he said, would their affective power be truly apparent.[17] In the preface to the Eighth Book, Monteverdi himself used rhythmic differences from slow to fast to distinguish his three *generi*: *molle*, *temperato*, and *concitato*. But even in his earliest madrigals, he played with tempo in various ways to contrast straightforward statements with their emotional consequences. For example, in "Se nel partir da voi, vita mia, sento" (First Book), the initial movement in half notes and quarter notes (minims and crotchets) slows to whole notes and half notes (semibreves and minims) at the "harsh torment" felt by the lover on leaving the beloved (see Ex. 2.1), and the same contrast appears later in the setting for the "so many pains" ("tanti guai") suffered in the same circumstance. Even if the beat stays the same, each musical event lasts twice as long.[18] Textual repetition can have a similar effect in halting the action. In "Cor mio, mentre vi miro" (Fourth Book), Guarini's point is that the beloved's beauty allows the lover's heart to be reborn—Monteverdi states "per te rinasce" six times with increasing intensity—but the ending is resigned: the heart dies upon each rebirth (two sad statements of "e per te nato, more").

"Or che 'l ciel e la terra e 'l vento tace" (Eighth Book) also plays with time as the insomniac lover veers between anger and grief. Monteverdi stretches out its first

---

[16] Compare McClary, "Doing the Time Warp in Seventeenth-Century Music." Cypess (*Curious and Modern Inventions*, 184) discusses the manipulation in Frescobaldi's toccatas of "clockwork time" and "subjective, private time," which she associates with spiritual meditation and prayer. Calcagno (*From Madrigal to Opera*, 226) notes the "temporal expansion typical of psychological time" in the handling of the refrain in "Qui rise, o Tirsi, e qui ver' me rivolse" (Sixth Book).

[17] Fabbri, *Monteverdi* (1985), 152–53, from Aquilino Coppini, *Epistolarum libri sex* (Milan: Archiepiscopal Press, 1613), fol. 101r: "Qui sunt à Monteverdio, longiora intervalla, et quasi percussiones inter canendum requirunt. Insistendum tantisper; indulgendum tarditati; aliquando etiam festinandum. Ipse moderator eris. In iis mira sanè vis commovendorum affectuum." Van den Putte had provided (as Erycius Puteanus) a Latin poem praising Artusi included in the prefatory material to *L'Artusi, overo Delle imperfettioni della moderna musica* (1600); see Carter, "Cerberus Barks in Vain," 468–71.

[18] The effect is clear not just in the longer note values but also in the handling of the separate elements of suspensions, whether at the quarter note (crotchet) or the half note (minim). Compare DeFord's discussion (*Tactus, Mensuration, and Rhythm in Renaissance Music*, 416–17) of Cipriano de Rore's "Hor che 'l ciel e la terra" (1542), building on the distinction between a "theoretical *tactus*" and a "compositional" one.

quatrain (the world sleeps) over twenty-three measures without any textual repetition. The next two lines (the lover tosses and turns) span thirty-five, but only because half plus one of them ("e chi mi sface . . .") are repeated seven times in whole or in part while the lover obsesses over what causes him such sweet pain. As in "Cor mio, mentre vi miro," the lover's anguish replays itself over and over: he dies and is reborn a thousand times a day ("mille volte il dì moro e mille nasco"). Monteverdi splits that line into two—"mille, mille volte il dì moro" and "e mille, mille nasco"— and while he does not quite get to a "thousand," "mille" appears thirty-four times in different voice groupings.[19] Moreover, in the final statement of the line, he slows everything to a complete halt on "moro" before rather cheekily picking up the pace at "e mille, mille nasco" with four statements in SSA, TTB, SSA, and the full ensemble. This usually brings a smile to both performers and listeners.

The changes of pace throughout "Or che'l ciel," and Monteverdi's recursive approach to separate lines of the text, represent the typical temporal disjunctions of any lover's fantasy. In "Altri canti di Marte e di sua schiera" (Eighth Book), however, he finds a different reason to extend the musical moment. The final line of the *seconda parte* makes a request to Love: that if he brings death to the heart, he should give life to song ("se desti morte al cor, da vita al canto"). The last tercet of the sonnet is delivered twice, once by the solo bass and then by the SSATTB ensemble. In both cases, Monteverdi plays with the obvious juxtaposition of "morte" and "vita," but he is more interested in giving life to song. The bass has three statements of "da vita al canto," with an elaborate roulade for "canto" in the first that gets extended in the third. This is about as much as a solo song can take. The full ensemble is a different matter, however. On the repeat of the tercet, Monteverdi dispatches the first two lines in eight homophonic measures. The last line has two statements covering thirty-one measures. But in each case, "se desti morte al cor" takes up only three, and for the rest, Monteverdi returns to that bass roulade and develops it contrapuntally across all the voices in elaborate combinations, including an extended one for two tenors that makes a fairly direct reference to, or provides a model for, the two tenors' "exaltabitur in gloria" in the first "Beatus vir" setting in the *Selva morale*.[20] Monteverdi seems to want to delay the final double bar, giving life to song for as long as he can.

The *Lamento della ninfa* takes matters still further. The text itself is complicated enough with its mixed verbal tenses that place a sad event in temporal limbo: a nymph emerged from her dwelling, her pale face revealed her grief, she let forth a sigh, she wandered here and there, thus she laments her lost love, she speaks in the first person, but for the narrators this is what she said. The music creates additional ambiguity. Monteverdi's distinction between the "time of the hand" (for the first three stanzas and the last) and the "time of the emotion" for the nymph

---

[19] This almost doubles the number of thousandfold "ohimè"s (eighteen) at the end of "Oimè, se tanto amate" (Fourth Book).
[20] This is the "Beatus vir" that also borrows its instrumental ritornello (as it were) and other passages from the canzonetta "Chioma d'oro" (Seventh Book).

makes a clear distinction between the two, but that "emotional time" is constructed by placing and then displacing the nymph within the regular metrical framework of the four-measure ostinato in triple meter. Time is in effect caught in a logic error that causes it to hang in a loop, stretching out the moment just before dawn when—as so many of Monteverdi's madrigals reveal—love matches are either sealed or broken.

At some point, however, music must move on or stop. The lamenting nymph would rather it ended sooner than later—"ah, be silent" ("ah, taci"), she says to herself—although the text has one stanza still to go so as to reveal the lesson drawn from her tale by her three witnesses: that Love pours fire and ice into the hearts of lovers. It is a rather shopworn conclusion, and Monteverdi gives it short shrift. But he finds a different solution to the problems of an ending in the last of the five Italian settings in the *Selva morale*: "Chi vòl che m'innamori." This is one of the three that have two violin parts. In "O ciechi, il tanto affaticar che giova?" they largely double the upper voices save where they flesh out the accompaniment in the solo passages (for T, S^2, and B). At the beginning of "Voi ch'ascoltate in rime sparse il suono," the violins echo each gesture in the voice as if to represent the wordless "suono" (sound) of the sighs in Petrarch's "scattered rhymes" (and later, they fill out the harmony when things get tricky in terms of tuning). Only in "Chi vòl che m'innamori," however, do the instruments have music independent of the text.

This is a canzonetta in three stanzas, each with a varied refrain that contrasts what happens "today" with "tomorrow" (laughter turns to tears, light to shadow, and birth to death). Monteverdi chooses not to allocate the stanzas to different voices as he did with other of his canzonettas: this is too serious a text for that. But at "hoggi" ("si ride," "sian luce," "si nasce"), Monteverdi shifts to a dance-like triple time over the *ciaccona* ground bass heard in "Zefiro torna e di soavi accenti," and then back to a solemn duple time for the consequences "tomorrow" ("e poi diman . . ."); this happens twice in each stanza, given Monteverdi's repetition of its last two lines.[21] The situation here is similar to "È questa vita un lampo," playing the present ("hoggi") against the future ("diman"), although the strophic text forces a threefold emphasis on the inevitable.

The words of "Che vòl che m'innamori" offer scant ground for optimism: time destroys everything, terror fills the heart, and life is all in vain. Monteverdi finds a way to compensate, however. He provides the canzonetta with two instrumental ritornellos: the first is an eight-measure galliard (in triple time) at the beginning and between the stanzas, and the second serves for the end of the piece ("Ritornello secondo che serve per la fine dela detta canzonetta"). This second ritornello adds to the beginning of the galliard a solemn, and solemnly beautiful, fourteen-measure pavane. Instrumental ritornellos had long been characteristic of the canzonetta: the

---

[21] Tarquinio Merula's strophic setting (in duple time) published in 1638 is much more straightforward; see his *Curtio precipitato et altri capricii (1638)*, ed. Jevtovic, 40. Merula also has the correct "siam luce" for Monteverdi's "sian luce."

1607 *Scherzi musicali* is full of them, and Monteverdi came up with some neat ritornello variations for the two canzonettas in the Seventh Book, "Chioma d'oro" and "Amor, che deggio far." In those last two cases, as also in "Questi vaghi concenti" (Fifth Book), the setting ends with the last line of the text delivered by the voices.[22] "Chi vòl che m'innamori," however, speaks beyond its vocal double bar: the new pavane is appropriately serious, but the last notes heard are the sprightly galliard that seems intended to offer some comfort. The instrumental sighs in "Voi ch'ascoltate in rime" have changed into something else. One might read this as some attempt to muse on life "today," or as invoking the dance of heavenly angels to come. But either way, it is pure sound that provides the last word. For all the importance of the poetic texts in Monteverdi's madrigals, it is music as music that matters most in the end.

---

[22] "Tempro la cetra, e per cantar gli honori," at the head of the Seventh Book, is an exception: the initial sinfonia returns at the end and leads to a dance sequence, probably because the setting draws on the model of operatic prologues.

Bibliography

Agee, Richard J., "The Venetian Privilege and Music-Printing in the Sixteenth Century," *Early Music History* 3 (1983): 1–42.

Arrigoni, Giovanni Giacomo, *Concerti di camera a 2. 3. 4. 5. 6. 7. 8. 9. (Venice, 1635)*, edited by Pyrros Bamichas, http://epapers.bham.ac.uk/3311/1/Arrigoni_edition.pdf (2019).

Artioli, Umberto, and Cristina Grazioli (eds.), *I Gonzaga e l'Impero: itinerari dello spettacolo*, "Storia dello spettacolo: Fonti" 4 (Florence: Le Lettere, 2005).

Badolato, Nicola, "Soluzioni metriche e motivi poetici nei testi intonati da Benedetto Ferrari e Nicolò Fontei," *Recercare* 30 (2018): 33–62.

Barbieri, Patrizio, "'Chiavette' and Modal Transposition in Italian Practice (c. 1500–1837)," *Recercare* 3 (1991): 5–79.

Baroncini, Rodolfo, "Monteverdi a Venezia: l'azione in città," in *Monteverdi a San Marco*, ed. Baroncini and Di Pasquale, 155–83.

Baroncini, Rodolfo, "Monteverdi in Venice: New Documents and Perspectives," *Early Music* 45/3 (August 2017): 365–76.

Baroncini, Rodolfo, and Marco Di Pasquale (eds.), *Monteverdi a San Marco: Venezia 1613–1643*, "ConNotazioni" 13 (Lucca: Libreria Musicale Italiana, 2020).

Bates, James, "Monteverdi, the Viola Bastarda Player," in *The Italian Viola da Gamba: Proceedings of the International Symposium on the Italian Viola da Gamba*, edited by Susan Orlando (Solignac: Ensemble Baroque de Limoges, 2002), 53–70.

Bertolini, Manuel, "Censurare la musica: una prospettiva di ricerca attraverso la Congregazione Oratoriana," in *La musica dei semplici: l'altra Controriforma*, edited by Stefania Nanni (Rome: Viella, 2012), 217–47.

Besutti, Paola, "Claudio Monteverdi cittadino mantovano: *Tirsi e Clori*, le feste del 1615 e il 'novo ordine generale'," *Philomusica On-line: Rivista del Dipartimento di Musicologia e Beni Culturali [Università di Pavia]*, 17 (2018), http://riviste.paviauniversitypress.it/index.php/phi/issue/view/165.

Besutti, Paola, "'Cose all'italiana' e alla tedesca 'in materia di ricreatione': la circolazione di strumenti, strumentisti e balli fra Mantova e i territori dell'Impero Romano germanico (1500–1630)," in *I Gonzaga e l'Impero*, ed. Artioli and Grazioli, 239–72.

Besutti, Paola, "The 'Sala degli Specchi' Uncovered: Monteverdi, the Gonzagas and the Palazzo Ducale, Mantua," *Early Music* 27/3 (August 1999): 451–65.

Bianconi, Lorenzo, "Struttura poetica e struttura musicale nei madrigali di Monteverdi," in *Congresso internazionale sul tema "Claudio Monteverdi e il suo tempo"*, ed. Monterosso, 335–48.

Blackburn, Bonnie J., and Laurie Stras (eds.) *Eroticism in Early Modern Music* (Farnham, U.K.: Ashgate, 2015).

Bosi, Kathryn, "Adriana's Harp: Paintings, Poetic Imagery, and Musical Tributes for the *Sirena di Posilippo*," *Imago musicae* 30 (2018): 75–104.

Calcagno, Mauro, *From Madrigal to Opera: Monteverdi's Staging of the Self* (Berkeley: University of California Press, 2012).

Carter, Tim, "Another Monteverdi Problem (and Why It Still Matters)," in *Fiori musicali: liber amicorum Alexander Silbiger*, edited by Claire Fontijn and Susan Parisi, "Detroit Monographs in Musicology: Studies in Music" 55 (Sterling Heights, Mich.: Harmonie Park Press, 2010), 83–94.

Carter, Tim, "Artusi, Monteverdi, and the Poetics of Modern Music," in *Musical Humanism and Its Legacy: Essays in Honor of Claude V. Palisca*, edited by Nancy Kovaleff Baker and Barbara Russano Hanning (Stuyvesant, N.Y.: Pendragon Press, 1992), 171–94.

Carter, Tim, "Beyond Drama: Monteverdi, Marino, and the Sixth Book of Madrigals (1614)," *Journal of the American Musicological Society* 69/1 (Spring 2016): 1–46

Carter, Tim, "Cerberus Barks in Vain: Poetic Asides in the Artusi–Monteverdi Controversy," *Journal of Musicology* 29/4 (October 2012): 461–76.

Carter, Tim, "'E in rileggendo poi le proprie note': Monteverdi Responds to Artusi?" *Renaissance Studies* 26 (2012): 138–55.

Carter, Tim, "Epyllia and Epithalamia: Some Narrative Frames for Early Opera," *The Italianist* 40/3 (October 2020): 382–99.

Carter, Tim, "Improvised Counterpoint in Monteverdi's 1610 Vespers," in *"Uno gentile et subtile ingenio": Studies in Renaissance Music in Honour of Bonnie J. Blackburn*, edited by M. Jennifer Bloxam, Gioia Filocamo, and Leofranc Holford-Strevens (Turnhout: Brepols, 2009), 29–35.

Carter, Tim, "Intriguing Laments: Sigismondo d'India, Claudio Monteverdi, and Dido *alla parmigiana* (1628)," *Journal of the American Musicological Society* 49/1 (Spring 1996): 32–69.

Carter, Tim, "Lamenting Ariadne?" *Early Music* 27/3 (August 1999): 395–405.

Carter, Tim, "Listening to Music in Early Modern Italy: Some Problems for the Urban Musicologist," in *Hearing the City in Early Modern Europe*, edited by Tess Knighton and Ascensión Mazuela-Anguita (Turnhout and Tours: Brepols, 2018), 25–49.

Carter, Tim, "Monteverdi and Some Problems of Biography," *Journal of Seventeenth-Century Music* 18 (2012), http://sscm-jscm.org/jscm-issues/volume-18-no-1.

Carter, Tim, "Monteverdi, Early Opera and a Question of Genre: The Case of *Andromeda* (1620)," *Journal of the Royal Musical Association* 137 (2012): 1–34.

Carter, Tim, *Monteverdi's Musical Theatre* (New Haven and London: Yale University Press, 2002).

Carter, Tim, *Music in Late Renaissance and Early Baroque Italy* (London: Batsford, 1992).

Carter, Tim, "Ottavio Rinuccini's *Narciso*: A Study and Edition," *Journal of Seventeenth-Century Music* 30 (2024), https://sscm-jscm.org/jscm-issues/volume-30-no-1.

Carter, Tim, "'Sfogava con le stelle' Reconsidered: Some Thoughts on the Analysis of Monteverdi's Mantuan Madrigals," in *Claudio Monteverdi: studi e prospettive; atti del convegno, Mantova, 21–24 ottobre 1993*, edited by Paola Besutti, Teresa M. Gialdroni, and Rodolfo Baroncini, "Accademia Nazionale Virgiliana di Scienze, Lettere e Arti: Miscellanea" 5 (Florence: Olschki, 1998), 147–70.

Carter, Tim, "Singing *Orfeo*: On the Performers of Monteverdi's First Opera," *Recercare* 11 (1999): 75–118.

Carter, Tim, "Some Notes on the First Edition of Monteverdi's *Orfeo* (1609)," *Music and Letters* 91/4 (November 2010): 498–512.

Carter, Tim, "Two Monteverdi Problems, and Why They Matter," *Journal of Musicology* 19/3 (August 2002): 417–33.

Carter, Tim, "The Venetian Madrigals," in *The Cambridge Companion to Monteverdi*, ed. Whenham and Wistreich, 179–94.

Carter, Tim, "Winds, Cupids, Little Zephyrs, and Sirens: Monteverdi and *Le nozze di Tetide* (1616–17)," *Early Music* 39/4 (November 2011): 489–502.

Carter, Tim, and Richard A. Goldthwaite, *Orpheus in the Marketplace: Jacopo Peri and the Economy of Late Renaissance Florence* (Cambridge, Mass.: Harvard University Press, 2013).

Cascelli, Antonio, "Place, Performance and Identity in Monteverdi's *Combattimento di Tancredi e Clorinda*," *Cambridge Opera Journal* 29/2 (July 2017): 152–88.

Chafe, Eric T., *Monteverdi's Tonal Language* (New York: Schirmer, 1992).

Chater, James, "'Un pasticcio di madrigaletti'? The Early Musical Fortune of *Il pastor fido*," in *Guarini, la musica, i musicisti*, ed. Pompilio, 139–55.

Chew, Geoffrey, "A Model Musical Education: Monteverdi's Early Works," in *The Cambridge Companion to Monteverdi*, ed. Whenham and Wistreich, 31–44.

Chew, Geoffrey, "The Perfections of Modern Music: Consecutive Fifths and Tonal Coherence in Monteverdi," *Music Analysis* 8/3 (October 1989): 247–73.

Coluzzi, Seth J., "Black Sheep: The Phrygian Mode and a Misplaced Madrigal in Marenzio's Seventh Book (1595)," *Journal of Musicology* 30/2 (April 2013): 129–79.

Coluzzi, Seth J., *Guarini's "Il pastor fido" and the Madrigal: Voicing the Pastoral in Late Renaissance Italy* (New York: Routledge, 2023).

Coluzzi, Seth J., "Licks, Polemics, and the *Viola bastarda*: Unity and Defiance in Monteverdi's Fifth Book," *Early Music* 47/3 (August 2019): 333–44.

Coluzzi, Seth J., "'Se vedesti qui dentro': Monteverdi's 'O Mirtillo, Mirtillo anima mia' and Artusi's Offence," *Music and Letters* 94/1 (February 2013): 1–37.

Coluzzi, Seth J., "Structure and Interpretation in Luca Marenzio's Settings of *Il pastor fido*" (PhD diss., University of North Carolina at Chapel Hill, 2007).

Cusick, Suzanne, "'There was not one lady who failed to shed a tear': Arianna's Lament and the Construction of Modern Womanhood," *Early Music* 22/1 (February 1994): 21–41.

Cypess, Rebecca, *Curious and Modern Inventions: Instrumental Music as Discovery in Galileo's Italy* (Chicago: University of Chicago Press, 2016).

Dahlhaus, Carl, *Studies on the Origins of Harmonic Tonality*, translated by Robert O. Gjerdingen (Princeton, N.J.: Princeton University Press, 1990).

DeFord, Ruth I., *Tactus, Mensuration, and Rhythm in Renaissance Music* (Cambridge, U.K.: Cambridge University Press, 2015).

Di Pasquale, Marco, "La cappella dogale di San Marco: significato, funzione e struttura," in *Monteverdi a San Marco*, ed. Baroncini and Di Pasquale, 5–57.

Di Pasquale, Marco, "Le compagnie dei musici marciani," in *Monteverdi a San Marco*, ed. Baroncini and Di Pasquale, 185–224.

Dolata, David, "Bellerofonte Castaldi (1580–1649) of Modena: Musician, Poet, and Adventurer," *Acta musicologica* 79 (2007): 85–111.

Dolata, David, *Meantone Temperaments on Lutes and Viols* (Bloomington: Indiana University Press, 2016).

Doni, Giovanni Battista, "Trattato della musica scenica," in *De' trattati di musica di Gio. Battista Doni*, edited by Anton Francesco Gori, vol. 2 (Florence: Stamperia Imperiale, 1763), 1–144.

Dragosits, Anne Marie, *Giovanni Girolamo Kapsperger: "Ein ziemlich extravaganter Mann"* (Lucca: Libreria Musicale Italiana, 2020).

Duffin, Ross W., *How Equal Temperament Ruined Harmony (And Why You Should Care)* (New York: W. W. Norton, 2007).

Durante, Elio, and Anna Martellotti, *Cronistoria del concerto delle dame principalissime di Margherita Gonzaga d'Este*, 2nd ed. (Florence: S.P.E.S., 1989).

Fabbri, Paolo, "Inediti Monteverdiani," *Rivista italiana di musicologia* 15 (1980): 71–86

Fabbri, Paolo, *Monteverdi* (Turin: EDT/Musica, 1985).

Fabbri, Paolo, *Monteverdi*, trans. Tim Carter (Cambridge, U.K.: Cambridge University Press, 1994).

Georis, Christophe, *Claudio Monteverdi "letterato" ou les métamorphoses du texte*, "Bibliothèque de littérature générale et comparée" 113 (Paris: Honoré Champion, 2013).

Giles, Roseen, *Lettera amorosa: Music in the Epistolary Mode* (Cambridge, U.K.: Cambridge University Press, forthcoming).

Giles, Roseen, *Monteverdi and the Marvellous: Poetry, Sound, and Representation* (Cambridge, U.K.: Cambridge University Press, 2023).

Haramaki, Gordon, "Beyond the *Seconda prattica*: Claudio Monteverdi and the Poetics of Genre after *Orfeo*" (PhD diss., University of California Los Angeles, 2008).

Harrán, Don, *Salamone Rossi: Jewish Musician in Late Renaissance Mantua* (Oxford and New York: Oxford University Press, 1999).

Henson, S. Matthew, "Foreign Songs for Foreign Kings: The Manuscript Scorebook of Angelo Notari" (PhD diss., Florida State University, 2012).

Holman, Peter, "'Col nobilissimo esercitio della vivuola': Monteverdi's String Writing," *Early Music* 21/4 (November 1993), 576–90.

Holzer, Robert R., "'Sono d'altro garbo . . . le canzonette che si cantano oggi': Pietro della Valle on Music and Modernity in the Seventeenth Century," *Studi musicali* 22 (1992): 253–306.

Horden, Peregrine (ed.), *Music as Medicine: The History of Music Therapy since Antiquity* (Aldershot, U.K.: Ashgate, 2000).

Ingegneri, Marc'Antonio, *V libro di madrigali a 5 voci*, edited by Gloria Joriini and Marco Mangani, "Marc'Antonio Ingegneri: opera omnia" II/v (Lucca: Libreria Musicale Italiana, 2006).

Jacobsen, Karin, and Jens Peter Jacobsen (eds.), *Claudio Monteverdi: Il quinto libro de madrigali* (Denmark: Edition Egtved, 1985).

Johnstone, Andrew, "'High Clefs' in Composition and Performance," *Early Music* 34/1 (February 2006): 29–54.

Kirkendale, Warren, *The Court Musicians in Florence during the Principate of the Medici, with a Reconstruction of the Artistic Establishment*, "'Historiae musicae cultores' biblioteca" 61 (Florence: Olschki, 1993).

Kurtzman, Jeffrey, "Monteverdi's Missing Sacred Music: Evidence and Conjectures," in *The Musicologist and Source Documentary Evidence: A Book of Essays in Honour of Professor Piotr Poźniak on His 70th Birthday*, edited by Zofia Fabiańska et al. (Kraków: Musica Iagellonica, 2009), 187–208.

Kurtzman, Jeffrey, *The Monteverdi Vespers of 1610: Music, Context, Performance* (Oxford: Oxford University Press, 1999).

La May, Thomasin, "Imitazione in Monteverdi's Canzonettas and the Madrigals, Books I–III" (PhD diss., University of Michigan, 1987).

La Via, Stefano, "Monteverdi esegeta: rilettura di *Cruda Amarilli/O Mirtillo*," in *Intorno a Monteverdi*, edited by Maria Caraci Vela and Rodobaldo Tibaldi (Lucca: Libreria Musicale Italiana, 1999), 77–99.

Lax, Éva (ed.), *Claudio Monteverdi: Lettere*, "Studi e testi per la storia della musica" 10 (Florence: Olschki, 1994).

Leach, Elizabeth Eva, *Sung Birds: Music, Nature, and Poetry in the Later Middle Ages* (Ithaca, N.Y.: Cornell University Press, 2006).

Levenberg, Jeffrey, "*Seconda pratica* Temperaments, *Prima pratica* Tempers: The Artusi–Monteverdi Controversy and the Retuning of *Musica moderna*," *Acta musicologica* 92 (2020): 21–41.

Long, Megan Kaes, *Hearing Homophony: Tonal Expectation at the Turn of the Seventeenth Century* (New York: Oxford University Press, 2020).

Luoma, Robert G., "Relationships between Music and Poetry (Cipriano de Rore's 'Quando signor lasciaste')," *Musica disciplina* 31 (1977): 135–54.

McClary, Susan, "Doing the Time Warp in Seventeenth-Century Music," in *Music in Time: Phenomenology, Perception, Performance*, edited by Suzannah Clark and Alexander Rehding (Cambridge, Mass.: Harvard University Department of Music, 2016), 237–56.

McClary, Susan, *Modal Subjectivities: Self-Fashioning in the Italian Madrigal* (Berkeley: University of California Press, 2004).

Mantoan, Diego, "Prove generali di teatro musicale in laguna: il contesto musicale veneziano del primo Seicento e il ruolo di Monteverdi nella nascita del melodramma a Venezia," *Venezia arti: bollettino del Dipartimento di Storia delle arti e conservazione dei beni artistici "Giuseppe Mazzariol" dell'Università Ca' Foscari di Venezia* 22–23 (2013): 84–88.

Meier, Bernhard, *The Modes of Classical Vocal Polyphony Described According to the Sources*, translated by Ellen S. Beebe (New York: Broude Brothers, 1988).

Merula, Tarquinio, *Curtio precipitato et altri capricii (1638)*, edited by Phoebe Jevtovic, "Recent Researches in the Music of the Baroque Era" 177 (Middleton, Wisc.: A-R Editions, 2012).

Miller, Roark, "New Information on the Chronology of Venetian Monody: The 'Raccolte' of Remigio Romano," *Music and Letters* 77/1 (February 1996): 22–33.

Mischiati, Oscar, *Indici, cataloghi e avvisi degli editori e librai musicali italiani dal 1591 al 1798*, "Studi e testi per la storia della musica" 2 (Florence: Olschki, 1984).

Monterosso, Raffaello (ed.), *Congresso internazionale sul tema "Claudio Monteverdi e il suo tempo": relazioni e comunicazioni* (Verona: Valdonega, 1969).

Moore, James H., "*Venezia favorita da Maria*: Music for the Madonna Nicopeia and Santa Maria della Salute," *Journal of the American Musicological Society* 37/2 (Summer 1984): 299–355.

Morales, Jorge, *Sigismondo d'India et ses mondes: un compositeur italien d'avant-garde; histoire et documents* (Turnhout: Brepols, 2019).

Newcomb, Anthony, "The Ballata and the 'Free' Madrigal in the Second Half of the Sixteenth Century," *Journal of the American Musicological Society* 63/3 (Fall 2010): 427–98.

Newcomb, Anthony, *The Madrigal at Ferrara, 1579–1597*, 2 vols. (Princeton, N.J.: Princeton University Press, 1980).

Nuti, Giulia, *The Performance of Italian Basso Continuo: Style in Keyboard Accompaniment in the Seventeenth and Eighteenth Centuries* (Aldershot, U.K.: Ashgate, 2007).

O'Rourke, Russell Joseph, "Representation, Emotion, and the Madrigal in Sixteenth-Century Italy" (PhD diss., Columbia University 2020).

Ossi, Massimo, "Between *Madrigale* and *Altro genere di canto*: Elements of Ambiguity in Claudio Monteverdi's Setting of Battista Guarini's *Con che soavità*," in *Guarini, la musica, i musicisti*, ed. Pompilio, 13–30.

Ossi, Massimo, *Divining the Oracle: Monteverdi's "Seconda prattica"* (Chicago: University of Chicago Press, 2003).

Ossi, Massimo, "Monteverdi as Reader of Petrarch," *Journal of Medieval and Early Modern Studies* 35/3 (Fall 2005): 663–79.

Ossi, Massimo, "Monteverdi, Marenzio, and Battista Guarini's 'Cruda Amarilli,'" *Music and Letters* 89/3 (August 2008): 311–36.

Ossi, Massimo, "'Pardon me, but your teeth are in my neck': Giambattista Marino, Claudio Monteverdi, and the *Bacio mordace*," *Journal of Musicology* 21/2 (April 2004): 175–200.

Ossi, Massimo, "A Sample Problem in Seventeenth-Century Imitation: Claudio Monteverdi, Francesco Turini and Battista Guarini's 'Mentre vaga Angioletta,'" in *Music in Renaissance Cities and Courts: Studies in Honor of Lewis Lockwood*, edited by Jessie Ann Owens and Anthony M. Cummings (Sterling Heights, Mich.: Harmonie Park Press, 1997), 253–70.

Owens, Jessie Ann, "Marenzio and Wert Read Tasso: A Study in Contrasting Aesthetics," *Early Music* 27/4 (November 1999): 555–74.

Parisi, Susan Helen, "Ducal Patronage of Music in Mantua, 1587–1627: An Archival Study" (PhD diss., University of Illinois at Urbana–Champaign, 1989).

Patuzzi, Stefano, "'S'a queste d'Este valle': Claudio Monteverdi and a *Mascherata* of 1607 in Mirandola," *Early Music* 31/4 (November 2003): 541–56.

Petrobelli, Pierluigi, "'Ah, dolente partita': Marenzio, Wert, Monteverdi," in *Congresso internazionale sul tema "Claudio Monteverdi e il suo tempo"*, ed. Monterosso, 361–76.

Pirrotta, Nino, "Monteverdi's Poetic Choices" (= "Scelte poetiche di Monteverdi," 1968), in *Music and Culture in Italy from the Middle Ages to the Baroque*, by Nino Pirrotta (Cambridge, Mass.: Harvard University Press, 1984), 271–316.

Pompilio, Angelo (ed.), *Guarini, la musica, i musicisti*, "ConNotazioni" 3 (Lucca: Libreria Musicale Italiana, 1997).

Privitera, Massimo, "'Leggete queste note': la *lettera amorosa* di Achillini e Monteverdi," postface to Claudio Achillini, *Poesie (1632)*, facs. edited by Angelo Colombo (Rome: Edizioni di Storia e Letteratura, 2010), 225–46.

Privitera, Massimo, "*Piagn'e sospira*: forme della 'seconda pratica' nel Quarto Libro di Monteverdi," *Il Saggiatore musicale* 6 (1999): 39–62.

Pryer, Anthony, "Monteverdi, Two Sonnets and a Letter," *Early Music* 26/3 (August 1997): 357–71.

Puliti, Gabriello, *Ghirlanda odorifera (1612)*, edited by Ivano Cavallini, "Monumenta artis musicae sloveniae" 46 (Ljubljana: Muzikološki inštitut Znanstvenoraziskovalnega centra Slovenske akademije znanosti in umetnosti, 2004).

Reese, Gustave, *Music in the Renaissance*, rev. ed. (New York: W. W. Norton, 1959).

Rosand, Ellen, "The Descending Tetrachord: An Emblem of Lament," *Musical Quarterly* 65/3 (July 1979): 346–59.

Rosand, Ellen, "Monteverdi's Mimetic Art: *L'incoronazione di Poppea*," *Cambridge Opera Journal* 1/2 (July 1989): 113–37.

Saunders, Steven, "New Light on the Genesis of Monteverdi's Eighth Book of Madrigals," *Music and Letters* 77/2 (May 1996): 183–93.

Schneider, Federico, "Rethinking Claudio Monteverdi's Seventh Book of Madrigals (1619) via Giovan Battista Marino's *La lira* (1614)," *Journal of Seventeenth-Century Music* 24 (2018), https://sscm-jscm.org/jscm-issues/volume-24-no-1.

Schrade, Leo, *Monteverdi: Creator of Modern Music* (New York: W. W. Norton, 1950).

Seifert, Herbert, "Rapporti musicali tra i Gonzaga e le corti asburgiche austriache," in *I Gonzaga e l'Impero*, ed. Artioli and Grazioli, 219–27.

Siegele, Ulrich, "*Seconda pratica*: Counterpoint and Politics," *Journal of Seventeenth-Century Music* 18 (2012), https://sscm-jscm.org/jscm-issues/volume-18-no-1.

Sogliani, Daniela, "La Serenissima e il Ducato: arte, diplomazia e mercato nel carteggio tra Venezia e Mantova (1613–1630)" (PhD diss., University of Verona, 2017).

Solerti, Angelo, *Le origini del melodramma: testimonianze di contemporanei* (Turin: Fratelli Bocca, 1903; repr. Hildesheim: G. Olms, 1969).

Stevens, Denis, "*Madrigali guerrieri, et amorosi*: A Reappraisal for the Quartercentenary," *Musical Quarterly* 53/2 (April 1967): 161–87.

Stevens, Denis, "Monteverdi's Necklace," *Musical Quarterly* 59/3 (July 1973): 370–81

Stevens, Denis (ed.), *The Letters of Claudio Monteverdi*, 2nd ed. (Oxford: Clarendon Press, 1995).

Strainchamps, Edmond, "The Life and Death of Caterina Martinelli: New Light on Monteverdi's 'Arianna'," *Early Music History* 5 (1985): 155–86.

Strainchamps, Edmond, "New Light on the Accademia degli Elevati of Florence," *Musical Quarterly* 62/4 (October 1976): 507–35.

Stras, Laurie, *Women and Music in Sixteenth-Century Ferrara* (Cambridge, U.K.: Cambridge University Press, 2018).

Strocchia, Sharon T., *Forgotten Healers: Women and the Pursuit of Health in Late Renaissance Italy* (Cambridge, Mass.: Harvard University Press, 2019).

Tibaldi, Rodobaldo, "La musica a Cremona all'epoca di Monteverdi," *Philomusica On-line: Rivista del Dipartimento di Musicologia e Beni Culturali [Università di Pavia]*, 17 (2018), http://riviste.paviauniversitypress.it/index.php/phi/issue/view/165.

Tomlinson, Gary, "Madrigal, Monody, and Monteverdi's 'Via naturale alla immitatione'," *Journal of the American Musicological Society* 34/1 (Spring 1981): 60–108.

Tomlinson, Gary, *Monteverdi and the End of the Renaissance* (Oxford: Oxford University Press, 1987).

Vassalli, Antonio, and Angelo Pompilio, "Indice delle rime di Battista Guarini poste in musica," in *Guarini, la musica, i musicisti*, ed. Pompilio, 185–225.

Walker, D. P. (ed.), *Musique des intermèdes de 'La pellegrina': les fêtes de Florence—1589* (Paris: Éditions du Centre national de la recherche scientifique, 1986).

Watkins, Glenn E., and Thomasin La May, "Changing Concepts of Originality in the Madrigals of Gesualdo and Monteverdi," in *Claudio Monteverdi: Festschrift Reinhold Hammerstein*, edited by Ludwig Finscher (Laaber: Laaber-Verlag, 1986), 453–87.

Watty, Adolf, "Zwei Stücke aus Claudio Monteverdis 6. Madrigalbuch in handschriftlichen Frühfassungen," *Schütz-Jahrbuch* 7 (1985–86): 124–36.

Welker, Lorenz, "'Con che soavità': Claudio Monteverdi und die Bedeutung des Instrumentalen im Madrigal," in *Wie semantisch ist die Musik? Beiträge zu Semiotik, Pragmatik und Ästhetik an der Schnittstelle von Musik und Text*, edited by Florian Mehltretter (Freiburg im Breisgau: Rombach, 2016), 47–68.

Whenham, John, *Duet and Dialogue in the Age of Monteverdi*, "Studies in British Musicology" 7, 2 vols. (Ann Arbor, Mich.: UMI Research Press, 1982).

Whenham, John, and Richard Wistreich (eds.), *The Cambridge Companion to Monteverdi* (Cambridge, U.K.: Cambridge University Press, 2007).

Wistreich, Richard, "'Inclosed in this tabernacle of flesh': Body, Soul, and the Singing Voice," *Journal of the Northern Renaissance* 8 (2017), https://northernrenaissance.org/issues/issue-8-2017.

Wistreich, Richard, "'La voce è grata assai, ma . . .': Monteverdi on Singing," *Early Music* 22/1 (February 1994): 7–19.

Wistreich, Richard, "Of Mars I Sing: Monteverdi Voicing Virility," in *Masculinity and Western Musical Practice*, edited by Ian Biddle and Kirsten Gibson (Farnham, U.K.: Ashgate, 2009), 67–94.

Index of Monteverdi's Works

For the benefit of digital users, indexed terms that span two pages (e.g., 52–53) may, on occasion, appear on only one of those pages.

Notes are indicated by "n" following the page number. Tables are indicated by an italic *t* following the page number. Poets are given where the identification is secure (or reasonably so).

A che tormi il ben mio (I), 17n.10, 82
A Dio, Florida bella, il cor piagato (VI; G. B. Marino), 98–99, 197–98
    bass voice in, 63n.36
    birds, 128
    confused ending, 98
    continuo instrument, 179n.40
    contrappunto alla mente, 98
    "T'amo mia vita!" motive, 100n.41
Ah, che non si conviene (VII), 37, 206
Ah, dolente partita! (IV; B. Guarini), 88–90, 204
    clefs, 60, 89n.17
    context in *Il pastor fido*, 90n.22, 113, 114
    first published (1597), 31–32n.10, 60
    gender-neutral text, 90
    monologue or dialogue, 89–90, 113
    other settings, 82, 88
    perhaps for Pellizzari ensemble, 60
    possibly for Third Book, 34–35, 54
    variants, 36n.17, 89n.20
Ahi come a un vago sol cortese giro (V; B. Guarini), 62, 63, 118, 122, 204
    Coppini's contrafact, 204–5
    gender-neutral text, 120
    and Pallavicino, 21
    playing with time, 222
    refrain, 120–21, 200
Al lume delle stelle (VII; T. Tasso), 154–55
Altri canti d'Amor, tenero arciero (VIII), 78n.81, 201
    bass "I," 182, 201–2
    clumsy text, 10, 145–46
    descending tetrachord, 213
    Monteverdi speaks, 77
    reference to Vienna, 202
    string instruments, 182
Altri canti di Marte e di sua schiera (VIII; G. B. Marino), 10
    singing, 224
    text changed, 153n.21
Amor, che deggio far (VII), 46, 226
Amor, per tua mercé, vattene a quella (I; G. M. Bonardo), 16
Amor, se giusto sei (V), 62, 118–19
    bass "I," 118, 201
Amor, s'il tuo ferire (I), 16, 18n.13
Andromeda (1620; E. Marliani), 47
Anima del cor mio (IV), 41n.33, 54n.10, 167–69
    and "Cor mio, mentre vi miro," 167–68
    female poetic voice, 90n.22
Anima dolorosa, che vivendo (IV; B. Guarini), 60, 178–79
    handling questions, 108n.55
Anima mia, perdona (IV; B. Guarini)
    criticized by Artusi, 6, 60, 112, 159
    emphasis on upper voices, 60
    female poetic voice, 90n.22
    text changed, 113, 152
Apollo (1620; A. Striggio), 69, 70*t*, 73
A quest'olmo, a quest'ombre et a quest'onde (VII; G. B. Marino), 200–201, 218
    bass "I," 46, 201
    echoes of the Sixth Book, 201n.34
    instruments, 44
    nostalgic, 43
    position in Seventh Book, 36–37, 43–44
    text changed, 146n.11
Ardo, e scoprir—ahi lasso!—io non ardisco (VIII), 137–38, 205
    falling thirds, 206n.41
Ardo sì, ma non t'amo (I; B. Guarini), 16, 17n.8
    compared with Ingegneri, 18–19
    preeemptive entries, 82, 83
Arianna (1608; O. Rinuccini), 4, 55, 70*t*, 100–101, 188, 212, 213
    revived in Venice (1640), 70*t*, 219
    See also Lasciatemi morire

Armato il cor d'adamantina fede (*Scherzi musicali*, 1632; VIII; IX), 27, 74–75n.65
Armida abbandonata (1627?; T. Tasso), 28n.3, 111
   Rapallini as Ubaldo, 69, 70*t*, 111n.61
Augellin che la voce al canto spieghi (VII), 128–29
   distempered, 178, 183n.48
A un giro sol de' belli occhi lucenti (IV; B. Guarini), 60, 89n.18
   consecutive fifths, 167
   harmonic range, 177

Baci soavi e cari (I; B. Guarini), 16, 17, 26, 81n.5
Ballo delle ingrate (1608; VIII; O. Rinuccini), 4, 55, 169n.19, 192, 216
   representative, 27–28, 187–88
   revised for Vienna, 28, 76
Batto, qui pianse Ergasto. Ecco la riva (VI; G. B. Marino), 46n.51, 196, 198–99, 200, 210
   continuo instrument, 179–80
   not dramatic, 197n.30
   Tirsi as speaker, 199
Beatus vir I (*Selva morale e spirituale*), 9, 224
Bel pastor dal cui bel guardo (IX; O. Rinuccini), 72, 75, 208

Cantai un tempo, e se fu dolce il canto (II; P. Bembo), 22–23, 24, 27
Ch'ami la vita mia nel tuo bel nome (I), 16, 22n.20, 41
Che dar più vi poss'io (V), 92n.23, 113–14n.68
Chioma d'oro (VII), 36, 44, 75, 190, 224.20, 226
   not "Chiome," 9n.23
Ch'io non t'ami, cor mio? (III; B. Guarini), 58, 59
   Phrygian mode, 165
   textual misreading, 149
Ch'io t'ami, e t'ami più de la mia vita (V; B. Guarini), 114–15
   arranged by Notari, 62
   dissonances, 173–74
   See also Deh, bella e cara (2p); Ma tu, più che mai dura (3p)
Chi vòl aver felice e lieto il core (VIII; B. Guarini), 216, 218
Chi vòl che m'innamori (*Selva morale e spirituale*), 219, 225–26
Chi vuol veder d'inverno un dolce aprile (*Canzonette a tre voci*), 14n.3
Chi vuol veder un bosco folto e spesso (*Canzonette a tre voci*), 14–16
Christe, adoramus te (Bianchi, *Libro primo de motetti*, 1620), 175n.29

Combattimento di Tancredi e Clorinda (1624; VIII; T. Tasso), 36, 72, 104, 105, 123, 146, 197, 214
   cantastorie, 182
   concitato genere, 136, 184
   continuo instruments, 181
   differences between score/parts, 39, 145, 148n.13, 158
   editorial problems, 145
   final cadence, 181–82, 194
   first performance, 28n.4, 74, 76
   harmonic range, 181, 184
   narrative issues, 192–94
   "Notte" stanza, 192, 222
   ornamentation, 48, 78, 222
   playing with time, 222
   representative, 27–28, 187–88
   and Sigismondo d'India, 111
   string instruments, 74, 101n.43, 181–82, 184, 214
Come dolce oggi l'auretta (*Proserpina rapita*; IX; G. Strozzi), 72, 73–74, 208n.47
Con che soavità, labra odorate (VII; B. Guarini), 42, 43, 75
   harmonic range, 132, 182–83
   Muses, 63, 182–83
   playing with time, 222
   scoring, 44
   "T'amo mia vita!" motive, 100n.41
   voicing Caterina de' Medici, 46
Cor mio, mentre vi miro (IV; B. Guarini), 66
   and "Anima del cor mio," 167–68
   diapente descents, 165–66, 167
   gender-neutral text, 86n.11
   mode, 163, 165
   playing with time, 223
   quoted in "O Mirtillo," 161–63, 170
Cor mio, non mori? E mori! (IV; B. Guarini), 118
   gender ambiguity, 54n.11, 90n.22
Così sol d'una chiara fonte viva (VIII; 2p of "Or che 'l ciel")
   chromatic ascents, 175–76
   textual misreading, 144–45
   tuning issues, 176, 179, 183
Cruda Amarilli, che col nome ancora (V; B. Guarini), 41, 61–62, 113, 114, 161n.7
   amaryllis for Rome, 112
   arranged by Notari, 62n.31
   criticized by Artusi, 6, 112, 159, 170–71
   dissonances, 113, 160, 170–174
   high clefs, 61
   mode, 171
   Monteverdi's affection for, 117
   and Pallavicino, 171

Crudel, perché mi fuggi (II; B. Guarini), 17
  as dialogue, 85–86, 90, 121
  and Marenzio, 19–20
  and Pallavicino, 19, 20–21

Damigella (*Scherzi musicali*, 1607;
  G. Chiabrera), 138
Darà la notte il sol lume alla terra (VI; 3p of
  "Incenerite spoglie"), 166n.14
Deh, bella e cara e sì soave un tempo (V: 2p of
  "Ch'io t'ami, e t'ami più")
  textual misreading, 115n.74, 153
Dice la mia bellissima Licori (VII;
  B. Guarini), 137
Ditelo, o fiumi, e voi ch'udiste Glauco (VI; 2p
  of "Incenerite spoglie"), 152
Dolcemente dormiva la mia Clori (II;
  T. Tasso), 24n.22, 34, 91
  Kauffmann's anthology, 31–32n.10
  playing with time, 221
  voicing, 83–84
Dolcissimi legami (II; T. Tasso), 18n.14
  gender ambiguity, 86n.11
Dolcissimo uscignolo (VIII; B. Guarini), 128*t*,
  130, 218
Donna, nel mio ritorno (II; T. Tasso), 18n.14, 81
Donna, s'io miro voi, ghiaccio divengo (I),
  18n.13, 81

Ecco di dolci raggi il sol armato (*Scherzi
  musicali*, 1632), 27
Eccomi pronta ai baci (VII; G. B. Marino), 209
Ecco mormorar l'onde (II; T. Tasso), 34,
  128*t*, 133–34
  Laura Peverara, 133
  text changed, 153n.22
  and Wert, 21
Ecco, Silvio, colei che in odio hai tanto (V;
  B. Guarini), 114–15
  arranged by Notari, 62
  high clefs, 61, 114
  See also Ferir quel petto (5p); Ma se con la
    pietà (2p)
Ecco vicine, o bella tigre, l'hore (VII;
  C. Achillini), 183–84n.48
E così, a poco a poco (V; B. Guarini), 120
  refrain, 121, 200
È questa vita un lampo (*Selva morale e
  spirituale*; A. Grillo), 220–21, 225
  circle of fifths, 178
Era l'anima mia (V; B. Guarini), 113–14n.68
  criticized by Artusi, 6, 112, 136, 160
  dissonances, 172n.25
  gender ambiguity, 95
  playing with time, 222

Et è pur dunque vero (*Scherzi musicali*, 1632),
  140n.27

Ferir quel petto, Silvio? (V; 5p of "Ecco, Silvio,
  colei"), 114n.70
  handling questions, 108n.55
Filli cara et amata (I; A. Parma), 16n.7, 53,
  54n.11, 118
  compared with Pallavicino, 19–20
  preemptive entry, 16, 82–83
Fornito ha 'l corso aprile (lost), 190–92
Fumia la pastorella (I; A. Allegretti), 17n.8,
  26, 209–10
  homophony for direct speech, 92
  about singing, 132

Gira il nemico insidïoso Amore (VIII;
  G. Strozzi), 206n.42

Iam moriar, mi fili (contrafact of "Lasciatemi
  morire"; *Selva morale e spirituale*), 219
I bei legami (*Scherzi musicali*, 1607;
  G. Chiabrera), 138
Il ritorno d'Ulisse in patria (1640;
  G. Badoaro), 3, 219
Incenerite spoglie, avara tomba (Sestina; VI;
  S. Agnelli), 40n.29, 101, 169, 195
  Caterina Martinelli, 10, 40
  text changed, 152
  See also Darà la notte (3p); Ditelo, o fiumi
    (2p); Ma te raccoglie (4p)
intermedi for *Aminta* (1628; C. Achillini and
  A. Pio di Savoia), 110
Interrotte speranze, eterna fede (VII;
  B. Guarini), 42n.40, 44n.42
Intorno a due vermiglie e vaghe labra (II), 17,
  18, 128*t*
Io ch'armato sin hor d'un duro gelo. *See* Ecco
  di dolci raggi
Io, che nell'ozio nacqui e d'ozio vissi (VIII; 2p
  of "Ogni amante è guerrier"), 76n.71
  bass "I," 202
  text revised for Vienna, 76–77n.73
Io mi son giovinetta (IV; B. Guarini), 41n.33,
  99, 110, 128*t*
  compared with Luzzaschi, 67
  consecutive fifths, 167
  narrative structure, 93–94
  perhaps for Alfonso II d'Este, 60
  about singing, 133
Io pur verrò là dove sète; e voi" (III; 3p of
  "Vivrò fra i miei tormenti"), 105
Io son pur vezzosetta pastorella (VII; G. F.
  Ferranti), 44–45, 47
  Caterina de' Medici, 46, 75

La bocca onde l'asprissime parole (II;
　　E. Bentivoglio), 27, 34
La finta pazza Licori (1627; G. Strozzi), 221
La giovinetta pianta (III; T. Tasso), 13,
　　24n.22, 34
　Kauffmann's anthology, 31–32n.10
　perhaps for Pellizari ensemble, 57–58
Lamento d'Arianna. See Lasciatemi morire
Lamento della ninfa. See Non avea Febo ancora
Lamento d'Olimpia. See Voglio, voglio morir
La mia turca che d'amor (Milanuzzi, Quarto
　　scherzo delle ariose vaghezze, 1624), 140
La piaga c'ho nel core (IV; A. Striggio), 151
　poet, 151n.18
　textual misreading, 149n.15
Lasciatemi morire (S; Lamento d'Arianna,
　　1623; O. Rinuccini), 116, 183n.47, 191–
　　92, 212
　contrafacts, 219
　publication, 36n.18, 72
　stile rappresentativo/recitativo, 188, 189
Lasciatemi morire (SSATB; Lamento
　　d'Arianna; VI; O. Rinuccini), 40, 100,
　　116, 174n.27, 187, 195, 213
　bass voice in, 63n.36
　compared with solo-voice version, 101–3
　Doni on, 102
La vaga pastorella (I), 132–33
La violetta (Scherzi musicali, 1607;
　　G. Chiabrera), 138
Le nozze d'Enea con Lavinia (1641), 3, 219
Le nozze di Tetide (unfinished; 1616–17;
　　S. Agnelli), 61n.25
L'incoronazione di Poppea (1643; G. F.
　　Busenello), 3, 142, 175, 219
Longe da te, cor mio (IV), 41n.33, 54n.11, 118
Luci serene e chiare (IV; R. Arlotti), 87–88, 90,
　　121, 155
　neighbor-note prolongation, 169
Lumi, miei cari lumi (III; B. Guarini), 58,
　　59n.21

Ma dove (o lasso me!) dove restaro (III; 2p of
　　"Vivrò fra i miei tormenti"), 104–6
Ma se con la pietà non è in te spenta (V; 2p of
　　"Ecco, Silvio, colei")
　added text, 115
　continuo at ending, 118
　criticized by Artusi, 6, 112, 160
Ma te raccoglie, o Ninfa, in grembo 'l cielo
　　(VI; 4p of "Incenerite spoglie"), 174
Ma tu, più che mai dura (V; 3p of "Ch'io t'ami,
　　e t'ami più"), 118n.83
　change of system, 178n.35

Mentre vaga Angioletta (VIII; B. Guarini), 53,
　　77–79, 122–24, 130, 133
　nightingales, 125, 128t
　other settings, 78
　triple time, 123–24, 136
Mentr'io mirava fiso (II; T. Tasso), 34, 90
　and Ingegneri, 18–19
M'è più dolce il penar per Amarilli (V;
　　B. Guarini), 114–15
　Monteverdi's statement, 117
Misero Alceo, del caro albergo fore (VI; G. B.
　　Marino), 210
　continuo instrument, 179n.40
　German manuscript, 40, 185–86
　moves sharpward, 180–81
　narrative structure, 196–97, 198
　not dramatic, 197n.30
　strophic variation, 186, 197
　text changed, 196–97
　typographical error, 144
Movete al mio bel suon le piante snelle. See
　　Volgendo il ciel

Ninfa, che scalza il piede e sciolta il crine
　　(VIII), 207
Nisi Dominus (1610 "Vespers"), 98n.34
Non avea Febo ancora (incl. Lamento della
　　ninfa; VIII; O. Rinuccini), 72, 209–16
　canzonetta, 29, 210
　ground bass, 213, 215–16
　known in Vienna, 76
　layout in partbooks, 37n.20, 214
　other settings, 210, 212, 217
　performance instructions, 78n.81, 214
　playing with time, 214–16, 217,
　　224–25
　representative, 187
　text published by Romano, 191n.13, 210
　voyeurism, 209, 216
Non è di gentil core (VII), 36–37, 75n.69
　added lines, 154
Non giacinti o narcisi (II; G. Casoni), 17
Non m'è grave il morire (II;
　　B. Gottifredi), 82n.7
Non partir, ritrosetta (VIII), 176, 207, 216
　chromatic ascent, 175
Non più guerra, pietate (IV; B. Guarini), 60
Non si levava ancor l'alba novella (II; T. Tasso),
　　18n.14, 27, 34, 41, 117, 128t
　ballata, 17–18
　bass for direct speech, 83
　counterpoint, 14
　Kauffmann's anthology, 31–32n.10
　narrative structure, 94–95

Non sono in queste rive (II; T. Tasso)
   loses track of syntax, 149n.16
   about singing, 130–31, 133
Non vedrò mai le stelle (VII), 37, 137

Occhi, un tempo mia vita (III; B. Guarini)
   for Pellizari ensemble, 57
   textual misreading, 149n.15
O ciechi, il tanto affaticar che giova? (*Selva morale e spirituale*; Petrarch), 219–20, 225
O come è gran martire (III; B. Guarini), 24n.22
   falling minor sixth, 96
   gender-neutral text, 87
   three sopranos, 58
O come sei gentile (VII; B. Guarini), 75n.69
   birdsong, 128
   missing text, 155–57
O dolce anima mia, dunque è pur vero (III; B. Guarini), 57
Ogni amante è guerrier: nel suo gran regno (VIII; O. Rinuccini), 28, 128t, 154, 202–3
   bass "I," 202
   originally addressed to Jacopo Corsi, 202–3
   text changed, 146, 202–3
   for Vienna, 76, 202
   See also Io, che nell'ozio (2p)
Ohimè, ch'io cado, ohimè (Milanuzzi, *Quarto scherzo delle ariose vaghezze*, 1624), 72n.57, 140
Ohimè, dov'e 'l mio ben, dov'e 'l mio core? (VII; B. Tasso), 46, 75, 167n.17
Oimè il bel viso, oime 'l soave sguardo (VI; Petrarch), 169, 195
   composed 1607(?), 40, 63n.33
Oimè, se tanto amate (IV; B. Guarini), 90, 224n.19
   dissonances, 171–72
O Mirtillo, Mirtill'anima mia (V; B. Guarini), 113–14, 160–66, 170, 173
   criticized by Artusi, 6, 112, 159, 160–61
   mode, 160–61, 163, 164, 165
   quotes "Cor mio, mentre vi miro," 161–63
   response to "Cruda Amarilli," 161–62n.7
O primavera gioventù de l'anno (III; B. Guarini), 157n.30
   sets early version of text, 88n.14, 112
Or, care canzonette (*Canzonette a tre voci*), 41
Or che 'l ciel e la terra e 'l vento tace (VIII; Petrarch), 111n.60, 128t, 135–36
   circle of fifths, 178n.37
   concitato genere, 136
   harmonic range, 183

known in Vienna, 76
   playing with time, 223–24
   See also Così sol d'una chiara fonte (2p)
Orfeo (1607; A. Striggio), 3, 4, 9, 62n.30, 63n.33, 65, 130
   and the *Combattimento*, 181–82
   formalism, 9, 121n.87
   harmonic shifts, 105–6n.51
   printed score, 6n.13, 30, 37, 180n.42, 180–81n.43
   and "Questi vaghi concenti," 63
   singers in, 59n.22, 61, 63, 65
   songs in, 139
O rossignuol ch'in queste verdi fronde (III; P. Bembo), 128
   perhaps for Pellizari ensemble, 57–58, 128
   textual misreading, 148
O sia tranquillo il mare o pien d'orgoglio (VIII), 138, 142, 205
O viva fiamma, o miei sospiri ardenti (VII), 44n.42, 75, 205
   Caterina de' Medici, 46
   text revised, 45–46

Parlo, misero, o taccio? (VII; B. Guarini), 130
   bass voice, 63n.36, 201
   as dialogue, 47
Perché fuggi tra' salci (VII; G. B. Marino), 44n.42, 137, 183–84n.48
   circle of fifths, 178n.37
   comic, 206
Perché se m'odiavi (S; *Arie de diversi*, 1634), 72, 75, 208–9
Perché se m'odiavi (TTB; IX), 72, 75, 208–9
Perché ten fuggi, o Fillide (VIII), 207, 216
Perfidissimo volto (III; B. Guarini), 59
Piagn'e sospira; e quand'i caldi raggi (IV; T. Tasso), 173, 221n.10
   chromaticism, 109n.56, 174–75
   playing with time, 221–22
   as response to Artusi, 6, 41
Pianto della Madonna. *See* Iam moriar, mi fili
Più lieto il guardo (*Arie de diversi*, 1634), 140n.25
Poiché del mio dolore (I), 16, 18n.13
Presso un fiume tranquillo (VI; G. B. Marino), 41, 96–98, 99, 101, 128t, 197–98
   bass voice in, 63n.36
   compared with Dognazzi, 67, 97
   continuo instrument, 179–80
   German manuscript, 40, 48n.58
Proserpina rapita (1630; G. Strozzi), 72, 73–74, 208n.47. *See also* Come dolce oggi l'auretta

Qual si può dir maggiore (*Canzonette a tre voci*), 41
Quel'augellin, che canta (IV; B. Guarini), 41n.33, 128*t*, 193n.20
   avoids consecutive fifths, 167
   contrappunto alla mente, 93n.27
   and *Il pastor fido*, 112
   perhaps for Alfonso II d'Este, 60
Quel'ombra esser vorrei (II; G. Casoni), 18n.15
Quel sguardo sdegnosetto (*Scherzi musicali*, 1632), 140n.27
Questa ordì il laccio, questa (I; G. B. Strozzi), 53
Questi vaghi concenti (V), 128*t*, 129–30, 226
   bass "I," 201
   compared with Gastoldi, 63n.34, 130
   for Monteverdi's musicians in Mantua, 55, 61–62, 63, 129
   sinfonia, 63, 129–30
Qui rise, o Tirsi, e qui ver' me rivolse (VI; G. B. Marino), 199–200
   continuo instrument, 179n.40
   Ergasto as speaker, 199
   playing with time, 222, 223n.16
   refrain, 121, 222, 223n.16
   scoring, 63, 199–200
   text changed, 199n.32

«Rimanti in pace» a la dolente e bella (III; L. Celiano [= A. Grillo]), 95–96, 99, 175n.28, 198
   echoes Tasso, 106–7n.53
   falling minor sixth, 96
   harmonic range, 177

S'andasse Amor a caccia (II; T. Tasso), 18n.14
Se i languidi miei sguardi (*lettera amorosa*; VII; C. Achillini), 154, 190
Se 'l vostro cor, Madonna (VII; B. Guarini), 42n.40
Se nel partir da voi, vita mia, sento (I; G. M. Bonardo), 14–16, 18n.13, 81
   playing with time, 223
Se per avervi, oimè, donato il core (I; G. M. Bonardo), 18n.13
Se per estremo ardore (III), 59
Se pur destina e vòle (*partenza amorosa*; VII; O. Rinuccini), 154, 169n.19, 190
Se pur non mi consenti (I; L. Groto), 18n.13, 82–83
Sestina (VI). *See* Incenerite spoglie
Se tu mi lassi, perfida, tuo danno! (II; T. Tasso), 34
   grammatical problem, 22n.20

Sfogava con le stelle (IV; O. Rinuccini), 91–92
   Coppini's contrafact, 172n.24
   counterpoint for direct speech, 92, 137
   dissonances, 172
   falsobordone, 91–92
   line removed, 153
   other settings, 66, 67n.46, 172n.23
   textual misreading, 172
Sì, ch'io vorei morire (IV; M. Moro), 60, 90, 178n.38
   Coppini's contrafact, 194
   harmonic range, 177–78
   poet, 90n.21
Sì dolce e 'l tormento (Milanuzzi, *Quarto scherzo delle ariose vaghezze*, 1624), 140–41, 142
Sì, sì, ch'io v'amo (IX), 69
Sovra tenere erbette e bianchi fiori (III), 95, 96n.32
   counterpoint for direct speech, 92
   Kauffmann's anthology, 31–32n.10
   for Pellizari ensemble, 57
Spuntava il dì (*Selva morale e spirituale*; F. Balducci), 219
Stracciami pur il core (III; B. Guarini), 59
   gender ambiguity, 86n.11
   Kauffmann's anthology, 31–32n.10
Su, su, su, pastorelli (SSA; VIII), 72, 128*t*, 216
   missing lines, 154
Su, su, su, pastorelli (TTB; IX), 72, 154

Taci, Armelin, deh taci (*Madrigali del signor cavaliero Anselmi*, 1624), 207
«T'amo mia vita!», la mia cara vita (V; B. Guarini), 67, 99–100, 197n.30
   Claudia Cattaneo, 99
   compared with Pallavicino, 100n.40
   diapente descent, 100, 166
   motive in other works, 100n.41
   musical reference, 130
Tempro la cetra, e per cantar gli honori (VII; G. B. Marino), 36, 44n.42
   changes to text, 44n.45, 146
   improvising poet-singer, 182n.43
   instruments, 130, 182n.45, 226n.22
   as prologue to Seventh Book, 43
   strophic variation, 192
Tirsi e Clori (VII), 44n.42, 137, 188, 218
   composed for Mantua (1615), 43
   performance instructions, 48–49, 54–55, 192
   reconciling Ferdinando Gonzaga and Caterina de' Medici, 47
   strophic variation, 192
"T'amo mia vita!" motive, 100n.41

INDEX OF MONTEVERDI'S WORKS

Tornate, o cari baci (VII; G. B. Marino), 151, 179–80n.41, 209n.48
Tra mille fiamme e tra mille catene (I), 22n.20
Troppo ben può questo tiranno Amore (V; B. Guarini), 67, 119–20, 139, 187
Tu dormi? Ah crudo core (VII), 175, 183n.48
Tutte le bocche belle (II; F. Alberti), 131n.18

Una donna fra l'altre onesta e bella (VI), 63, 196
   composed in 1607(?), 63n.33
   continuo instrument, 179n.40
   Coppini's contrafact, 40, 196
Usciam, Ninfe, omai fuor di questi boschi (I), 17, 132

Vaga su spina ascosa (VII; G. Chiabrera), 44n.42
Vago augelletto che cantando vai (VIII; Petrarch), 69, 124, 128*t*
   refrain, 143–44
   textual misreading, 143, 145
Vattene pur, crudel, con quella pace (III; T. Tasso), 39, 104, 105, 106–10, 148
   chromaticism, 175
   diegesis and mimesis, 108–9, 198–99
   not dramatic, 110
   omits stanzas, 107, 193, 200
   for Pellizari ensemble, 57
Vivrò fra i miei tormenti e le mie cure (III; T. Tasso), 39n.26, 59, 59n.21, 104–6, 109, 195
   homophony, 105, 115

   mimetic, 104
   perhaps for Pellizari ensemble, 57
   See also Io pur verrò (3p); Ma dove (2p)
Voglio di vita uscir, voglio che cadano, 4n.6
Voglio, voglio morir, voglio morire (*Lamento d'Olimpia*), 4n.6
Voi ch'ascoltate in rime sparse il suono (*Selva morale e spirituale*; Petrarch), 69, 111n.60, 219
   instruments, 225, 226
Voi pur da me partite, anima dura (IV; B. Guarini), 60, 62n.29, 66n.45, 90
   durus, 178
   harmonic range, 177
Volgea l'anima mia soavemente (IV; B. Guarini), 60, 149–50, 157n.30
Volgendo il ciel per l'immortal sentiero (*ballo*; VIII; O. Rinuccini), 188, 192
   textual misreading, 147–48
   Viennese references, 76, 148n.13
Vorrei baciarti, o Filli (VII; G. B. Marino), 152, 206n.41, 209n.48

Zefiro torna e di soavi accenti (*Scherzi musicali*, 1632; IX; O. Rinuccini), 75, 135, 148
   ciaccona, 27, 76n.71, 135, 146, 225
   "ime," 147
   "odori," 146
Zefiro torna e 'l bel tempo rimena (VI; Petrarch), 128*t*, 134, 195
   change of system, 178n.35
   composed 1607(?), 40, 63n.33

General Index

For the benefit of digital users, indexed terms that span two pages (e.g., 52–53) may, on occasion, appear on only one of those pages.

Notes are indicated by "n" following the page number. Tables are indicated by an italic *t* following the page number.

Accademia degli Incogniti (Venice), 77n.75
Accademia degli Intrepidi (Ferrara), 6, 30*t*, 60
Achillini, Claudio, 154, 190
Agnelli, Scipione, 10, 40
Alberto da Parma, 20, 82
Aldegati, Domenico, 67–68
Allegretti, Antonio, 26, 92, 209
Amadino, Ricciardo, 6, 6n.11, 30*t*, 31, 32
   continuo figures, 37
   errors in Monteverdi editions, 38, 89n.20, 105n.50, 144n.4
   formats, 33–36
   other composers/anthologies, 21, 31n.8, 32n.12, 41n.35, 63n.34, 67n.46, 209
Ambrosini, Pietro, 13, 31
Amigoni, Giovanni, 63n.36, 69, 69n.55, 70–71*t*
Andreini, Virginia, 101, 101n.42
anthologies
   Arie de diversi (1634), 38, 68, 70–71*t*, 72, 72n.58, 75, 140, 140n.25, 209
   De floridi virtuosi d'Italia (1583–86), 21–22, 41n.35
   Fiori del giardino (1597), 31, 34, 36n.17, 88, 89n.18, 89n.20
   Il maggio fiorito (1623), 72n.59
   Milanuzzi, *Quarto scherzo* (1624), 72, 140
   Morsolino, *Il primo libro delle canzonette* (1594), 32n.12, 60n.23
   Spoglia amorosa (1584), 22
Antwerp, 30*t*, 118n.82
Apollo, 1, 44, 73n.60, 146
Arcadelt, Jacques, 80–81
aria (musical style), 68, 72, 210, 213, 218
aria (poetic structure), 27
arie da cantar ottave, 104
arie da cantar sonetti, 134n.21
Ariosto, Ludovico, 125n.7
Aristotle, 185n.50
Arlotti, Ridolfo, 87

Arrigoni, Giovanni Giacomo, 76, 77
Arrigoni, Pompeo (cardinal), 5
Artusi, Giovanni Maria, 5–8, 116, 159–60, 166, 169, 172, 195
   on "Anima mia, perdona," 6, 60, 112
   as Antonio Braccino da Todi, 6, 160, 195n.22
   criticizes Bottrigari, 5, 177
   criticizes Monteverdi, 5–8, 32, 33, 41, 50, 112, 117, 159–60, 185, 186
   on "Cruda Amarilli," 5, 41, 112, 170–71
   on "Era l'anima mia," 6, 112, 136, 160
   ignores texts, 159
   L'Artusi, overo Delle imperfettioni della moderna musica (1600), 5, 116n.80, 159, 161n.5, 176–77, 223n.17
   on "Ma se con la pietà," 6, 112, 160
   on "O Mirtillo," 5, 112, 160–61, 163–64
   Seconda parte dell'Artusi . . . (1603), 5, 7n.16, 159–60, 160n.3
Atti, Francesco degli, 154n.24
Audi, Pierre, 222n.14
Augustine of Hippo, St., 125

Bacchino, Teodoro, 57n.16, 62
Balducci, Francesco, 219
ballata, 17, 22, 26, 27, 93, 120n.85, 154n.24
Banchieri, Adriano, 8, 208
Barbarino, Bartolomeo, 68, 69, 70–71*t*
Bardi, Giovanni de', 188
Bardi, Pietro de', 188
Baroni, Mutio, 64
Basile, Adriana, 44–45n.46, 61n.25, 66n.44, 72, 75, 77
   arrives in Mantua, 40n.29, 217
   performs with Mantuan singers, 64–65
   songs known by heart, 65
Basile, Giovanni Battista, 64
Basile Lelio, 64
Basile, Margherita, 75, 77

Basile, Vittoria, 64, 75
basso continuo, 8, 29, 36, 48n.58, 130,
    177n.33, 187
  bottom-up thinking, 185–86
  figuring, 37, 176, 179n.39, 180, 181
  frees voices, 96, 119, 187, 196
  instruments, 44n.44, 49, 124, 138–
    39, 179–82
  omit thirds from triads, 177, 183
basso seguente, 29, 118, 179n.39, 195, 221
bass voice as poetic "I," 80–81, 82, 83, 105, 115,
    200–203
  "Altri canti d'Amor," 145–46, 182, 201–2
  "Altri canti di Marte," 224
  "Amor, se giusto sei," 118, 201
  "A quest'olmo," 44, 46, 201
  "Augellin che la voce," 129
  as Monteverdi, 145–46, 202, 207
  "Ogni amante è guerrier," 202–3
  "Parlo, misero, o taccio?", 47
  "Questi vaghi concenti," 201
  "Sfogava con le stelle," 92
Belli, Girolamo, 88
Bembo, Gian Matteo, 73, 74, 75
Bembo, Pietro, 22, 23, 27, 128, 148
Benedetti, Piero, 208n.46
Bentivoglio, Enzo, 111n.60
Bentivoglio, Ercole, 27
Bertani, Lelio, 22n.20, 41n.35
Berti, Giovanni Pietro, 68, 70–71*t*, 140
Bianchi, Giulio Cesare, 61, 64
Biancosi, Gerardo, 68, 70–71*t*
Bisucci, Giovanni Battista, 61n.26
Boccaccio, Giovanni, 93, 128*t*, 167
Bologna, 5, 8, 61n.26, 69n.55, 177, 188
Bonardo, Giovanni Maria, 10*t*, 18n.13
Bonini, Severo, 218
Boniventi, Bonivento, 68, 69, 70–71*t*
Borlasca, Bernardino, 188
Bottrigari, Ercole, 5, 177
Bozzola, Pietro, 31
Braccino da Todi, Antonio. *See* Artusi
Brandi, Antonio, 217n.1
Brescia, 31
Brevio, Giovanni, 22
Brunelli, Antonio, 210, 212, 213, 217

Caberloti, Matteo, 68n.51, 78, 124
Caccini, Giulio, 60, 72, 217
  Euridice (1600), 188
  Le nuove musiche (1602), 66–67,
    112n.64, 139
Caccini, Settimia, 72, 75
Caletti, Giovanni Battista, 78n.78
Camonzoli, Margherita, 45n.47

Campagnolo, Francesco, 61, 65, 66n.44
Campeggi, Ridolfo, 188
Canini Valcarenghi, Stefano, 13
cantastorie, 182, 213
cantata, 64n.39, 72, 140
canto alla francese, 130, 139, 218
canzone (poetic), 17n.8, 26, 28, 40, 92, 96, 129,
    148, 209, 209n.49
canzonetta (poetic), 26, 28, 29, 77, 210
  expansion in the 1620s, 139–40
Capello, Pietro, 30*t*
Cardi, Giulio, 60
Casola (Cassola), Bassano, 39, 63, 64, 79
Casoni, Girolamo, 10*t*
Castaldi, Bellerofonte, 72n.56
  admires Monteverdi, 69n.53, 185
Casulana, Maddalena, 80
Cattaneo, Claudia, 24, 60, 62
  death, 64
  "T'amo mia vita!", 99
Cattaneo, Giacomo, 24, 56
Catullus, Gaius Valerius, 101
Cavalli, Francesco, 68, 69, 70–71*t*, 75
Celiano, Livio. *See* Grillo, Angelo
Cesareo, Gioseppe, 80–81n.3
Cesena, 68
Chiabrera, Gabriello, 26, 138–39, 210n.50, 213
chiavette, chiavi naturali. See clefs
Chieppio, Annibale, 79
chitarrone, 8, 48–49, 116n.78, 117, 118, 139,
    179, 180, 192
  Monteverdi plays, 185
  tuning, 177n.33, 180, 180–81n.43
Christine of Lorraine (Grand Duchess of
    Tuscany), 44, 57
ciaccona, 4n.6, 27, 76n.71, 135, 146, 225
clefs, 33, 40, 51–52, 55
  C1 clef for solo songs, 72, 190, 209
  C3 clef for alto or tenor, 86n.10
  chiavette, 19, 21, 51–54, 58–60, 61–62, 83,
    87, 89, 105, 106, 114, 200
  chiavi naturali, 19, 21, 51–54, 58–60,
    61–62, 63, 89
  other combinations, 53–54
  transposition, 53, 61, 138, 210
Clement VIII (pope), 125n.9
concerto delle dame (Ferrara), 58, 77, 87, 133,
    159n.1
  Luzzaschi's music for, 55, 58–59, 67, 80
concitato genere, 76, 97–98, 136, 182, 183, 184,
    202, 220, 223
continuo. *See* basso continuo
contrabasso. See violone
contrapposti, 16, 19, 82
contrappunto alla mente, 14, 93n.27, 98

GENERAL INDEX   243

Coppini, Aquilino, 40, 63n.33
   contrafact technique, 49, 172n.24, 194–95, 196, 205
   on Monteverdi, 195, 223
Corradi, Flaminio, 68n.49
Corsi, Jacopo, 76–77n.73, 202, 203
Costantini, Antonio, 45n.47
Crasso, Nicolò, 44–45n.46, 77n.75
Crema, 70–71*t*
Cremona, 1–2, 4, 11, 13, 38, 63
   other musicians in/from, 19, 24, 32n.12, 38n.22

Dal Pozzo, Cassiano, 125n.9
Dante, 28
Danyel, John, 156, 157
Danyel (Daniel), Samuel, 156
D'Arco, Livia, 159n.1
"Dichiaratione" (1607), 6–7, 23n.21, 36, 50, 126, 139n.22, 164. See also *seconda pratica*
diegesis, 91–93, 95, 98, 101, 177, 198, 210, 211
   in epic, 91, 104, 106, 108, 192
   more amenable to music, 109
   not dramatic, 110, 197n.30
Dina, Virginio, 9n.21
D'India, Sigismondo, 111
Dognazzi, Francesco, 61, 61n.25, 64, 77
   Il primo libro de varii concenti (1614), 43, 65, 97
   sings with Sacchi, 65, 67
Donato, Baldassare, 22
Doni, Giovanni Battista, 188n.3, 192, 218
   Monteverdi's correspondence, 7, 185
   on the *Lamento d'Arianna*, 102, 189, 195
   on *stile recitativo*, etc., 189–90, 194
Dymoke, Edward, 156n.27

enargeia, 91, 195
Este, Alfonso II d' (Duke of Ferrara), 7, 58, 60, 67, 125n.7, 164
Este, Alfonso III d', 74
Este, Cesare I d' (Duke of Modena), 74–75n.65
Este, Laura d', 62

Fabriano, 70–71*t*
falsobordone, 91–92
Farina, Carlo, 69, 70–71*t*
Farina, Luigi, 70–71*t*
Farnese, Odoardo I (Duke of Parma), 2
Farnese, Ottavio (Duke of Parma), 22
Ferdinand II (emperor), 2, 41–42, 76, 202, 218
Ferdinand III (emperor), 30*t*, 41, 76, 154, 182, 202, 203
Ferranti, Giovanni Francesco, 44–45n.46

Ferrara, 6, 7, 30*t*, 32, 56, 60, 63, 70–71*t*, 164
   Artusi in, 5, 112, 116, 159–60
   Vincenzo Gonzaga models on, 7, 58–59
   See also *concerto delle dame*
Ferrari, Benedetto, 70–71*t*, 72
Ferrari, Cherubino, 5
Festa, Costanzo, 14
Ficino, Marsilio, 7
Fiorini, Ippolito, 159n.1
Fiorino, Gasparo, 14
Florence, 8, 31n.9, 37, 44–45n.46, 57, 58, 102, 213, 218
   and Caterina de' Medici, 44, 45, 48n.56
   Monteverdi and, 2, 65–66
   singers in/from, 55–56n.12, 57n.18, 60, 65, 217
Flori, Georg (Giorgio Florio), 78n.78
Follino, Federico, 55–56, 58, 59, 64n.38, 101
Fondazione Claudio Monteverdi (FCM)
   edition, 14n.2, 18n.11, 90n.21, 105n.50, 179n.39
   errors in, 16n.7, 38n.23, 38n.24, 85n.9, 94n.28
Fontanelli, Alfonso, 32, 217
Fornaci, Giacomo, 209
Fraganesco, Alessandro, 13
Frescobaldi, Girolamo, 223n.16

Gabrieli, Andrea, 31–32n.10
Gabrieli, Giovanni, 31–32n.10
Gaffurius, Franchinus, 7
Gagliano, Marco da, 64n.39, 208n.46
Galilei, Vincenzo, 7, 185, 188
Gallo, Vincenzo, 18
Gardano, Angelo, 17, 30*t*, 31, 33–35
Gastoldi, Giovanni Giacomo, 2n.3, 24, 31n.8, 31–32n.10, 57
   Concenti musicali (1604), 63n.34, 130, 132n.19, 132n.20
   handling questions, 108n.55
   music for *Il pastor fido*, 113n.67, 116n.77, 117
Gatti, Alessandro, 151n.18
Gatti, Aurelio, 151n.18
generi (*molle*, *temperato*, *concitato*), 136, 184–85, 223. See also *concitato genere*
Genoa, 4, 40, 63, 78–79
Gesualdo, Carlo, 32, 87–88
Gesualdo da Traetto, Giovanni Andrea, 45
Ghirlinzoni, Lelio, 217n.1
Giacobbi, Girolamo, 188
Gibbons, Orlando, 157n.31
Giovannelli, Ruggiero, 22
Giovanni, Scipione, 68n.52
Giuliani, Giovanni, 69, 70–71*t*

GENERAL INDEX

Giunti (Florentine printers and booksellers), 31n.9
giustiniana, 160n.3, 207–8
Giustiniani, Lorenzo, 73
Giustiniani, Vincenzo, 218
Gonzaga, Camillo, 117n.81
Gonzaga, Eleonora (empress), 2, 76
    dedicatee of *Selva morale*, 218
    recruits Mantuan musicians, 77
Gonzaga, Ferdinando (cardinal, then Duke of Mantua), 39, 43–44, 45, 47, 50n.2, 63n.36, 65
    as poet and composer, 64
Gonzaga, Francesco IV (prince, then Duke of Mantua), 2, 28n.5, 40, 55, 100
    as dedicatee, 6, 30*t*, 50
Gonzaga, Guglielmo (Duke of Mantua), 19, 56
Gonzaga, Margherita (Duchess of Ferrara), 58, 60n.23
Gonzaga, Vincenzo I (Duke of Mantua), 2, 5, 7n.17, 41, 62, 67n.47, 76, 101, 102
    commissions Sestina, 10, 40
    as dedicatee, 13, 24, 30*t*, 116–17
    and Ferrara, 6, 7, 56, 58
    his musicians, 2, 19, 21, 24, 50, 56–57, 59, 60–61, 62
    summer visits, 4, 40, 63, 79, 139
Gonzaga, Vincenzo II (Duke of Mantua), 77
Goretti, Antonio, 5
    in Ferrara, 6, 116, 159
    Monteverdi's assistant in Parma, 3, 38
Grande, Pandolfo, 61
Grandi, Alessandro, 206n.40
Grassi, Bernardo Pasquino, 77
Grene, Anne, 156n.26
Grillo, Angelo (Livio Celiano), 66n.44, 73n.60, 95, 106–7n.53, 220–21
    praises Monteverdi, 8, 66
Grimani, Antonio, 70–71*t*
Groto, Luigi, 18n.13, 77n.75
Guarini, Battista, 9–10, 25, 116, 120, 125, 128*t*, 199
    and England, 156, 157n.31
    other settings of, 19, 21, 66n.45, 67, 77n.75, 78n.78, 85n.9, 86n.11, 100n.40
    stylistic issues, 81n.5, 111n.62, 152–53, 204
    textual variants, 25n.23, 67n.47, 77n.77, 85n.9, 86n.11, 87n.12, 88n.14, 112, 119n.84, 123n.3
    See also *Il pastor fido*; Index of Monteverdi's Works
guitar (Spanish), 65, 139

Habsburg court, 2, 41–42, 76
    performers at, 77, 78
harp, 48, 56, 57, 60, 65

harpsichord, 8, 53, 123n.4, 183, 185, 218
    as continuo instrument, 44n.44, 48, 117–18, 139, 179, 180–81
Haydn, Franz Joseph, 33
Henri IV (King of France), 76, 148n.13, 202
hexachords, 88n.13, 163n.9, 168n.18, 184
Homer, 199
Humanism, 1, 7–8

Iberti, Annibale, 4n.5, 40, 48, 54, 63n.33
Il pastor fido (Guarini), 27, 112–17, 156n.27, 221n.10
    controversial, 112
    cuts, 116
    Gastoldi's music in, 116n.77, 117
    lyric prose, 115
    Mantuan performance (1598), 5, 88, 112, 116
    other musical settings from, 61n.27, 82, 88–89, 112n.65, 113, 114n.70, 116n.78
Ingegneri, Marc'Antonio, 13
    Monteverdi emulates, 18–19
    and Rore, 22–23, 24
    teaching Monteverdi, 2, 13–25, 29, 32, 103, 131, 164
    teaching Pallavicino, 19
Isabella di San Martino, 64
Isacchino della Profeta, 56

Jacquet of Mantua, 14

Kapsperger, Giovanni Girolamo, 78, 210, 211n.53, 212, 213, 217
Kauffmann, Paul, 31, 34, 36n.17, 88, 89n.18, 89n.20
Kircher, Athanasius, 126n.10

Lake Garda, 64
Lassus, Orlande de, 22
Le Jeune, Claude, 139
Lercari, Giovanni Carlo, 24n.22
Licino, Giovanni Battista, 25n.23, 95n.29, 120n.85, 177
lira da braccio, 65, 182
L'Ottuso, 5, 7n.16, 159–60
Lucretius (Titus Lucretius Carus), 127
Luzzaschi, Luzzasco, 32, 159n.1
    madrigals sent to Mantua, 58–59, 64n.37, 67n.47
    music for the Ferrarese *concerto*, 55, 67, 80, 87

Madama Eufemia (Neapolitan singer), 92n.25
Madama Europa (Mantuan singer), 56, 58, 60
madrigal (poetic), 26, 139n.23, 141
madrigal book, 10, 22, 28, 55
    formats, 32–37

organization of, 39, 40–41
production, 38
Magli, Giovanni Gualberto, 217n.1
Magni, Bartolomeo
  errors in 1632 *Scherzi musicali*, 27, 38
  and Monteverdi, 30*t*, 31, 34, 36n.18, 72, 75, 188
  other composers/anthologies, 9n.21, 43, 75n.66, 76, 207, 210n.51
Malgarini, Federico, 61n.25
Malipiero, Gian Francesco, 34n.16, 38n.24, 89n.20, 105n.50
Manelli, Francesco, 70–71*t*, 72
Mantua, 11, 24–25, 58–59, 70–71*t*, 111
  Monteverdi dissatisfied with, 2, 67n.48, 73, 101
  Sala degli Specchi, 50, 64
  S. Barbara, 2n.3, 57
  See also performers (Mantua)
Marenzio, Luca, 16, 22n.20, 31–32n.10, 32, 46n.50, 85n.9, 87, 112n.65, 175n.30
  compared with Monteverdi, 30, 46n.51, 82, 88–89, 114, 131
  "Cruda Amarilli," 61n.27, 113
  in the 1589 Florentine *intermedi*, 57
  Monteverdi borrows from, 10, 19–20, 85
  setting Tasso, 103–4
  "Tirsi morir volea," 22, 80
Margaret of Austria (Queen of Spain), 5, 112
Margherita of Savoy (Duchess of Mantua), 28n.5, 55, 100
Maria Magdalena of Austria, 191
Marino, Giambattista, 9, 10, 40, 47, 128, 156, 196n.26, 206
  L'Adone, 128n.16
  other settings of, 67, 76n.71, 77n.75, 97, 209n.49
  Rime boscherecce, 46n.51, 199, 200
  See also Index of Monteverdi's Works
Marinoni, Giovanni Battista (bass in Mantua), 63
Marinoni, Giovanni Battista (tenor/theorbist in Venice), 63n.32, 68n.51, 69, 70–71*t*
Marliani (Marigliani), Ercole, 47
Martinelli, Caterina, 56n.15, 62
  death, 64, 101n.42
  recruited to Mantua, 56n.15
  Sestina (Sixth Book), 10, 40, 169
  taught by Monteverdi, 60
Masotti, Paolo, 80n.3
Massaino, Tiburtio, 78n.78
Mazzocchi, Domenico, 218
Medici, Caterina de' (Duchess of Mantua), 72
  musical training, 43, 48n.56
  pregnancies, 45

and Seventh Book, 30*t*, 42–48, 66, 75, 146, 155, 190
Medici, Cosimo II de' (Grand Duke of Tuscany), 191
Medici, Eleonora de' (Duchess of Mantua), 76
Medici, Ferdinando I de' (Grand Duke of Tuscany), 44, 57, 58
Medici, Francesco de' (prince), 44–45n.46
Medici, Margherita de' (Duchess of Parma), 2
Medici, Maria de' (Queen of France), 76–77n.73
Melli, Domenico Maria, 97n.33
mensuration signs, 160
Merula, Tarquinio, 225n.21
Merulo, Claudio, 22, 31–32n.10
Milan, 4, 24, 194
Milanuzzi, Carlo, 68n.52, 70–71*t*, 72
  compared with Monteverdi, 140–42
mimesis, 40n.29, 91–96, 99, 100–101, 110, 112
  in epic, 103–6, 115, 192–93
  less amenable to music, 109
  in "Non avea Febo ancora," 210, 211
  in the Sixth Book, 197, 198
Miniscalchi, Guglielmo, 140
Mocenigo, Girolamo, 28, 73–74, 75, 76, 222
Mocenigo, Giustiniana, 73
mode, 19, 40, 51–54, 160–61, 163–65, 170, 177–78, 184–85, 213
  authentic vs. plagal, 52, 164, 171n.21
  cadences, 15–16, 166, 171n.21
  diapente descents, 16n.5, 106, 165–69, 171
  difference from major/minor scales, 52–53
  epic Dorian, 105
  mixture, 161, 164, 166, 169, 171n.21
  modern treatments of, 88n.13, 163n.9, 168n.18
  Phrygian as special case, 164–65
Monferrato, 24n.22, 45n.47, 61, 65
  War of, 43
Monte, Philippe de, 18n.13, 22, 31–32n.10, 113
  Monteverdi borrows from, 16
MONTEVERDI, 1: Biography (etc.)
  character, 11, 68, 121, 219
  edits Arcadelt, 80–81n.3
  festivities in Parma (1628), 2, 3, 5, 38, 70–71*t*, 72, 110, 111
  foreigner in Venice, 68
  funeral commemoration, 68n.51, 78, 220n.7
  his *concerto delle donne*, 62
  in Hungary, 62–63
  insists on rehearsals, 64, 79
  maestro della musica (Mantua), 2, 7, 21, 50–51, 60–62, 63–64, 73, 117, 129
  maestro di cappella (Venice), 2, 67–68, 79, 141
  Mantuan citizen, 2, 68

MONTEVERDI, 1: Biography (etc.) (*cont.*)
  ordained, 41n.36
  and Pallavicino, 19–21, 85, 100n.40, 121, 171
  pension (Mantuan), 2, 41, 42, 76
  personal tragedies, 101
  plays chitarrone, 185
  plays string instruments, 2, 13, 24, 50
  sends music to Vienna, 76–77
  social circles in Venice, 68–72
  students, 60, 61, 68, 69
  studies with Ingegneri, 2, 13–25, 29, 32, 103, 131, 164
  and Thirty Years' War, 42, 219, 220
  treatise on the *seconda pratica*, 6, 7, 185
  viola bastarda, 50, 62n.28
  See also *seconda pratica*
MONTEVERDI, 2: Musical issues
  alto parts (wide-ranging), 54n.10, 57, 59, 60, 61, 86
  arrangements, 62, 101n.44
  arranging aria for five voices, 102
  canzonettas (strophic or through-composed), 26, 27, 75, 140, 207–9, 213–14, 225
  canzonetta textures (as basis for madrigals), 15–16, 55, 83, 167
  chromaticism, 109, 151, 168, 169, 175–76, 186
  circles of fifths, 163n.9, 178, 180, 183, 184
  clef combinations (unusual), 53–54, 55, 61, 69, 219
  comic settings, 129, 175n.29, 206–9
  compositional process, 4, 14
  concitato genere, 76, 97–98, 136, 182, 183, 184, 202, 220, 223
  consecutive fifths, 19, 167, 171n.20
  continuo frees voices, 96, 119, 187, 196
  contrapposti, 16, 19, 82
  dissonances, 16, 82, 89, 141, 170–74, 215, 216
  fingerprints, 16, 19, 96, 106, 132, 163, 169, 171–72, 178n.28, 206n.41
  gamut, 163, 177, 178, 180, 181
  harmonic juxtapositions, 105
  instrumental music, 9, 130, 182n.45, 226; ritornellos, 43, 130, 138–39, 140n.27, 182n.45, 224n.20, 225–26; sinfonias, 63, 129–30, 201, 222, 226n.22
  larger-scale settings of texts set by others, 66–67, 111n.60
  mode, 19, 40, 53, 54, 160–70
  models, 14, 16, 17n.10, 19–23, 43, 77
  neighbor-note progressions, 167–70, 180
  preemptive entries, 16, 82–83, 197, 206; for dialogue, 85–86, 92, 95–96
  prefers duets, 29, 62, 204
  refrains, 9, 120–21, 143–44, 200, 222; in canzonettas, 29, 75n.67, 208, 210–12, 219, 225
  self-quotation, 100n.41, 161–63, 167–68, 170
  strophic variation, 27, 140, 186, 192, 197, 208, 222
  tempo, 16, 37, 48, 214, 223, 224
  transposing musical units, 88, 100, 166, 167
  triple time as expressive force, 138, 141, 213; for "change," 92; as "singing," 123–24, 135, 136–42, 201
MONTEVERDI, 3: Text setting
  adds text, 115, 154–55
  "alas," 169, 171, 172n.25, 224n.19
  ambiguities of poetic voice, 86n.11, 91, 94, 121, 138
  aversion to "odori," 146
  changes texts, 44n.42, 46, 76–77, 146, 151–54, 156, 192, 196–97, 199n.32, 200, 203, 219n.6
  contiguous texts in poetic sources, 22n.20, 120n.86, 199, 209n.48
  cuts texts, 114, 115, 153–54, 190, 202
  dangerous texts, 90
  direct speech, 83, 91, 99, 104, 138, 149, 212; change of scoring for, 84, 93, 96, 120, 149–50, 155, 197, 198–99; contrapuntal, 91–92, 137; homophonic, 92, 108
  "disse" (etc.) as interjection, 93, 98–99, 110, 198–99, 214
  enjambment, 107, 143, 148, 150, 215
  exclamations, 16, 87, 96, 105–6, 171–72; bass voice for, 14, 82, 115; harmonic shifts, 162, 169, 193
  gender-neutral texts, 45, 54n.11, 58, 75, 86–88, 90, 95, 119, 120, 132
  imperatives, 82, 102, 108, 120
  misreads texts, 18, 98, 115n.74, 119n.84, 143–54, 172, 201, 212
  parenthetical insertions, 18, 114n.72, 149, 151
  questions inflected musically, 16, 108
  resistance to complex syntax, 82, 149–53
  textual superimposition, 16, 18, 81–83, 89, 103, 152n.20, 187
  vocatives, 16, 45, 80, 81, 82, 114, 137, 149, 163, 193, 205, 219; voicing, 82, 92, 120
  word-painting, 83, 123, 133, 135, 147, 187, 204
  See also diegesis; mimesis
MONTEVERDI, 4: Publication issues
  editions, 6, 29–32, 34, 36, 38, 72, 118n.82; manuscript sources for, 37, 38–39,

78n.81, 145, 148n.13, 179n.40, 181n.44, 188n.2; variants in, 38, 89n.20, 105n.50, 144n.4
marketability, 27–28, 29, 31–32, 48, 50
ordering of madrigals, 40–42, 124, 216
printing errors, 38, 39, 98n.35, 143, 144, 180n.42

MONTEVERDI, 5: Madrigal books
First (1587), 13, 18, 30*t*, 81; canzonetta textures, 14, 53; clefs, 53–54, 118; dedication, 13, 24, 41; fingerprints, 16; models, 16, 22–23; poetic choices, 16–17, 26–27; poetic voices, 54n.11, 86; references to music, 132–33; two tenors, 54, 118

Second (1590), 17, 30*t*, 128*t*; clefs, 54, 57–59; dedication, 13, 38; engages with competition, 19–21, 24n.22; gender-neutral texts, 86; models, 17–19, 21–24; poetic choices, 17, 26–27; printing issues, 34; Tasso, 18, 24; wide-ranging alto, 59n.21

Third (1592), 30*t*, 32, 128*t*; *basso seguente* added, 118n.82; clefs, 54; dedication, 13, 24; epic poetry, 25, 27, 103–4; gender-neutral texts, 86; for Mantua, 5, 13, 24–25, 55; poetic choices, 24–25, 27; printing issues, 34, 39n.26; successful, 30–31; two ensembles, 57–59; wide-ranging alto, 59, 61

Fourth (1603), 30*t*, 32, 128*t*; *basso seguente* added, 118n.82; clefs, 54; dating of contents, 5, 60; dedication, 60; dissonances, 171–73; erotic, 90; Ferrara, 60, 67; gender-neutral texts, 54n.11, 86; ordering, 40–41, 167; poetic choices, 27, 111; printing issues, 36; response to Artusi, 5–6, 32; title page, 2n.3; two tenors, 54, 118; vocal scoring, 60, 62n.28; wide-ranging alto, 59n.21, 60

Fifth (1605), 30*t*, 128*t*; arrangements, 62; *basso seguente*, 118, 179n.39; bass singer, 61–62; chamber performance, 50, 117; clefs, 53, 61; competes with Pallavicino, 21; continuo madrigals, 8, 9, 29, 63, 96, 117–21, 187, 196, 201, 222; corrected edition, 38; dating of contents, 33; dedication, 6, 50; dissonances, 170, 173; *Il pastor fido*, 111, 112–17; mode, 165; not dramatic, 116–17; postface, 6–7, 11, 50; praised by Coppini, 195; printing issues, 36; response to Artusi, 5–6, 32; tenors, 61, 62, 118, 120, 204; title page, 2n.3, 179; vocal scoring, 41, 55, 63, 118; wide-ranging alto, 59n.21

Sixth (1614), 27, 30*t*, 31, 82, 97, 128*t*, 178n.37, 200; basso continuo, 179–81, 195; bass singer, 63n. 36, 201; clefs, 53, 63; *concertato* madrigals, 29, 36, 61, 196–97, 222; corrected edition, 38; dating of contents, 5, 40, 63n.33; Marino, 10, 40n.29, 199, 201n.34; music for Mantua, 4, 5; named characters, 196; no dedication, 7, 38, 42; organization, 40, 195n.24; printing issues, 36, 38, 144; privilege, 36n.18; putting Mantua behind, 42, 101; sent to Grillo, 220n.8; wide-ranging alto, 59n.21

Seventh (1619), 4, 9, 28–29, 30*t*, 38, 42–49, 72, 74–75, 128*t*, 178n.37; avoids five-voice writing, 27, 218; basso continuo, 49, 179, 180–81n.43; bass singer, 63n.36, 201; for Caterina de' Medici, 42–45, 47–48, 66, 75, 155, 190; clefs, 53; compared with Dognazzi, 43, 69; dedication, 42–43, 44, 45n.47; flowers, 44n.42, 205; organization, 36–37, 42, 43, 209n.48; possible performances in Venice, 75; printing issues, 36–37; reward, 47–48; "Tirsi" and "Clori," 46–47, 155; title, 27; triple time, 137

Eighth (1638), 9, 29, 30*t*, 31, 38, 75, 128*t*, 179, 180–81n.43, 188, 201; avoids five-voice writing, 218; clefs, 53; compared with Arrigoni, 76–77; dating of contents, 4, 28, 41, 76; dedication, 76–77; descending tetrachord, 213; editorial problems, 39, 144–45, 147–48; organization, 10, 41–42, 77, 124, 201, 205, 216; performance instructions, 74, 78–79, 123, 214; preface, 28n.4, 136, 184–85, 223; printing issues, 36, 37, 39; privilege, 36n.18; scribal patterns, 39, 145, 148n.13, 153n.21; title page, 27–28, 187; triple time, 137; unmarketable, 32; Vienna, 41–42, 76–77, 78. See also *generi*

Ninth (1651), 4, 30*t*, 208; leftover pieces, 4, 31; privilege, 36n.18

See also Index of Monteverdi's Works

MONTEVERDI, 6: Other works
Canzonette a tre voci (1584), 26; clefs, 51; dedication, 41
contrafacts, 40, 49, 63n.33, 172n.24, 194–95, 196, 205, 219
Lamento d'Arianna, etc. (1623), 72, 188, 189n.8; privilege, 36n.18
lost, 3, 4, 65–66, 73, 74–75, 110, 111, 190–92, 220n.8
Madrigali spirituali (1583), 31
in manuscript, 4n.6

MONTEVERDI, 6: Other works (cont.)
   Messa... et salmi (1650), 4, 70–71t
   in other prints, 32n.12, 38, 60n.23, 70–71t, 72, 75n.66, 140, 207
   Sacrae cantiunculae (1582), 13, 14, 31
   Sanctissimae Virgini Missa... ac Vespere (1610), 4, 7, 9, 40
   Scherzi musicali a tre voci (1607), 6, 26, 30t, 50, 121n.87, 138–39, 225–26; canto alla francese, 139; folio, 36; for Monteverdi's concerto, 62. See also "Dichiaratione"
   Scherzi musicali (1632), 27, 30t, 72, 75; badly printed, 38; privilege, 36n.18
   Selva morale e spirituale (1640–41), 4, 31, 219; dating, 218n.4; dedication, 76, 218
Monteverdi, Francesco, 69, 70–71t, 78, 124, 140
Monteverdi, Giulio Cesare, 2, 6n.13, 26, 30t, 64, 138–39, 159
   Il rapimento di Proserpina (1611), 65
   See also "Dichiaratione"
Monteverdi, Massimiliano, 48n.55, 70–71t
Morales, Cristóbal de, 14
Moro, Mauritio, 90n.21
Morsolino, Antonio, 32n.12, 60n.23
Morsolino, Uomobuono, 32n.12
Mozart, Wolfgang Amadeus, 33
Muses, 1, 44, 63, 146, 182

Nanino, Giovanni Maria, 22, 31–32n.10
Naples, 64, 217
Negri, Marc'Antonio, 209
Nenna, Pomponio, 209
Nola, Giovanni Domenico da, 22
Notari, Angelo, 62
Nuremberg, 31

ode, 28, 191, 210n.50, 213
Olina, Giovanni Pietro, 125–26, 127, 129
Orlandi, Santi, 43
Orologio, Gerolamo, 30t
Orsini, Paolo Giordano II (Duke of Bracciano), 38n.22, 141
ottava rima, 26, 28, 43, 104, 145
   Monteverdi's settings of, 27, 28, 106, 137, 167n.17, 222
Ovid (Publius Ovidius Naso), 76, 101–2, 125, 154, 190, 199, 202–3

Padua, 68n.52
Palestrina, Giovanni Pierluigi da, 22
Pallavicino, Benedetto, 2n.3, 19, 21n.17, 24, 31n.8, 31–32n.10, 56, 82
   "Cruda Amarilli," 61n.27, 113
   and Monteverdi, 19–21, 85, 100n.4, 121, 171
   "T'amo mia vita!", 100n.40
partbooks, 33, 37, 49, 51, 72
   format, 17, 33–36
partitura, 36, 39, 49, 159, 214
Paul V (pope), 7
Parma, 5, 22
   1628 festivities, 2, 3, 5, 38, 70–71t, 72, 110, 111
Pellizzari (Pelizari) family (singers: Annibale, Antonio, Bartolomeo, Isabetta, Lucia), 56, 57, 58, 59, 60, 105, 128
performance issues, 29, 37, 48, 49, 74n.63, 131n.18, 151
   pitch, 52–53
   proportional shifts, 160
   tempo, 37, 189, 214–15, 223
   transposition, 53, 61
   See also basso continuo
performers (Mantua), 50, 55–67
   altos, 56, 59, 61, 86n.10
   basses, 56, 61–62, 63, 63n.36, 69
   castratos, 56, 59, 60, 62, 64, 65
   different ensembles, 59, 62, 63
   female singers, 55–56, 59, 60, 64–65, 75, 105
   Monteverdi recruiting, 50, 56n.15, 60–61, 62, 69n.55
   string band, 56, 61, 63, 70–71t
   tenors, 56, 59, 60–61, 62, 65, 118
   wind band, 61
performers (Venice), 50, 67–75
   compagnie, 67–68
   Monteverdi favors male voices, 69, 72–73, 208–9, 219
   prejudice against foreigners, 68
   St. Mark's, 67–68
performers (Vienna), 76–77
Peri, Jacopo, 48n.56, 66, 217n.1
Perla, Giulio Cesare, 56
Pesenti, Martino, 39n.27, 68n.52
Petracci, Pietro, 77n.75, 151n.18
Petrarch (Francesco Petrarca), 9–10, 17, 23, 28, 45, 128t, 156, 199n.32, 200n.33.
   See also Index of Monteverdi's Works
Petratti, Francesco, 38n.22, 141
Peverara, Laura, 77, 133, 159n.1
Phalèse, Pierre, 30t, 118n.82
Philip III (King of Spain), 5
Piazza, Giovanni Battista, 210n.51
Piazza, Paulo, 229n.7
Pico, Alessandro I (Principe di Mirandola), 62
Pirrotta, Nino, 9–10

GENERAL INDEX

Plato, 7, 126, 127, 164, 185, 185n.50
Pliny the Elder (Gaius Plinius Secundus), 78, 125, 127, 128n.16
Plutarch, 101
poetic meters, 26, 138–40, 184, 194
    versi sdruccioli, 27n.2, 207n.43, 213n.56
    versi tronchi, 139–40, 141, 211n.53, 215
Poland, 2
Porto, Bernardino da, 32n.12
Possenti, Pellegrino, 8–9
Prevesa, 70–71*t*
prima pratica, 7, 8, 159
printing, 29–42
    errors, 38, 39, 98n.35, 143, 144, 180n.42
    formats, 32–37
    limitations, 37, 48, 49
    reprints, 31n.7
psalm tones, 164
Puliti, Gabriello, 208, 209
Putte, Henrik van den (Erycius Puteanus), 223

Quintilian (Marcus Fabius Quintilianus), 195n.23

Rapallini, Giacomo, 69n.55, 70–71*t*
    in *Armida abbandonata*, 69, 111n.61
Rasi, Francesco, 57n.18, 60–61, 192
    composer, 61n.25, 65, 66n.45, 188
    in *Il rapimento di Proserpina*, 65
    in *Orfeo*, 63, 65
Raverii, Alessandro, 30*t*, 31, 34
recitative, 27, 116, 139, 140n.25, 189–94, 197, 213, 214, 215, 218
Recupito, Ippolita, 192
Reggio nell'Emilia, 70–71*t*
Remedio, Vincenzo, 69, 70–71*t*
Rena, Orazio della, 56n.15
Ricardi, Giacomo, 13, 24, 30*t*
Richards, Jonathan, 156n.26
Rinuccini, Ottavio, 2, 8, 10*t*, 65–66, 128*t*, 191, 213
    "Fornito ha 'l corso aprile," 190–92
    on madrigals, 217–18
    See also Index of Monteverdi's Works
Rivieri, Stefano, 69, 70–71*t*
Romanesca, 27, 43, 46, 167n.17
Romano, Remigio, 46n.52, 73n.60, 139, 190–91, 192, 210
Rome, 37, 56n.15, 80–81n.3, 112, 126, 189
Ronsard, Pierre de, 139
Rore, Cipriano de, 22–24, 68, 223n.18
    and Ingegneri, 22
    and *seconda pratica*, 7, 22, 23n.21, 164
Rossi, Francesco, 68n.49

Rossi, Matteo, 63n.36
Rossi, Salamone, 24, 31n.8, 56, 61, 64
    composer, 61n.25, 67n.46, 118, 146n.11, 172n.23
    settings from *Il pastor fido*, 113, 116n.78
    voice ranges, 59n.21, 63n.36
Rovetta, Giovanni, 69, 70–71*t*
Rovetta, Vito, 68n.49
Rovigo, Francesco, 31–32n.10
Rubini, Giovanni Battista, 61, 77
Rubini, Lucia, 77
Rubini, Orazio, 61, 77
Ruggiero (aria di), 43
Rusticucci, Girolamo (cardinal), 125n.9

Sabbio, Vincenzo, 31
Sacchi, Giovanni Battista, 60, 64–65, 67
Sampierdarena, 40, 63, 64
Sances, Giovanni Felice, 68, 70–71*t*, 78
Sannazaro, Jacopo, 199
Schrade, Leo, 3
Schütz, Heinrich, 40
seconda pratica, 5–9, 11, 115, 126, 127, 139, 144, 159, 195
    Monteverdi's treatise, 6, 7, 185
    not *prattica*, 7n.17
    Rore, 22, 23n.21, 164
    serva/padrona, 7n.17
    See also "Dichiaratione"
sestina (poetic form), 26, 152
Simonetti, Leonardo, 70–71*t*, 75n.66
Solferino, Marquis and Marchioness of, 64
sonnet (poetic form), 26, 28, 134n.21
Spa, 139
Spataro, Giovanni, 7
spinetta, 44n.11, 49, 180n.43, 182n.46
Stivori, Francesco, 22n.20, 67n.46
Strambali, Bartolomeo, 68n.49
Striggio, Alessandro (the elder), 22, 56
Striggio, Alessandro (the younger), 3
    "La piaga c'ho nel core," 151
    Monteverdi's letters to, 28n.3, 61n.25, 61n.26, 67n.48, 69, 70–71*t*, 73, 102, 111, 188, 221
    and the Seventh Book, 42n.39, 47
strophic variation, 27, 140, 186, 192, 197, 208, 222
Strozzi, Giulio, 73–74, 208n.47, 221
system, 40, 160–61, 163, 164–65, 168n.18, 171
    cantus mollis/durus, 178n.35, 184

tactus, 37, 124, 160, 189, 214–15, 222, 223
Tarditi, Orazio, 68n.52
Taroni, Antonio, 209
Tasso, Bernardo, 46

Tasso, Torquato, 9–10, 18, 24–25, 128*t*, 156, 199
    Aminta, 110, 111, 156n.27
    "Aretia" (eclogue), 24n.22
    Gerusalemme conquistata, 6, 109n.56, 192, 221n.10
    Gerusalemme liberata, 27, 39, 103–4, 106, 109n.56, 111n.61, 145, 147, 158, 192
    other settings of, 18, 19, 22n.20, 24n.22, 92n.24, 103–4, 105n.50, 105–6n.51, 108, 111
    speaks to his characters, 107, 193
    speaks to the reader, 94, 107, 193, 200
    See also Index of Monteverdi's Works
Tempesta, Antonio, 125n.9
terza rima, 26, 219
Terzi, Serafino, 56, 63
Testi, Fulvio, 74–75n.65
theorbo. *See* chitarrone
Thirty Years' War, 42, 220
Tivoli, 70–71*t*
Tomlinson, Gary, 3
Tresti, Flaminio, 24, 87n.12
tuning and temperament, 5, 132, 134, 160n.3, 174–83, 225
Turini, Francesco, 78n.78

Uberti, Gratioso, 126–27, 137
Ugolini, Vincenzo, 209
Urbana, Lucrezia, 56n.15, 60

Valerio da Ferrara, 63
Valli da Todi, Antonio, 125
Varoli, Benedetto, 77n.77, 123n.3
Vecchi, Orazio, 14, 22n.20, 31–32n.10, 208
Venice, 2, 3, 30*t*, 36n.18, 38, 66n.44, 75n.66, 111, 140, 191
    opera in, 3, 219
    patrician households, 28, 73–74, 75
    plague, 38, 68, 218n.4

St. Mark's Basilica, 2, 4, 42, 50, 63n.32, 63n.36, 67–68, 69, 70–71*t*, 75, 78, 79
    See also performers (Venice)
Verità, Marco, 13, 24, 30*t*, 41
Verona, 22, 24, 65n.42
Vicentini, Antonio, 69, 70–71*t*
Vicenza, 32n.12, 56, 70–71*t*
Vienna, 28, 37. *See also* Habsburg court
villanella, 19, 26, 167
Vincenti, Alessandro, 4, 30*t*, 31, 32n.11, 38, 75
    and the *Combattimento*, 39, 76, 145
    See also anthologies: *Arie de diversi*
Vincenti, Giacomo, 21, 31
viola bastarda, 50, 62n.28
viole da braccio (violin family), 44n.44, 49, 61, 63, 77, 101n.44, 177, 181, 182
viole da gamba (viol family), 44n.44, 177, 181, 182
violin, 44, 62, 77, 101n.44, 124, 139, 183, 201, 219, 225
violone, 49, 124, 181

War of Mantuan Succession, 77
War of Monferrato. *See* Monferrato
Wert, Giaches de, 22, 24, 31n.8, 31–32n.10, 32, 134
    "Ah, dolente partita!", 82, 88–89
    compared with Monteverdi, 21, 30, 82
    "Cruda Amarilli," 61n.27, 111
    handling questions, 108n.55
    position in Mantua, 2n.3, 21, 56
    setting Tasso, 92n.24, 103, 105n.50, 105–6n.51, 108, 111
Willaert, Adrian, 14

Zacconi, Lodovico, 124, 126
Zanetti, Sigismondo, 70–71*t*
Zarlino, Gioseffo, 7, 165, 171n.21